Wrox's SQL Server™ 2005 Express Edition Starter Kit

Wrox's SQL Server™ 2005 Express Edition Starter Kit

Rajesh George and Lance Delano

WILEY

Wiley Publishing, Inc.

Wrox's SQL Server™ 2005 Express Edition Starter Kit

Published by
Wiley Publishing, Inc.
10475 Crosspoint Boulevard
Indianapolis, IN 46256
www.wiley.com

Published simultaneously in Canada

ISBN-13: 978-0-7645-8923-2
ISBN-10: 0-7645-8923-7

Manufactured in the United States of America

10 9 8 7 6 5 4 3 2

1B/SR/RS/QV/IN

Library of Congress Cataloging-in-Publication Data
George, Rajesh, 1974-
 Wrox's SQL server 2005 : express edition starter kit / Rajesh George and Lance Delano.
  p. cm.
 Includes index.
 ISBN-13: 978-0-7645-8923-2 (paper/CD-ROM+online)
 ISBN-10: 0-7645-8923-7 (paper/CD-ROM+online)
 1. SQL server. 2. Client/server computing. 3. Database management.
 I. Delano, Lance, 1957- . II. Title.
 QA76.9.C55G46 2005
 005.2'768--dc22

                                    2005025426

For general information on our other products and services please contact our Customer Care Department within the United States at (800) 762-2974, outside the United States at (317) 572-3993 or fax (317) 572-4002.

Wiley also publishes its books in a variety of electronic formats. Some content that appears in print may not be available in electronic books.

About the Authors

Rajesh George is one of the founders of the SQL Server Express project within Microsoft, and has been involved in many of the key design decisions. He worked as a program manager on the SQL Server team responsible for various functionalities in SQL Server Express, MSDE, and SQL Data Access layers. He has spoken at several conferences and has authored the SQL Server Express Overview white paper on Microsoft.com. With prior software development experience in the Windows team at Microsoft as well as companies such as Nortel Networks and Netscape, he is currently a development manager at Amazon.com. Rajesh holds a Masters in Computer Science from Mississippi State University and MBA from University of Washington. You can reach him directly at contactgeorger@yahoo.com.

Lance Delano is a lead program manager in Visual Studio. Lance has an extensive background in database tools including database design and query tools. He is heavily involved in the customer research, proposals, specification, and program management of SQL Server Express.

Credits

Executive Editor
Robert Elliott

Development Editor
Sara Shlaer

Technical Editor
Andrew Watt

Production Editor
Felicia Robinson

Copy Editor
Kathryn Duggan

Editorial Manager
Mary Beth Wakefield

Production Manager
Tim Tate

Vice President & Executive Group Publisher
Richard Swadley

Vice President and Executive Publisher
Joseph B. Wikert

Project Coordinator
Ryan Steffen

Graphics and Production Specialists
Jonelle Burns
Carrie Foster
Laura Goddard
Mary Gillot Virgin
Lynsey Osborn
Alicia B. South

Quality Control Technician
Jessica Kramer

Proofreading and Indexing
TECHBOOKS Production Services

To my mother, Valsa George. Her determination and sacrifice remains an inspiration.

—Rajesh George

Thanks Natalie, and thanks kids, for the sacrifice you made so I could write this book. Now, let's go camping.

—Lance Delano

Contents

Acknowledgments	**xvii**
Introduction	**xix**
Who Should Read This Book	**xix**
What This Book Covers	**xix**
How This Book Is Structured	**xx**
Introduction to Concepts	xx
Rich Database Applications Development with SQL Server 2005 Express	xxi
Setup and Deployment	xxi
Developing Multi-User Applications	xxii
Appendix	xxii
What's on the CD-ROM?	**xxii**
Conventions	**xxiii**
Source Code	**xxiii**
Errata	**xvi**
p2p.wrox.com	**xvi**
Part I: Introduction and Concepts	**1**
Chapter 1: Getting Started with SQL Server 2005 Express Edition	**3**
Introducing SQL Server 2005 Express Edition	**3**
SQL Server 2005 Express Edition Highlights	5
Upgrading from Other Products	5
Features and Benefits of SSE	**6**
SSE User Scenarios	**7**
Desktop Application with Single-User SSE	8
Client/Server Application with Multi-User SSE	9
Application Replicating with a Central Office	10
Single-User ASP.NET Applications	11
ASP.NET Third-Party Hosting	12
Server Database Application	13
Licensing and Support	**14**
Visual Basic or C#	**14**

Contents

Installing SSE and Visual Basic Express   **15**

Hardware and Software Requirements for SSE   15

Hardware and Software Requirements for Visual Basic Express 2005   15

Installation Steps   16

Summary   **18**

Exercises   **18**

Chapter 2: Database Basics with SQL Server Management Studio Express Edition   **19**

Basic Database Concepts   **19**

Introduction to SQL Server Management Studio Express Edition   **22**

Using SSMS-EE for the First Time   22

Using Transact-SQL (T-SQL) with Query Editor   **27**

Using Data Definition Language (DDL)   29

Using Data Manipulation Language (DML)   31

Stored Procedures and Functions   34

Using Table Relationships   37

Querying on Multiple Tables   38

Using a View   40

Summary   **42**

Exercises   **42**

Chapter 3: Creating a Simple Database Application   **43**

Creating Your First Application   **44**

Adding a Database to Your Project   46

Working with Your Database in Database Explorer   47

Configuring a Data Source   50

Creating a Windows Form   52

Building and Debugging Your Application   53

Fixing up the Properties   53

Testing Your Application   55

Summary   **56**

Exercises   **56**

Part II: Rich Database Applications Development with SQL Server Express   **57**

Chapter 4: Developing a Rich Client Database Application   **59**

Designing Your Database in VB Express   **59**

Creating a Master-Detail Form   **63**

Contents

Working Directly with Components	**69**
Working with the Binding Source	73
Using DataSet and DataTable	74
Working with TableAdapter	76
Printing	**77**
Summary	**78**
Exercises	**79**

Chapter 5: Developing a Rich Web Database Application   81

Creating a Web Application Using Web Express	**82**
Master Pages	**83**
Adding a Database	**85**
Filtering Data	**88**
Inserting Data	**91**
Working with Master Detail	**93**
Help with More Complex Queries	**96**
Summary	**98**
Exercises	**99**

Chapter 6: Understanding Xcopy Deployment and User Instance Model   101

Introduction to Xcopy	**101**
Automating Connectivity to the SSE Instance	102
Understanding the User Instance Model	104
Getting Deeper into User Instances	**106**
ADO.NET Extensions for User Instance	107
Initialization of a User Instance	107
A Security Model Using File Permissions	108
Who Can Connect to a User Instance?	110
Using SSEUtil	111
How Is User Instance Different from a SSE Instance Running as a Service?	113
T-SQL Extensions for Managing User Instance	115
Summary	**116**
Exercises	**117**

Chapter 7: Using XML in Your Database Application   119

Creating an XML Schema Definition	**120**
Creating a Schema Collection in SSE	**124**
Creating a Column with an XML Data Type	**126**

Contents

Populating an XML Column with Data   **128**
Querying an XML Column   **130**
Summary   **132**
Exercises   **132**

Chapter 8: Debugging Database Applications   133

Basic Verification   **134**
Tracing Output   **135**
VB Express Debugger   **137**
Assertions   **140**
T-SQL Debugging   **141**
SQL CLR Debugging   **143**
Summary   **144**
Exercises   **144**

Part III: Setup and Deployment   145

Chapter 9: Understanding SQL Server Express Setup   147

Installing SSE with the Setup Graphical User Interface   **147**
Post-Installation Verification   **162**
Silently Installing SSE   **163**
    Using Command Line Parameters to Install SSE Silently   163
    Using INI Files to Install SSE   169
    Understanding Log Files and Dealing with Setup Errors   169
    Detecting SSE Programmatically   170
Adding or Removing SSE 2005 Features   **170**
Uninstalling SSE   **175**
Summary   **177**
Exercises   **178**

Chapter 10: Deploying Your Application   179

Deploying Your Application   **180**
Updating Your Application   **183**
Publishing Your Web Application   **188**
Summary   **191**
Exercises   **191**

Contents

Chapter 11: Migrating from Microsoft Desktop Engine (MSDE)   193

Understanding Microsoft Desktop Engine (MSDE)   **193**
MSDE Concurrency Workload Governor   194
Usage Scenarios   195
Comparing MSDE and SSE   195
Migrating Applications to SSE   198
MSDE Setup and Servicing   201
Upgrading MSDE to SSE   **204**
MSDE to SSE Upgrade Rules   204
Automatically Upgrading MSDE to SSE   207
Manually Upgrading MSDE to SSE   216
Summary   **218**
Exercises   **219**

Chapter 12: Migrating from Jet and Microsoft Access to MSDE and SSE   221

Introduction to Microsoft Access and Jet   **221**
Comparing SSE, MSDE, and Jet   **223**
Introduction to Access Project Development with MSDE   **228**
Migrating from Jet to MSDE or SSE   **235**
Upgrading from Access Database to Access Projects   236
Upgrading Database Objects   236
Upgrading Application Objects   238
Mapping DAO to ADO   239
Summary   **245**
Exercises   **246**

Part IV: Developing Multi-User Applications   247

Chapter 13: Securing Your Multi-User Database Application   249

Introduction to SSE Security   **249**
SSE Objects Hierarchy   250
Principals Who Can Access the SSE Objects   252
Permissions   259
Access Control   262
SSE Security Model   **264**
Connecting to SSE   265
Authentication Modes Supported by SSE   266
Permissions Hierarchy   267
Verifying Permissions   271
Summary   **272**
Exercises   **272**

Contents

Chapter 14: Upgrading from SSE to Other SQL Server 2005 Editions   **273**

Introducing SQL Server 2005 Editions   **273**
Reasons to Upgrade from SSE   **275**
Features Offered by SQL Server 2005 Editions   **276**
    Manageability   276
    Scalability   277
    High Availability   277
    Performance   278
    Business Intelligence   279
    Messaging and Notification   280
Upgrading from SSE to Editions of SQL Server 2005   **280**
    Upgrading Your Database Application   280
    Upgrading SSE Using the Graphical User Interface   287
Summary   **292**
Exercises   **293**

Chapter 15: Building Robust Multi-User Database Applications   **295**

Choosing and Creating Primary Keys   **295**
Creating Alternate Keys   **304**
Creating Constraints   **305**
Views   **306**
Table-Valued Functions   **308**
Transactions   **310**
Moving Your SSE Application to a Server   **313**
Summary   **315**
Exercises   **315**

Appendix A: Exercise Answers   **317**

Index   **339**

Acknowledgments

First of all I would like to thank the staff at Wiley. Many thanks to Robert Elliott, the executive editor, for the direction, and helping this project gain momentum. Words of appreciation to Sara Shlaer, Andrew Watt, Felicia Robinson, and Kathryn Duggan for help with editing, deadlines, and project management.

At different stages of research and book preparation, many colleagues, friends, and reviewers helped in various ways. My appreciation goes to: Michael Edwards, James Hamilton, and Tanmoy Dutta.

Finally, I would like to thank my family for the support and encouragement. I could not have done this without you.

Rajesh George

October 2005

I would like to acknowledge all of the people in SQL Server who helped make SQL Server Express a reality. While many people worked on hard on this, two people who really came through in the end were Tanmoy Dutta and George Li. Additionally, I would like to thank the staff and management of Wiley for help in working through the manuscripts. In particular, I would like to call out Sara Shlaer for her help. And, most of all, I thank my family – and especially my wife – for their support and encouragement.

Lance Delano

October 2005

Introduction

SQL Server 2005 Express Edition (SSE) is the desktop version of Microsoft's very popular SQL Server 2005 database product. SSE is free to use and redistribute and is packed with easy to use features. Microsoft has taken big steps in making SSE approachable and usable by all types of developers, from beginners to advanced users. Also all editions of Visual Studio 2005 accommodate SSE naturally in the project system so that developers will find it much easier to build and deploy local data applications with SQL Server by using SSE. If you want to understand how to use the free version of one of the world's most popular and powerful databases, then this book is for you.

Who Should Read This Book

This book assumes you have very little background with either databases or programming. You may never have created a single application of any kind. Alternatively, you may have only created simple databases in Access. No prior programming experience is required, but you should have an aptitude for working with software and a desire to learn. If you have a desire to learn and an interest in storing information in a database—and in creating drop-dead simple applications to work with the data—this book has a lot to offer. The step-by-step samples cover all the major scenarios SSE is designed for, from installation and development to debugging and deployment.

Alternatively, if you are a more experienced developer, you may find this book useful because it describes a number of new features that are unique to SSE that make working with SSE much easier than with its predecessor, MSDE. You get an insight into the SSE design and architecture from the authors who are intimately involved in the creation of many of these features. In addition, you will find useful information about the various deployment and programmatic features that are not properly documented.

What This Book Covers

This book focuses on using SSE to design and build your desktop and web applications. In addition to the tools supplied with SSE, Visual Basic Express 2005 and Web Express 2005 are used to for application development. The features that are unique to SSE such as Xcopy, User Instances, and deployment are also covered in detail. The Microsoft SQL Server Books Online focuses primarily on other editions of SQL Server, and the details specific to its free edition is often lost. You can use this book not only to jump start your database application development, but also as a reference on SSE features.

In building and releasing SSE, the SQL Server team worked very closely with another division in Microsoft, the Visual Basic programming language team. Two resulting products, SQL Server 2005 Express Edition and Visual Basic 2005 Express Edition (VB Express), were designed to be released simultaneously. VB Express is a programming environment that is tailored to work well with SSE. Visual Basic, as a programming language, targets people who want to write code with a minimum of hassle, who want to get the right job done quickly and easily. This book then, is about building and working with databases using SSE and VB Express. Working with VB Express is not a requirement for working with SSE. If you choose, you can just read and use the sections on SSE.

In this book, you learn how to:

- ❑ Design and work with basic database objects
- ❑ Install and start working with SSE
- ❑ Create simple database applications (without a single line of code)
- ❑ Create rich database applications (with a small amount of code)
- ❑ Create web-based applications that use your database
- ❑ Deploy your application and your database
- ❑ Use XML in your database
- ❑ Develop secure database applications
- ❑ Upgrade from Microsoft Access or previous versions of MSDE
- ❑ Move your SSE database to higher versions of SQL Server

How This Book Is Structured

There are four major areas in this book. The first part is a basic introduction to SQL Server, VB Express, and some basics of working with databases. Next, you move into richer application development topics. In the third part, you will learn some of the details of setting up and distributing SSE in scenarios that are more sophisticated. Finally, there is a section on developing multi-user applications.

The following sections introduce each part in more detail.

Introduction to Concepts

Chapter 1 is about getting started with SQL Server Express. Everyone should read this chapter because it quickly outlines the high-level features, benefits, and usage scenarios intended for SSE. It gives an overview of the licensing and support policies and gets you started installing SSE on your machine.

Chapter 2 introduces basic database concepts that are important to understand in designing your database. It also shows you how to install and work with SQL Server Management Studio Express Edition (SSMS-EE), the management tool for SSE. Chapter 2 also gives you an overview of all the basic database objects and how to create and manipulate them using Transact-SQL. This includes databases, tables, views, queries, and stored procedures. You should read this chapter if you want to understand how to use SSMS-EE to manage your database and create your objects.

Chapter 3 walks you through the basics of using VB Express to create a simple, single table, database application without writing a single line of code. VB Express has graphical tools that allow you to create the same database objects, including the database itself, tables, views, queries, and stored procedures. In this chapter, you will build and debug a very simple, but fully functional, database application. You should read this chapter if you want to know how to work with VB Express to create simple database applications.

Rich Database Applications Development with SQL Server 2005 Express

Chapter 4 is a continuation of your experience in working with VB Express. The database you created in the previous chapter will be used in this chapter to develop a rich client database application. The application you build in this chapter is more "real world." You should read this chapter if you want to know how to use VB Express to build richer database applications.

Chapter 5 moves you to the web development experience. Using the same basic application that you built in Chapter 4, you will create a rich web-based database application. In particular, you will learn about how to work with SSE in web applications. You will also learn about master pages and other web controls.

Chapter 6 explains the details behind the Xcopy feature of SSE. It is the Xcopy feature that allows you to treat your database like a normal file. You can copy the database and your other associated files from one machine to another like you do any other windows file. In particular, you will learn about the auto-attach, autoclose, and the user instances features along with the security model around it. You will also learn about the SSEUtil tool that can connect and work with User Instances.

Chapter 7 explains how you can use XML in your database. XML is a very popular storage and transmittal data format. SSE allows you to store and query XML data in your database. In this chapter, you will create an XML Schema Definition (XSD) file in VB Express and then store it in SSE. Then, when you define a column that has an XML data type, you will reference that XSD. With the XML column defined, you will insert data into it and then query it.

Chapter 8 instructs you on how to debug your database application. You learn basic validation and verification techniques to ensure that your database is being updated correctly. You also learn how to use trace flags, assertions, and the VB Express debugger.

Setup and Deployment

Chapter 9 explains the many options available for setting up SSE. Some options you will learn about include what instance to use, how to get the right tools, how to use the command-line silent install, and networking and authentication options. If you have specialized needs on how you install or redistribute SSE along with your application, you should read this chapter.

Chapter 10 is an extension, in some ways, of the previous chapter. In this chapter, you learn how to deploy both your application and SSE. VB Express has a new ClickOnce feature that enables you to publish and deploy both your rich client application and SSE to your user's machines. This chapter will be particularly important to you if you plan to distribute your application to multiple people.

Chapter 11 shows you how to migrate your data from MSDE to SSE. Because the feature set in SSE is not exactly the same as MSDE, you should be careful of some things. There are a number of choices to consider, including whether you upgrade manually or automatically and whether your MSDE database qualifies for an automatic upgrade. This chapter is important to anyone currently using MSDE.

Chapter 12 explains how to move from Microsoft Access to MSDE and SSE. It is important to know what you can actually transfer from an Access application. Some things will move and some will not. In order to know what you can transfer, this chapter will explain the key differences between the two programs and walk you through the upgrade wizard. If you want to move up from an Access application, read this chapter to get an idea of what to expect.

Developing Multi-User Applications

Chapter 13 introduces you to the basics of securing your database application. SSE has many different types of security features and you will learn about the SQL Server security models including authentication and authorization features. In addition, ensuring your data is secure is an important step in moving your database to a multi-user scenario. You should read this chapter if you intend to make your database publicly accessible.

Chapter 14 shows you how to move up from SSE to a higher-level version of SQL Server. There are a number of different editions of SQL Server and this chapter explains the differences between them. It also explains how to actually upgrade your application to work with higher-level versions of SQL Server.

Chapter 15 shows how to build your database application for situations where multiple users or multiple applications simultaneously use the database. Here you should consider things like how you design your primary keys, and the use of views and transactions. If you will use your database in a multi-user environment or target multiple applications to use the same database, you should understand this chapter.

Appendix

Appendix A has the answers to exercises found at the end of each chapter.

What's on the CD-ROM?

You will need the following software, which is included on the CD that accompanies the book:

- ❑ Visual Basic 2005 Express Edition
- ❑ SQL Server 2005 Express Edition

You will also need access to the Internet. There are some downloads referenced in the book which will require Internet access. In particular, you will need to download SSEUtil, a command-line utility that works with SSE as well as SQL Server Management Studio Express edition, the GUI tool for SSE. Details on how to download it are included in the book.

Note that Web Express 2005 is not on the CD. Web Express 2005 is used in Chapter 5. If you would like to follow the examples in Chapter 5, you will need to obtain a copy of Visual Web Developer 2005 Express Edition. You can get information on how to obtain it from `http://msdn.microsoft.com/ vstudio/express/vwd`.

Conventions

To help you understand how this book is formatted, there are a number of conventions used through the book.

❑   Certain elements, such as methods, commands, and parameters, are presented in a special code font, like this:

This can be verified by looking at the `SERVER=(local)\SQLExpress` connection string entry.

❑   Special tips or notes appear as italicized paragraphs:

In order to attach a read-only database, the log file must pre-exist. SSE does not regenerate the log file for a read-only database.

❑   Warnings or other very important notes appear in boxes:

> **If you are an interactive user on the machine, you can use user instance mode without any additional configuration changes even if you are a not an administrator on the box.**

The book makes use of Wrox's special Try It Out and How It Works features as well.

Try It Out

A Try It Out section is an in-place exercise that will help you understand the concepts quickly.

1.   Each Try It Out has a series of numbered steps to lead you through the exercise.

2.   Code is shown like this:

```
SELECT * FROM MyTable
```

How It Works

After each Try It Out, there is a How It Works section that explains what happened and discusses the key concepts in more depth.

Source Code

You can download the source code for the examples from http://www.wrox.com. At that URL, locate the book title and click on the Download Code link on the book's detail page.

Errata

While we make every effort to ensure that the book is accurate, if we do discover errors we need to fix after the book has gone to print, we will post them to the http://www.wrox.com site on the details page for the book. On the book details page, click the Book Errata link. This page shows you all of the errata that has been submitted.

If you don't see the error you have found on that page, go to www.wrox.com/contact/techsupport.shtml and complete a submittal form. We will check the information and post any fixes necessary.

p2p.wrox.com

Wrox maintains a programmer-to-programmer forum at www.p2p.wrox.com that allows you to post messages about Wrox books and related topics. At this site, you can ask or answer questions. To join the forums, follow these steps:

1. Go to www.p2p.wrox.com and locate the login/register section on the left. Click the Register Now link for new users. This will take you to the Terms of Use Agreement page.

2. On the Terms of Use Agreement page, click Agree. This will take you to the registration form. Fill it out and click Submit. This will cause the site to send you email with additional instructions.

3. When the email arrives, click on the link in the mail. This will take you to a final page that will confirm your registration. You can now start using the forums with your username and password.

Part I:

Introduction and Concepts

Chapter 1: Getting Started with SQL Server 2005 Express Edition

Chapter 2: Database Basics with SQL Server Management Studio Express Edition

Chapter 3: Creating a Simple Database Application

Getting Started with SQL Server 2005 Express Edition

This book introduces you to SQL Server 2005 Express Edition (SSE), the free edition of SQL Server 2005 that is designed for smaller systems. SSE is intended as a replacement for MSDE, a free database product based on SQL Server 2000. SSE is designed to have smaller disk and memory utilization than MSDE, and has features targeting Visual Studio VB and C# programmers who typically treat databases just like files. SSE serves as a database for both desktop and server applications; it is easy to use in all stages of your application life cycle.

This chapter covers the following topics:

- ❑ Introducing SQL Server 2005 Express Edition
- ❑ Important features in SQL Server 2005 Express Edition
- ❑ Key scenarios and the audience for SQL Server 2005 Express Edition
- ❑ Hardware and software requirements for installing SQL Server 2005 Express Edition
- ❑ Installing SQL Server 2005 Express Edition

Introducing SQL Server 2005 Express Edition

The SQL Server 2005 family, shown in Figure 1-1, includes the Workgroup, Standard, Enterprise, and Developer editions along with SQL Server 2005 Express Edition. Some editions of SQL Server 2005 are offered for both 32-bit and 64-bit Windows operating systems. Only SSE is free for use in development, production, and redistribution and is targeted at developers deploying simple database applications. The Workgroup edition is meant for smaller departments and businesses looking for an affordable database with good price performance ratio and rich features such as replication publishing and backup log shipping. The Standard and Enterprise editions are used by large departments or enterprises looking for business-critical solutions. The Developer edition has all the features of the Enterprise edition, but cannot be used in production. Each higher-level edition contains all the features offered by the edition immediately below it in the hierarchy. The only exceptions to this rule are the user instance and Xcopy deployment features that are present only in SSE. Chapter 6 covers these features in detail.

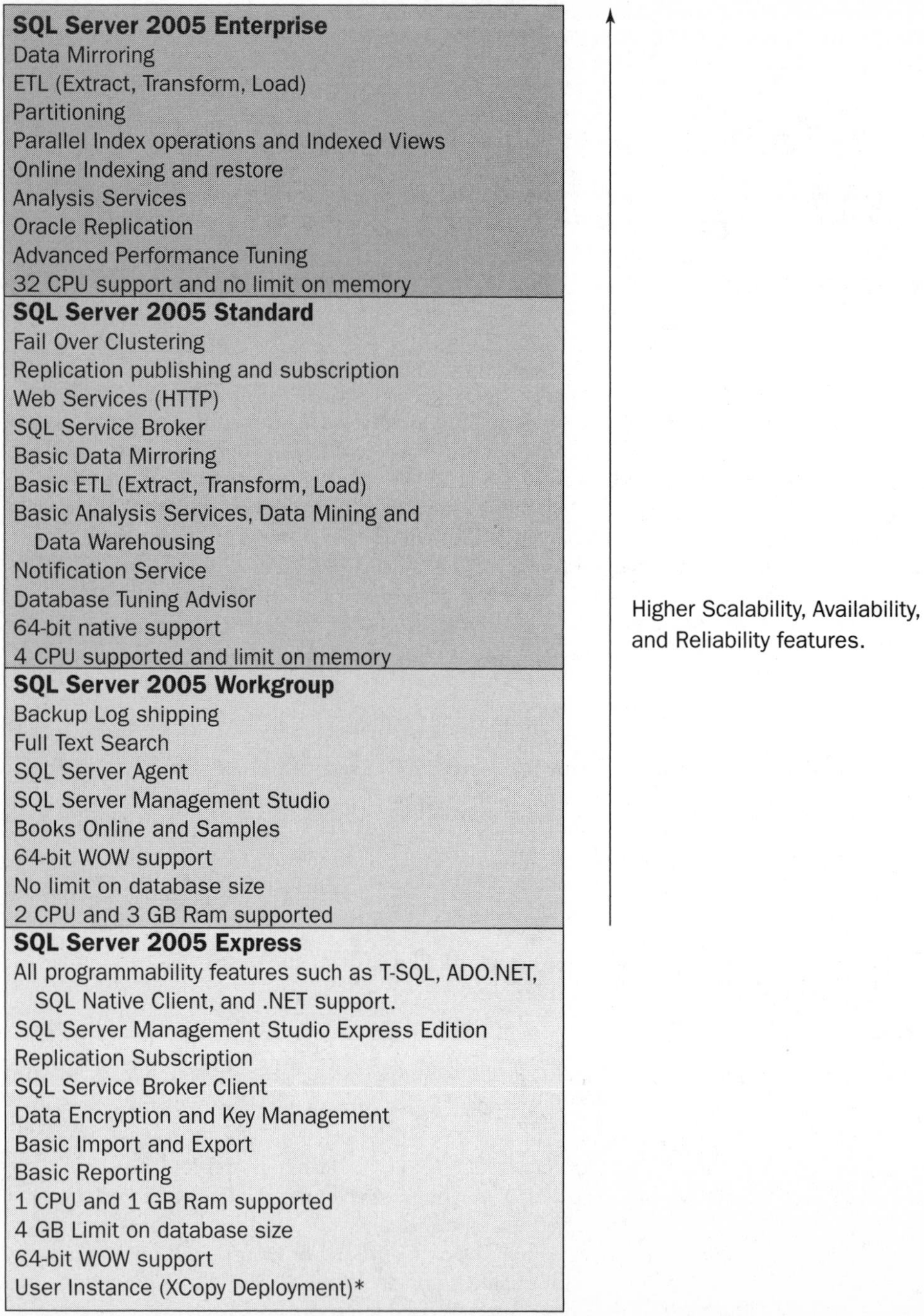

SQL Server 2005 Enterprise
Data Mirroring
ETL (Extract, Transform, Load)
Partitioning
Parallel Index operations and Indexed Views
Online Indexing and restore
Analysis Services
Oracle Replication
Advanced Performance Tuning
32 CPU support and no limit on memory

SQL Server 2005 Standard
Fail Over Clustering
Replication publishing and subscription
Web Services (HTTP)
SQL Service Broker
Basic Data Mirroring
Basic ETL (Extract, Transform, Load)
Basic Analysis Services, Data Mining and
    Data Warehousing
Notification Service
Database Tuning Advisor
64-bit native support
4 CPU supported and limit on memory

SQL Server 2005 Workgroup
Backup Log shipping
Full Text Search
SQL Server Agent
SQL Server Management Studio
Books Online and Samples
64-bit WOW support
No limit on database size
2 CPU and 3 GB Ram supported

SQL Server 2005 Express
All programmability features such as T-SQL, ADO.NET,
    SQL Native Client, and .NET support.
SQL Server Management Studio Express Edition
Replication Subscription
SQL Service Broker Client
Data Encryption and Key Management
Basic Import and Export
Basic Reporting
1 CPU and 1 GB Ram supported
4 GB Limit on database size
64-bit WOW support
User Instance (XCopy Deployment)*

Higher Scalability, Availability, and Reliability features.

*All the features except for User Instance (XCopy Deployment) are present in higher level editions.

Figure 1-1

SQL Server 2005 Express Edition is a free database management system based on Microsoft SQL Server 2005 that allows you to define, store, and manipulate data in an integrated fashion. It enables you to share data with others, while preserving user security and permission features. You can store data in an application-independent manner while making sure that redundancy and inconsistency are reduced and that data integrity is maintained. Data access APIs that follow industry-wide standards, such as ODBC and OLE DB, are provided in both native and managed code so that it is easy to import and export data from different sources.

SQL Server 2005 Express Edition Highlights

SQL Server 2005 Express Edition is a great database for developers, and includes all the important programming features present in other SQL Server 2005 editions. In fact, SSE contains the same database engine that ships with other SQL Server 2005 editions. The SQL Server 2005 database engine contains support for the networking protocols, T-SQL, and the storage layer. Advanced features such as .NET support, the XML data type, stored procedures and triggers, and replication subscription are also present. SSE supports databases up to 4GB. An application developed using SSE typically works seamlessly with other editions of SQL Server 2005. There is no limit on the number of user connections to the database, but performance is limited by the use of a single CPU and 4GB RAM. Typically applications using SSE can scale to 25 concurrent users.

Easy-to-use graphical interfaces provided with the SQL Server Management Studio Express Edition (SSMS-EE) Graphical User Interface (GUI) management tool simplify the basic database operations. This tool contains a query editor that enables you to interactively work with data inside the database. SQL Server Configuration Manager allows you to configure networking options. The SSE setup offers extensive graphical interface tools that allow you to configure the installation. Silent installs are also supported so that you can transparently install SSE with your application. Servicing of SSE is integrated with Windows Update and is almost automatic for the user.

There is deep integration of SQL Server 2005 Express Edition with all editions of Visual Studio, including Visual Basic Express and Visual Web Developer 2005 Express. The rich data controls provided automate simple tasks so that you can develop a forms-based application that uses a SSE database without writing a line of code. The single-user scenario that is commonly used for desktop clients and web users is simplified by the Xcopy feature in SSE that enables the database files to be copied and moved like normal windows files. Xcopy deployment simplifies the deployment of your application so that you can just zip up your application and database file and email it to the destination user. The recipient copies the unzipped file to her machine and double-clicks the application to run it.

Upgrading from Other Products

If you are currently using Microsoft Desktop Engine (MSDE), this book is important to you because SSE is the free upgrade path to use the SQL Server 2005 functionality. The workload governor present in MSDE is removed in SSE and there are no limits on the number of concurrent operations at any given time. Because earlier versions of MSDE had licensing ambiguities, SSE has a simple licensing structure and is free for production and distribution. The SSE setup is greatly improved, with new dialogs guiding you through the installation process. Deployment is also simplified by features such as Xcopy and integration with Visual Studio ClickOnce that allows you to create a deployment package with a simple click of a mouse. The introduction of SQL Server Management Studio Express Edition (SSMS-EE) is also an important milestone, as MSDE did not have a graphical user interface management tool.

If you are currently using the Jet database with Access or Visual Basic applications, switching to SSE may offer some advantages. Use SSE instead of Jet for scaling in multi-user scenarios and improved security features. .NET support is available only with SSE, so that you can program with C# or VB .NET on both the client and the server. Upgrading your applications to SQL Server is also easy if you use SSE. Jet is preferred over SSE in scenarios where you are highly concerned about the storage space or system memory, or where there are strict web download requirements. Chapter 12 provides more information about upgrading your applications to SSE.

Features and Benefits of SSE

Although SSE is the most basic member of the SQL Server 2005 family, it contains features necessary for database users ranging from beginner students to Independent Software Vendors (ISVs) developing complex redistributable applications. The following list points out some of SSE's best features:

❑ **Data types:** As mentioned, SSE ships with the same database engine that is behind the SQL Server 2005 Enterprise Edition and supports data types such as User-Defined data types (UDT), the XML data type, and VarChar(MAX). UDTs enable you to define new complex data types in C# or VB .NET. SSE supports the native XML data type that allows you to directly manipulate or query XML on the server, while the VarChar(MAX) data type allows you to store large character objects with a maximum size of 2GB. A complete list of the data types supported by SSE is provided in Chapter 2.

❑ **Language independent:** Supporting .NET inside SSE allows you to use your favorite .NET language such as C#, VB .NET, or J# for database development. Your VB .NET application runs inside SSE and queries the database engine using the ADO.NET APIs. ADO.NET exposes .NET classes in all your favorite programming languages to connect to a database instance as well as to create and manipulate database objects such as tables and schemas. Using .NET, your ADO.NET functions can now run inside SSE, not just on your client machine. Use this feature for procedural code where individual records are manipulated one at a time.

❑ **Ease of deployment:** Xcopy deployment allows you to copy, move, and delete database files just like normal Windows files. There is support for SSE with all Visual Studio editions so that it is possible to develop simple desktop and web database applications without writing a line of code. Building, debugging, and deploying your application is possible with a few mouse clicks from within Visual Basic Express or Visual Web Developer Express. Chapter 3 guides you through the steps for developing your first client application. Application deployment becomes very easy with Xcopy deployment and Visual Studio ClickOnce support. You can learn more about deployment in Chapters 6 and 10.

❑ **User instance functionality:** SSE supports the Run as Normal User scenarios, where a non-administrator on the local machine can use the functionality of SSE without having to involve the system administrator. This is enabled using the user instance functionality that provides for a private instance of SSE running in each user's context. These user instances are automatically started up by the application using the database owned by the user. One of the goals for the user instance is to make the single-user scenario very simple; the application developer need not worry about the complicated SQL Server Security model. SSE supports a file-based permission model which means that the read and write permissions on the physical database file are used to assign user permissions and privileges. SSE can also be used as a server where multiple users can connect to the server database; the performance characteristics of the server are governed by the limits on the CPU and memory usage. An instance of SSE can use only one CPU and 4GB RAM.

❑ **Security:** Much thought was given to making SSE install and run securely on your machine. Only local machine access is enabled by default because a majority of the SSE use cases are for local data. SSE runs under a low privilege service account. The user instance feature described earlier ensures that SSE runs under the context of each user for single-user scenarios. For multi-user scenarios, the SQL Server security model ensures appropriate access to authenticated users. Advanced security features including encryption are also included in the product.

❑ **Replication and messaging capabilities:** SSE supports offline capabilities by supporting replication subscription. Retail branches can subscribe to central offices with synchronization between the servers occurring at regular intervals. The SQL Service Broker feature supported by SSE provides asynchronous messaging capabilities so that SSE can send a message to SQL Server. This is particularly relevant for B2B web services.

❑ **Management tools:** The SQL Server Management Studio Express Edition tool, which is available via web download, offers capabilities to develop and test against SSE. It has a query editor that allows you to execute arbitrary T-SQL statements. SQL Server Configuration Manager allows you to change networking protocol settings and the SQL Service options. Rich command line facilities are available with the SQLCMD command line tool, while the SQL Bulk Copy (BCP) tool provides bulk transfer features.

❑ **Easy setup options:** SSE provides a reliable and robust setup user interface that guides you through the various setup and configuration options. A silent setup option is available where little or no user interface is shown. In a silent install you have to pass in the relevant configuration values as command line parameters or in setup initialization files. The silent option is typically preferred by ISVs who want to completely control the user experience, for instance, they want their application logo to show on the screen during installation.

SSE User Scenarios

SSE targets three main user segments:

❑ Developers building simple web applications

❑ ISV/ Developers redistributing SQL Server 2005 Express Edition as a client data store

❑ Small or medium business IT developers building transactional web and client server applications

Additionally, there are secondary user segments such as academics using SSE for education and server application developers using SSE as a cheap database server. Usage patterns differ for each of these user segments.

Web developers use SSE to store application data; SSE could be installed on a local or remote box. The application is deployed on the local machine during development, testing, and debugging. A remote web-facing machine is typically selected for production. The user can also use a third-party hosting provider, in which case the database is already provisioned and the user is responsible for copying the application files as well as updating the SSE database.

Desktop users primarily use SSE as a client database for storing application data on the local machine. For example, a photo album application might store an images database in SSE. Most of these applications are single-user applications.

ISVs typically use SSE as the database for their single-user or multi-user applications. Typically SSE is used with desktop editions of the application. For example, a 5-user edition of a customer-service application may use SSE, but the 50-user edition of the same application is likely to use SQL Server Standard. A seamless upgrade to other editions of SQL Server such as SQL Server 2005 Standard and Enterprise is important in this scenario.

The user gets SSE either from tools supplied by Microsoft like Visual Basic Express and Visual Web Developer 2005 Express, or as a web download from the Microsoft site. SSE can also be installed with third-party applications that redistribute it. The CD accompanying this book contains a version of SSE that can be used in both single-user and multi-user modes.

The following sections describe some of the common scenarios for using SSE.

Desktop Application with Single-User SSE

In this scenario, a simple single-user application running on your desktop or laptop uses SSE to store application data locally. For example, a tax preparation application might store tax information inside an SSE database. Many desktop applications developed with Microsoft Visual Basic Express and Microsoft Access fall into this category. The cost of licensing other editions of SQL Server for this scenario typically overwhelms the cost of the application itself, making SSE the most viable option.

If you are developing a desktop application, you can simply zip it up and email it to an end-user. Double-clicking the application executable on the user's computer launches the application. No extra configuration is required by the recipient. An ISV commercially developing software can also use the Visual Studio ClickOnce technology to deploy the application to one or more desktops. ClickOnce invokes the SSE setup utility, which is designed to install both client and server components on the local machine. The deployment process installs SSE on behalf of the user at the same time the application is itself installed if SSE is not already present on the machine. Multiple applications can share SSE, but each user on the local machine gets a private copy of the SSE instance using the user instance feature.

When you attempt to use a database in single-user mode, a user instance is spawned in the user context so that the database gets attached to the private instance. File-based permissions on the database file are used to verify whether a particular user can access the database file. The user spawning the user instance is a system administrator on this private instance. No other user can access this private instance and the physical database file cannot be shared by another user concurrently. Figure 1-2 shows a sample home desktop where the father and child have separate user instances for their applications.

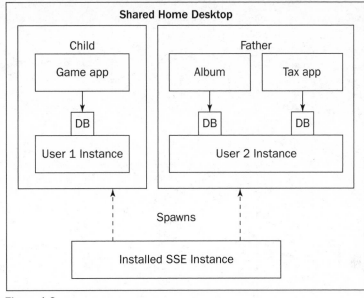

Figure 1-2

Certain SSE features are disabled when using user instances. For example, only Windows-based credentials are used for authentication. Features such as replication and SQL Server Service Broker will not work. Remote machine access using the TCP/IP or Named Pipes protocols is also not possible. The advantages of using the user instance feature include the ease of application development as well as the Run as Normal User scenarios. In the Run as Normal User scenario, a non-administrator on the local machine can develop, debug, and deploy SSE-based applications without any administrator-provisioned privileges. Chapter 6 covers user instances in more detail.

Typically, the application user need not worry about administering, installing, or servicing SSE because the application developer or ISV takes care of all the installation and configuration. Servicing of SSE is enabled using Windows Update so that you do not have to worry about getting the latest bits.

Client/Server Application with Multi-User SSE

Some desktop applications use a single SSE instance running as a Windows service to support a small workgroup of users. All users read and write data to a shared database instance residing on a file server, or on a workgroup member's own computer. SSE is installed only on the computer sharing the data. This scenario includes an application that is intended from the beginning to be used in a workgroup situation, as well as applications "growing up" by popular demand. An example of the latter category is a project-tracking application that grows in popularity within a firm so that the user base increases over time. A project-tracking application used by applications running on three desktops is shown in Figure 1-3.

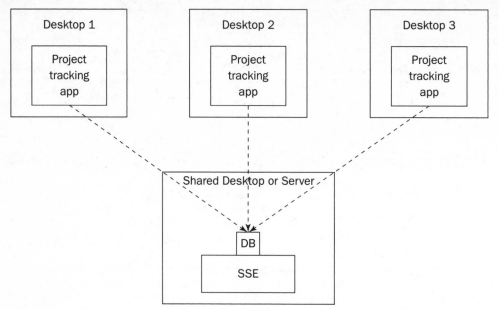

Figure 1-3

This scenario also includes ISV applications using Visual Studio tools to create and deploy client-server applications for small workgroups where other editions of SQL Server 2005 are too expensive.

SSE does not have any concurrency or user limits; limits are based on the hardware on which it is installed. Typically, the growth in the number of users to more than 25 requires upgrading to other editions of SQL Server 2005. The upgrade process is easy since the database engine as well as the client and server programming logic is similar across the different editions of SQL Server 2005.

Application developers developing multi-user applications must understand and deal with the SQL Server security model since the user instances security model is strictly single-user based. SQL Server 2005 Express Edition running as a service can handle multiple users accessing a shared resource concurrently. The application developer must handle the concurrency issues and define the permissions on shared objects. Security is covered in Chapter 13, while the issues surrounding concurrency are covered in Chapter 15.

The ClickOnce deployment feature exposed by Visual Basic Express is enabled for SSE, and client server applications are typically deployed using the setup.exe created by ClickOnce deployment. Chapter 10 deals with ClickOnce deployment in detail.

Application Replicating with a Central Office

In this scenario, the multi-user application explained in the scenario above is expanded to replicate a single, per-store, shared database with a centralized SQL Server backend. For example, in a retail store application replicating with the central office scenario, each store has one or more computers (such as checkout stations) accessing or modifying data in the shared database. Replication will periodically download new pricing and catalog data while uploading sales data. Connection to the central office may be periodically interrupted for hours or days for various reasons. In this scenario, each computer may have its own SSE database, or there may be only one SSE database that is shared by multiple computers. Synchronization is typically conducted on a regular schedule, such as nightly, but can be interrupted on occasion by unexpected outages. Figure 1-4 illustrates this scenario.

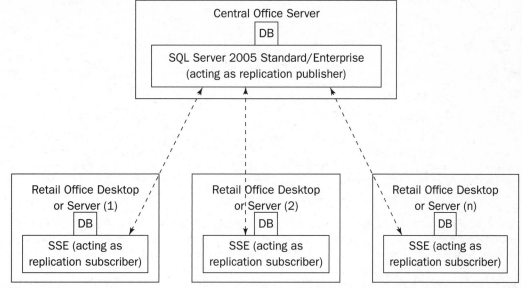

Figure 1-4

The disconnected sales force application is a related scenario where the remote computers are laptops used by the sales force and data is periodically replicated back to the central office. Various customer or sales data can be stored locally in either a read-only or a read-write access mode. In this case the laptop may be periodically synchronized with a central database at indeterminate intervals.

No tools are supplied with SSE to set up or administer replication. However, the replication tools supplied with other editions of SQL Server can be used with SSE as long as the SSE instance is replicating back to an edition of SQL Server 2005 higher than SSE.

Replication is outside the scope of this book and is not covered further.

Single-User ASP.NET Applications

You can develop web ppplications using the Visual Web Developer Express provided with the book. SSE has tight integration with Visual Web Developer to create ASP.NET applications. It is so easy to use that you can create data sources and build and debug applications without writing a single line of code. Chapter 5 guides you through creating ASP.NET applications.

After the ASP.NET web application is debugged and tested on the local machine, you can copy the relevant application and database files using the copy database or deploy database features in Visual Web Developer. The ability to treat database files just like regular Windows files, or Xcopy deployment, enables these copying scenarios. This is illustrated in Figure 1-5.

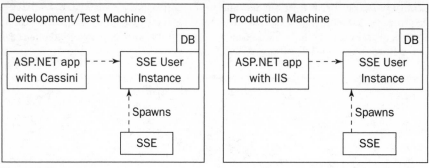

Figure 1-5

A web application runs under the context of a web server like IIS that translates a URL either into a URL or into an executable name, and then sends its output back. ASP.NET web applications support using IIS Web Server for remote scenarios and Cassini Web Server for local machine scenarios. Cassini is a secure, local web server introduced by Microsoft that supports local development and debugging scenarios. You can easily copy or deploy your ASP.NET application to a local or remote machine with only a few mouse clicks.

A user hosting a web application on his machine installs IIS and deploys the web application. This is often called a *dedicated hosting scenario* because the web server is dedicated to the applications that the user is knowledgeable about. There are no applications that are unknown or untrusted by the user on that machine. The dedicated hosting scenario typically uses the user instance feature in SSE because all connectivity to the database happens under the context of a single user, ASP.NET. The user must have copy, deployment, and debugging privileges on the working directory and machine.

It is important to understand what a single user means in the context of a web application. Although anonymous users over the Internet are accessing a web application, typically all database access is done under the context of a single user. The exception to this happens when the user impersonation feature is turned on so that the database access happens in the context of the Internet user who is accessing the website.

For example, consider a MyGarageSale web application that uses SSE to store the catalog of items sold and their prices. When the user accesses the MyGarageSale website, information is retrieved from the SSE database. Because the user's credentials may not be known ahead of time, the database access occurs under the context of a single user, ASP.NET.

ASP.NET Third-Party Hosting

This scenario involves the use of a third-party hosting provider when developers typically lease space on a web server host machine in return for administration services and a quality of service guarantee. The service is provided at a reduced cost by sharing the web server resources across several sites at once. Once you sign up as a user, you get a user directory to place your files, as well as a login and password with relevant privileges. This is a shared user scenario where there are untrusted applications running on the same machine. Each machine used by the third-party hosting provider could contain a large number of websites and users unknown to each other. To avoid name conflicts and the prospect of one user trampling on another user's files, this environment is tightly controlled by the administrator and each user is granted only the minimum required privileges.

Because most web applications are data-driven, it is common for a developer to purchase one or more databases from the hosting provider as part of their hosting contract. These databases are provisioned ahead of time and provide users with a connection string for accessing their databases. Most hosting providers provide web-based administration tools for creating and modifying schema and data.

> **Do not use the SSE user instance feature in a multi-user or third-party hosting scenario. For explanations refer to Chapter 6.**

Server Database Application

The server database application scenario refers to an economical deployment of a large-scale, SQL Server-based server application where components are installed in a simpler, cheaper, server configuration. They could be web-facing applications. There are three typical sub-scenarios including usage: as evaluation copies, single-user or small-user editions, and low-volume web applications.

The evaluation scenario covers the case of a server application that must be deployed on a single machine for evaluation or demo purposes. For example, the evaluation edition of a customer service application can ship with SSE or SQL Server Evaluation edition. The application development scenario is a subset of the evaluation scenario that involves the usage of SSE only in the design and development phase of a SQL Server application. ISVs develop applications using free SSE licenses while relying on their customers to purchase SQL Server licenses for testing and production deployment. This scenario enables development to proceed on client operating systems on desktops or laptops. The SQL Server 2005 Evaluation edition can also be used for this purpose. The Evaluation edition contains all the features of SQL Server 2005 Enterprise edition and has a trial period of 120 days.

The single-user or limited-user edition scenario is similar to the evaluation scenario, except that the deployment is used in production for a small number of users. This is commonly required to cover the low-volume scenario of a server application that requires SQL Server 2005 for its data access. The low-volume web application scenario typically includes web applications deployed on web servers with low concurrent usage patterns. However, this includes a model where the server application stores configuration or other data that does not get directly queried by remote clients, and hence the SSE use is typically low-volume. The SQL Server compatibility for easy scalability as well as the price point provides the primary attraction for SSE in this scenario.

Whereas the previous scenarios involve end-users installing applications on desktop operating systems, the server scenarios generally involve more knowledgeable end-users or even IT staff, and will always include installation on server operating systems. Thus the deployment environment will more closely match that of other editions of SQL Server 2005; however, the end-user will still not be as typically skilled or experienced as the SQL Server administrator in a server environment.

Licensing and Support

SSE is free to deploy in production environments, and you can redistribute it along with your application. However, the default web download license does not allow you to redistribute it. You must register for free at http://www.microsoft.com/sql/howtobuy/default.asp to get a license to redistribute SSE. Registration is required for redistribution in order to ensure that Microsoft can disseminate critical security information to partners if necessary.

Similarly the tools supplied with SSE, such as SSMS-EE, are free to use and redistribute. Any tool like SQL Server Management Studio (SSMS) that does not ship with SSE can be used with SSE only when SSE is used in conjunction with another edition of SQL Server 2005. For example, SSMS-EE does not have any replication-related tools even though SSE supports replication subscription. To use the replication tools inside SQL Server Management Studio, SSE has to be a replication subscriber to another edition of SQL Server 2005. Whenever you use SQL Server Express to connect to another licensed non-express edition of SQL Server 2005, Client Access License (CAL) is required. It does not matter whether the users are connecting directly or indirectly either through SQL Server Express or a website. For example if five users connect to SQL Server 2005 Standard edition using a terminal server, five CALs are required even though only a single machine is used to connect to the database instance.

SSE is fully supported by Microsoft via websites and newsgroups. Support via email and phone is also available for a fee.

Visual Basic or C#

A couple of words about the choice of programming language are appropriate here. Either Visual Basic 2005 or C# 2005 will work just fine; you should be able to get all your database application work done in either language. But, the teams developing these languages have different goals and you should keep those goals in mind when you select your language.

Visual Basic 2005 is targeted as an upgrade path for the millions of existing Visual Basic 6.0 users. The language syntax and features are specifically designed with that customer in mind. The Visual Basic language has rapid productivity, simplicity, and ease-of-learning as primary goals. The Visual Basic team is interested in making sure that everyone from first-time users to developers of corporate IT database applications are happy with the language's features.

C# 2005 is targeted as a home both for the C++ and Java developers. The C# language syntax is intended as a modern, general purpose, object-oriented language (with special emphasis on general purpose). The C# team is interested in making sure that C# remains at the forefront of the object-oriented programming world by introducing practical modern language innovation to the programming public.

You can choose to write in either Visual Basic or C#. The examples in this book will all use Visual Basic, but it should be very easy to find or create the exact same elements for C#.

You can use the Visual Basic 2005 Express edition for most of the examples in this book. The Express editions of Visual Studio are inexpensive. The higher-level editions of Visual Studio make building data-centric applications even easier with some advanced features. Specifically, higher-level editions of Visual Studio enable connections to remote databases for all languages, enable T-SQL debugging, and allow for database projects. If you want to try out these features, you'll need to get a higher-level edition of Visual Studio than the Express editions.

Installing SSE and Visual Basic Express

This section introduces you to the hardware and software requirements of SSE and Visual Basic Express along with the basic steps used to install these products on your local machine. If you encounter any issues during the installation process, please refer to Chapter 9 for more information about the setup procedures for SSE.

Hardware and Software Requirements for SSE

The following table lists the minimum hardware and software requirements for running Microsoft SQL Server 2005 Express Edition on a 32-bit machine.

Hardware	Minimum Requirements
Computer	Intel or compatible Pentium 600 MHz (recommended: Intel or compatible 1 GHz or higher)
Windows version	Windows Server 2003 SP1, Windows XP SP2, Windows 2000 SP4
Memory (RAM)	192MB minimum (recommended: 256MB or higher)
Hard disk space	525MB
Monitor	VGA or higher resolution 1,024x768
Pointing device	Microsoft mouse or compatible pointing device
CD-ROM drive	Required for CD installation

Support for SQL Express is limited to the Windows on Windows (WOW) 32-bit subsystem on 64-bit operating systems.

> **The proper version of .NET Framework 2.0 must be installed prior to installing SQL Server 2005 Express Edition. You should remove any previously installed version of .NET Framework 2.0 before installing a later version.**

Hardware and Software Requirements for Visual Basic 2005 Express Edition

The following table lists the minimum hardware and software requirements for running Microsoft Visual Basic 2005 Express Edition on a 32-bit machine. The hard disk size includes the .NET Framework installation.

Hardware	Minimum Requirements	Recommendation
Computer	Intel or compatible Pentium 600 MHz	Intel or compatible 1 GHz or higher
Windows versions	Microsoft Windows 2003 Server Windows XP SP2 Windows 2000 SP4	Microsoft Windows 2003 Server Windows XP SP2 Windows 2000 SP4
Memory (RAM)	128MB minimum	256MB or higher
Hard disk space	500MB typical, up to 1.3GB may be required	1.3GB free space
Monitor	VGA or higher resolution 800x600 256 colors	VGA or higher resolution 1,024x768 Hi Color -16-bit
Pointing device	Microsoft mouse or compatible pointing device	Microsoft mouse or compatible pointing device
CD-ROM drive	Required for CD installation	Required for CD installation

Installation Steps

After verifying that you have the necessary hardware and software, follow these steps to install SSE and Visual Basic 2005 Express Edition on your local machine:

Warning: If you have any previous versions of Visual Basic 2005 Express Edition, SSE, or .NET Framework 2.0 on your computer, they must be uninstalled prior to installing SSE and VB .NET.

1. Insert the CD that comes with this book and double-click vbsetup.exe. Click Run when the Internet Explorer Security Warning popup appears.

2. On the Welcome page of the Installation Wizard, click Next.

3. The Licensing (EULA) page appears next. Read the license carefully before selecting the check box, which activates the Next button.

4. In the Installation Options dialog that appears, check the box for Microsoft SQL Server 2005 Express Edition and click Next (see Figure 1-6).

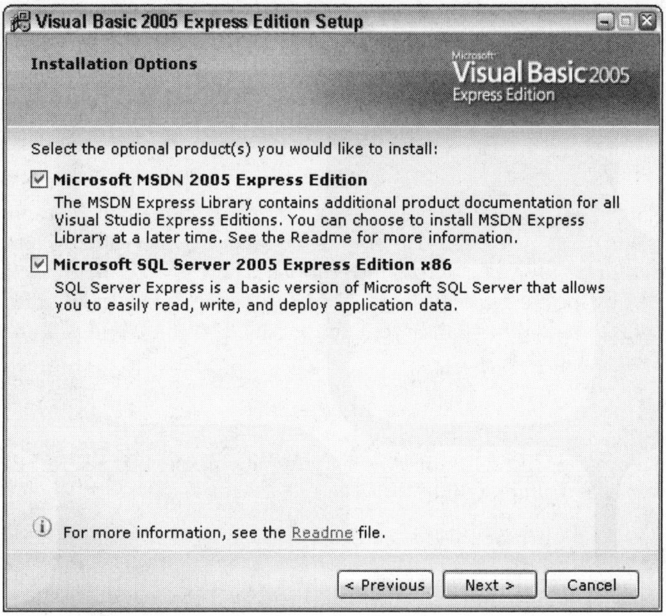

Figure 1-6

5. In the Destination Folder dialog box, click Install. You need not change the default destination location (see Figure 1-7).

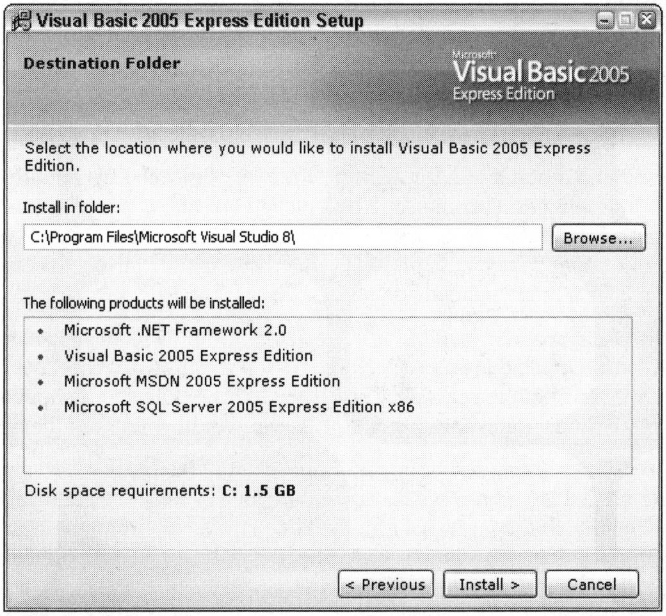

Figure 1-7

6. A progress bar is displayed to show that the Visual Basic 2005 Express Edition installation is in progress. Click Exit when the Setup Complete dialog appears.

Summary

This chapter introduced SQL Server 2005 Express Edition and some of its features, such as Xcopy and .NET support. SSE has the same database engine as the other SQL Server 2005 editions so that all the programmability features are similar across the editions. There is no limit on the number of users; the only limit is imposed by the hardware utilized. The relationship of SSE to other SQL Server 2005 editions, as well as its advantages over other databases such as MSDE and Jet, is also mentioned. This chapter addressed the following topics:

❑ SSE and its key features

❑ Important scenarios like Desktop Application with single-user SSE, ASP.NET hosting, and Client Server Application with multi-user SSE

❑ Licensing and support for SSE

❑ Hardware requirements for installing SSE and VB .NET

❑ Installing SSE and Visual Basic 2005 Express Edition on your machine

In the next chapter, you learn more about the basic database features supported by SSE.

Exercises

Try the exercises that follow to test your understanding of the material covered in this chapter. You can find the solutions to these exercises in Appendix A.

1. You are the chairperson for a university alumni association and want to figure out the appropriate SQL Server 2005 edition to use for a photo album application. This application is an interface for digital photographs and is expected to be installed on each member's desktop. There is no sharing of the application between members, as each person gets a personal copy of the database and the application. Annually the databases are updated and emailed to each member. What edition of SQL Server 2005 would you use?

2. You are the IT department head of Joe's Auto Parts. Your 75 retail shops are distributed in multiple states across the United States, and each retail shop requires two checkout counters that have the latest information about the catalog. The central office requires daily updates of sales information from the retail shops. What editions of SQL Server would you use in the retail and central offices?

3. You are an ISV deploying server applications to small businesses with one to five users. You want to move to the medium business segment supporting a larger number of users. Currently you are using SSE in the multi-user mode. How easy is it to move to higher editions of SQL Server?

Database Basics with SQL Server Management Studio Express Edition

Microsoft SQL Server 2005 Management Studio Express Edition (SSMS-EE) is a new database management tool for SQL Server 2005 Express (SSE). This simple-to-use tool is a simplified version of SQL Server Management Studio that ships with other versions of SQL Server 2005. It is designed for SSE customers who want an easy and intuitive graphical user interface (GUI) for doing the basic database management operations. This chapter is intended as an introduction to this tool, and explains the basic database objects that the user should know when dealing with SSE. This chapter covers the following topics:

❑ Databases and objects within the database

❑ SSMS-EE features such as Object Explorer and Query Editor

❑ Using Transact-SQL to develop simple queries

❑ Using the Query editor to create, delete, and modify common database objects such as databases, tables, views, stored procedures, and functions

Basic Database Concepts

Data in SSE is stored in a relational format inside a database. A *relational database* stores all its data in tables and all the operations on data are performed on these tables. A *table* is a grid of rows and columns. Each row is called a record, and contains values for the different columns. Some of these values could be NULL. A column is also called a field and defines the type of data that will be stored in that column. For example, in the top table in Figure 2-1, the columns define the fact that each row will contain an ID, Last Name, First Name, and Title. The third row or record, for example, will contain the values 10003, Borne, Peter, and Software Engineer. You define each column to be a particular type. For example, ID contains integers, while the Last Name, First Name, and Title store character data.

Customer Table

ID	Last Name	First Name	Title
10001	Gajanan	Piyush	Manager
10002	Chekov	Pasha	Administrator
10003	Borne	Peter	Software Engineer

→ Row or record

Unique   Column
primary key   or field

Ship to Customer Table

Ship ID	Customer ID	Ship Description	Street Address	State	Country	Zip
50001	10002	Book	1111 44th Ave	WA	US	98116
50002	10001	CD	2222 30th Ave	WA	US	98199
50003	10003	Antique	44200 32nd Ave	WA	US	98007

Unique   Foreign Key:
primary key   Customer ID
related to ID in
Customer Table

Figure 2-1

To distinguish between records, it is typical to define a field called the *primary key* that is unique. For example, in the Customer table shown in the figure, the ID field is the primary key. Duplicates are not allowed in the primary key, and hence you can uniquely refer to each record using the primary key. Sometimes multiple fields are used in the definition of the primary key. These primary keys are also useful to define relationships between tables. For example, the ShipToCustomer table contains a field called CustomerID. Each entry in CustomerID refers to an entry in the ID field of the Customer table. CustomerID is called a *foreign key* because it is a primary key defined in another table. Any data in a foreign key column must have corresponding data in the table where that column is the primary key. This mapping makes sure that there is no ShipToCustomer row without a valid customer.

When designing tables, three simple rules called the *three normal forms* are often used. These rules are:

1. All column values are single or atomic.

2. All column values depend on the value of the primary key.

3. No column value depends on the value of any other column except the primary key.

Consider the ShipToCustomer table in Figure 2-1. The customer shipping address details such as Street Address, State, Country, and Zip (zip code) are stored in separate columns. This is useful, for example, in calculating the shipping cost based on the Zip and country. If a single column is used to store this information, you have non-atomic values and calculation of shipping cost becomes difficult. To conform to the first normalization rule, you typically split the column with a collection of information into separate columns.

If you use one table to store both Customer and ShipToCustomer information with CustomerID as the primary key, you violate the second and third rules. Some of the columns in such a combined table, like Title, would depend only on the customer ID, while the others like ShipDescription depend only on ShipID. If the ShipID value in a row changes, the ShipDescription will also change. This design is also inefficient because the customer information has to be entered again for repeat purchases. To conform to the second and third normalization rules, you should first identify the dependencies between columns. Now split the large table with columns depending on fields other than the primary key into two or more distinct tables. You can use the foreign key concept described earlier to maintain the relationship between tables. To satisfy the third rule, do not store any calculated values.

When you apply the three rules, the database is *normalized*. A normalized database generally improves performance, lowers storage requirements, and makes it easier to change the application. Some specialized databases like decision support systems and data warehouses are explicitly built in violation of the three rules. They are called *de-normalized* databases, and are used because the data changes infrequently and because you are dealing with huge amounts of data used for reports or analysis. These special de-normalized database applications are not covered in this book.

An *index* can speed the search for a particular row or set of rows. Similar to a book index, an index to a database makes it easy for you to retrieve the data. Indexes are typically defined on specific columns so that the data retrieval on that column is fast. When you have defined a primary key in a table, SSE automatically creates a unique index on the primary key columns so that no two rows have the same value for this index. In the Customer table presented in Figure 2-1, SSE automatically creates an index on ID. It is a good idea to define non-unique indexes on the foreign keys because some of the foreign key values can be repeated. For example, a non-unique index on the CustomerID field of the ShipToCustomer table is useful for queries looking at active orders of a particular customer. Create indexes for improving performance of commonly used queries, but do not create unnecessary indexes since these could adversely affect database performance.

To insert a new Customer into the Customer Table or to create a new table for Inventory, use the *Structured Query Language (SQL)* programming language. SQL Server 2005 uses a dialect of SQL that is called either Transact-SQL or T-SQL. Transact-SQL (T-SQL) is an extension of the SQL standards authorized by the American National Standards Institute (ANSI) and the International Organization for Standardization (ISO). You will learn more about using T-SQL later in this chapter.

At first glance, T-SQL may seem complex. But once you understand the difference between a *procedural* and *declarative* language, it becomes simple. Visual Basic .NET is a procedural language, which means that you describe exactly the operations to be executed. An example would be using a `for` loop to read all the data from a text file. In a declarative language like T-SQL, you declare what you are looking for using the `SELECT` keyword, and SSE figures out how to get it. For example, the following SQL statement returns all rows from the Customer table where the Last Name is *Borne*. The explanations for the elements in this statement are provided later in this chapter.

```
SELECT * FROM Customer WHERE LastName='Borne'
```

A procedure or function is used in Visual Basic .NET to store a sequence of reusable code. SSE supports similar functionality for storing reusable units of T-SQL code. The *stored procedures* or *functions* in SSE contain a sequence of T-SQL statements that are stored inside the SSE database. They allow passing parameters and can be executed as a unit. SSE functions can return values that are in a table format, but stored procedures do not support this.

Introduction to SQL Server Management Studio Express Edition

SQL Server Management Studio Express Edition (SSMS-EE) is a free download from the Microsoft website, and is used to manage SSE. SSMS-EE includes the following features:

- ❑ A single, integrated, easy-to-use GUI for simple database operations
- ❑ Wizards for managing and creating objects like databases and tables
- ❑ The capability to view the objects within a database using the Object Explorer
- ❑ A robust query editor that supports multiple result sets

SSMS-EE is released separately from the SQL Server 2005 Express releases. The first version of SSMS-EE is expected to be released to the web a few months after the SSE launch in November 2005. SQL Server Management Studio, supplied with other editions of SQL Server, can be downloaded from http://www .microsoft.com/sql/2005/default.mspx and can be used against SSE in certain cases. Please refer to the licensing section for additional information.

> **You must be an administrator on the machine or be the system administrator (sysadmin) in SSE to use the examples in this chapter.**

Using SSMS-EE for the First Time

From the Start menu, select All Programs ➪ SQL Server 2005 ➪ SQL Server Management Studio to start SSMS-EE. This section explains the graphical user interfaces in detail.

Connection Dialog

When you start SSMS-EE, you see a connection dialog similar to Figure 2-2. The first item you should select is the correct instance of SSE. Multiple installations of SQL Server can run concurrently on a single machine, and each such installation is called an instance. For example, if you installed SSE according to the instructions in Chapter 1, the instance name used is *SQLExpress*. Supply a value of (local)\SQLExpress in the Server name field, or select <yourMachineName>\SQLExpress from the dropdown menu.

Next, choose how you want to login to SSE. There are two possible options: *Windows Authentication* and *SQL Server Authentication*. When using Windows Authentication mode, SSE uses the windows credentials that you supplied during login to your machine. This is the default authentication mode, and you do not have to pass in any additional information. If you choose SQL Server Authentication, you have to provide a user ID and password that is known to SSE.

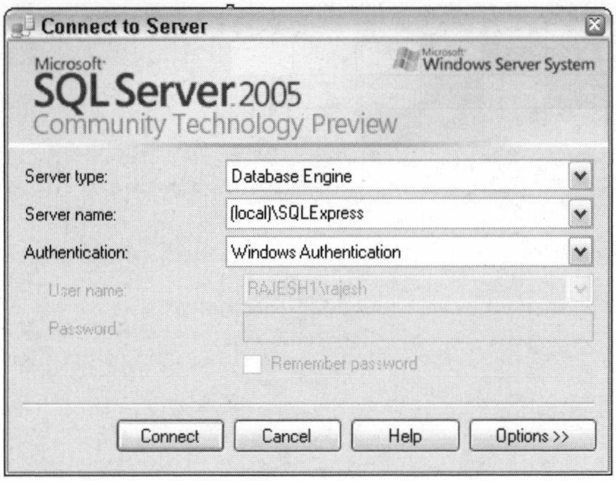

Figure 2-2

> Whenever possible, use Windows Authentication. SQL Server Authentication is disabled when you install SSE for the first time.

The authentication modes are described in detail in Chapter 13. Refer to that chapter for additional details on enabling SQL Authentication.

Click Connect to proceed with the connection, so that SSMS-EE connects to the specified server using the authentication properties provided. Clicking the Cancel button or the X icon will close the connection dialog.

SSMS-EE can only connect to SQL Servers that are running; no functionality is provided to start servers that are currently not running. You can use SQL Server Configuration manager to start and stop the services.

Object Explorer

Once you connect to an SSE instance using SSMS-EE, you will see a two-pane window similar to Figure 2-3. The left-hand pane, called the Object Explorer, contains details about your connection, databases, and security. This window is used to enumerate and display the most commonly referenced objects in the SSE instance. The Object Explorer is made up of the following components:

❑ The *Node window* uses a tree-like structure to represent SSE objects such as databases and tables. All the databases currently attached to the SSE instance and available to the user are listed in the database dropdown box. When users select a database, the Nodes window is populated with the database objects like tables and views for that database.

❑ When you right-click any of the objects displayed, you will get a Context Menu that exposes functionality available for that object.

❑ A toolbar is provided at the top with buttons for global functionality.

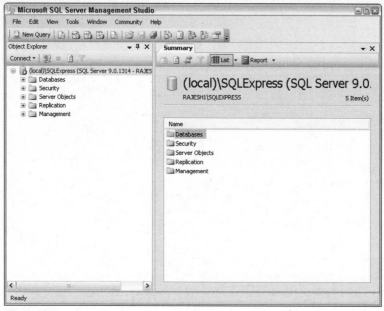

Figure 2-3

Node Window

The Node window displays database and security information for the SSE instance in a hierarchical fashion. The Databases node contains all the databases currently attached to the SSE instance that the user has permissions to connect to.

The important objects visible under an individual database node include:

- ❑ **Tables:** Expanding this node returns all the tables currently in the database. Expanding a table node retrieves all the columns and indexes on that table; columns are listed first followed by indexes.

- ❑ **Views:** Expanding this node returns all the views currently in the database.

- ❑ **Programmability:** Expanding this node returns all the programmability objects such as stored procedures and functions currently in the database.

- ❑ **Security:** Expanding this node returns all the security objects such as users defined in the database.

Right-clicking the objects at any level of the tree displays a context menu that contains operations that can be performed on that object. For instance, right-clicking the Databases node gives you the option to create a new database. Selecting this option launches the wizard for creating the new database as explained in the following Try It Out.

Try It Out   Creating, Renaming, and Deleting a Database Using SSMS-EE

1. From the Start menu, select All Programs ⇨ SQL Server 2005 ⇨ SQL Server Management Studio.

2. Enter the instance name in the Connection dialog and click Next. Typically, the instance name is (local)\SQLExpress.

3. Right-click the Databases node in the Object Explorer and select New Database.

4. Type **MyDatabase** for the database name and then click OK.

5. Expand the Databases node in the Object Explorer and verify that the database is present. Right-click MyDatabase and select Rename. Type the new name for the database (such as MyRenamedDatabase).

6. Right-click the same database again and select Delete. Confirm the action by clicking OK in the Delete Object dialog.

How It Works

This example demonstrates how easy it is to work with SSE databases using SSMS-EE. For example, you just need to specify the database name in order to create it. The Rename operation is similar to the renaming of a Windows file. There is an extra dialog when you try to delete the database to prevent user errors; if you do not want to delete the database, click Cancel.

Toolbar

The Toolbar for the Object Explorer contains functionality that is global in nature, and is independent of the selected node. The toolbar buttons and their behavior are described in the following list:

❑ **Connect:** Opens the connection dialog described earlier. This option allows users to choose which SQL Express server instance to connect to.

❑ **Refresh:** Refreshes the objects displayed in the object Explorer. The Refresh option is also available as a context menu for each object.

Query Editor

Although SSMS_EE provides an extensive graphical interface for managing SQL Express databases, many database users prefer to manage their servers using the T-SQL language supported by SSE. The Query Editor allows users to develop and execute T-SQL statements (see the right-hand pane in Figure 2-3). Groups of statements called *scripts* can also be executed against SSE. There are two main windows, *Editor window* and the *Results window*:

❑ The Editor window is used to develop and execute T-SQL statements and scripts. It can recognize and color-code T-SQL reserved words. A toolbar specifies the current database and options for displaying the results.

❑ The Results window displays the results of executing a query. Results are displayed as a grid, a text file, or can be saved to disk. Any messages or errors from executing the code are seen in the Message View.

The following Try It Out explores the query editor feature in SSMS-EE. You learn to execute simple queries, and use the drag-and-drop features in SSMS-EE.

Try It Out   Exploring the Query Editor

1. Click the New Query button to start the Query Editor.

2. Click the dropdown menu in the Editor window toolbar. You will see the list of databases attached to SSE. Make sure master database is selected.

3. Type the following SELECT command into the Query Editor (the first line is simply a comment). Notice the color-coding on the screen.

```
--The statement below shows the list of currently attached databases
SELECT * FROM sysdatabases
```

4. Press the hotkey F5 or use the Execute button to execute the statement.

5. Go to the Results window and look at both the Results and Messages tabs.

6. Go to the toolbar and select Results To File. Press the hotkey F5 or use the Execute button to execute the statement. Enter a name in the Save Results Dialog (such as TestResult) and click Save. Verify the Messages tab.

7. Go to Start ⇨ Run and type **notepad.exe**. Open the TestResult.rpt file that you just saved. Look at the results.

8. Verify the drag-and-drop feature in the Query editor using the following steps:

    a. Select the master database under Databases ⇨ System Databases. Hold down the mouse button and drag the node into the Query Editor.

    b. Select the dbo.spt_values table under Databases ⇨ System Databases ⇨ master ⇨ Tables ⇨ SystemTables. Hold down the mouse button and drag the node into the Query Editor.

    c. Select the name column under Databases ⇨ System Databases ⇨ master ⇨ Tables ⇨ SystemTables ⇨ dbo.spt_values ⇨ Columns. Hold down the mouse button and drag the node into the Query Editor.

How It Works

The context menu for the Editor window provides simple editor functionalities such as Cut, Copy, Paste, Undo, Redo, Font, and Save. In addition, you can execute a query, check the syntax of a query, or cancel a query execution using the context menu. You can also select the results display options such as Results To Text, Results To Grid, or Results To File.

The dropdown menu in the Editor window toolbar contains the list of all databases attached to the SSE. When a user selects a database, the Query Editor implicitly inserts a Transact-SQL USE database command with the database selected. The USE command points to the current database context. If one or more USE database statements are used in the query, the database dropdown menu changes to the database specified by the last USE statement.

The comments, or the statements that do not execute, are enclosed using the characters /* and */ or are preceded by two dashes (--).You can specify the display characteristics of the results using the three options available in the toolbar, described in the following list. These options are mutually exclusive, meaning that only one can be selected at any time.

❑ When Results To Text is selected, the query results are displayed inside a non-editable text area.

❑ When Results To Grid is selected, the query results are displayed inside a non-editable grid.

❑ When Results To File is selected, the standard Save As dialog is launched before every query execution. The query results are saved to the text file specified by the user.

You can drag the name of any object in the Object Explorer and drop it inside the Query Editor. Dragging objects such as a table or a column inserts the name of the object into the Query Editor.

Using Transact-SQL (T-SQL) with Query Editor

T-SQL is the language used by SSE to create, delete, modify, and access data inside the databases. T-SQL commands fall into two main categories: *Data Definition Language (DDL)* and *Data Manipulation Language (DML)*. DDL contains the commands used to create and destroy databases and database objects like tables. After the objects are created with DDL, you use DML to insert, delete, modify, or retrieve the data (see Figure 2-4).

| **DDL is used with Table Definition**
e.g CREATE TABLE Inventory (ID int PRIMARY KEY, name varchar(20) NULL, type varchar(20) NULL)

Sample Operations:
Create New Inventory Table: Creates the table definition and empty table.
Delete Inventory Table: Deletes the table definition and table.
Alter Inventory table: Changes the table definition; the corresponding table is also modified. If a column is deleted, all the values corresponding to the actual column are also deleted. Similarly, if a column is added, default values specified by user are assigned.
When DDL is executed, the actual table values could be affected. | **DML is used with Actual Table Data**
e.g. Inventory Table data is shown below

<table><tr><th>ID</th><th>Name</th><th>Type</th></tr><tr><td>1</td><td>FriendsVol 1</td><td>DVD</td></tr><tr><td>2</td><td>ER Vol 1</td><td>DVD</td></tr><tr><td>3</td><td>ER Vol1</td><td>VHS</td></tr><tr><td>4</td><td>Sixth Sense</td><td>VHS</td></tr></table>
Sample Operations:
View Table Data: Show the table data similar to the example above. You can select a subset of rows, subset of columns, or both.
Add New Record: A new row is inserted into the table
Delete Existing Record: An existing Row is deleted.
Update Existing record: Modify the value of any field inside a record.
There is no change to table definition when any of the DML commands are executed |

Figure 2-4

Each column, local variable, or parameter in SSE has a related data type, which is an attribute that specifies the type of data that the object can hold. The data types supported by SSE are described in the following table.

Data Type	Range/ Size	Description
bigint	-2^{63} to $2^{63}-1$ (size of 8 bytes)	Stores integer data
int	-2^{31} to $2^{31}-1$ (size of 4 bytes)	Stores integer data
smallint	-2^{15} to $2^{15}-1$ (size of 2 bytes)	Stores integer data
tinyint	0 to 255 (size of 1 byte)	Stores integer data
bit	1 or 0 value	Stores a 1 or 0 value
decimal, numeric	$10^{38} +1$ to $10^{38} -1$ (size depends on precision: maximum 17 bytes)	Stores decimal numbers
money	-2^{63} to $2^{63}-1$ (size of 8 bytes)	Stores monetary or currency values
smallmoney	-214,748.3648 to +214,748.3647 (size of 4 bytes)	Stores monetary or currency values
float	-1.79E + 308 to -2.23E - 308, 0, and 2.23E - 308 to 1.79E + 308 (size of 8 bytes)	Stores floating point data
real	-3.40E + 38 to -1.18E - 38, 0, and 1.18E - 38 to 3.40E + 38 (size of 4 bytes)	Stores floating point data
datetime	January 1, 1753, to December 31, 9999 (size of 8 bytes)	Stores date and time data
smalldatetime	January 1, 1900, through June 6, 2079 (size of 4 bytes)	Stores date and time data
char	Maximum of 8000 bytes	Stores non-Unicode character data
varchar	Maximum of 8000 bytes	Stores non-Unicode character data
nchar	Maximum of 4000 bytes	Fixed length Unicode string
nvarchar	Maximum of 4000 bytes	Variable length Unicode data
varchar(MAX)	Maximum 2GB	Variable length non-Unicode data
nvarchar(MAX)	Maximum 2GB	Variable length Unicode data
text	$2^{31}-1$ characters (8000 bytes long)	Stores variable length non-Unicode data
ntext	$2^{30}-1$ characters (4000 bytes long)	Variable length Unicode data
binary	8000 bytes	Fixed length binary data
varbinary	8000 bytes	Variable length binary data
varbinary(MAX)	Maximum 2GB	Variable length binary data

Data Type	Range/ Size	Description
image	2^31 − 1 bytes (8000 bytes long)	Variable length binary data
sql_variant	Maximum of 8016 bytes	Stores values of various SQL Server-supported data types, except text, ntext, timestamp, and sql_variant
timestamp	8 bytes	A database-wide unique binary number that gets updated every time a row gets updated
uniqueidentifier	16 bytes	Stores GUID (globally unique identifier)
XML Data Type	Maximum 2GB	Native data type for storing XML
User Defined Data type	Maximum 2GB	Stores data types defined by the user (e.g., zip code)

Using Data Definition Language (DDL)

Take a look at the basic commands used to create and destroy database objects. The basic DDL statements are:

❑ The CREATE command is used to create new objects like a database or a table.

❑ The DROP command allows you to permanently delete an object like a database or a table.

❑ The ALTER command is used to modify the definition of an object. For example, you can add or delete columns in an existing table using the ALTER statement.

The database name as well as the names of the objects within the database like table, view, variables, parameters, and index cannot exceed 128 characters. These names, called *identifier names,* must be unique and cannot be a T-SQL reserved word. The naming rules are as follows:

❑ The first character must be a letter, underscore (_), at sign (@), or the number sign (#).

❑ The characters after the first can be a letter, decimal numbers, underscore (_), at sign (@), dollar sign ($), or the number sign (#).

❑ Embedded spaces or special characters are not allowed in names.

You can get more information about T-SQL at http://msdn.microsoft.com/SQL/sqlreldata/TSQL/default.aspx. The following Try It Out gives you some practice using these commands.

Try It Out   Using CREATE, DROP, and ALTER Statements

1. Open the SSMS-EE Query Editor. To create a new database, type the following inside the editor.

```
CREATE DATABASE testDb
```

Highlight the statement, and then press the hotkey F5 or use the Execute toolbar button to execute the statement.

29

2. To create a new table inside the database, type the following, highlight the statement, and execute it by pressing F5.

```
USE testDb
CREATE TABLE Inventory (ID int PRIMARY KEY, name varchar(20) NULL, type varchar(20)
NULL)
```

3. Right-click the Databases node and select Refresh. Notice the new testDb database. Select the nodes testDb Í Tables Í Inventory Í Indexes. You will see an index entry corresponding to the primary key selected. Alternatively, view the index information by executing the following statement from the query window:

```
EXEC sp_helpindex Inventory
```

4. To add a new column to the Inventory table, type the following statement, highlight it, and execute it by pressing F5. Right-click Columns under Inventory and select Refresh. Verify that the new column is added.

```
ALTER TABLE Inventory ADD Description varchar(20) NULL
```

5. To remove the Description column from the Inventory table, type the following statement, highlight it, and execute it by pressing F5. Right-click Columns under Inventory and select Refresh. Verify that the column is removed.

```
ALTER TABLE Inventory DROP COLUMN Description
```

6. To remove the table, type the following statement, highlight it, and execute it by pressing F5. Right-click Tables under Inventory and select Refresh. Verify that the table is removed.

```
DROP TABLE Inventory
```

7. To remove the database, type the following statement, highlight it, and execute it by pressing F5. Right-click Databases and select Refresh. Verify that the database is removed.

```
USE master
DROP DATABASE testDB
```

How It Works

In this example, you use the T-SQL CREATE, ALTER, and DROP commands to create, modify, and destroy a database and a table. To execute a statement, highlight the statement and then press the Execute button on the toolbar or press the hotkey F5.

> If you do not highlight the statement before pressing F5, SSE executes all the statements in the query window, including the ones previously executed.

When the CREATE DATABASE statement is executed, the testDb database is created in two Windows files called testdb.mdf and testDb_log.ldf. The file with the .mdf extension is the data file, while the other file is the log file. The USE command is used to specify the database you wish to work with. Notice that the database dropdown list on the query window's toolbar is automatically changed to reflect the new database context.

The Inventory table is created inside the database testDb when the CREATE TABLE statement is executed. An index is created using the primary key automatically. In Steps 4 and 5, the ALTER statement is used to add and remove a column to the test table. Finally, use the DROP statement to delete the table and the database.

> **Use the DROP statement with care since it destroys the entire object. If you want to delete individual records, use the DELETE command.**

Using Data Manipulation Language (DML)

Now that you can create a table, you can use Data Manipulation Language (DML) to insert, delete, or modify table records. Typical DML statements are shown in the following list, and the Try It Out following demonstrates their usage.

- ❑ The SELECT command allows you to view a subset of columns; the columns specified after SELECT are shown when the statement is executed (see Figure 2-5). It is typically used along with the FROM clause. SSE runs the query against the table or view specified after FROM. * is a special wildcard character that indicates to SSE that all the columns are to be shown.

- ❑ The WHERE command allows you to obtain a subset of rows (see Figure 2-5). The rows returned are filtered using the criteria in the WHERE clause. The WHERE clause can be used with all the other commands like SELECT, UPDATE, DELETE, and INSERT. The typical operators used when specifying the criteria in the WHERE clause are mentioned in the following table.

- ❑ The INSERT command allows you to insert records into objects specified by the FROM clause.

- ❑ The DELETE command allows you to delete records specified by the FROM clause.

- ❑ The UPDATE command allows you to update the values inside a record or groups of records.

Original Table

ID	Name	Type	Qty	Publisher
1	FriendsVol 1	DVD	2	Prentice Hall
2	ER Vol 1	DVD	8	Warner
3	ER Vol 1	VHS	10	Warner
4	Sixth Sense	VHS	12	NULL

Subset of Rows (WHERE Publisher = Warner)

ID	Name	Type	Qty	Publisher
2	ER Vol 1	DVD	8	Warner
3	ER Vol 1	VHS	10	Warner

Subset of Columns (SELECT, Name, Type)

Name	Type
FriendsVol 1	DVD
ER Vol 1	DVD
ER Vol 1	VHS
Sixth Sense	VHS

Figure 2-5

Common Operators	Description
+	Addition
-	Subtraction
*	Multiplication
/	Division
%	Returns the integer remainder of a division (Modulo operator)
=	Equal to, assign value
>	Greater than
<	Less than
>=	Greater than or equal to
<=	Less than or equal to
<>	Not equal to
!=	Not equal to
!<	Not less than
!>	Not greater than
AND	TRUE when both of the conditions are TRUE
NOT	Reverses the value of any other Boolean operator
OR	TRUE if either condition is TRUE
LIKE	Checks if a character string matches a given pattern

Try It Out   Using SELECT, WHERE, INSERT, DELETE, and UPDATE with a Table

In this Try It Out, you practice using the DML statements.

1. Before using the DML commands, you must create a database and a table. Type and execute the following statements in the SSMS-EE Query window:

```
CREATE DATABASE testDb
GO
USE testDb
CREATE TABLE Inventory (ID int PRIMARY KEY, name varchar(20) NULL, type varchar(20)
NULL)
```

2. Insert records into the Inventory table by typing and executing the following statements:

```
INSERT INTO Inventory VALUES (1,'Friends', 'DVD')
INSERT INTO Inventory VALUES (2,'Friends', 'VHS')
INSERT INTO Inventory VALUES (3, 'Apprentice', 'DVD')
GO
SELECT * FROM Inventory
```

3. Try to insert a record with a duplicate ID by typing and executing the following statement:

```
INSERT Inventory VALUES (3,'Wrong ID Value', 'DVD')
GO
```

You should receive an error message. The statement is not executed.

4. View the records in the table by typing and executing the following statements:

```
-- View the entire table
SELECT * FROM Inventory

-- View the row having a value of 1 for ID
SELECT * FROM Inventory WHERE ID=1

--View the rows having a value greater than 1 for ID
SELECT * FROM Inventory WHERE ID>1

--View only the name column in the Inventory table
SELECT name FROM Inventory
```

5. Update a record by typing and executing the following statements:

```
--The value of the type field is updated for the record with ID=2
UPDATE Inventory SET type='DVD' WHERE ID=2

--The value of the name field is updated for all the records in Inventory table
UPDATE Inventory SET name= name+'Vol 1'
GO
-- View the updated table
SELECT * FROM Inventory
```

6. Delete a record and view the updated table by typing and executing the following statements:

```
DELETE FROM Inventory WHERE ID=2
GO
-- View the updated table
SELECT * FROM Inventory
```

How It Works

The example demonstrates simple DML statements used against the Inventory table. The INSERT command is used to insert rows into the table. If an attempt is made to insert a record containing a duplicate primary key, you see the following error message:

```
Violation of PRIMARY KEY constraint 'PK__Inventory__7C8480AE'. Cannot insert
duplicate key in object 'Inventory'
```

SSE makes sure that the primary keys in a table are unique. The combinations of SELECT and WHERE commands in step 3 select subsets of columns and rows, respectively. The UPDATE command is used to modify a column value in a single record or a group of records. Finally, individual records are deleted in step 6 using the DELETE command. It is also possible to specify multiple records for deletion using the WHERE clause in a DELETE statement.

The three INSERT commands in step 1 are executed together as a single batch inside SSE since the GO command is specified after the third INSERT statement. A *batch* is one or more T-SQL statements that can be executed together on the server. This is better than executing one statement at a time because there is overhead involved in each client server interaction. The *batch terminator* for SSMS-EE is the keyword GO, which is case-insensitive. You cannot change this default setting.

> Use batches of T-SQL instead of executing one statement at a time. It is even better to use stored procedures or functions, as explained in the next section.

Stored Procedures and Functions

Stored procedures and functions contain T-SQL statements that are stored inside the database and are optimized for faster execution compared to a batch of T-SQL statements sent from the client. These statements are checked for syntax by SSE and are compiled the first time they get executed. This cached, compiled version is used for subsequent executions. Another advantage of using stored procedures is that if the T-SQL statements inside your stored procedure change, your application need not be recompiled. Stored procedures and functions can accept multiple parameters, just like a VB .NET function or procedure.

Stored procedures typically perform a single well-defined action and have all the error checks done within the code. Functions, on the other hand, can return a scalar or table valued result that can be used inside a SELECT, WHERE or FROM clause inside another T-SQL statement.

Use the CREATE PROCEDURE (CREATE PROC) and CREATE FUNCTION statements to create a stored procedure or function. They are invoked using the EXEC command. The following Try It Out demonstrates the use of stored procedures.

Try It Out   Creating and Using Stored Procedures

Use the database and table from the previous Try It Out in this example.

1. Declare variables used in the stored procedure by entering and executing the following T-SQL from the SSMS-EE Query window.

```
USE testDB
DECLARE @procID int
DECLARE @procName varchar(20)
DECLARE @procType varchar(20)
```

2. Create a stored procedure to view records by using the following T-SQL:

```
CREATE PROC sp_getRecords AS SELECT * FROM Inventory
```

3. Create a stored procedure to insert records using the following T-SQL:

```
CREATE PROC sp_insertRecord @procID int, @procName varchar(20), @procType
varchar(20) AS INSERT INTO Inventory VALUES (@procID, @procName, @procType)
```

4. Create a stored procedure to delete a record using the following T-SQL:

```
CREATE PROC sp_deleteRecord @procID int AS DELETE FROM Inventory WHERE ID=@procID
```

5. Create a stored procedure to update a record using the following T-SQL:

```
CREATE PROC sp_updateRecord @procID int, @procName varchar(20), @procType
varchar(20) AS UPDATE Inventory SET name=@procName, type=@procType where ID=@procID
```

6. Execute the stored procedures defined above by entering and executing the following statements:

```
--Insert records into the Inventory table by executing the following statements.
EXEC sp_insertRecord 4, 'ER Vol 1', 'DVD'
EXEC sp_insertRecord 5, 'ER', 'VHS'
EXEC sp_insertRecord 6, 'Sixth Sense', 'VHS'

--Delete record with ID=3
EXEC sp_deleteRecord 3

--Update record with ID=5
EXEC sp_updateRecord 5, 'ER Vol1', 'VHS'

--View the updated table
EXEC sp_getRecords
GO
```

Figure 2-6 shows the output from this procedure.

	ID	name	type
1	1	FriendsVol 1	DVD
2	4	ER Vol 1	DVD
3	5	ER Vol1	VHS
4	6	Sixth Sense	VHS

Figure 2-6

How It Works

This example demonstrates the use of stored procedures to create, delete, and modify records in a table. The variables used as parameters are declared using the DECLARE statement. The variable names must begin with an at sign (@) and they cannot be of a text, ntext, or image data type. The table data type is not allowed with a stored procedure, but can be used with a function. The scope of a local variable is the batch, stored procedure, or statement block in which it is declared.

The T-SQL statements contained by the stored procedure are specified after the AS keyword. The stored procedure is executed using the EXEC command. The parameters passed to a stored procedure are specified after the stored procedure name and are separated by commas.

SSE defines some *aggregate functions,* which summarize the results of a query, rather than listing all of the rows. Some commonly used aggregate functions are listed following.

❑ SUM () gives the total of all the selected rows for a given numeric column.

❑ AVG () gives the average of the given column.

❑ MAX () gives the largest figure in the given column.

❑   MIN () gives the smallest figure in the given column.

❑   COUNT(*) gives the number of rows satisfying the conditions.

❑   VAR gives the statistical variance of all the values in the expression.

❑   STDEV gives the statistical standard deviation of all the values in the expression.

Try It Out   Using Functions and Aggregate Functions

Use the database and table from the previous Try It Out in this example.

1.   Add a new column called quantity to the Inventory table by using the following statements:

```
USE testDB
--Add a new numeric column called quantity
ALTER TABLE Inventory ADD quantity numeric
GO
--Populate the new column
UPDATE Inventory SET quantity=ID*2

--View the updated table
SELECT * from Inventory
```

2.   Verify whether the old stored procedures still work against the updated table by using the following statements:

```
--Insert fails
EXEC sp_insertRecord 7,'ED', 'DVD'

--Select * succeeds
EXEC sp_getRecords
```

The sp_insertRecord stored procedure should fail because the table structure has changed. However, the stored procedure sp_getRecords succeeds since it has no dependency on the column structure because of the wildcard *.

3.   Create a new function called AverageQuantity that computes the average for a given type by using the following statements. This function uses the aggregate function AVG.

```
CREATE FUNCTION AverageQuantity(@funcType varchar(20))
RETURNS numeric AS
BEGIN
     DECLARE @average numeric
     SELECT @average = AVG(quantity) FROM Inventory WHERE type=@funcType
     RETURN @average
END
```

4.   Use the function AverageQuantity for determining the DVD items whose quantity value is greater than the average, as shown in the following statements:

```
SELECT ID, name, dbo.AverageQuantity('DVD') AS average from Inventory
WHERE quantity>dbo.AverageQuantity('DVD') AND type='DVD'
```

How It Works

The example illustrates the use of a function called `AverageQuantity` used to compute the average quantity for a given type in the Inventory table. Add a new field called "quantity" to the Inventory table to demonstrate the usage of this function. Once the table structure is changed, the stored procedure `sp_insertRecord` fails to execute.

> If you modify the table structure, then stored procedures and functions that are affected by the change in structure must also be modified if you want them to continue to work correctly.

Use `CREATE FUNCTION` to create the function. A variable called `@average` is defined, for storing the computed average. Because the numeric value corresponding to average is returned, this function can be used inside the `SELECT` and the `WHERE` statements. The dbo is a user that has permissions to perform operations on the database (you learn more about that in Chapter 13).

Using Table Relationships

You can now use the foreign key concept described earlier to define a relationship between two tables. The following Try It Out demonstrates the process.

Try It Out   Using Foreign Keys to Define Table Relationships

Execute the following T-SQL from the SSMS-EE Query Editor window.

1. Define a Publisher table with a `REFERENCES` constraint as shown in the following statements. (The table is not normalized for ease of demonstrating the foreign key concept.)

```
USE testdb
CREATE TABLE Publisher(ID int PRIMARY KEY, InventoryID int REFERENCES
Inventory(ID), pubName varchar(20) NULL)
```

2. Insert valid records into the Publisher table by using the following statements.

```
INSERT INTO Publisher VALUES (1, 1, 'Warner')
INSERT INTO Publisher VALUES (2, 4, 'Warner')
INSERT INTO Publisher VALUES (3, 5, 'Warner')
SELECT * FROM Publisher
```

3. Try to insert records into the Publisher table without a valid InventoryID, as shown following. Verify that this operation fails.

```
INSERT INTO Publisher VALUES (4, 2, 'InvalidInventoryID')
```

4. Try to delete records from the Inventory table that the Publisher table refers to by using the following statements. Verify that this operation fails.

```
DELETE * FROM Inventory WHERE ID=1
```

How It Works

First you define a new table called "Publisher." The foreign key is defined inside the Publisher table using the REFERENCES keyword followed by information about the referenced table (Inventory) and its primary key (ID). Once defined, the foreign key introduces constraints on the Inventory table for updates and deletes. By default, SSE prevents a delete or update of an Inventory row if the row's ID is referred to by the Publisher.

The REFERENCES clause used in the definition of the InventoryID makes sure that all the InventoryID values inside the Publisher table correspond to an ID value inside the Inventory Table. Hence when an attempt is made to insert a row into the Publisher table with no corresponding ID in the Inventory table, the statement fails. Similarly, a deletion of a row in Inventory fails when there is a referencing entry in the Publisher table.

By default, the earlier CREATE TABLE statement is equivalent to the following:

```
CREATE TABLE Publisher(ID int PRIMARY KEY, InventoryID int REFERENCES
Inventory(ID)ON UPDATE NO ACTION ON DELETE NO ACTION, pubName varchar(20) NULL)
```

NO ACTION means that the delete or update is prevented by default. Another possible value is CASCADE, which tells SSE to delete all matching rows in the referencing (Publisher) table if there is a delete on the Inventory table.

Unlike for a primary key, an index is not automatically built for the columns declared as foreign key. Also there is some performance degradation during upgrades and deletes because SSE has to verify the integrity of the tables during the operation.

You can also use a special stored procedure called a *trigger* to maintain relationships between tables. Triggers use T-SQL to store elaborate rules necessary to protect the integrity of data. While stored procedures are called by the user, triggers are invoked automatically by SQL Server. When an attempt is made to change the protected data object, the corresponding trigger is automatically invoked. The trigger can be invoked instead of the proposed action, or after the data is modified by the action. They are called *instead-of* and *after* triggers respectively. Defining and maintaining table relationships is just one application of triggers. If you use triggers, you have the capability to set all the referencing table values to NULL or a default value when a deletes or update occurs. You can also provide custom error messages when using triggers.

Querying on Multiple Tables

One of the advantages of building the table relationships using a foreign key is the ease of querying over multiple tables. T-SQL exposes a keyword called JOIN that uses the columns of matching rows in different tables to return a single table. You can also specify additional constraints using the WHERE clause.

Assume that the first table is called *left* table, while the second table in the JOIN is called the *right* table. A join condition defines the way two tables are related by specifying the column from each table that is used for the join. A typical join condition specifies a foreign key from one table and its associated key in the second table along with an additional constraint using the WHERE clause. When combining two tables, the following basic combinations exist and are further illustrated in Figure 2-7:

❑ The result contains only the rows that have a match in both tables. This is called INNER JOIN or JOIN. The order of the tables is not significant in this case.

❑ All rows in the *left* table are included, but only the matching rows in the *right* table are present. This is called LEFT OUTER JOIN.

❑ All rows in the *right* table are included, but only the matching rows in the *left* table are present. This is called RIGHT OUTER JOIN.

❑ All the rows from both the tables are included. This is called the FULL OUTER JOIN.

❑ The result is the Cartesian product of the rows from both the tables, so there is a row for each possible combination. This is called the CROSS JOIN. You can get more information about using JOIN from the following link: http://msdn.microsoft.com/library/en-us/acdata/ac_8_qd_09_610z.asp.

Try It Out   **Using JOIN**

1. Execute the following statements to create two sample tables called "Inv" and "Pub" in the SSMS-EE Query Editor. There is no foreign key constraint defined on Pub so that we can demonstrate RIGHT JOIN. Each table contains an ID value that is not present in the other table. For example, Inv table contains an ID of 2, while the Pub table contains an ID of 3.

```
USE testdb
CREATE TABLE Inv(ID int PRIMARY KEY, name varchar(20))
CREATE TABLE Pub(PubID int PRIMARY KEY, InvID int)
INSERT INTO Inv Values (1, 'Friends')
INSERT INTO Inv Values (2, 'ER')
INSERT INTO Pub Values (1, 1)
INSERT INTO Pub Values (3, 3)
--view the tables
SELECT * FROM Inv
SELECT * FROM Pub
```

2. Try the five different JOIN combinations by using the following statements:

```
SELECT * FROM Inv AS I JOIN Pub AS P ON I.ID=P.InvID
SELECT * FROM Inv AS I FULL OUTER JOIN Pub AS P ON I.ID=P.InvID
SELECT * FROM Inv AS I LEFT OUTER JOIN Pub AS P ON I.ID=P.InvID
SELECT * FROM Inv AS I RIGHT OUTER JOIN Pub AS P ON I.ID=P.InvID
SELECT * FROM Inv AS I CROSS JOIN Pub
```

3. Add a WHERE clause as an additional constraint to FULL OUTER JOIN as shown:

```
SELECT * FROM Inv AS I FULL OUTER JOIN Pub AS P ON I.ID=P.InvID WHERE I.ID=2
```

How It Works

This example demonstrates the different combinations of JOIN (previously illustrated in Figure 2-7). The right and the left tables are specified on either side of the JOIN clause. The ID in Inv table is matched with the InvID of the Pub table using the ON clause, which is often called the join condition. Inv table contains an ID of 2 that is not present in the Pub table. Similarly, the Pub table contains an InvID of 3 that is not present in the Inv table. In Figure 2-7, these values are highlighted to emphasize the different conditions for JOIN.

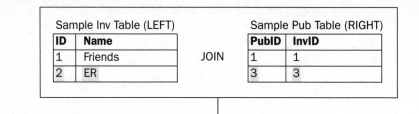

INNER JOIN OR JOIN Results

ID	Name	PubID	InvID
1	Friends	1	1

Explanation: Only the rows with ID value of 1 are present in both tables.
This is similar to an intersection operation.

LEFT OUTER JOIN Results

ID	Name	PubID	InvID
1	Friends	1	1
2	ER	NULL	NULL

Explanation: Rows with ID value of 1 are present in both tables similar to INNER JOIN. RIGHT table does not have InvID value 2, and hence NULL is used.

RIGHT OUTER JOIN Results

ID	Name	PubID	InvID
1	Friends	1	1
NULL	NULL	3	3

Explanation: Rows with ID value of 1 are present in both tables similar to INNER JOIN. LEFT table does not have ID value 3, and hence NULL is used.

FULL OUTER JOIN Results

ID	Name	PubID	InvID
1	Friends	1	1
2	ER	NULL	NULL
NULL	NULL	3	3

Explanation: Rows from both tables are present. NULL is used as a filler when there is no corresponding ID.

CROSS JOIN Results

ID	Name	PubID	InvID
1	Friends	1	1
2	ER	1	1
1	Friends	3	3
2	ER	3	3

Explanation: Row 1 and 2 from LEFT are combined with Row 1 from RIGHT. Then Row 1 and 2 from LEFT are combined with Row 2 from RIGHT.

Figure 2-7

Using a View

A *view* is a useful object supported by SSE that allows you to work with data defined by a SELECT query. The SELECT statement used for view definition must have at least one column after the SELECT keyword, and at least one table in the FROM clause. Once defined, this view can be treated just like a table, and you can use it in other queries. However, the actual data accessible through a view is not stored as a distinct object. Only the SELECT statement that created the view is stored, so the results are created at run-time from tables that are often called the *base tables*.

Use the CREATE VIEW statement to create a view. An index is not created for a view by default. You must specify SCHEMABINDING for any view on which you create an index. The SCHEMABINDING option prevents the base tables referenced by the view being changed without adjusting the view. The following Try It Out demonstrates a view that uses a JOIN of the Inventory and Publisher tables.

Try It Out   **Using Views**

This example uses the Inventory and Publisher tables defined in an earlier Try It Out.

1.   Create a view using the Inventory and Publisher tables by entering and executing the following statements in the SSMS-EE Query Editor.

```
USE testDB
GO
CREATE VIEW InventoryPublisherView AS
(SELECT * FROM Inventory AS I FULL OUTER JOIN Publisher AS P ON I.ID=P.InventoryID)
```

2.   Use the view in a SELECT command as shown:

```
SELECT * from InventoryPublisherView
SELECT Name, type, quantity, pubName from InventoryPublisherView
```

3.   Try to delete a record from the view, using the following line. You will get an error.

```
DELETE FROM InventoryPublisherView WHERE ID=1
```

4.   Alter the view by selecting only some of the columns, as shown:

```
ALTER VIEW InventoryPublisherView AS
(SELECT ID,name,type,quantity,pubName FROM Inventory AS I FULL OUTER JOIN Publisher
AS P ON I.ID=P.InventoryID)
GO
SELECT * from InventoryPublisherView
```

5.   Delete the view using the following statement:

```
DROP VIEW InventoryPublisherView
```

How It Works

This example demonstrates the creation and usage of the InventoryPublisherView that contained columns from resulting from an OUTER JOIN of the Publisher and Inventory tables. You can see that the view can be used in the FROM clause just like a table. However, there are some restrictions for INSERT, DELETE, and UPDATE. INSERT and UPDATE are allowed only if the data modification statements affect one base table. DELETE is not allowed in a multitable view. If you attempt such a deletion you will see an error message like the following:

```
Error on delete:  View or function 'InventoryPubisherView' is not updatable because
the modification affects multiple base tables.
```

Summary

This chapter introduced the basic database features supported by SSE. The SQL Server Management Studio Express Edition (SSMS-EE) GUI tool allows you to view and manage database objects such as tables, views, stored procedures, and functions. Commonly used graphical features in SSMS-EE were explained in this chapter. You also learned about the basic Transact SQL (T-SQL) statements so that you can use the Query Editor to develop and maintain tables and stored procedures. In this chapter you learned to

- ❏ Create and manipulate databases, tables, columns, rows, primary keys, and foreign keys

- ❏ Use the Connection Dialog, Object Explorer, and Query Editor user interfaces in SSMS-EE

- ❏ Use T-SQL with Query Editor to do simple Data Definition Language (DDL) and Data Manipulation Language (DML) queries

- ❏ Develop and use stored procedures and functions using the Query Editor

- ❏ Define table relationships using a foreign key

- ❏ Query across multiple tables using JOIN

- ❏ Create and use a view

In the next chapter, you learn more about creating a simple database application using Visual Basic Express.

Exercises

Try the exercises that follow to test your understanding of the material covered in this chapter. You can find the solutions to these exercises in Appendix A.

1. Create an Employees table. Each Employee is defined by an Employee ID and has a Last Name, First Name, office number, and salary as attributes. Insert five distinct rows into the table. Create a stored procedure that updates the salary of all the employees. A numeric number passed as a parameter to this stored procedure indicates the percentage salary increase. Increase the salary of all the employees by 5% using this stored procedure.

2. Find all the employees' customers with a last name starting with *S* (hint: use LIKE).

3. Create an Office table that has the attributes of office number, area in square feet, phone number, and whether it has a window or not. Insert five rows into the table. Write a query to find out which employees have a window in their office.

4. Create a view on the Employees and Office tables such that the Office number is matched from both the tables.

Creating a Simple Database Application

Chapters 1 and 2 introduced you to the basics of SSE. Next, you need to understand some basics of using Microsoft Visual Basic 2005 Express Edition or, more informally, VB Express. VB Express makes building data-centric applications very easy. Some applications, such as those you will build in this chapter, don't require that you write any code at all. Slightly richer applications require very little coding on your part. Creating a highly customized application will require much more code, depending on how much customization you want to provide. But creating a basic database-centric application is very easy; VB Express is a breakthrough in database programmer productivity.

Creating a database-centric application using a version of VB Express is as easy as creating a similar application in Microsoft Access. (In Chapter 12, you learn how to upgrade from Access to VB Express.) And, when you're done, your application in VB Express is easily extended with all the power of the .NET framework and programming environment, making it a suitable choice for corporate applications.

In this chapter, you get a brief introduction to VB Express and you will quickly build a simple database application. You will learn how to:

- ❑ Work with projects and the various tool windows in VB Express
- ❑ Create and work with tables and data directly from VB Express
- ❑ Create a WinForms application
- ❑ Build and debug your application

You need a couple of things to get started:

- ❑ SQL Server 2005 Express Edition
- ❑ Microsoft Visual Basic 2005 Express Edition

If you are doing all of the exercises in the book, you will have already installed both of these products in Chapter 1. Note that if you have any version of VB Express, you likely also have SQL Server Express installed as that product is bundled with VB Express.

Creating Your First Application

To create an application in VB Express, you create a new project. That project is placed in the Solution Explorer. Throughout this chapter and others, we may alternatively refer to either your Solution or your Project. In VB Express, you can only have one project per Solution. So, a reference to either your Solution or your Project means the same thing.

When you create your project, a WinForms form is automatically created in your Solution. Next, you will add an SSE database to your Solution. Then, you will create a table in the database from within VB Express. You will populate the table with data and then create a Data Source. With the Data Source, you can then create a grid control for your WinForm that is automatically bound to the Data Source. With all of that in place, and without writing a single line of code, you will build and run your application.

First, you must create a project.

Try It Out   Creating a New Project

This Try It Out shows you how to start up VB Express and create a new project. Follow these steps:

1. Launch VB Express by choosing: Start ➪ All Programs ➪ Visual Basic Express Edition 2005.

2. Select the File menu and choose New Project ➪ Windows Application.

3. At the bottom of the dialog, for the name of the application, type in the name **MyFirstApp** and click OK.

4. Once created, choose File ➪ Save All. This brings up the Save Project Dialog. Click Save.

Note that it may take a few seconds to initialize the development environment. Don't worry. It's common for applications to take a while the first time they are ever run on your machine. Generally, the first application to load on a machine that depends on the .NET Framework pays the price of loading common framework pieces for all applications that may use it at some point. When the project loads, it will appear similar to Figure 3-1.

Note a couple of things about the environment. The gray box in the middle is the WinForm form. It is on this form that you will create controls and other elements that will appear in your application. On the right, your new project appears in the Solution Explorer. The Solution Explorer holds the list of elements in your project. (VB Express is a low-end version of Visual Studio. Higher-level versions of Visual Studio allow you to store multiple projects in the Solution Explorer.) The list of elements is a summary list. In addition to what you can see, VB Express generates both code and directories that are hidden. You only see the elements necessary to do your work.

In the same window, but on a different tab, is the Data Sources window. You'll work with this window later on in this chapter to drag a data source onto the WinForm. Below both of these windows is the Properties window. In this window you set properties for items you have selected. On the bottom left is the Task List. If you have an error, it will show up here. Finally, on the upper left, is the Database Explorer. When you create a connection to the database, the connection will appear in this window. Except for the Task List, you will work with all of these windows in this chapter.

DataSources Window

Database Explorer   WinForm Form   Solution Explorer Window

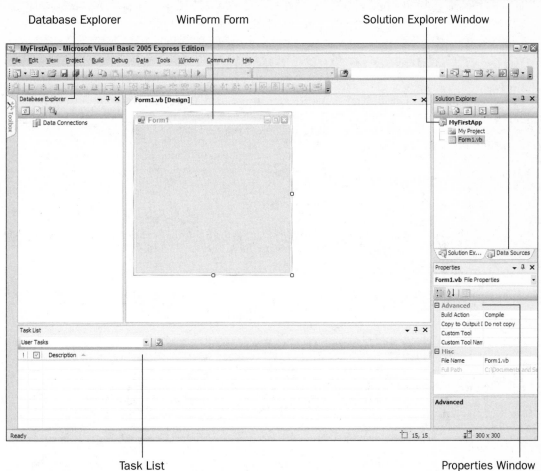

Task List   Properties Window

Figure 3-1

How It Works

VB Express does a lot of work in the background to set things up for you. There are more files created than those you see in the Solution Explorer. If you want to see all the files in your project, select the second icon from the left on the Solution Explorer window and the list expands, as shown in Figure 3-2.

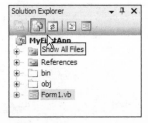

Figure 3-2

You should now see a bin folder and an object folder added to the files that were previously visible. Expand the various nodes in the Solution Explorer tree. Note that when you open the Form1.vb node, you see a Form1.Designer.vb file. This is the generated code for Form1.

Adding a Database to Your Project

Because you're going to create a database application, you need to add a database to your project. Your project is a collection of the files necessary for your application. When you choose to create a Windows application, VB Express automatically puts in the set of files necessary for to create a WinForm. But, VB Express doesn't assume you are necessarily going to create a database application. So, you must explicitly add a database file to your project.

Try It Out   Adding a New Database

To add a database to your project, follow these steps:

1. Right-click on the top node titled MyFirstApp in the Solution Explorer and choose Add ⇨ New Item from the context menu. This brings up the Add New Item dialog.

2. In the Add New Item dialog, select the Database icon.

3. At the bottom of the dialog, for the name of the database, type **MyDB.mdf** and click Add. After a few seconds, your database will be added to your Solution and the Data Source Wizard will come up.

4. Cancel the Data Source Wizard. Do not make any choices in it at this time.

> Note: if you get a "Timeout expired" error, and this is the first time you have run SSE under your account, simply follow the steps again. It should connect the second time.

It may take a few seconds for VB Express to respond after you add the database to your Solution. Note that you should now have both a database added to your Solution and a connection to it in the Database Explorer. Open the Database Explorer and view the contents of the database (which should be empty at this point).

How It Works

VB Express does a lot of work for you behind the scenes. First, when you add a new database to your Solution, VB Express communicates with SQL Server Express and issues the commands to directly create a new database in your Solution directory. Second, after the database is created in that directory, VB Express then creates a connection to the database and puts it into the Database Explorer, which appears on the left. Further, if it is the first time you have ever used SQL Server Express under your account, there is an additional — one time per user — time delay while SQL Server configures itself to work with your user account. SQL Server Express copies some administration files to your local user account directories.

If you still have Show All Files enabled in the Solution Explorer, you will see that MyDB.mdf is also a node. If you open that node, you will see a MyDB_log.LDF file. This is a log file. A log file must always be present with SQL Server databases. It is the file to which SQL Server logs transactions before they are transferred to the database itself (that is, the .MDF file). VB Express ensures that these two files are copied as a pair when you work with them.

> *Note that if you have an existing database, you can choose Add ⇨ Existing Item and then point to an existing database you want to add to your project. VB Express will copy it (and the associated .LDF file) to your Solution folder. If no .LDF file is present in the location you are copying the .MDF from, SQL Server Express will create a new .LDF for the .MDF in the new location.*

Working with Your Database in Database Explorer

The Database Explorer lists the connections you currently have available for use. If you expand the connections node, you will see an additional list of folders for database tables, views, stored procedures, functions, and so on. From the Database Explorer, you can create tables, views, stored procedures, and all the relevant database objects you need for development purposes. You can even populate the database with data.

VB Express provides a very rich environment for designing and populating your database. The following Try It Out shows you how to add a new table to your database.

Try It Out   **Creating a Table**

Start by creating a very simple application that stores people's names, addresses, and phone numbers. To add a new table, follow these steps:

1. Navigate to the Database Explorer and expand the MyDB.mdf node. If the Database Explorer is not visible, choose View ⇨ Database Explorer.

2. Right-click on the Tables folder node under your connection node and choose Add New Table to bring up the Table Editor.

3. Enter the information from the following table into the Table Editor. The result should look like Figure 3-3.

Column Name	Data Type
PersonID	Int
FirstName	nvarchar(50)
LastName	nvarchar(50)
Firstline	nvarchar(50)
Secondline	nvarchar(50)
City	nvarchar(50)
State	nvarchar(50)
Phone	nvarchar(50)

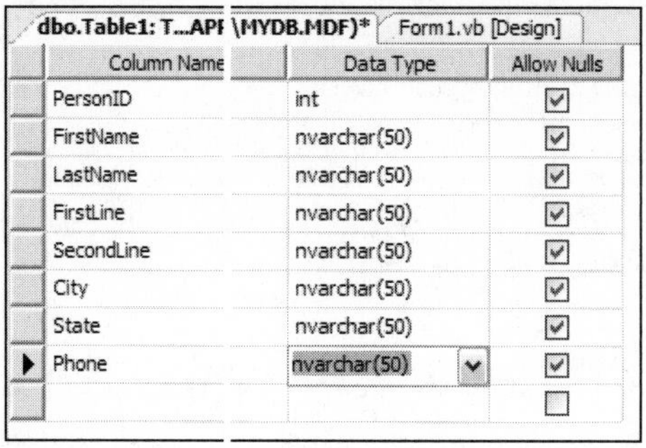

Figure 3-3

4. Right-click the PersonID row marker and set the PersonID column as the Primary Key, as shown in Figure 3-4.

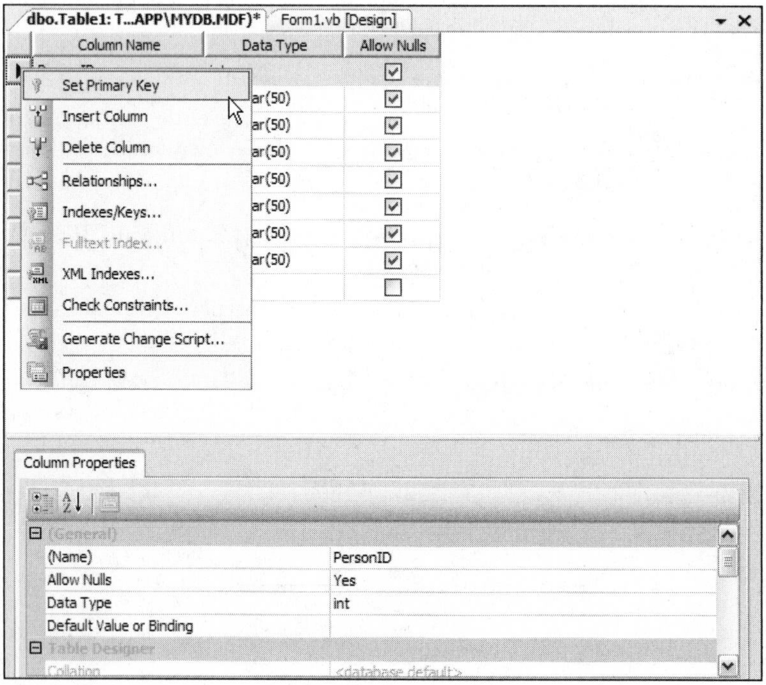

Figure 3-4

5. From the menu, choose File ⇨ Save Table1. This will bring up a Choose Name dialog. Type in the name **Person** as the table name and click OK.

The Person table is now in the database. To convince yourself that this is true, look over at the Database Explorer on the left. Note that it now has a Person node under the Tables folder. Expand the Person node and note that the columns you added in the table editor now show up in the Database Explorer.

How It Works

The Database Explorer shows what is currently in the database; it is a live view of the current database objects. Any change you make in the Database Explorer will be directly reflected in the database. In addition to creating database tables, you can create foreign key relationships between tables; get help with writing queries, writing views, and writing stored procedures; and more. Also directly available from the Database Explorer is the capability to manipulate the data in the database. (You will do all this in Chapter 4.) VB Express provides a table data editor for SQL Server that you can use to insert, update, and delete data directly. The following Try It Out shows you how to add data to your table using this feature.

Try It Out   **Adding Data to the Person Table**

To enter some data for your application, follow these steps:

1. Right-click the Person node in the Database Explorer and choose Show Table Data. This will bring up a table data editor.

2. Enter data from the following table directly in the grid until your table looks the one in Figure 3-5:

Person ID	First Name	Last Name	Firstline	Second-line	City	State	Phone
1	George	Washington	1 Cherry Lane	NULL	Washington	DC	1 000 1234567
2	Abe	Lincoln	2 Log Rd	3rd house	Chicago	IL	1 000 2345678
3	Thomas	Jefferson	3 Monticello Ct	NULL	Charlottesville	VA	1 000 3456789

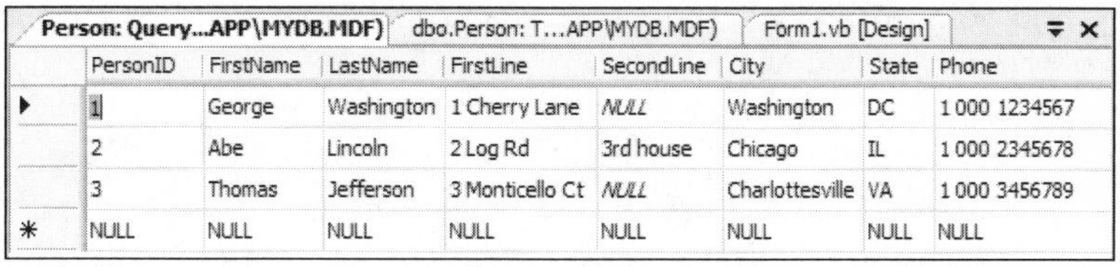

Figure 3-5

Make sure you move out of the last line so it does not show that it is still being edited. Do not select Save or Save All in the environment. Close the Table Data grid by closing the window. You will not be prompted to save the data. Now, reopen the Table Data grid by choosing Show Table Data from the Person Table in the Database Explorer node. The data you just entered will all be there.

How It Works

When you click Show Table Data, you actually bring up the Query Designer Results Pane. The Query Designer is a general query tool you can use to write queries and when you click Show Table Data, the Query Designer is actually running and the Query Designer menu appears on the menu bar. Also, if you right-click on the background of the Results Pane, you can choose to show other panes, such as the Criteria Pane. While it is specifically a pane in the Query Designer, you can think of it as a table data editor. You don't need to deal with the other aspects of the Query Designer simply to update the data in your table.

When you add data in the Results Pane, as soon as you move to a different row, VB Express immediately updates the database so that the grid is always as up-to-date as possible.

> **When you update the data in the Results Pane, it is updated directly in the database. You can't undo an update directly. You must manually make the change to revert it back to an old value. You can still undo your actions up until the time you leave the row. Once you leave the row, the row is updated into the database.**

Configuring a Data Source

Now that you've created a database and entered data into it, you're ready to configure a Data Source. A *Data Source* is the object a grid on a form in your application references to get data from your database. When you configure a Data Source, it automatically creates a DataSet for you that can work with your database. A *DataSet* is an in-memory database that your application can work with directly. Just like your database on disk, a DataSet will have a copy of your data, but only in-memory. A DataSet has tables and rows and, in this case, points directly to your database. A DataSet can also point to a web service, or an assembly.

The following Try It Out shows you how to configure a Data Source, which will automatically create a DataSet for your database.

Try It Out   Configuring a Data Source

1. On the menu bar, choose Data ⇨ Show Data Sources. (Alternatively, you can choose the tab next to the Solution Explorer window.) This will bring up the Data Sources window on the IDE.

2. In the Data Sources window, choose Add New Data Source, as shown in Figure 3-6, to bring up the Data Source Configuration Wizard.

Figure 3-6

3. In the Choose a Data Source Type step of the Data Source Configuration Wizard, choose the Database (the default) and click Next.

4. In the Choose Your Data Connection step of the Data Source Configuration Wizard, choose the data connection you created for MyDB.mdf and click Next.

5. In the Save the Connection String to the Application Configuration File step of the Data Source Configuration Wizard, choose to save the connection to the Application Configuration File (the default) and click Next.

6. In the Choose your Database Objects step of the wizard, shown in Figure 3-7, check the Tables node, which has the Person table under it, and click Finish. VB Express will work for a while and update the DataSet for the Person table you just added.

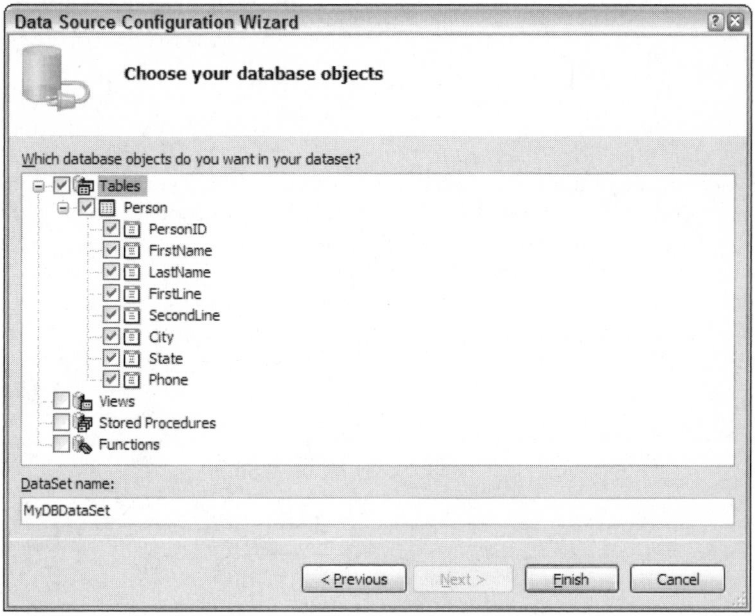

Figure 3-7

Note that for a large DataSet, VB Express may work quite a while. Don't worry; it's better to have VB Express create the code automatically than for you to have to create it by hand.

How It Works

Behind the scenes, VB Express configures the DataSet to include the table you just added. A DataSet is an in-memory database; it is the middle stopping ground for your data as it travels to and from the database. With a DataSet, you can work with data from your database in an offline fashion. Databases are one type of data source you can use to populate a DataSet. The other types of data sources are a web service and an object. DataSet code is generated by VB Express to work specifically with your application. Each time you reconfigure your DataSet, VB Express must regenerate the DataSet code.

Creating a Windows Form

With a DataSet now fully configured, you can now take the next step in creating your application by adding controls to your form. One way to add controls to a form is to add them from the ToolBox and then bind those controls to your DataSet. However, the faster way is to directly drop the DataSet objects you want from the Data Sources window onto the form. VB Express will drop the controls for you and do the data binding automatically, as you can see in the following Try It Out.

Try It Out   **Dropping Controls onto a Form**

1. Open the Solution Explorer and double-click Form1.vb. This brings up the window for the form.

2. Open the Data Sources window and drag the Person table from the Data Sources window onto the form. This creates a ToolStrip and a Data Grid View on the form that is bound to your DataSet.

3. Resize the grid and form so that the grid fits well on the form.

How It Works

A number of very important things happened in this exercise. When you dragged the Person Table from the Data Sources window onto Form1, VB Express created a lot of code for you. The DataGridView was created on your form, which is where the data will be displayed. A ToolStrip was created for you as well. A ToolStrip holds buttons such as Add, Delete, and the navigational controls. All of these controls work together. So, for instance, choosing the Add button on the ToolStrip will add a new record in the database. Note also that at the bottom of the Form1.vb you can see the Component Tray, a gray area with four components, as shown in Figure 3-8.

Figure 3-8

The first component is MyDBDataSet. You already know about DataSets. A DataSet is the code necessary to create and hold the in-memory database of your data. A reference to the DataSet is now added to your Solution. Additionally, several other components are added:

❏   One component is the PersonBindingSource, which is a BindingSource. *BindingSources* sit between the controls on your form and the DataSet. They encapsulate or hold the binding sources for a specific form. The form controls are bound to a BindingSource, which, in turn, is usually targeted at a specific table in a DataSet.

❏   Another component added is the PersonTableAdapter, which is a TableAdapter. *Table Adapters* sit between the DataSet and the actual data source (in this case, MyDB.Mdf). They hold the query, insert, update, and delete statements necessary to work with your DataSet. A TableAdapter can have multiple queries (for example, to get filtered views of a table's data or to get data from two different tables).

❏   The final component created is the PersonBindingNavigator, which is a DataNavigator. *DataNavigators* enable navigation through records in the DataSet. They also enable the addition, deletion, and editing of records. From a UI perspective, the DataNavigator functionality is exposed through the DataNavigator control (informally referred to as the VCR control). The DataNavigator is the component used to ensure that all data bound controls work synchronously with each other.

Building and Debugging Your Application

Now that you have a form with data bound controls, a configured DataSet, and a database, you're ready to build and debug your application.

Try It Out   Building and Debugging

This Try It Out shows you how to debug your application.

1.   Press F5 or choose Debug ⇨ Start to start the application in debug mode.

VB Express may work a while but, eventually, your application will come up in debug mode. The ToolStrip that was added automatically for you is operational on the data grid. Try choosing the next, previous, first, and last buttons. They all work automatically with your data grid. The Add new row button is also operational. It will add new rows to the grid. Or, you can add them directly to the grid itself by typing data in * (new) row. If you choose the Save Data button on the ToolStrip, the data will be saved to the database.

2.   When you have finished working with the application in debug mode, either close the application or choose Debug ⇨ Stop Debugging to stop debugging.

How It Works

When you press F5, VB Express performs a couple of tasks. First, if your application has not been built yet, VB Express will build it into an executable program. When it builds the executable program, it translates your source code files from Visual Basic into machine-executable code that is placed in an output directory. When you are debugging, the output directory is beneath the source files in a directory named "bin." This is where your executable program is placed.

Your database files are also copied there (as well as your configuration files.) When you debug your application, or when you just run it after having built it (which you'll do next), your application uses the database that is in the same directory as the application itself. When you do enter data that is saved, it will be saved in the version of the database that is in the same directory as the executable. This process is covered in more detail in Chapter 8.

For now, navigate to the bin folder under your Projects directory:

```
C:\Documents and Settings\<user name>\My Documents\Visual
Studio\Projects\MyFirstApp\MyFirstApp\bin
```

In that directory, you see two key files used for your database: MyDB.mdf and MyDB_log.ldf. These are the database files that are copied as a pair into your output and other directories.

Fixing up the Properties

You should fix up some other properties of the application to make it behave well. Virtually every programming object in VB Express (DataGridView, ToolStrip, and so on) has properties. These properties are usually available for you to set directly in the Properties window.

One key thing to understand when you make these changes is that the Properties window shows the properties for the item that currently has focus in the IDE.

Try It Out   Setting Properties for the Grid

1. Right-click the DataGridView in your form and choose Properties. This should set the focus and selection to the Properties window on the right-hand side of the IDE and display the properties for the DataGridView.

2. Scroll down to the Dock property to Fill, as shown in Figure 3-9.

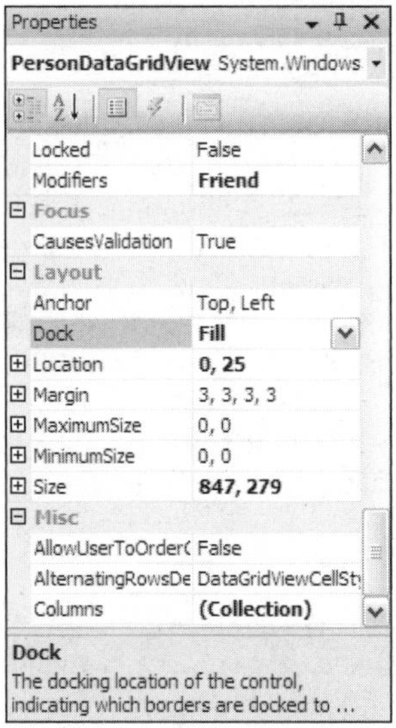

Figure 3-9

3. Press F5 (or choose Debug ⇨ Start) and verify that the grid now fills the window. (You can choose Control+F5 if you want to run the application without debugging.)

    Now the grid looks a lot better in the application form.

4. Next, select the form itself. In the Properties window, in the Appearance section, set the Text property to MyFirstApp.

5. Choose File ⇨ Save All to save all project properties.

How It Works

The key thing to keep in mind is that the properties for all of the controls and components that you work with are available in the Properties window. When you change a property, it changes the way your application will behave. Some of the changes may be minor, such as cell color or background. However, other changes may make the program behave very differently. For instance, if you want to make your application read-only, you simply set the following properties:

1. In the Behavior section of the Properties window, set both the AllowUserToAddRows and the AllowUserToDeleteRows properties to False.

2. Ensure that the ReadOnly property is also set to True.

3. Finally, to remove the Add, Delete, and Update buttons from the ToolStrip, select each of the buttons in the ToolStrip (that is, bindingDataNavigatorDeleteItem, bindingDataNavigatorSaveItem, and bindingDataNavigatorAddNewItem). Bring up the Properties window, find the Behavior section, and set the Visible property to False.

If you take these steps and rebuild your application, you will see that the DataViewGrid has become read-only. Take some time to browse through the properties available to you. You can set the cell colors, margins, and many other properties. Take some time to explore the various properties of the controls you use. You may be surprised at the functionality already available for them that you can choose just by changing a property.

Testing Your Application

While you have run your application by pressing F5, you are now ready to test your application as it will run on users' machines.

Try It Out   **Testing Your Application**

1. Open MyDocuments and navigate down to your project directory. The path will be something like the following:

```
C:\Documents and Settings\<yourName>\My Documents\Visual Studio\Projects\
MyFirstApp\MyFirstApp.
```

2. Under the MyFirstApp directory is a bin folder with two other folders: debug and release. Open the release directory. This directory holds all of the files you will normally distribute to end-users.

3. In the release directory, double-click MyFirstApp.exe. This should bring up the application.

Congratulations! Your application should run in much the same way that it did in debug mode, however, it is running without VB Express. It is now an application you can copy to another place on disk (or send to a friend via email) and run. The key is to copy all the files (remember, you need both the .MDF and .LDF database files).

How It Works

A very important point to understand is that the connection string that instructs SQL Server on which database the application should connect to actually specifies the MyDB.mdf file via a relative path (using a DataDirectory macro). So, whether the application is run in your bin directory, or whether you copy the files along with the database and send it to someone else to run on their machine (they must have SQL Server Express running on their machine as well), it will just work. You learn more about how to deploy SQL Server Express with your application in Chapter 10 in the discussion of ClickOnce Deployment.

If you are familiar with SQL Server, and databases in general, another point to understand is that most connection strings require you to specify the logical name of the database you want to connect to. The physical name is often irrelevant because the database is usually already connected. With this style of connection, the logical database name is left blank. The logical name is generated from the physical name and current path of the .MDF. Thus the logical name is always unique for the physical name and location. This style of connection also forces a new attach of the database so that your application can work with it. When your application is finished working with it, and the application domain shuts down, SQL Server auto closes the database and the physical write lock on the database is released. This makes the .MDF and .LDF available for copying purposes.

Summary

In this chapter, you learned how to create a straightforward read-only database application using Microsoft Visual Basic 2005 Express Edition. And it didn't require you to write a single line of code! To be clear, there is a lot of code behind the scenes that is generated for you, but VB Express does all that work, making the creation of a simple database application very easy.

In this chapter, you learned how to:

- ❑ Create a new project
- ❑ Work with the Database Explorer and Table Designer
- ❑ Add data to your table
- ❑ Work with the Data Sources window
- ❑ Create a WinForms application
- ❑ Build your application
- ❑ Run and debug your application

In Chapter 4, you learn how to develop a rich client database application.

Exercises

Try the exercises that follow to test your understanding of the material covered in this chapter. You can find the solutions to these exercises in Appendix A.

1. Assume you want to use an existing database for your application instead of creating a new one. Try adding an existing one with Add ➪ Existing Item. (Hint: Search your machine for *.mdf files.)

2. Assume you want to take a starter kit approach and build off of other people's applications. Using File ➪ New Project, in the New Project section, create a new database application using the My Movie Collection Starter Kit.

3. Using File ➪ New Project, create and build your own database structure and sample data from scratch and create a new sample read-only database.

Part II:

Rich Database Applications Development with SQL Server Express

Chapter 4: Developing a Rich Client Database Application

Chapter 5: Developing a Rich Web Database Application

Chapter 6: Understanding Xcopy Deployment and User Instance Model

Chapter 7: Using XML in Your Database Application

Chapter 8: Debugging Database Applications

Developing a Rich Client Database Application

Visual Basic Express (VB Express) makes it easy to build complex data-centric applications. In Chapter 3, you built a simple data-centric application that required no coding on your part. In this chapter, you build a more complex data-centric application and also walk through the basics of using VB Express to design and create a richer database.

In this chapter you learn to:

❑ Design and create a richer database using VB Express

❑ Create an updateable master-detail data-centric application

❑ Use more complex WinForm controls

When you're done, you will be able to build more complex create data-centric applications fairly easily and quickly with VB Express. While this chapter gives you the basics, there are still many other topics for you to pursue in building rich data-centric applications.

Designing Your Database in VB Express

To build a richer database using VB Express, you will start with the database you created in Chapter 3 and modify it. You will add a second table, Book, and link it to the Person table. When you're done, your database will look like the diagram shown in Figure 4-1.

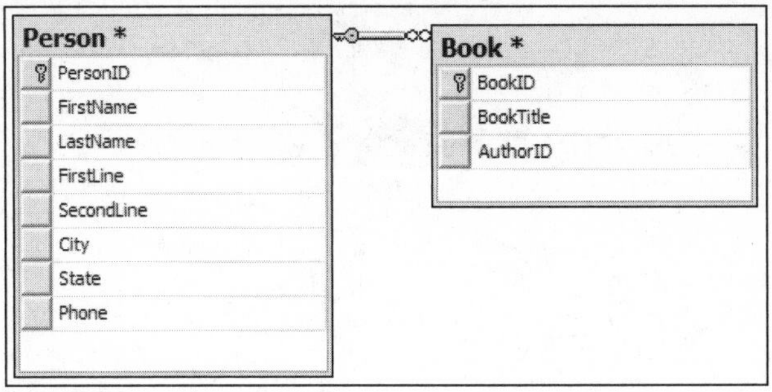

Figure 4-1

Try It Out   Creating a Second Table

To create the second table in your database, follow these steps:

1. Using the same connection you made earlier to the database in the temporary directory, add a new table with the structure shown in the following table and name it Book. Set BookID as the primary key.

2. Choose File ⇨ Save Table2 to save the table you have created. Name the table Book.

> If you have opened your MyFirstApp project from Chapter 3, it should still retain the connection you made to your database. If it is not present in Database Explorer, double-click MyDB.mdf in the Solution Explorer to reopen a connection to the database. Also, recall that to create a new table, you right-click the Tables folder in the Database Explorer. If your MyFirstApp project is not open, you can create a direct connection to your database by right-clicking the Data Connections node in the Database Explorer. Choose Add Connection and then browse to the MDF in your old project.

Column Name	Data Type	Allow Nulls
BookID	int	No
BookTitle	nvarchar (50)	No
AuthorID	int	No

How It Works

When you create your table, the first choice you make is the *column name*. The column name should have no spaces in it (that is, use BookID rather than Book ID). The names you create for tables shouldn't contain spaces either. SQL Server will allow you to create and use a column or table name with spaces. However, if you use a column or table name with spaces, it makes query code you might write later difficult to read because you must bracket, or delimit, the name like so: [Person Name]. Compact names (ones without spaces) make queries easier to read and less prone to error since you don't have to remember to delimit the names.

The second choice you must make is the *data type* for the column. For this application, you have selected the data types of int, nvarchar (50), and varbinary(MAX). int is an abbreviation for a 32-bit integer. nvarchar (50) is a Unicode variable-length character data type with a maximum size of 50 characters. varbinary(Max) allows for the storage of variable length binary data to the maximum size allowed by SQL Server 2005. This makes it ideal for the storage of picture data such as bitmaps. An important point to understand is that when you choose a data type for a column, SQL Server allocates space in the .MDF file for the type of data you wish to store. Depending on the type of data you store, SQL Server can optimize both the space needed and the speed with which it accesses data. You can find more information about the data types available to you in SQL Server in Chapter 2. You can also find information by using SQL Server Books Online. SQL Server Books Online is not bundled with SQL Express by default. You must download it separately from the Internet. The online documentation comes with SQL Server Express Manager, and is available on the web at http://lab.msdn.microsoft.com/express/sql/.

The third choice you typically make is how you will *uniquely identify* information in your table. In this application, you have designated PersonID and BookID as the unique identifiers for the Person and Book tables, respectively. You did this by setting those columns as the primary key.

Also, when you created your primary key, an index was automatically added to the table for you. Indexes enable very fast lookup of values. This is critical for primary keys. If there are other columns in your table that could serve as an alternate key (that is, if the data in that column is also unique like the data in the primary key column), consider creating an index for that column, too, since you may want to search your table data using that column's value instead of the primary key data. To do this, bring up the Table Designer and right-click on the background to bring up a context menu. On the context menu, choose Indexes/Keys and create an index for your alternate key column.

Finally, you must choose whether the user must put in data for a given column or whether data is *optional*. In the Book table example all of the columns are required. So, the Allow Nulls setting is NO for all of them. However, for the Person table, all of the columns are optional except for the primary key.

Now that you have a Book table, link it to the Person table with a foreign key, as shown in the following Try It Out. The foreign key will point from the Book table to the Person table.

Try It Out   Linking the Person and Book Tables

To link the Book table to the Person table from the Database Explorer in VB Express, follow these steps:

1. While in the Table Designer for the Book table, right-click somewhere in the table designer window to bring up the context menu. In the context menu, choose Relationships to bring up the Foreign Key Relationships dialog.

2. In the Foreign Key Relationships dialog, choose Add. This adds a new *unconfigured* foreign key. On the right-hand side of the dialog, at the bottom of the list of properties for the newly created relationship, choose the Tables and Columns Specification property builder to bring up the Tables and Columns dialog.

3. In the Tables and Columns dialog, choose Person as the primary key table (on the left). Move to the dropdown combo box below Person and choose PersonID. The foreign key table on the right is Book. Tab to the right and, below Book, choose AuthorID.

4. Click OK to close the Tables and Columns dialog and Close to close the Foreign Key Relationships dialog. You have now created a foreign key relationship between the Book and Person tables.

5. Add the data to the table as is shown in the table below (right click on the Book table in the Database Explorer and choose Show Table Data).

BookID	BookTitle	AuthorID
1	How to Chop a Cherry Tree	1
2	Valley Forge Snow Angels	1
3	Martha and Me	1
4	Summer Job Surveying Virginia	1
5	Log Chopping in Illinois	2
6	Registry of Visitors to the White House	2
7	My Favorite Inventions	3
8	More Favorite Inventions	3
9	Inventions for which the World Is Not Ready	3
10	The Path to the White House	2
11	Why I Don't Believe in Polls	2
12	Doing the Right Thing Is Hard	2

6. Finally, close the connection in the Database Explorer to the MyDB.mdf database in the temporary directory.

How It Works

When you create a foreign key, what you have done — in simple English — is to tell SQL Server that any values in the foreign key reference column in the Book table must match a valid record in the Person table. Any book recorded in the Book table must be written by a person recorded in the Person table. Specifically, you are saying that the values in the Book table's AuthorID column (such as 1, 2, and 3) are constrained. Each value in the Book table AuthorID column must match a PersonID value in the Person table (that is, 1, 2, or 3), which are values used in this application to uniquely identify a person. But note that it does not have the inverse meaning. It does not mean that all of the values in the PersonID table must match each of the values in the Book AuthorID column. So, potentially, there may be values in the PersonID column that are not referenced in the AuthorID column. Or, put more simply, some persons may not have written any books.

Creating a Master-Detail Form

The relationship between Person and Book is generally referred to as *master-detail*. In this example, the Book table is dependent on, or subject to, the Person table for information. The Book table information is incomplete; the Book table AuthorID column points to the Person table to complete its information. Hence, the Person table is master and the Book table is detail. This master-detail pattern occurs quite frequently in software. Another simple example is the information contained generally on a Purchase Order (for example, date of the purchase, who is purchasing, where they live, and so on) and Purchase Order Line details (what specific items they are purchasing). While in Chapter 3 you added a single table to a form, now you will add two tables, Person and Book, to your form. The first step, however, as in Chapter 3, is to get the database into your project. Use the database you created in Chapter 3 as a starting point.

| Try It Out | Creating a Project with Add Existing Item |

1. Create a new project. Name it MasterDetail and save it.

2. In the Solution Explorer, right-click the MasterDetail node to bring up the context menu.

3. Copy the MyDB.mdf database from your project in Chapter 3 by choosing Add ⇨ Existing Item from the context menu. Change the Files of Type dropdown to Data Files (*.xsd; *.xml; *.mdf; *.mdb) to see MDF files in directories. Then, navigate to the temporary directory where you stored the now modified version of MyDB.mdf and choose Add. This should add the MyDB.mdf to your project. It will also bring up the Data Source Configuration Wizard.

> You should close any connections that are currently open in the Database Explorer to MyDB.mdf. Choose the MyDB.mdf database, right-click, and then detach. Then choose Delete. This detaches the database and then closes the connection. VB Express will actually work with the old connection present; however, you may find it confusing to have two MyDB.mdfs present in your Database Explorer.

4. In the Data Source Configuration Wizard, check the Tables check box and click Finish. This selection will include both the Person and Book tables and will add the MyDBDataSet to your project.

How It Works

VB Express copies the database from your old project into your new project. When it copies the database, it automatically looks for the .LDF file as well (the LDF is the log file for your database) and copies it too. VB Express creates the DataSet for you automatically as well. If you open the Data Sources window, you'll see a node for both the Book and Person tables.

Now you are ready to create an updateable master-detail form for Person and Book. As in Chapter 3, you work from the Data Sources window.

Making a Master-Detail Form

To create the master-detail form, follow these steps:

1. Change the Person node in the Data Sources window from the default of a DataGridView to Details. Right-click the Person node and choose Details as illustrated in Figure 4-2. This will change what is placed (DataGridView or Details) on the form when you drag the node to the form.

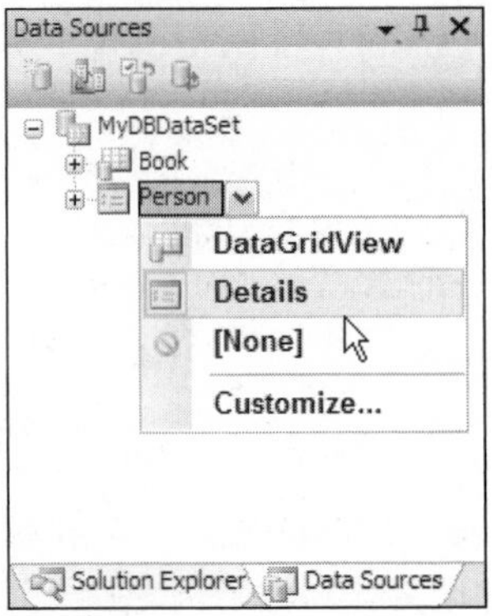

Figure 4-2

2. Drag the Person node from the Data Source window onto the form. This step populates your form with the details for Person.

3. Drag the Book node from the Data Sources window onto the form below the Person details. This places a grid on the form showing book details. Before dropping the grid on the form, you should resize the form so that the grid will fit. You may also want to rearrange the detailed Person fields on the form.

4. Select the small arrow for the Book grid to expand into the DataGridView Tasks, as shown in Figure 4-3.

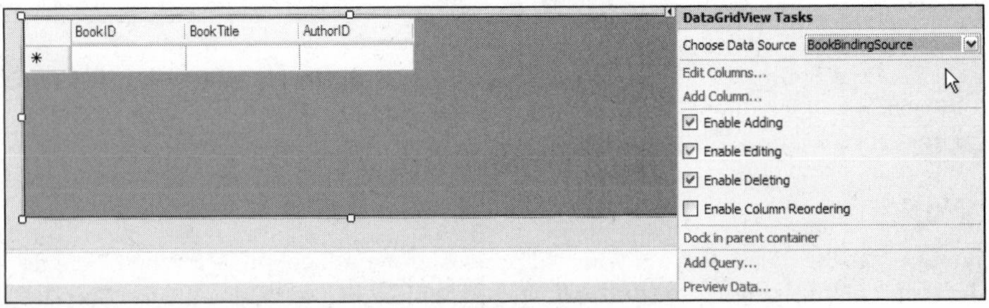

Figure 4-3

5. Select the dropdown combo box for the Choose Data Source and expand the PersonBindingSource to expose the FK_Book_Person foreign key relationship, as shown in Figure 4-4. Select the Foreign key as the binding source and click outside the form to close the menu.

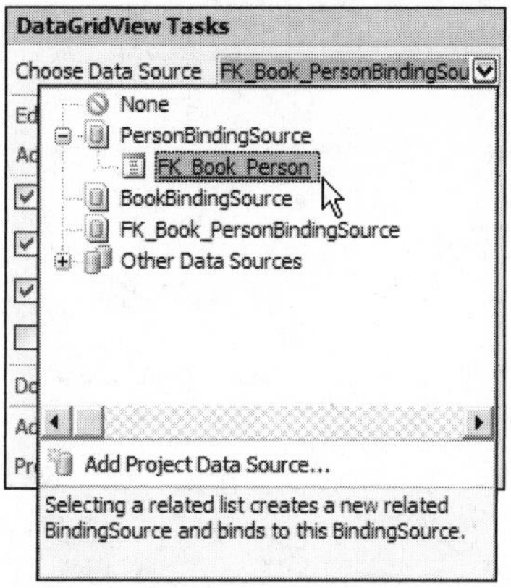

DataGridView Tasks

Choose Data Source FK_Book_PersonBindingSou ▼

- ⊘ None
- ⊟ PersonBindingSource
    - FK_Book_Person
- BookBindingSource
- FK_Book_PersonBindingSource
- ⊞ Other Data Sources

Add Project Data Source...

Selecting a related list creates a new related BindingSource and binds to this BindingSource.

Figure 4-4

> **Note:** You can avoid steps 4 and 5 if you take a short cut. The short cut is to drag the Book node that sits under the Person node in the Data Sources Window onto the form. In the Data Sources Window, first expand the Person node. You will see all of the fields for Person and a node at the bottom for book. Dragging this node over is the same as doing steps 3 – 5 at the same time. However, if you accidentally drag over a node, you need to know how to configure it once dropped and positioned. You need to know how to do steps 4 and 5.

6. Select the grid for the Book and press F4 to bring up the Properties window. In the Miscellaneous section at the bottom, select the builder button for the Columns Collection. This should bring up the Edit Columns property editor. For the BookID, BookTitle, and AuthorID columns, change the property values as indicated in the following table:

Column Name	Change the Property Values to:
BookID	Layout Width = 50
BookTitle	Layout = 400
AuthorID	Layout = 50

7. Choose File ➪ Save All.

8. Close the Properties window and press F5 to build your application.

How It Works

When your application runs, you will see both the Person information and the correctly associated book information. When you specify the foreign key as the binding source for the Book grid, VB Express uses that information to create a number of components that work closely together to create a master detail application for you. If you have the Form window up, you will notice an area at the bottom of your screen that is populated with icons and descriptions much like those in Figure 4-5.

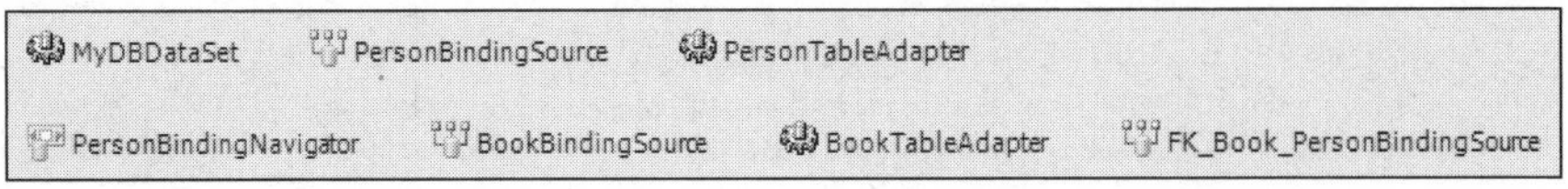

Figure 4-5

Included in this area are the non-UI components such as DataSet, BindingSource, TableAdapter, BindingNavigator, and the BindingSource for both the Person and the Book tables. Select any one of these components and the Properties window will display its properties. If you select a TableAdapter or the DataSet, you will see a little arrow leading to a context menu pop-up that you can use to perform additional tasks for these components such as editing in the designer or adding new queries.

It is very important to note that while you can see the information correctly displayed in your form, it does not mean the data will save correctly to the database. Unfortunately, the generated code only really handles the information in the Person grid. It does not correctly handle the information in the Book grid. While you can choose the Save button in the form while it is running, if you check carefully, you will see that the data in the database is not updated. VB Express automatically handles a single table update for you, but multiple table updates are left to the developer.

This is the end of the free ride with the designers. To get this form to save correctly to the database, you will need to write some code. Fortunately, the code is not very difficult. The following Try It Out shows how to make your master-detail form updateable.

Try It Out   Making a Master-Detail Form Updateable

To make your master-detail form updateable, follow these steps:

1. On the Form1.vb designer, double-click the Save button. This opens the code editor with Form1.vb and puts you in the `SaveItem` Subroutine. (Alternatively, you can just open Form1.vb directly and navigate to the `SaveItem` Subroutine.)

2. At the top of the file (above Public Class Form1), add the following `Imports` statement:

```
Imports System.Data
```

3. Replace the existing `SaveItem` code with the following code. Note also the `Imports System.Data`, which goes above the class declaration.

```
Imports System.Data
Public Class Form1

    Private Sub bindingNavigatorSaveItem_Click(ByVal sender As System.Object, _
```

```
ByVal e As System.EventArgs) Handles bindingNavigatorSaveItem.Click

    If Validate() Then

        Me.BookBindingSource.EndEdit()
        Me.PersonBindingSource.EndEdit()

        Try
            'Delete records in the child table
            Me.BookTableAdapter.Update(Me.MyDBDataSet.Book.Select("", "", _
                DataViewRowState.Deleted))
            'Handle Add, Update, and Delete in parent table
            Me.PersonTableAdapter.Update(Me.MyDBDataSet.Person.Select("", "", _
                DataViewRowState.Added Or _
                DataViewRowState.ModifiedCurrent Or _
                DataViewRowState.Deleted))
            'Handle Add & Update in child table
            Me.BookTableAdapter.Update(Me.MyDBDataSet.Book.Select("", "", _
                DataViewRowState.Added Or _
                DataViewRowState.ModifiedCurrent))
        Catch ex As Exception
            MessageBox.Show(ex.Message)
        End Try

    End If
End Sub
...
Private Sub BookDataGridView_DataErrorEvent(ByVal sender As System.Object, _
    ByVal e As System.Windows.Forms.DataGridViewDataErrorEventArgs) _
    Handles BookDataGridView.DataError

    MessageBox.Show(
        "Error: Check that a valid record number has been input. Save Person
information first")

    End Sub
...
End Class
```

4. In the same Form1.vb file, find the `Form1_Load` subroutine. Reverse the load order of the Book and Person tables. By default, the generated code puts the detail Book table first and the master Person table second. Reverse the order so they appear as follows, with the Person table being filled first and then the Book table.

```
Me.PersonTableAdapter.Fill(Me.MyDBDataSet.Person)
Me.BookTableAdapter.Fill(Me.MyDBDataSet.Book)
```

5. Next, open the Data Sources window and right-click MyDBDataSet and then click the Edit DataSet with Designer menu item. This will bring up the DataSet Designer.

6. Double-click the relationship arrow between the Book and Person data tables. This will bring up the Relation dialog.

7. In the Relation dialog, click the Both Relation and Foreign Key Constraint radio button. Then set the Update Rule, Delete Rule, and Accept/Reject Rule to Cascade as shown in Figure 4-6.

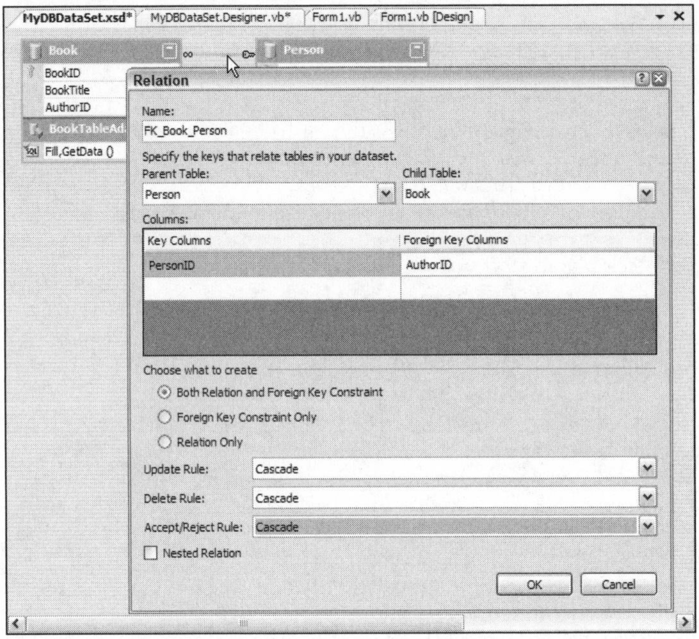

Figure 4-6

8. Click OK to close and save your settings.

9. Choose File ⇨ Save All.

10. Press F5 to build and debug.

11. Press Shift F5 to stop debugging or close the application.

How It Works

This procedure makes your master-detail form updateable. To add new Book records, simply add a new record at the bottom of the Book grid. To delete a row, select the entire row and press the Delete key. Now that you have changed the SaveItem code, you can make changes to either the Person or the Book records, and clicking the Save button on the ToolStrip of your MasterDetail Form application will save all of your changes to the database. Note that for entirely new records, you need to still save the Person information first before adding new Book info.

The code you entered to update the database is specifically ordered in such a way that conflicts are avoided. So, first, any records in Book (or detail) that are to be deleted are removed. Then, any adds, modifications, or deletes are made to the Person (master) table. Finally, any new records to be added to Book or updates are made to the Book table. Working in this order means that the foreign key constraint (that all records in the Book table must point to a valid record in the Person table) will not be violated.

Note also that in the DataSet designer, you had to explicitly also choose for the DataSet to honor the foreign key in the database. If you don't, when you delete a record in the Person table, you will find that that DataSet will not mark any dependent records in the Book table as records that must be deleted. And when you try and save your changes, you will get an error.

You added a custom error message to deal with the case where a data error occurs. Note that it has a message for two separate cases. One where the user neglects to put in a record number for a BookID and the other when the user attempts to add Book information for a Person that has not yet been saved into the database.

Finally, note that you reordered the load order of the Person and Book tables. You did this by telling the DataSet to honor the foreign key. Therefore, you want the Person table loaded before you load the Book table, because the Book table has records that point to the Person table. Otherwise, you will get an error when you load the records.

Working Directly with Components

In the preceding section, you wrote some code that directly accessed components such as `TableAdapters`. There are a number of components generated for you automatically. You can further customize and extend your application by working directly with those components as you did in the last section. Most of the kinds of calls you will make to customize your application are quite simple. The programming model developed for building data-centric applications is very extensive. In this section, you further extend and customize your application by directly working with these components.

As it stands, the application returns all the records in your database. If your database is of significant size, you may want to filter the database records that you are looking at. The following Try It Out shows you how to do so.

Try It Out   Filtering Your Records

To filter your records, follow these steps:

1. Right-click on the ToolStrip and choose Edit Items to bring up the Items Collection Editor.

2. Select a separator from the dropdown menu and click the Add button to add the separator to the Members list.

3. Next, add a Label and click the Add button to add the label ToolStripLabel1 to the Members list.

4. Select ToolStripLabel1 in the members list. The properties for the label appear on the right-hand side of the dialog.

5. In the properties grid, in the Appearance section, find the Text property and set it to the text Filter Criteria.

6. Add another item to the Members list. First, select TextBox from the item list and add it to the Members list. Ensure that the `Text` property of the TextBox is set to blank (that is, no text).

7. Add a final item to the Members list. First select a button from the item list and add it to the Members list. Set the `Text` property of the button in the Properties window on the right to Filter Now. Then, set the `Display Style` property to `Text`. When you are finished, the Items Collection Member list should appear as shown in Figure 4-7.

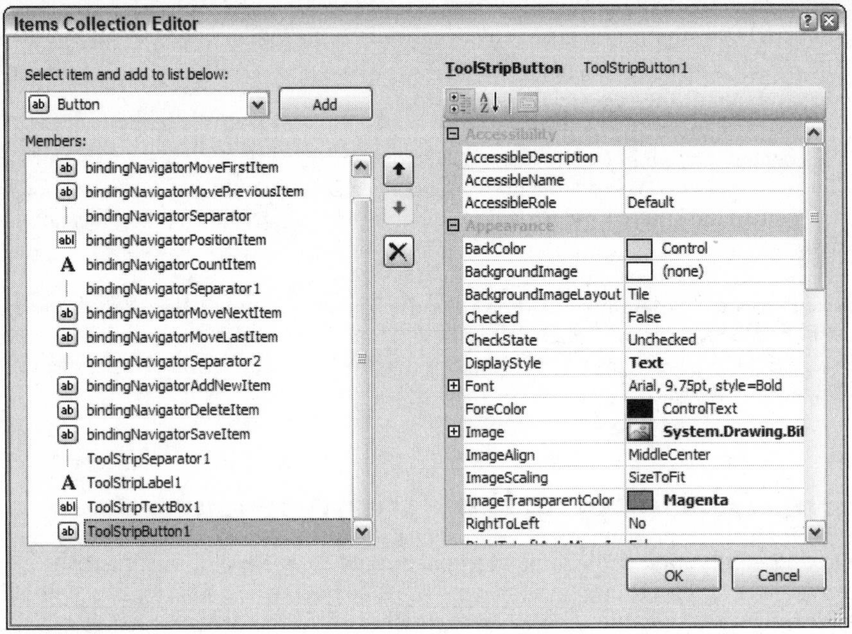

Figure 4-7

8. Click OK to close the Items Collection editor to take you back to the Form1 designer.

9. Double-click the Filter Now button you just added on the ToolStrip. This brings up the code editor for Form1.vb and creates a click-event handler for you on the ToolStrip.

10. In the click-event handler, add the following code:

```
Try

    PersonBindingSource.Filter = ToolStripTextBox1.Text
    PersonBindingSource.ResetBindings(False)

Catch ex As Exception

    MessageBox.Show(ex.Message)

End Try
```

11. Choose File ➪ Save All.

12. Debug your application (press F5).

13. While debugging your application, enter the types of search criteria listed in the following table and observe the results:

Search Criteria
FirstName like 'g%'
PersonID > 2
Garbagetext

How It Works

Your search criteria are passed directly to SSE. If the criterion is illegal (as in the `Garbagetext` case), the exception is caught and the message is displayed in a message box. Note that the search operators used above (such as `like 'g%'` and `> 2`) are legal T-SQL expressions for a T-SQL `WHERE` clause. Therefore, searches such as `FirstName LIKE 'G%' AND PersonID > 2` and `PersonID > 2 OR LastName like 'J%'` are also legal.

The code you wrote to filter the records uses the BindingSource component. In addition to setting the filter, you can also set the sort order. In the following Try it Out, you add the sorting code to the form load handler code.

Try It Out   Sorting Your Records

To sort your records, follow these steps:

1. Right-click Form1.vb in the Solution Explorer and choose View Code to bring up the `Form1.vb` code.

2. Find the `Form1_Load` event handler and add the following code after the `fill` statements:

```
Me.PersonBindingSource.Sort = "LastName ASC, FirstName DESC"
```

3. Press F5 to debug your application.

How It Works

Note that your application now comes up with last names sorted first. Note also the syntax of the code that you have entered. Again, the command text inside the quotes is an SQL statement applicable to sorting. Note the `ASC` and `DESC` keywords in the code. They stand for *ascending* and *descending*, respectively. The `ASC` following `LastName` means that the LastName column data will be sorted in an ascending order. This is the primary way in the table data will be sorted. The `DESC` following `FirstName` means that the FirstName column data will be sorted in descending order wherever LastName data is identical.

As the final example in this section, you add the ability to find a specific record.

Try It Out   Finding and Navigating to Specific Records

To find a specific record with a specific primary key value, follow these steps:

1. Right-click on the ToolStrip and choose Edit Items to bring up the Items Collection Editor.

2. Select a separator from the item list and click the Add button to add the separator to the Members list.

3. Choose a Label from the item list and click the Add button to add the label ToolStripLabel2 to the Members list.

4. Select ToolStripLabel2 in the Members list. The properties for the label appear on the right-hand side of the dialog.

5. In the Appearance section of the properties grid, find the `Text` property and set it to the text `Find Criteria`.

6. Add another item to the Members list: Select a TextBox from the item list and add it to the Members list. Set the `text` property to `<Search Value>` and set the `(name)` property to `FilterInput`.

7. Next, select a button from the item list and add it to the Members list. Set the `text` property to `Find Now`, the `Display` property to `Text`, and the `(Name)` property to `FindNow`.

8. Double-click the Find Now button you just added to the ToolStrip. This brings up the code editor for Form1.vb and creates a click-event handler for the button.

9. In the click-event handler, add the following code:

```
Try

    Dim PKvalue As String = FilterInput.Text
    Dim RowLocated As DataRow = Me.MyDBDataSet.Person.Rows.Find(CType(PKvalue,
Integer))
    If Not (RowLocated Is Nothing) Then
        MessageBox.Show(CType(RowLocated(1), String))
  Else
        MessageBox.Show(PKvalue & " record not located")
    End If

Catch ex As Exception
    MessageBox.Show(ex.Message)
End Try
```

10. Save your code and press F5 to bring up your application. Enter primary key values in the Filter Search area and try it out. Try values such as `1`, `2`, or `15`.

How It Works

With the number of controls you've added, things may be a bit crowded. You can work around this by resizing the form. The code you have entered is for a click-event handler. This handler will catch any click on the button and then allow you to execute your code. The code you entered will take the string entered into the FindNow text box and use it to search the MyDBDataSet. If the string is located, the program will navigate to that record and present a message that the record was found. Otherwise, it will show a message that the record was not located.

Working with the Binding Source

The binding source is a central record currency binding service for controls on your form. Rather than having your grid control, for instance, bind or directly reference records in the DataSet, it instead relies on the binding source to provide the service of keeping the reference to records in the DataSet. By default, all of your controls use the same binding source so it coordinates, for all your controls, which record is currently being referenced so that the controls all work harmoniously. As you saw in the last section, the binding source provides the ability for you to specify filters and sort. In addition, it also provides record currency management (as just described), change notifications, and other services.

It is useful to understand the relationship of the various components in your application to each other. The primary components in your WinForm application are the WinForm, the controls on your form, the BindingSource, Binding Navigator, DataSet, and TableAdapter, as shown in Figure 4-8.

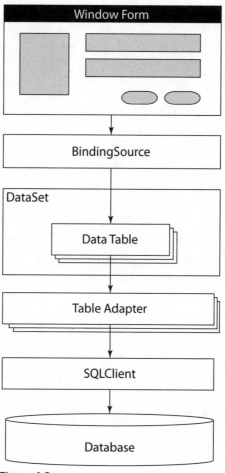

Figure 4-8

Using DataSet and DataTable

In Figure 4-8, the component below the BindingSource is the DataSet. As mentioned in Chapter 3, the Data Set is an in-memory version of your database. It contains a number of DataTables (each DataTable directly corresponds to a table in your database) and the relationships between them. In a DataSet, specific queries or methods can be associated with a specific DataTable. In particular, each DataTable has both a `Fill` and `GetData` method associated with it. These are the methods called in the form load handler where you added the sorting statement. You can see these methods in the DataSet Designer, and you can preview data, add new queries, and perform other actions as well.

To edit the DataSet in the Designer, follow these steps:

    1.   Open the Data Sources window and right-click on the background. Choose Edit DataSet with Designer to bring up the DataSet Designer, shown in Figure 4-9.

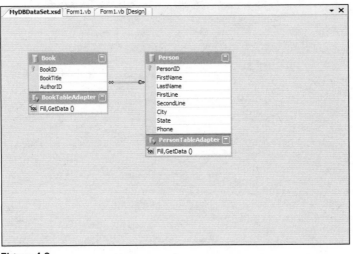

Figure 4-9

    2.   Right-click the Person DataTable and choose Configure to bring up the TableAdapter Configuration Wizard.

In the TableAdapter Configuration Wizard, you can directly alter the SELECT statement used to load data into the DataTable. You can further use the graphical query designer to build the query for you automatically.

Try It Out   **Using the Graphical Query Designer**

To use the graphical query designer:

    1.   While in the Table Adapter Configuration Wizard, choose the Query Builder button. This launches the Query Builder, shown in Figure 4-10.

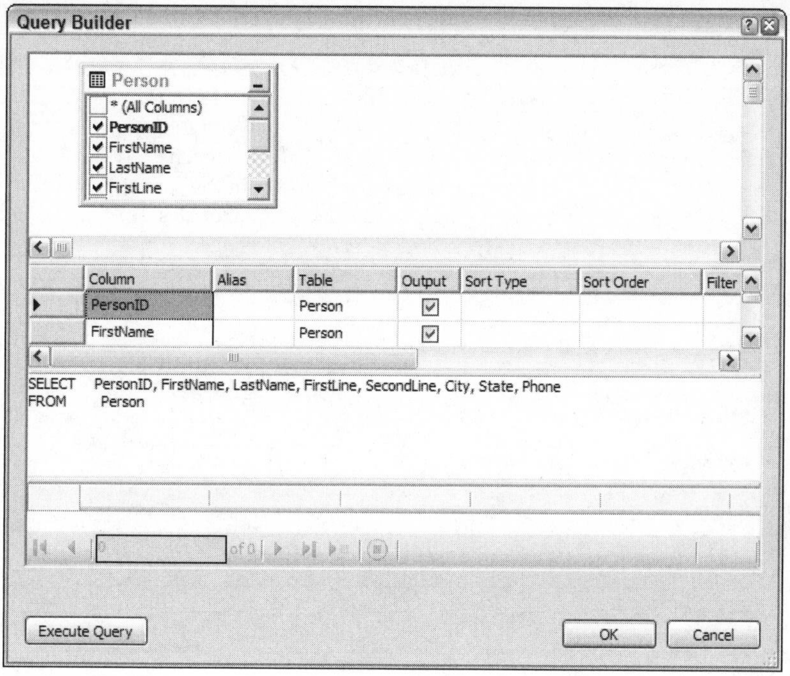

Figure 4-10

2. On the PersonID row, in the Filter column, add the text >2 and click OK.

3. Click Finish in the Configuration Wizard.

How It Works

Note that while you can use the graphical query designer to help you get a correct query, you can also directly edit the SQL text in the Configuration Wizard. In either case, if you change this SQL, it will change the values loaded into the DataSet from the Database. In this case, if you leave this change in place, the data in the dataset will not contain the PersonID = 1 or 2 records.

An important way to check that your data is coming into the DataSet correctly is to use the Preview Data menu item on the Data menu.

Try It Out   Previewing Your Data

To preview the data for your DataTable, follow these steps:

1. While in the DataSet Designer, right-click the Person DataTable and choose Preview Data to bring up the Preview Data dialog, shown in Figure 4-11.

2. Click the Preview button to preview the data for your DataTable.

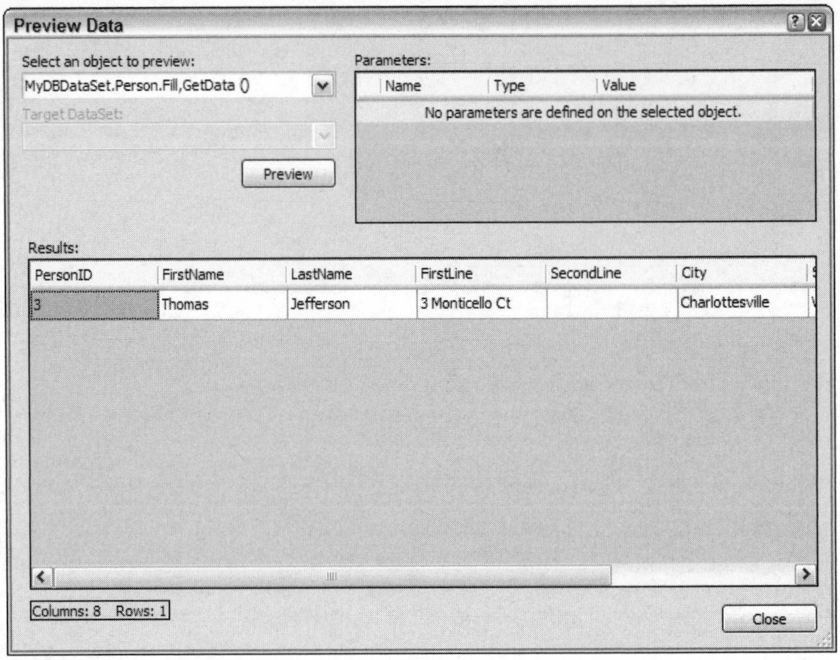

Figure 4-11

3. Close the Preview Data dialog to go back to the DataSet Designer.

4. Right-click the Person DataTable and choose Configure. Clear the WHERE (PersonID > 2) clause from your query and click Finish.

How It Works

This exercise illustrates that you can use an arbitrary SELECT statement to populate your form. You do not have to select all the records.

Working with TableAdapter

There are several other options available to you in the DataSet Designer. In particular, you can add new queries or stored procedures and associate them directly with a specific DataTable. Then, in your code, you can call them with the pattern of TableAdapter.*newStoredProcedure*. Chapter 15 provides an example of how to do this.

The TableAdapter is the primary bridge between the DataSet and the database. Recall that it was the TableAdapter that you called to update the Database with changes (adds, deletes, and modifications) to the Person and Book tables.

Printing

No application would be complete without the ability to print. Adding printing functionality to your form is conceptually easy, but in practice can be quite difficult.

Adding reporting is also significantly easier in the Standard and higher versions of Visual Studio; however, the reporting control is not available in VB Express.

To add menus and printing capabilities for your application, follow these steps:

1. Open the ToolBox and find the Printing section. Add the PrintDocument component to your component tray.

2. With the ToolBox still open, from the Menus & Toolbars section add a menu strip to your form. After you place the menu strip, you may need to rearrange the other fields so that they fit correctly.

3. With the menu strip positioned at the top of your form, you can now type directly into the field. Type the word **File**. This will expand the menu strip so that you can type to the right of and below the text.

4. Below the menu item File, type the word **Print**. It should look like the diagram in Figure 4-12.

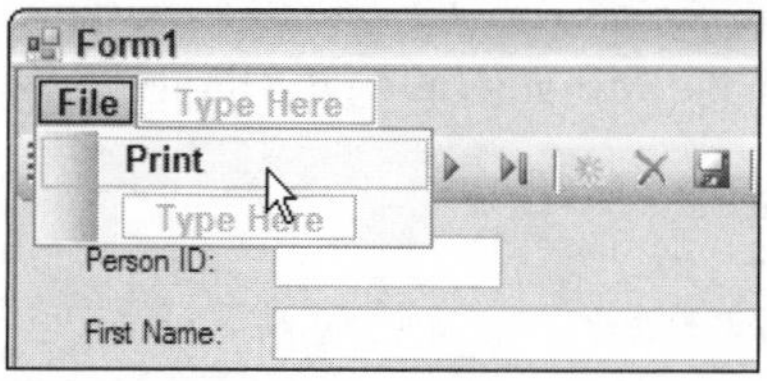

Figure 4-12

5. Double-click the Print menu item to create an event handler for the Print menu. In the event handler, add the following code:

```
Try
    PrintDocument1.Print()

Catch ex As Exception
    MessageBox.Show(ex.Message)
End Try
```

6. Next, you need to add a new event handler called PrintDocument1_Print. Double-click the PrintDocument1 component in the component tray. That will create the event handler for you. In the event handler, add the following code:

```
e.Graphics.DrawString(PersonIDTextBox.Text(), New Font _
("Arial", 30, FontStyle.Bold), Brushes.Black, 150, 125)

e.Graphics.DrawString(FirstNameTextBox.Text(), New Font _
("Arial", 30, FontStyle.Bold), Brushes.Black, 150, 200)

e.Graphics.DrawString(LastNameTextBox.Text(), New Font _
("Arial", 30, FontStyle.Bold), Brushes.Black, 150, 250)
```

With what you have done here, you can print an individual record. However, at this point, you're pretty much at the bare knuckles print code level. It is not very pretty to write although it's very flexible and powerful. Note that since this is graphics-level printing, you control every aspect of where and how something is printed. You must specify the XY location of every print element.

> The reporting control available in Standard and higher versions of Visual Studio is very powerful and easy to use. With the reporting control, you get reporting functionality similar to Microsoft Access. For instance, you can easily specify report headers, repeating elements, subtotals, and so forth. You can choose to simply display the report to screen or print to a printer. Furthermore, the report definitions you specify for the reporting control are directly transferable and useable in SQL Server's report server.

Summary

In this chapter, you have learned some of the critical elements of writing a single-user, SSE-based application. A great deal of your application code is actually generated for you. And the small parts of code that you have actually written are very modest in comparison. There is a great deal of power available to you both directly in the designers and with modest amounts of code.

In particular, this chapter addressed:

- ❑ Designing and creating a richer database using VB Express
- ❑ Creating an updateable master-detail data-centric application
- ❑ Using more complex WinForm controls
- ❑ Adding an existing database to your project
- ❑ Creating foreign key relationships between tables in VB Express
- ❑ Creating an updateable master-detail relationship on a form
- ❑ Filtering and sorting your data
- ❑ ADO.NET components and how they are related
- ❑ Using the graphical query designer in VB Express
- ❑ Printing

In the next chapter, you learn how to create a web database application.

Exercises

Try the exercises that follow to test your understanding of the material covered in this chapter. You can find the solutions to these exercises in Appendix A.

1. Add more dialogs, menus, and such to finish up your application. Each dialog may either allow you to work with a specific table in your database or display certain information. Start by creating an About dialog that you can launch from the menu and that will display appropriate credit information.

2. Make sure that your application is accessible to those that cannot use a mouse well. This means that you must add accelerators to the menu and ensure that tabbing works throughout the application in a smooth manner. Start by adding accelerators to the existing Print and File menus. Use the ShowShortCutKeys property. When you add an ampersand to a menu name, the ampersand marks the accelerator (for example, &Print).

3. There are several printers available to your users. You need to make your application capable of using all those printers. There is code readily available on the Internet that can help you add the code you need. As a hint, go to http://msdn.microsoft.com/library and search for PrintDialog.ShowDialog. Add the Print Dialog component to your application and allow the user to choose a Printer.

Developing a Rich Web Database Application

Visual Basic Express makes it easy to build complex data-centric applications. In Chapter 4, you built a richer data application that required some code on your part. However, the designers provided a great deal of the heavy lifting. In a similar way, the designers in Visual Web Developer 2005 Express Edition ("Web Express") provide the same kinds of productivity gains as well. In this chapter, you build a rich web application and take advantage of the tight integration of SSE and Web Express.

Specifically, in this chapter you learn to:

- ❑ Use the local web server for Visual Web Developer development
- ❑ Create an updateable master-detail data-centric application for the web

You need Visual Web Developer 2005 Express Edition for this chapter. This is not included on the CD with the book.

When you are done, you will be able to build complex web data-centric applications quickly and easily with Web Express 2005. While this chapter gives you the basics, there are still many other topics for you to pursue in building rich web applications.

In this chapter, first you will create a very simple web application. Next, you will learn how to use master pages to make your web application more consistent. Then you will add a database to the project and create the same type of application you created in Chapter 4, including the use of filtering on your data.

A web application is not identical to a rich-client type of application. The UI is not as responsive, and you rely on communication with the server for the display of each page you navigate to. However, the benefit is that you only have to change your application in a single place. You have no explicit deployment of the application to end-users' machines.

Chapter 5

Creating a Web Application Using Web Express

To illustrate the creation of a web application, use the database you created in Chapter 4. You will try to get to the same kind of functionality in the web application as you created in the rich client database application in Chapter 4. Additionally, you will use some features unique to ASP .NET.

Try It Out   Creating a New Web Application

To create a new web application, follow these steps in Visual Web Developer:

1. Choose File ➪ New Web Site. This brings up the New Web Site dialog.

2. In the lower left corner of the New Web Site dialog, ensure that the dropdown for Location is File System and that the Language is Visual Basic.

3. Type in the name of your web page to the right of the Location field. Enter the name **Presidents** at the end of the default path and click OK. This will create your web application and open the editor to display the source for the default page. The default path with the President web application name should be something like the following:

```
C:\Documents and Settings\<name>\My Documents\Visual Studio
2005\WebSites\Presidents
```

4. In the lower left-hand corner of the screen, find the Design tab and click it to bring up the design surface for the web page.

5. On the design surface, type the following text: **Presidents and their Favorite Books**.

6. If the Formatting Toolbar is not open, open it by choosing View ➪ Toolbars and checking the box next to the Formatting Toolbar. With the Formatting Toolbar open, format the text you just entered as bold, 24 pt text.

7. Press Ctrl+F5 to bring up your web page as shown in Figure 5-1.

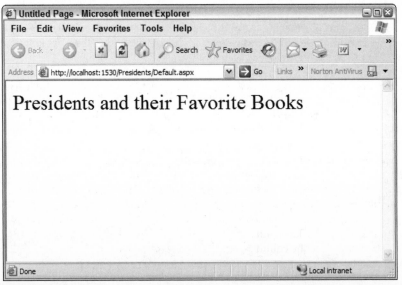

Figure 5-1

How It Works

In previous versions of Visual Studio, you needed an IIS server running and configured to build and debug web applications. You also had to place your application in a virtual application root such as `c:\inetpub\wwwroot\`.

No more.

Web Express ships with a lightweight built-in web server. Note that when you first created your web project, instead of choosing File System as the location, you could have chosen an http or FTP site. Because Web Express ships with a built-in web server, you are able to save your website locally in a My Documents folder. Thus, all web development can be local—as long as you have all the files necessary for your web application on your local machine. When it comes time for deployment, you can publish your web application to any location you choose.

Choosing Control+F5, rather than F5, brings up the website directly without launching the debugger. You'll find that if you are dealing primarily with the built-in controls provided by the framework, you won't often need the debugger since many errors will be displayed plainly on a web page somewhere. On the other hand, if you are adding code behind the web pages, the debugger can provide useful help.

Master Pages

Because you are building a web application that will have multiple pages, you should build your application in the right way: You should use *master pages*. Master pages make it easy to ensure that your application has a common look across all pages by allowing some content and styling to remain the same across all pages. The following example shows you how to create and use a master page.

Try It Out   **Using Master Pages**

To start working with master pages, follow these steps:

1. Open Solution Explorer. Right-click the `Default.aspx` file and click Delete.

2. Right-click the c:\Presidents node at the top of the Solution Explorer and choose Add New Item to bring up the Add New Item dialog.

3. In the Add New Item dialog, choose Master Page, leave the Name as MasterPage.master, and click Add.

4. Once the Source view comes up in the Document Window, click the Design tab in the lower left-hand corner. This opens the designer for the master page. You should see a ContentPlaceHolder1 at the top of the designer.

5. Open the Toolbox Window on the left and expand the HTML section. Add a table below ContentPlaceHolder1.

6. The table, when added, will be quite small. Expand the table by dragging the right-hand edge of the table to the right.

7. Delete two columns in the table (leaving only one). First, select the smart tag that appears over a column (when you place your mouse in a column) to select the column. With the column selected, right-click the column and choose Delete ⇨ Columns.

8. Select the ContentPlaceHolder1 and move it (by selecting the move icon in the upper left-hand corner) into the middle table cell. The table will automatically resize to handle the ContentPlaceHolder1.

9. In the top cell, type the following text: **Presidents and their Favorite Books**. Format the text with 24 pt text. In the bottom cell, type the text **created by** followed by your name. Center both text strings in their respective cells.

10. Add a new page to the solution that depends on the master page. In the Solution Explorer, right-click the c:\Presidents node and choose Add New Item.

11. In the Add New Item dialog, choose Web Form, and then check the Select Master Page check box, and finally, click Add. This brings up the Select a Master Page dialog.

12. In the Select a Master Page dialog, select the MasterPage.master item and click OK.

13. Select the newly added page and choose the Design tab to bring up the designer. The page should look like Figure 5-2.

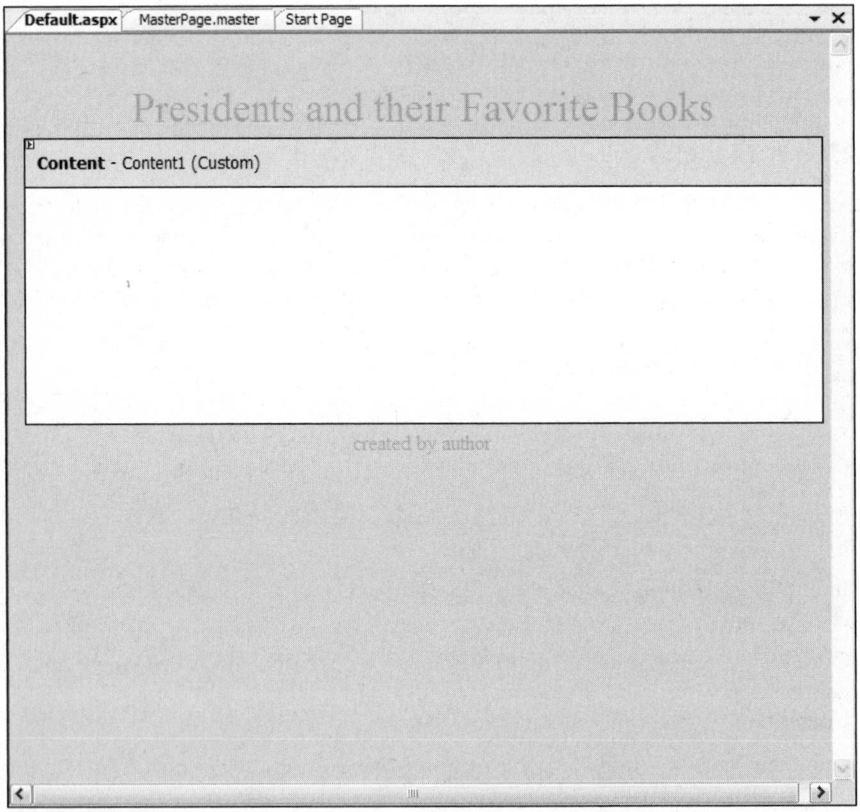

Figure 5-2

14. Choose Ctrl+F5 to bring up the web page in your browser.

How It Works

The displayed web page should look very similar to the first web page you built. The difference, however, is significant. You will continue to use this web page as the basis for the rest of this chapter. With master pages you have the ability to keep the title, or common header, the same on all pages. Many complex web pages use this type of arrangement for pages that, for instance, need to keep the header and left side the same across a number of pages. When you select one or more cells you can choose to merge cells, delete rows, delete columns, and so on. You can create most any type of structure you want to be constant across multiple pages. Additionally, while you found ContentPlaceHolder1 already on the page when you created a content page, you can add additional ContentPlaceHolders from the ToolBox's Standard section.

With a master page now built and a default page created, you are ready to add data to your web application.

Adding a Database

Adding a database to a web application is similar to adding a database for a Windows application. As with WinForms, to create a basic data web application, you can use the designers exclusively, as in the following Try It Out.

Try It Out   **Adding a Database to Your Web Application**

To add a database to your application, follow these steps:

1. Add the database you created in previous chapters to your web application. Right-click the App Data node in the Solution Explorer. (Caution: Be sure to choose App Data node.) Choose Add Existing Item to bring up the Add Existing Item dialog.

2. Navigate to and select a copy of the MyDB.MDF that you created in Chapter 4 (the one that has both the Person and the Book tables) and click Add. This adds both MyDB.MDF and MyDB_Log.LDF to your solution.

How It Works

When you choose to add the existing MyDB.MDF database, it is copied to the App_Data directory. If you do not add the MyDB.MDF database to the App_Data directory, the solution will only hold a reference to the database at the location you point to. It will not copy the database to your project. If you try to publish your website, the database will not be deployed with it. The App_Data directory does not sit in your project directory. It is in the WebSites subdirectory. The WebSites directory is a peer-level directory with the Projects directory. It is in this directory that you will find not only your database, but your other aspx pages as well.

With a database now available in your solution as a data source, you can now add GridView controls to your web pages.

Try It Out   Adding and Configuring a GridView Control

To add a GridView control to your application, follow these steps:

1. Make sure you are on the Default.aspx page (not the master page), and then open the ToolBox window. From the Data section, drag the GridView into the ContentPlaceHolder1 area. This will add the control and open the GridView Tasks menu. It should appear as displayed in Figure 5-3. (Note that if the GridView Tasks menu does not come up automatically, you can bring it up by selecting the GridView and selecting the smart tag.)

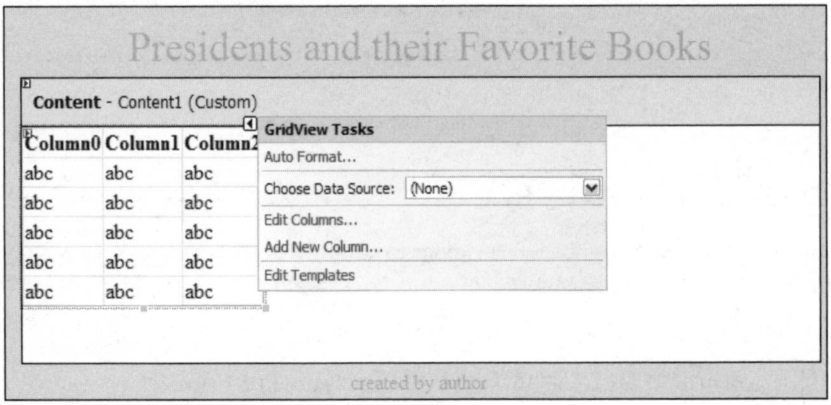

Figure 5-3

2. Select the Choose Data Source dropdown list and choose New Data Source. This brings up the Data Source Configuration wizard.

3. On the first screen of the Data Source Configuration dialog, choose Database and click OK to bring up the Configure Data Source wizard.

4. Choose from the Data Connection dropdown list to select MyDB.MDF as the data connection and click Next.

5. Choose to save the connection with the default suggested name. Click Next.

6. Configure the Select Statement by taking the default Specify columns from a table or view, and then select * from the Persons table.

7. Click the Advanced button and first check the Generate Insert, Update, and Delete statements check box, and then the Use Optimistic Concurrency check box. Click Next.

8. Click the Test Query button to test the query that has been generated for you automatically and if it works correctly, click Finish. If it doesn't work correctly, go back and recheck steps 4 – 7. If you get a message that the web service cannot be started, close down Visual Web Developer and restart it again.

9. In the GridView Tasks menu, choose to enable Sorting, Editing, Deleting, and Selection. Close the GridView Tasks menu by clicking on the background of the page.

10. In the GridView Tasks menu, choose AutoFormat and pick a scheme, such as Slate. Click OK.

11. Press Ctrl+F5 to start your application and test it. It should appear as shown in Figure 5-4.

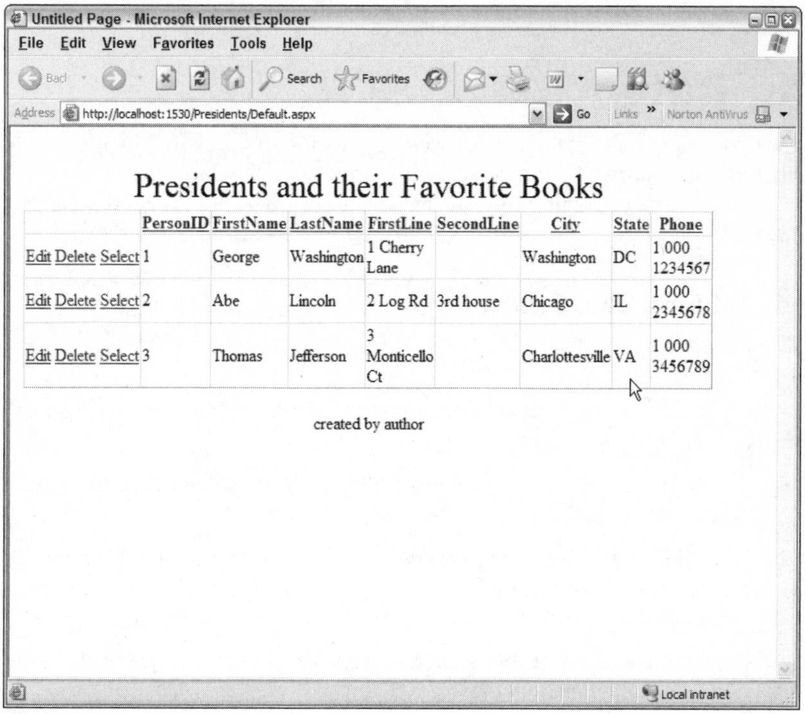

Figure 5-4

How It Works

By making a few choices in some dialogs, you have now enabled a fully functioning web page that does updates and deletes of database records for a single table. This is a huge productivity gain. If you select the Source tab in the document window for Default.aspx (your current web page), you can see all of the code that Web Express generates for you automatically. While you can write all of this by hand, it is much faster to simply generate it via the designer.

You should be aware of a few details. First, if you do not want the records to be updateable, don't check the Edit or Delete check boxes. Second, if you do not click the Advanced button in the Configuration and check the option to Generate Insert, Update, and Delete statements, you will not have the options in the GridView menu to enable editing and deleting of your data.

Third, you can always go back and reconfigure the Data Source by choosing the smart tag for the GridView and then choosing Configure Data Source. Therefore, if you did not check some option during the initial configuration process, you can always go back and make desired changes.

And, finally, it may seem a little strange to check Use Optimistic Concurrency when you are the only one using the database at this point. However, when you publish the website for access by other users, you will want optimistic concurrency working on your users' behalf.

At this point, you have put together a basic web page that will get all the data from a table. If your database table has a large number of records, your next step is to filter that data.

Filtering Data

There are several ways to filter data for your web application. If you know in advance how the data should be filtered (for example, by the person who is querying the database, by the city they live in, and so on), you can simply statically filter the data as part of the query that is generated for you, as shown in the following Try It Out.

Try It Out   Filtering Data Statically

To add a filter to your existing application, follow these steps:

1. Use the smart tag on the GridView to open the GridView Task menu and choose Configure Data Source.

2. Click Next to move to the Configure Select Statement page, and click the WHERE button. This brings up the Add WHERE Clause dialog.

3. In the Add WHERE Clause dialog, choose the PersonID for the Column field. Choose the Greater Than operator, and choose None for the Source. On the right, in the Parameter properties value field, type **1**. Click Add and then OK.

4. Click Next to move to the next page in the wizard and test your query. It should show just the records 2 and 3 in the Person table.

5. Cancel out of the wizard and do not save your changes.

How It Works

You could save your changes at this point, but you do not need to save the changes and re-run the web page just to see exactly the same records that come up in test query page. And, you want the rest of the records around for the rest of the chapter. If you do save your changes, you need to re-run the configuration wizard and remove the WHERE clause from the query.

When you filter your data this way, you generate a fixed T-SQL query that will always return the data filtered in a particular way. In this example, you fixed the WHERE clause of the SQL query so that it eliminated the first record. But, the content of the WHERE clause could be anything. You could set it so that it returns all records of presidents that lived in Virginia. Or, you could set it to return all presidents whose names include the string George. If you want to find rows that contain specific characters, for instance all the records that have an S, you use the LIKE operator and put the **S** in the value field.

Additionally, if you click the Order By button in the Configure Data Source wizard, you can specify the order in which the data is returned from the database. The wizard will add an ORDER BY clause to your T-SQL query. Currently, data is returned to the web page in the order in which data is stored in the database. That may not be the order you want to show items to the user. In this example, you might want to order the records by last name.

The previous approach works for filtering requirements that you know in advance. But often you want to enable the user to filter records dynamically. The following example shows you how to do that.

Try It Out   Filtering Data Dynamically

In this Try It Out, you add a new DropDownList control and create a separate new Data Source. Then, you configure the GridView's Data Source to bind to the filter control. To filter records dynamically, follow these steps:

1.   Open the `Default.aspx` page in Design view. Click to the right of the GridView, inside the Content1 cell and press the left arrow twice, and then press Enter. This should move the GridView down in the cell and leave space above it.

2.   Open the ToolBox window and expand the Standard section. Drag the DropDownList control into the space above the GridView. This should place the DropDownList above the GridView and open the DropDownList Tasks menu. If the task menu is not open, use the smart tag on the DropDownList to open it.

3.   In the DropDownList Tasks menu, first check the Enable AutoPostBack option and then the Choose Data Source option. This opens the Data Source Configuration wizard for this control.

4.   For the Select a Data Source data source, choose a *<New data source ...>* from the dropdown combo box. This will bring up the Data Source Configuration Wizard dialog.

5.   In the Choose a Database Type step, choose Database and click OK Simply accept the default name and click Next.

6.   In the Choose Your Data Connection step, use the dropdown list to choose the *existing* connection string you previously created and click Next to bring up the Configure Select Statement page of the wizard. You only need a new Data Source, not a complete new connection to the database.

7.   In the Configure SELECT Statement page, check only State, and check the Return Only Unique Rows checkbox. State should be the only field that is returned.

8.   On the Test page, test your query. It should return the state codes. If it does not, you have configured your select statement incorrectly. When it is correct, click Finish. This should return you to the Choose a Data Source page of the configuration wizard.

> **Note that there are two other fields in the Choose a Data Source Wizard page: Select a Data Field to Display in the DropDownList and Select a Data Field for the value of the DropDownList. Both of these should get filled in automatically when you finish configuring your Data Source. This is because you will only return one field: State.**

At this point you have added the DropDownList control and you have created a new Data Source as the source for the DropDownList control. Now, you must configure the existing Data Source for the GridView.

9.   Select the GridView control and use the smart tag to bring up the Tasks menu and choose Configure Your Data Source.

10.   In the Choose Your Data Connection page, use the existing connection string and click Next. This takes you to the Configure SELECT Statement page of the wizard.

11. Choose the WHERE button to bring up the Add WHERE Clause dialog. In the dialog, choose State for the Column field, choose = for the Operator field, and choose Control for the source field. In the parameter properties section, choose DropDownList1 for the controlID and choose IL for the default value.

12. Click the Add button to add the SQL Expression and then click OK to close the dialog. Click Next to advance the wizard to the Test Query page.

13. Test your query by clicking the Test Query button. This brings up the Parameters Values Editor. You can either use the default IL value and simply run the query, or substitute a different value. If the query result is correct, click Finish. If the query result is not correct, check your options and try again.

14. Press Ctrl+F5 to run your application. It should appear as shown in Figure 5-5.

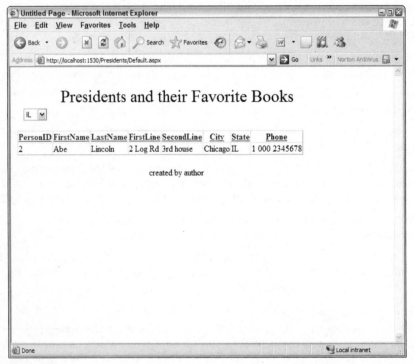

Figure 5-5

How It Works

With only three records in the Person table, the filtering is not that exciting. However, it is not hard to imagine what it would be like with more records. It is important to note the auto-post back you set for the control in the beginning of the steps. It is the posting back of the choice in the DropDownList control that allows the right records to be selected for display in the GridView.

When you created the dropdown control, you had to specify a new data source. The first data source was configured to return the results for the GridView. However, you did not have to specify a new connection. You can use the existing connection with a different query.

Also, although in this case you added only a single WHERE clause to your query that retrieves data, you can actually add several WHERE clauses. In other words, you can add additional controls and filters, and the extra filters will be additive. If you add an additional WHERE clause and then look at the generated code for the T-SQL statement in the SQL Expression page, you will see that the statements are combined with an AND operator. If you choose the Specify a Customer SQL Statement or stored procedure option in the Configure Data Source Wizard, you can directly create the T-SQL and use an OR instead of an AND for the combination of filters. Or, you can either change the T- SQL directly in the code, or first generate what you want using the AND syntax in the wizard and then copy the T-SQL and use it in building the custom SQL statement.

You should also note that while you get Delete and Edit functionality virtually for free in a web page using a GridView, you do not get the ability to add a new record. You must add this separately, as explained in the following section.

Inserting Data

You cannot use the GridView to insert new records. However, you can use the FormView. The FormView allows you to view data record by record. With the FormView you can edit, delete, and insert. In this example, given what you have already built, you only need the ability to insert. You still use the Form View because you can restrict the functionality to Insert by simply setting a property.

Try It Out   Inserting Data

To add a page to insert a new record, follow these steps:

1. Add a new web page by right-clicking the Solution Explorer, adding a New Item, and then choosing New Web Form. Name the web page **AddItem.aspx**, and click Add. Choose the MasterPage.master and click OK.

2. Navigate back to the Default.aspx Design view. Open the ToolBox, expand the Standard section, and add a LinkButton below the GridView.

3. Right-click the LinkButton and change the Text property to Add New Record.

4. Click the PostBackURL property cell and use the ellipses (...) button to bring up the Select URL dialog. Choose AddItem.aspx and click OK. This should place the "~/additem URL in the property value.

5. Open the AddItem.aspx Design page and add a FormView from the Data Section of the ToolBox. This will add the FormView to the page and bring up the FormView Tasks.

6. Select FormView Tasks ⇨ Choose Data Source ⇨ <New Data Source> to bring up the DataSource Configuration Wizard.

7. Select Database, use the default ID for the data source, and click OK. This brings up the Choose your Data Connection page of the wizard.

8. Use the dropdown list to select the already existing connection string and click Next to see the Configure SELECT Statement page of the wizard.

9. Choose the Person table, and then click the asterisk (*) for the columns. Click the Advanced button and select Generate Insert, Update, and Delete statements. Also select Optimistic concurrency and click OK. Click Next, test your query, and click Finish to complete the wizard.

10. Right-click the FormView control and choose Properties from the context menu. Find the DefaultMode property and change it to Insert. This should add two buttons, Insert and Cancel, at the bottom of the FormView.

11. Open the FormView Tasks menu, choose AutoFormat, and pick a format you like, such as Slate.

12. Add a LinkButton control from the ToolBox Standard Section below the AddItem control. Change the text property to Back to Master List and set the PostBackUrl to the `Default.aspx` page.

13. Press Ctrl+F5 to launch your web page. After the main page is up, click the Add New Record button. The `AddItem.aspx` page should appear as shown in Figure 5-6.

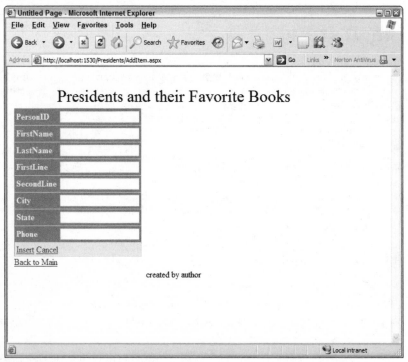

Figure 5-6

How It Works

Given what you have learned so far, this should all be pretty straightforward — linking between pages with inserts on a separate page. You have used, however, a new data control, the FormView. You can choose how the fields are laid out, rather than accept a strict tabular layout. From the Form View Tasks menu, you can choose to edit the template upon which the FormView is based to get a layout more suited to your liking.

In addition to the FormView, there are other data controls. For this task of adding a new record, you could have just as easily have used the DetailsView. It's a rectangular layout that works well for this type of task. The FormView is more freeform than the DetailsView. Another control is the DataList. This control lists the details of each record sequentially. With this control, you will almost certainly use paging. You can enable paging in all the data controls. Paging will limit the number of records displayed on a single page and automatically create links to allow the user to move back and forth among the records.

Working with Master Detail

You have now enabled viewing, editing, deleting, and inserting on a single table. The next step is to link pages that can deal with records in two different tables that are in a master-detail relationship. In the example you have been working with, you must now add a page that can handle books. The relationship between Presidents and Books is a master-detail relationship much like the relationship been a purchase order and purchase order details. This subject is discussed in more detail in Chapter 4.

Try It Out	Adding a Book Page

To add the Book page and link it with the Person page, follow these steps:

1. Add a new Web Form called `Book.aspx`.

2. Bring up the `Default.aspx` page designer and select the GridView. Then, select the smart tag to bring up the GridView Tasks and choose Edit Columns to see the Fields dialog.

3. From the Available fields window, choose to add a Hyperlink field. This will place the hyper-linked field in the Selected Fields window.

4. In the Properties Window for the selected field, set the properties as shown in the following table. After the property values have been set, click OK to close the Fields dialog.

Property Name	Value
HeaderText	Link
Text	Details ...
NavigateURL	~/book.aspx
DataNavigateURLFields	PersonID
DataNavigateURLFormatString	Book.aspx?personID={0}

5. On the Book.aspx page, add a new GridView and then select GridView tasks ➪ Choose Data Source ➪ <New Data Source ...>.

6. In the Data Source Configuration wizard, in the Choose a Database step, click the Database icon and then click Next. Then, in Choose Your Data Connection, select the existing connection string and click Next. This should take you to the Configure SELECT Statement step.

7. For the Book table, choose * to select all the fields. Then, click the WHERE button to bring up the Add WHERE Clause dialog.

8. In the Add WHERE Clause dialog, select AuthorID for the Column. The Operator field should be equals (=) and the Source should be QueryString. The QueryString field (on the right) should be PersonID, as shown in Figure 5-7. Click Add and then click OK.

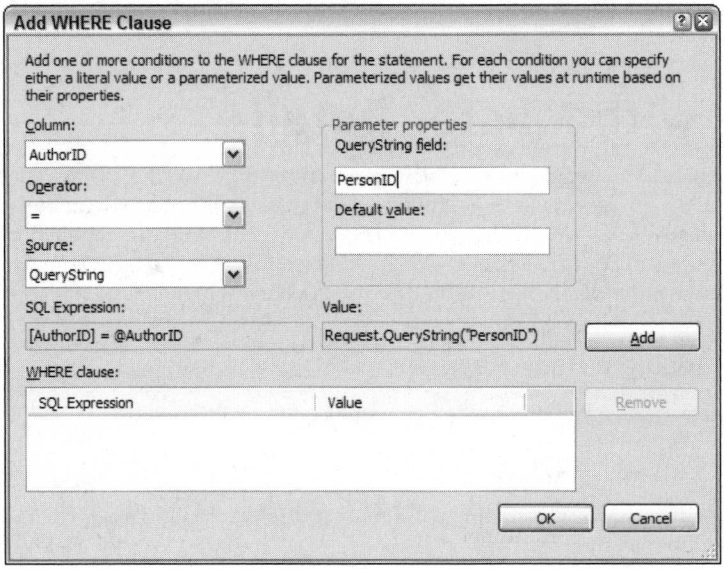

Figure 5-7

9. Click the Advanced button and select Generate Insert, Update, and Delete Statements and then click OK.

10. Test your query. If the results are correct, click Finish. If they are not, check your settings and try again.

11. In the GridView Tasks menu, choose to enable Editing and Deleting.

12. Press Ctrl+F5 and run your web application. The Book page should appear as shown in Figure 5-8.

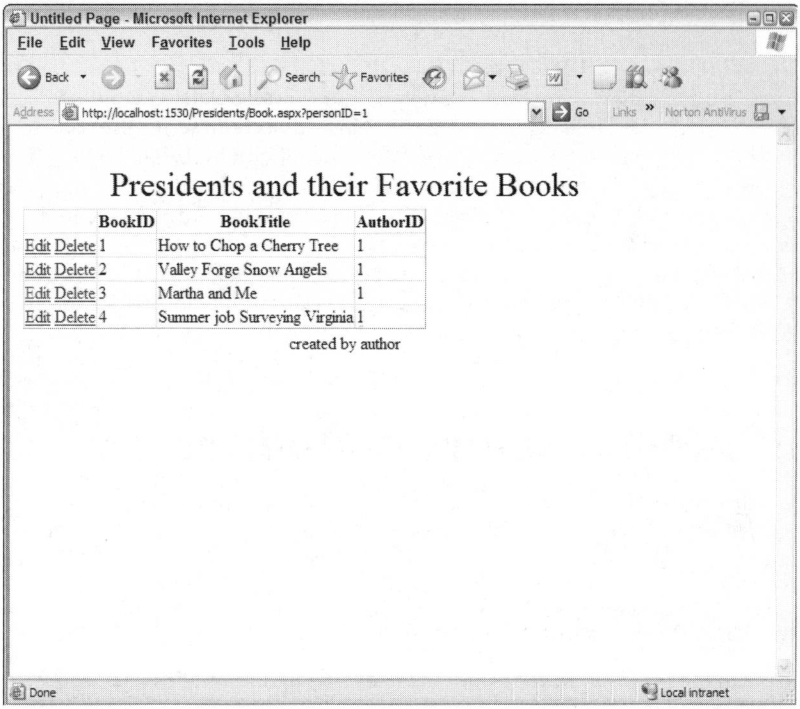

Figure 5-8

How It Works

There are a couple of important technical points that deserve attention. The way in which the master page communicates with the Book page is through the page request to the Book page. It has the details that specify which master record number should be used to filter the child records so that the correct child records are displayed.

You specified the information that would be used in the page request when you specified the `DataNavigateURLFormatString` to `Book.aspx?personID={0}` in the GridView on the default page. The more general form of that specification (if you are only sending one piece of information) is:

```
[ASPX page name].aspx?[field name of info to send]={0}
```

If you look at the request page that brings up the Book page, you will see an example of this syntax instantiated. For example, navigating to the first record for George Washington yields this request URL to the Book page on my machine:

```
http://localhost:38916/Presidents/Book.aspx?PersonID=1
```

It should be similar on your machine.

It is important to understand what you have done and what you have not done. What you *have* done is to split the master information away from the detail information onto two separate pages. That makes the update code easier — and in particular means you do not have to write any code to make this work. You can rely on the code generated for you. In a master detail update, when you update both the master table and the detail table at the same time, you must be careful to do things in the right order (delete child table records, then update master table info, then add and update child records). By splitting the pages, you can rely on the database to handle cascade updates and deletes on parent changes (if the child table has the foreign key set to cascade updates and deletes), and child table changes are constrained by what is in the parent table. For example, you cannot add a new child record that links to a parent record until it first exists in the database.

Help with More Complex Queries

The query you wrote to link the child and master tables was very simple. If you need to write a more complex query, one that traverses several tables, you may want to use a graphical query tool to help you define the query.

Try It Out   **Writing a Custom Query**

You will start with the previous example, but instead of using the WHERE clause button, you specify to create a custom T-SQL Statement.

To create a custom query for the Book page, repeat steps 1 through 6 of the previous Try It Out, and use the following steps for the remainder of the exercise:

7. On the Configure Select Statement page, choose to specify a custom SQL Statement or stored procedure and click Next to move to the Define Custom Statements or Stored Procedures page of the wizard. In this wizard, click the Query Builder button.

8. In the Add Table dialog for the Query Builder, choose to add the Book table and then click Close.

9. Expand the Query Builder to full screen so that you can easily see all the columns in the Grid Pane.

10. In the Diagram pane of the Query Builder, check all the columns in the Book table you want to appear in the GridView. Then, add @AuthorID in the Filter column to the right of the Book .AuthorID. When you're done, your screen should look like Figure 5-9. Click OK and then click Next to go to the Define Parameters page.

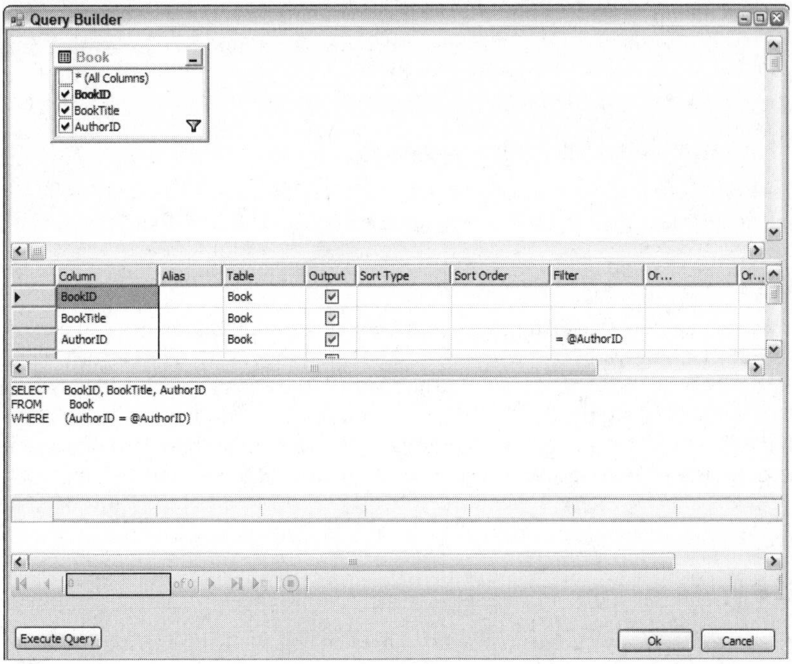

Figure 5-9

11. In the Define Parameters page of the Configure Data Source wizard, select the AuthorID item in the Parameters field and choose QueryString for the parameter source. The QueryStringField should be PersonID as shown in Figure 5-10.

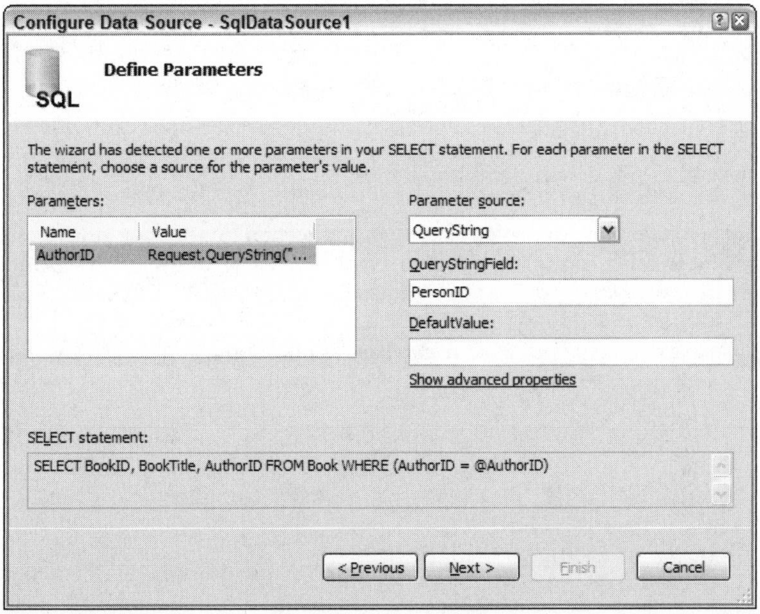

Figure 5-10

12. Click Next to advance to the next page in the Wizard so you can test your query. Click the Test Query button at the bottom to run the query. It will prompt you for a value. Enter **1** and click OK. If the query returns the correct results, click OK to close the Query Builder. Clicking OK will populate the SQL field with the generated SQL text.

13. Click Finish after you have tested your query.

14. Press Ctrl+F5 to run your web page. Once you are on the default page, follow a details link. The Book details page should appear with all the books written by that president.

How It Works

We have only specified how to use the QueryBuilder with a Select statement. You can use the Query Builder for Inserts, Updates, and Deletes as well. Just select the Insert, Update, or Delete tab in the Define Custom Statements or Stored Procedures page and launch the Query Builder from those tabs. The Query Builder will launch with the right T-SQL syntax; you just need to add the fields that should match up. Underneath the covers, it is the engine the QueryBuilder is based on that is used to automatically generate the SQL syntax for inserts, updates, and deletes in other parts of the wizard as well.

Summary

This chapter showed you how to create powerful data-centric web applications with zero coding. Specifically, this chapter addressed how to:

- ❑ Use the local web server in developing a web application
- ❑ Use master pages
- ❑ Add local SSE databases to a web application
- ❑ Add grid controls and bind them to the database
- ❑ Filter data on a web page
- ❑ Link pages with details
- ❑ Create master-detail relationships
- ❑ Use the tool to create more complex queries

The chapter did not cover how to deploy your web application to a hosting site, how to use styles, and how to use the host of other controls and features in ASP .NET. Those are subjects for other books. However, you can now quickly put together a data-centric application with ASP .NET.

In Chapter 6, you learn how to deploy your database application using the Xcopy feature.

Exercises

Try the exercises that follow to test your understanding of the material covered in this chapter. You can find the solutions to these exercises in Appendix A.

1. Specify the order in which the query results are returned, using the Order By button. Order the results by Last Name.

2. Add some records (for example, you can invent new presidents) and then add additional controls to filter. Use an OR conditional between WHERE statements instead of an AND conditional.

3. Change the properties for the LinkButton to make it look more like a traditional button.

4. With the FormView up, choose Edit Templates. You will see a list of templates that are used for Insert, Edit, and so on. Edit the Insert template with different label names and arrange the fields more attractively than the default layout.

Understanding Xcopy Deployment and User Instance Model

In Chapter 3 you learned about using SSE with Visual Basic Express. In this chapter, you learn about the Xcopy feature supported by SSE that makes it possible to handle SSE database files the same ways you do Windows files. The deployment of a database application using Xcopy is simple because the files can be copied or moved to a different location without any additional configuration. Xcopy also enables the *Run as Normal User* scenarios, which means that nonadministrators on the machine can use SSE without requiring any additional Windows privileges or permissions in SQL Server. However, this feature also introduces some conditions such as single-user access and Windows authentication. This chapter addresses the following topics:

- ❑ Introduction to Xcopy
- ❑ Enabling Run as Normal User scenarios using user instances
- ❑ Using Xcopy and user instances within your application
- ❑ Managing user instances
- ❑ Limitations of Xcopy and user instances

Introduction to Xcopy

Xcopy is a new feature in SSE that allows a local database to be moved, copied, or emailed along with the application. At the final destination the user double-clicks the database application to launch it. Internally, SSE takes care of attaching the database and log files automatically to an appropriate SSE instance so that you need not do any additional configuration.

This feature is intended for simple single-user database applications. You do not have to deal with the complexity that has traditionally resulted from having a full-blown relational database management system like SQL Server. Among other things, this model is as easy to use as Microsoft Access, where developers can copy their application and simply expect it to work. The SSE databases operate within the security context of the calling application. In general, the interaction with the database engine and the database files cannot cause effects on the system beyond those of the account that invokes the application.

You will appreciate this feature if you have tried deploying a SQL Server 2000-based desktop application. In addition to copying the files to the destination, you have to run T-SQL or DMO scripts that configure the SQL Server 2000 instance so that the application can run. Many of these configurations require privileges that are not available to normal users. This means that the administrator has to be involved for the setting up of desktop application.

There are two main mechanisms that enable Xcopy support in SSE: automating connectivity to the SSE instance, and the user instance model. Automating connectivity to SQL Server enables the databases to be treated like files, while the user instance model allows a nonadministrative Windows account to access SSE without any extra privileges.

Automating Connectivity to the SSE Instance

Before specifying the features in SSE that automate the connectivity, it is important to understand the *attach* and *detach* steps involved in database connectivity. SSE keeps track of the databases that it uses in an internal table. Before opening or using a database, the user must first attach the database to SSE . SSE updates the information about the database inside this internal table. The information stored includes details like the logical database name and the actual physical database name. For subsequent opening or closing of this database, SSE verifies that an entry is present inside this internal table. If you decide not to use a database anymore, you can use the sp_detach_db command to remove details about the database. Editions of SQL Server 2005 other than SSE maintain a lock on the user database once it is attached. This means that the database must be detached before it can be moved or copied. To automate connectivity to the SSE instance, attach and detach operations are automated.

Automating connectivity to the SSE instance is made possible by three features: the new AttachDBFilename option in the connection string, auto-naming of database and log file, and the AutoClose feature. Attaching the database automatically is taken care of by the AttachDBFilename syntax, while the AutoClose feature closes the file and relinquishes control from SSE the process. The automatic renaming of the database and log files permits these files to be copied on the local machine. The following sections examine each of these features in detail.

AttachDBFilename

AttachDBFilename is a new connection string entry present in the SQL Client managed provider. It allows you to directly specify a relative or absolute file path for the database. The database file automatically attaches to SSE when the connection is opened, and this database is the default database for that connection. If the database is already attached when the AttachDBFilename is invoked, then the attach operation is skipped. Refer to the next section for the actual rules employed.

Visual Studio supports a special macro called |DataDirectory| that is commonly used with AttachDBFilename. This macro is evaluated at run-time to point to the data directory of the application where database files are stored. This special string should be at the beginning of the file path and works only against a local file system.

Auto-naming the Database and Log File

SSE uses a logical name to identify databases attached to it. This name is different from the database file name, and typically the user can specify this name using the `database` or `initial catalog` connection string entry. SQL Server makes sure that each logical database name is unique. SSE also keeps track of the actual location of the database file so that it can be loaded on demand. When `AttachDBFilename` is used with the `database` or `initial catalog` entry specifying the logical database name, the following rules are used to determine whether the connection can succeed:

❏ If there is an existing entry in SSE for the logical name, the actual file paths are verified. If the file path of the database file specified matches the existing SSE entry, then the attach operation is skipped and the connection to the database proceeds. If the file path does not match, a new entry is created corresponding to the path and the connection request proceeds.

❏ If there is no existing entry with the same logical database name, a new entry is created in SSE and the connection request proceeds.

Given these rules, specifying a static logical name using the `database` or `initial catalog` connection string is problematic when using Xcopy, because there could be a previous logical database entry in the SSE instance that matches the connection string value. Hence, you explicitly specify the logical database name only in special cases where a static name is required, such as for replication, SQL Service Broker, or multiple-part names in T-SQL queries.

> When using Xcopy, do not use the database or initial catalog keywords in the connection string to specify the logical database name. The supported syntax in SSE includes database=; or initial catalog=; or the user can also omit them totally in the connection string. When the logical name is not specified, an automatic name is generated for the database file based on its location.

The logical name automatically generated for the database is based on the relative file path of the database (.mdf) file. For instance, if the database file is at c:\My application\mySSEDatabase.mdf, the logical database name will be based on the full path. If the file path is longer than 127 characters, the logical database name is shortened and prefixed with a character representation of a SHA-1 hash of the file path, ensuring a unique logical name. This is because the logical database name cannot exceed 127 characters. (Note that omitting the database name in previous versions of SQL Server such as SQL Server 2000 or MSDE would result in an error.)

The log file name (.ldf) is not explicitly specified when using `AttachDBFilename`. SSE expects its log file name to be of the format: *<databasePhysicalFilename>*_log.ldf. For instance, if the physical database file name is myDb.mdf, then the log file name should be myDb_log.ldf. The directory information is not used in the naming of log files, but existing log files must reside in the same directory as the database file. If SSE cannot find this file in the same directory as the database file, then a new log file of the same name is automatically created during attach. Hence, the user (automatically) attaching the database must have read/write permissions to the directory containing the database.

In addition to the name restrictions already mentioned, there are other limitations for SSE. Other editions of SQL Server support using multiple data and log files for a database so that these files can be distributed in multiple file groups. This is not supported in the `AttachDBFilename` syntax. Network shares, HTTP paths, or Universal Naming Conventional (UNC) remote databases are also not supported by SSE.

AutoClose

The AutoClose feature enables the database file to be in a copy-able state when it is not in use, by releasing the file handle of the user database files when there are no active connections. Thus, when the application is closed, the database is ready to be moved or copied. AutoClose existed in SQL 2000 and is enabled by default in SQL Server Express.

From the user's perspective, AutoClose does not always work when connection pooling is enabled. With connection pooling, connections are not actually closed when the user invokes the closing of the connection, but they are returned to the pool instead. In order to close all connections, typically the application domain has to be shut down or all the open connections have to be closed. ADO.NET also contains functions like `ClearPool` if you want to force manual resets within your application.

Understanding the User Instance Model

In the user instance model introduced in SSE, the SQL Server engine will run within the user's context and can be used only by that user. Since only a single user is allowed, even a nonadministrator user can use a user instance. SSE takes care of the initialization and destruction of user instances and the creation is done on demand.

On the other hand, the traditional SQL Server model relies on a common Windows service running on the machine. Multiple users connect to this service if they have the proper permissions and privileges. These permissions and privileges are explained in detail in Chapter 13. By default, a normal user on the machine has very few privileges on SQL Server and hence is unable to run applications using SQL unless the administrator provides the relevant security permissions first. This is a classic server scenario where multiple users share the same database server. Figure 6-1 illustrates the two models.

As shown in the figure, an existing SQL Express installation that runs as a service is used to create instances at run-time. The new SSE processes spawned under the user context do not run as a service. One user instance is created for each user. This idea is very similar to an application using a DLL, except that the user instance is a process running in its own address space. A new connection string entry is added to the SQL Client ADO.NET-managed provider allowing the user to initialize and use user instances. These instances are automatically deleted by SSE when they are no longer used. There are some T-SQL management functions that allow an administrator on the machine to view and manage these user instances.

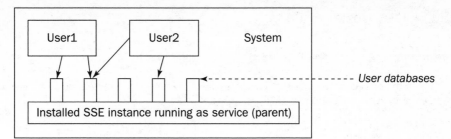

Traditional SSE as a Service Scenario

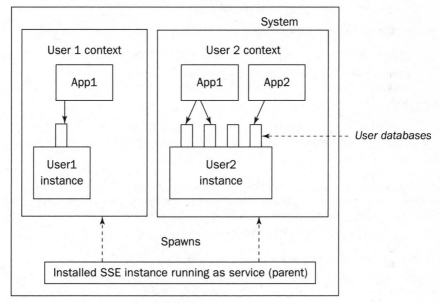

User Instance Model

Figure 6-1

Each SSE instance running as a service or as a user instance can use a maximum of 1GB RAM and one CPU. In other words, the memory limit of a particular user instance will have no impact on the memory limit of another user instance or SSE service.

Try It Out   User Instance

This Try It Out demonstrates the use of a user instance from within Visual Basic Express and allows you to move or copy a database project to a different location. Follow these steps:

1. Open the project from Chapter 3 using the File ➪ Open Project command from Visual Studio. Open the bin folder and run MyFirstApp.exe.

2. Open the app.config file. Find the `<connectionStrings>` section and verify that the connection string value contains `User Instance=true`.

3. Copy the contents of the bin folder by dragging the folder to the desktop.

4. Open the copied folder and run MyFirstApp.exe.

5. Delete the bin folder from the desktop.

6. Move the original bin folder to a different directory (for example, C:\).

7. Open the copied folder and run MyFirstApp.exe.

How It Works

In Chapter 3 you added a database to a project, and created and populated a table. Next you added the data source and displayed the table grid in a form. When you run the application, you can see the grid view of the table you just created.

You can verify that the application is Xcopy-deployable by looking at the `User Instance=true` value in the connection string entry. The application developer programs the connection string to point to the parent SSE instance, and the redirection happens internally. This can be verified by looking at the `SERVER=(local)\SQLExpress` connection string entry.

After you copy the bin folder to a new location, right-click the properties of this folder to verify that the copy was successful. When you run MyFirstApp.exe from the new location, you will see the same grid view layout of the table you had created earlier. Similarly, the move and delete steps work just like normal Windows files.

The remainder of this chapter discusses more detailed aspects of user instances.

Getting Deeper into User Instances

In this section you learn how SSE initializes and destroys the user instance. You will also learn to manage and use these instances using T-SQL, and ADO.NET. As explained earlier, SSE can work in both the user instance mode and the service mode. You should use the user instance mode in any of the following circumstances:

❑ You want nonadministrators on the machine to use the application.

❑ You want to copy, move, or email the application and database file to another location or user.

❑ You do not want to worry about the complicated security mechanisms in SQL Server 2005.

❑ Your application is single-user and uses Windows Authentication.

❑ You are not using the networking features of SSE, and the database is used only on the local machine.

❑ You are using the SQL Client managed provider for developing your application.

❑ You are not planning to use the application with other editions of SQL Server 2005, such as SQL Server Standard Edition or SQL Server Enterprise Edition.

ADO.NET Extensions for User Instance

The SQL Client managed provider in ADO.NET introduces a new connection string keyword, `user instance`, which can have a value of `true` or `false`. To invoke the user instance, the user has to explicitly use `User Instance=true` in the connection string. When this key word is omitted or `User Instance=false` is present in the connection string, no user instance support is in effect and SSE behaves in the same way as other editions of SQL Server 2005. The OLEDB- or ODBC-managed providers and non-managed APIs, such as SQL Native Access, OLEDB, ODBC, or ADO, do not support this feature.

Initialization of a User Instance

The SSE instance running as a service controls all user instances that may be created. This instance is called the *parent instance*. It spawns and destroys all its child user instances. All new connection requests from ADO.NET initially come to this instance, which decides whether to create a new user instance or reuse an existing one. The general sequence of actions that happens when the parent SSE instance gets a new connection request is described in the following list, and is illustrated in Figure 6-2.

1. When the application calls the `Open` method on a connection object, ADO.NET sends a new connection request to the parent SSE instance. The identity of the parent server is determined by the `server` keyword in the connection string. Connection pooling reuses an existing connection to the parent instance, but a connection reset is forced so that the following steps take place.

2. If the application has `User Instance=true` in the connection string, then the parent instance determines whether a user instance should be spawned or not. The rules governing the creation of user instances are described later in this section. The user creating the user instance is a sysadmin on that instance.

3. If the operation is successful, the instance name of the user instance is passed to ADO.NET along with the appropriate return code. If ADO.NET receives an error from the server, the connection open request fails and the `Open` method will throw a `SQLException`.

4. If the `Open` method (step 3) is successful, ADO.NET receives the name of the new user instance. It closes the connection to the parent SSE instance and opens a new connection to the user instance, which is returned to the user.

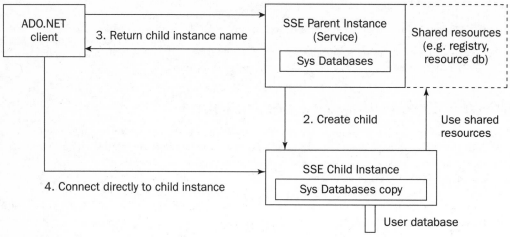

1. New Connection Request (User Instance = true)

Figure 6-2

The following rules are checked by the SSE server inside a built-in function to verify the credentials of the user and the appropriate application configuration. Failure to meet any of the conditions below results in an error:

❑   The user is a valid SSE login and can connect to the parent instance. By default, all interactive users on the machine can connect to the SSE instance.

❑   The user has relevant Windows file permissions on the database file. Typically the user must have read and write permissions on the database file specified in AttachDBFilename to enable application write to the database. If the user has read permissions only, the database is opened in the read-only mode and the application cannot update the database.

❑   Windows Authentication is used for connection.

❑   The application specifies the user instance keyword in the connection string.

When all these conditions are satisfied, the function checks to see whether there is an existing user instance already running under the context of the user initiating the connection. If such an instance exists, then the connection to this user instance is passed to ADO.NET. Otherwise, a new SSE process is spawned under the context of the calling user, and the name of the new user instance is passed to the user. SSE keeps track of the list of user instances on a machine, as well as their activity status.

A Security Model Using File Permissions

When you use user instances, SSE honors the Windows file permissions on your user database file. If you have full control on the database files (.mdf and .ldf), you do not need any additional SQL privileges. The user attaching the database using user instance is a sysadmin on the user instance and has full control on the database and its subdatabase objects. The user databases derive their read-only or read-write properties based on the file permissions of the mdf file.

The permission from the file is read by SSE only when the file is opened. Because of AutoClose, the database file handles are closed when there is no activity on the file. These permissions are verified the next time the file is opened.

On file systems such as FAT or FAT32 that do not have any security Access Control Lists (ACL), all local users have full control of the database when using user instances. This is one reason why we recommend the use of NTFS instead of either FAT file system. SQL authentication is disabled for user instance mode, which means that any authentication mechanism that relies on SQL authentication will not work. The user instance supports Windows authentication by default, and this is enforced by running the user instance under a trace flag.

The following Try It Out shows how easy it is to change the file permissions. The assumption is that you are the current owner of the MyDB.mdf file and that you want to provide Full Control permissions to a new account called TestAccount.

Try It Out   Changing File Permissions

1. Copy the MyDB.mdf and MyDB_log.ldf files from the preceding Try It Out to the folder c:\MyDB.

2. Open Windows Explorer and browse to C:\MyDB. Right-click the MyDB.mdf, click Properties, and then click the Security tab. If you cannot view the Security tab, do the following:

    a. Click Start, and then click Control Panel. Double-click Folder Options.

    b. On the View tab, under Advanced settings, clear the check box next to Use Simple File Sharing (recommended).

3. The TestAccount does not show up in the list of users, so click Add. Click the Advanced button, and then click the Find Now button. Select TestAccount from the list and then click OK. Click OK again.

4. View the default permissions given to TestAccount on the database file. Click the Full Control check box and then click OK.

5. To view the effective permissions, right-click MyDB.mdf, click Properties, and then click the Security tab. Click Advanced, and then click the Effective Permissions tab. Click the Select Button. Enter TestAccount as the name of a user and then click OK. The selected check boxes indicate the effective permissions of the user or group for that file or folder.

How It Works

In this example, you added a Windows account called TestAccount to the list of users for MyDB.mdf. By default, the TestAccount has Read & Execute, List Folder Contents, and Read permissions. In step 4, you give Full Control permissions to the user TestAccount. The last step explains how to check the effective permissions, that is, find out what permissions a user has on the file. The Effective Permissions calculation takes the permissions from the local and domain groups the user is a member of, as well as any permissions inherited from the parent object. The effective permissions that are granted to a user are indicated by a check mark. The effective permissions of TestAccount are shown in Figure 6-3.

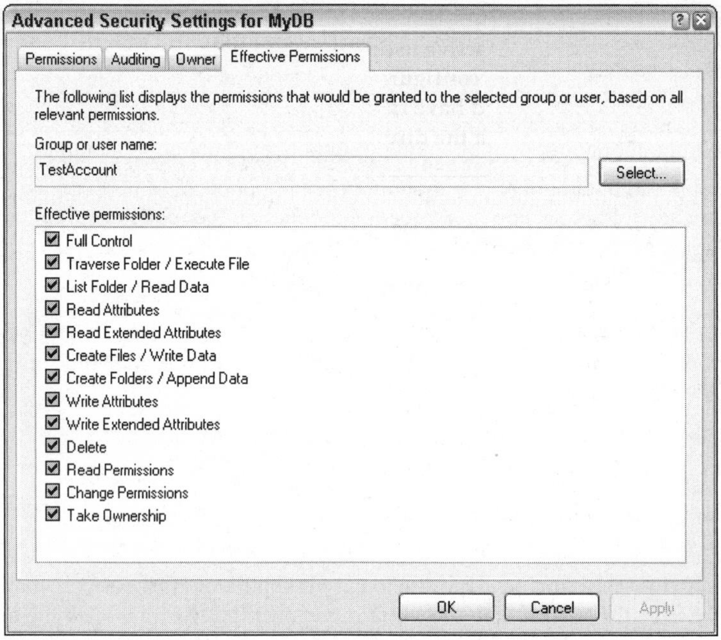

Figure 6-3

Who Can Connect to a User Instance?

This section offers an introduction to the various permissions and privileges automatically provided by SSE when using a user instance. This is an advanced section and assumes that you already know the basics of the SQL Server security mechanism covered in Chapter 13. The permissions in the following list are required on the parent SSE instance before a user can create a user instance.

❑   `sql connect` privileges to connect to the parent SSE.

❑   Read and Execute permissions on SQL Server binaries. These permissions are required so that users can run SSE inside their user context.

❑   Execute permissions on the built-in function that actually instantiates the user instance.

These permissions are given to Builtin\Users by default so that nonadministrator users having a valid login on the machine can use SSE. So if you are an interactive nonadministrative user on the machine, you automatically get all these permissions. In addition, you should also have `full control` permissions on the user database file as well as read and write permissions on the folder containing the database. The reason for requiring `full control` on the database is that SSE impersonates the user while accessing the database file. The security permissions from the file are mapped to the SQL Server security model at the time the file is opened. If a log file is absent, it is automatically created during attach, and hence the read and write privileges on the directory are required.

> In general, if you are an interactive user on the machine, you can use user instance mode without any additional configuration changes even if you are a not an administrator on the box. You should have full control on the user database file, as well as read and write permissions on the directory containing the database.

In order to attach a read-only database, the log file must pre-exist. SSE does not regenerate the log file for a read-only database.

Using SSEUtil

SSEUtil is a command line tool that allows you to connect and run commands on a user instance. It can not only find all the SSE instances installed on a local machine, but it also exposes functionalities to attach, detach, or list the databases on a SSE instance. SSEUtil can be used instead of sqlcmd when working with user instances because SSEUtil can automatically connect to the user instance and use the `AttachDBFilename`-type attach behavior. Sqlcmd can only connect to a user instance that is already running, and you have to explicitly specify the instance name in the command line. Specifying the instance name could be painful since the name is a GUID.

To install SSEUtil, follow these steps:

1. To download SSEUtil, click the SQL Server Express Utility link at http://msdn.microsoft.com/ SQL/downloads/tools/default.aspx. Click the Download button in the upper right-hand corner of this page to start the download. Note that the supported operating systems are similar to SSE, and .NET Framework v2.0 is required for this installation to proceed.

2. When the File Download and Internet Explorer security warning dialogs pop up, click Run.

3. Click Yes in the EULA (license dialog) after reading it.

4. You will be prompted to enter a location to save the extracted files. Type **c:\SSEUtil**. The .exe and the readme files are installed in this directory.

The various command line arguments passed to this tool are listed and described in the following table. All command line arguments are prefixed with a dash (-) sign, and only the first letter of the argument needs to be passed. Parameters are specified within angle brackets in the table.

Arguments	Description
`attach <DBfilepath>`	Attach a database file using `AttachDbFilename`
`create <DBfilepath>| name=<DBName>`	Create a database using the given name or file path
`list`	List all databases currently attached
`detach <DBFilePath>| name=<DBName>`	Detach all databases starting with the specified name

Table continued on following page

Arguments	Description
upgrade <filePath | directory>	Upgrade an individual database file or all database files in a folder
trace + | - <number>	Enable or disable the specified trace number for all client connections
childlist	List all the child user instances
console	Console mode allows you to type T-SQL statements
run <filename>	Run the named file, which can contain T-SQL and extended commands
version	Display the version of SSE
listsrv [remote]	List the local or remote instances of SQL Server and SSE
shrink <filename>	Shrink the given database file (and log file if present)
main	Use the parent SQLExpress instance to connect
child <username>	Connect to child instance for the current or specified user
log <logfile>	Use the specified log file for all input and output
server <server\instance,port>	Specify the server, instance name, and/or port to connect to
timeout<seconds>	Specifies the connection timeout in seconds.
Cmdtimeout<seconds>	Specifies the command timeout in seconds
user <name>	Specify the user name to connect with
pwd <password | ?>	Specify the password to connect with, or prompt for password if ? is passed as argument

In the following Try It Out, you attach and detach a database file to a user instance using SSEUtil.

Try It Out   Working with User Instance and SSEUtil

1. Copy the MyDB.mdf and MyDB_log.ldf from the earlier Try It Out exercise to the folder c:\MyDB.

2. Open a command line prompt by typing **cmd.exe** from Start ⇨ Run. Type the following from the command line:

```
SSEUtil -a "c:\MyDB\MyDB.mdf"
```

3. Type the following from the command line to list all the databases attached to the user instance. You should verify that the database attached in the previous step is visible. Notice that only the first letter of the command list is used.

```
SSEUtil -l
```

4. To verify the version of SSE you are connected to, type the following:

```
SSEUtil -version
```

5. To detach the file MyDB.mdf used with the previous example, type the following:

```
SSEUtil -d "c:\MyDB\MyDB.mdf"
```

6. Use the following T-SQL to make sure the database is detached. This example introduces you to running SSEUtil in the console mode where you can run arbitrary T-SQL Commands.

```
SSEUtil -c
Use master
go
Select * from sysdatabases
go
```

How It Works

In the previous Try It Out, you used Visual Studio to connect to a user instance. In this example, you use SSEUtil to connect to a user instance. SSEUtil focuses on SSE scenarios and can connect to the named instance called SQLExpress automatically. In step 2, you attach the database file using the AttachDBFilename syntax instead of the sp_attachDB syntax. A user instance is automatically created under the covers for you if one is not already running. SSEUtil provides you with the capability of listing the attached databases, as well as verifying the version of SSE. After detaching the database in step 5, you use the console mode of the SSEUtil to run arbitrary T-SQL commands. In step 6, you are querying the sysdatabases table in the master database to get the list of databases that are attached.

How Is User Instance Different from a SSE Instance Running as a Service?

A user instance is automatically named by SSE during the creation process using a GUID, which is a unique identifier. The user instance name is not easily identifiable compared to a SSE instance running as a service, since the latter uses an alphanumeric name provided by the user.

It is important to recognize that the user instance shares the executables and registry keys with the parent instance. If a service pack is applied to the parent instance, the user instances automatically get updated. In fact, you do not have to worry about servicing the user instances at all as long as the parent instance is serviced.

The user instance uses a *copy* of the system databases like master, model, and msdb instead of using the ones used by the parent SSE instance. When the user instance is first created for the user, the system databases are copied from the Template Data directory to the user's local application data directory. By default the destination for the data files is drive:\Documents and Settings\Username\Local Settings\Application Data\Microsoft\Microsoft SQL Server Data\SQLEXPRESS.

Your error log and tempdb database is also created every time the user instance initializes. The resource database is opened in a read-only mode. Only shared memory protocol is enabled for user-instances, which means that only local-box operations are possible. You cannot connect to a user instance from a remote machine or change any setting to enable the networking for user instances.

When there are no open connections for a period of time, the user instance shuts down automatically. The timeout period used depends on the `User Instance timeout` configuration option. The default value is five minutes. Thus, the lifetime of the user instance depends on the lifetimes of the application using it. After all the databases hosted by a user instance are auto-closed, the shutdown timer is activated and the user instance shuts down when the timer value reaches 0. Note that even if the user logs off, the user instance continues to be alive and goes through the time-to-live shutdown mechanism.

Every time a user instance is initialized, there is a small time spent initializing all the system databases and the SQL Server engine. This small performance hit when the application starts could be significant in some cases. Once the user instance is running, the performance is similar to SQL Server Express running as a service.

Because the user instance is hosted by the user, sysadmin privileges on this user instance are given to the user. So you are an administrator on the user instance you spawned, even if you are a nonadmin on the machine. Since the user instance is not shared, is running within your own context, and can only connect locally, this is secure.

A single-user instance can have multiple databases attached to it, but a single physical database cannot be used by multiple SSE instances at the same time. This means that multiple users on the same machine require different copies of the database if they want to run concurrently. A file-sharing model works only if the file is used sequentially. For example, suppose there are two users on the machine, and both of them have full control on the database file. The first user attaching the database will have exclusive control on the file. The second user is unable to use the database while the first user's application is running because the user instance is ensured single-user mode. The database auto-closes when the first user's application shuts down. Now the second user can start using the database; however, the first user application will fail to attach the database if used at this time. When SSE is running as a service, SQL Server controls access to the different users using permissions, and hence multi-user capabilities are possible. The following table outlines the differences in running SSE as a service versus as a user instance.

SSE Running as a Service	SSE Running as User Instance
Multi-user.	Single-user.
Usable by the administrator or users who are granted privileges by the administrator.	Usable by all normal interactive users on the machine. For a non-interactive user like ASP.NET, the administrator must explicitly grant permissions.
Windows and SQL Authentication.	Windows Authentication
The admin on the machine is sysadmin by default.	The user hosting the user instance and the administrator on the machine are sysadmin by default on the user instance.
The authentication and authorization models in SQL Server 2005 are used. Refer to Chapter 13 for additional details.	User must have full control on the database file and write permissions on the working directory. The permissions on the file are used for authentication.

SSE Running as a Service	SSE Running as User Instance
No automatic copying of system database files. Only a single copy is used at a time.	The system databases are copied when a user instance is created. Each user instance uses a separate copy of the system databases.
The installed instance should be serviced with Windows updates and service packs.	The installed instance (that is, the parent instance) should be serviced with Windows updates and service packs.
Remote networking possible.	Local machine access only.
All SSE features are supported.	Some SSE features such as replication are disabled.
Database applications are not Xcopy-deployable. Users may need additional privileges to use the application.	Database applications are Xcopy-deployable.
`server` and `database` (or initial catalog) entries passed in the connection string.	`User Instance=true` and `server` entries passed in the connection string. `database` (or initial catalog) entry is avoided
You have to modify the default Visual Basic Express connection string to use SSE as a service.	By default, Visual Basic Express uses the user instance mode for its applications.
Works with all the command line and GUI tools.	Works with command line and GUI tools only if the user instance is already started, and you know the GUID based instance name. SSEUtil can connect directly to the named SSE instance of SQLExpress.
The SQL Server Service is always running.	The user instance lifetime depends on the application lifetime. It is automatically started and closed by the parent SQL Server Service.
There is no delay during startup since the service is always running.	There is a slight delay in startup of user instance.

T-SQL Extensions for Managing User Instance

To enable administrators to manage user instances, a new virtual view called sys.dm_os_child_instances is introduced, which lists all the user instances spawned on the parent instance. This information is persisted in the master database metadata of the parent instance. SSE has the logic to determine the current status of the user instance, such as alive or dead. The status appears as part of the heart_beat column in the view. The various columns in this view are described below:

❑ owning_principal_name contains the name of the user who created this child instance

❑ owning_principal_sid is the security identifier (SID) of the principal defined by the owning_principal_name

❑ instance_name is the name of the user instance

❑ instance_pipe_name is the name of the connection string that can be used in your application to connect to this instance

❑ os_process_id is the windows process id

❑ os_process_creation_date is the date and time the user instance was created

❑ heart_beat refers to the dead or alive status of this user instance

New `sp_configure` options are also introduced for user instances. The `user instances enabled` configuration option allows you to enable or disable the user instance feature. For example, if you are using SSE in production to support multiple users, you may not need user instances. A value of 0 disables the creation of user instances. The `user instance timeout` configuration option allows you to specify the timeout period after which the user instance is terminated automatically in case there is no open connection to that user instance. Note that the timeout value can be specified in both the parent and the child instances. The child instance defaults to the timeout settings of the parent instance. However, you can specify a different timeout for the child once it is started. Run the following commands to see the current values for these configuration options.

```
sp_configure 'show advanced options', 1
reconfigure
go
sp_configure
```

The following table provides a summary of the common commands used with user instances.

Command/ Feature	Usage/Example	Description
sys.dm_os_child_instances view	SELECT * FROM sys.dm_os_child_instances	A view that lists all the user instances along with their status.
T-SQL SHUTDOWN	SHUTDOWN	The T-SQL SHUTDOWN command can be used to shut down SQL Server as well as user instances.
user instances enabled configuration	sp_configure 'user instances enabled', '1' sp_configure 'user instances enabled', '0'	A value of 1 enables the user instance feature in SSE, while a value of 0 disables this feature. This configuration value is 1 by default.
user instance timeout configuration	sp_configure 'user instance timeout', 500	The timeout value specified can be between 5 and 65535.

Summary

This chapter provided an introduction to the Xcopy feature supported by SSE. Automating the connectivity to the database is enabled using a combination of AttachDBFilename, auto-naming the logical database and the log file, and AutoClose. The functional aspects of user instances, including the ADO.NET extensions, the creation process, and the security model are covered in later sections.

In addition, this chapter addressed:

- ❑ Some key features such as SQL Authentication and remote networking that are not available when using the user instance

- ❑ The differences between running SSE as a service and as a user instance

- ❑ Using SSEUtil to connect to a user instance and perform simple operations such as detach and run T-SQL commands

- ❑ The T-SQL extensions that are useful for configuring and administering the user instances

In the next chapter, you learn more about using XML in your database applications.

Exercises

Try the exercises that follow to test your understanding of the material covered in this chapter. You can find the solutions to these exercises in Appendix A.

1. List the attached databases to a user instance as well as its parent instance.

2. Verify that the version of the parent instance and the user instance are the same.

3. List all SQL Server and SSE instances running on the local machine.

4. Detach all databases with names starting with d:.

7

Using XML in Your Database Application

XML is the newest storage paradigm to gain wide public acceptance. It is particularly useful for storing hierarchical data. A primary advantage of XML over relational data stores is that XML data is machine-independent. So, XML data defined and populated on an IBM mainframe can be sent to a Windows-based computer without any "fix-up" required by developers. Contrast this with the native and proprietary storage formats of relational databases. For instance, SQL Server cannot directly use an IBM DB2 database without some kind of import translation of the data and schema. As you might imagine, XML has become a favored choice for transporting data over the Internet. Further, XML can be typed or untyped. If it is typed, it means that the data in the XML file conforms to a specific developer-defined structure. If it is untyped, it may, or may not, conform to any defined structure. In SQL Server 2005 Express Edition, you have the capability to natively store and query XML data directly. You accomplish this by specifying a column in a table to have an XML data type, and then storing XML data in it. The number of options available when you use XML is quite large. This chapter will introduce a very common scenario of using XML.

In this chapter, you will learn to:

- ❑ Create and store typed XML data in SSE
- ❑ Insert XML data
- ❑ Query XML data

You will use SSE and VB 2005 Express for this chapter. This chapter does not address untyped XML. While there are valid scenarios for untyped XML, it is typed XML that is more useful. For instance, if XML data is typed, that is, it conforms to a known structure, and you have a lot of XML data in many records, you can query those records and rely on the known structure. If you are storing thousands of resumes, for example, you can retrieve the zip codes from all of them in a single query if you know that they all must have a zip code and that the zip code will be in a specific place in the XML data. Untyped XML is a useful way for someone to label or name parts of a document structure. While it may not conform to an externally defined structure, naming parts of a document is useful in its own right. Furthermore, a great deal of XML that exists today is untyped, so being able to store it in your database is important. When you have finished this chapter, you will be able to create and use XML Schema Definitions with XML in SSE.

Creating an XML Schema Definition

In this chapter, you will create an XML Schema Definition (XSD) for a resume, a common example to illustrate the need for an XSD. In this example, you assume that you want to structure all resume information such that, at a conceptual level, it enables the hierarchical structure shown following:

```
Name
Objective
Address
   Street
   City
   State or Province
   Country
   Postal Code
Work Experience
   Experience 1
   Experience 2
   Experience ... n
References
   Reference 1
   Reference 2
   Reference ... n
```

There are several ways to create an XSD file. You can write it by hand, or you can use an XSD text editor or XSD graphical editor to build it. Visual Basic Express does not have a built-in XSD graphical editor. That feature is available in higher-level versions of Visual Studio.

Most people design the information structures associated with XSDs from the top down as in the preceding example. But, when you write an XML Schema Definition, if you are using complex elements, such as the Address element in the example above, you first create those elements and then bring them together in a final XML definition at the bottom. So, in a sense, you write an XSD from the bottom up.

Try It Out   Creating an XSD in VB Express

To create an XSD for the resume concepts above, follow the steps outlined below:

1. Create a new Visual Basic project and name it XMLExample.

2. Right-click the XMLExample node in the Solution Explorer and choose Add New Item. Choose to add a new Text item, name it Resume.XML, and add it to your project.

3. Type the code in Listing 7-1 into the editor (or copy it from the Wrox website at www.wrox.com). This is the Resume XML Schema definition. The code should have none of the squiggly lines indicating an error showing in the editor. If you see such squiggles, check your code to make sure you haven't made an error.

Listing 7-1: XSD Definition

```
<?xml version="1.0" encoding="utf-16"?>
<xs:schema xmlns:xs="http://www.w3.org/2001/XMLSchema"
elementFormDefault="qualified" >

    <xs:element name="Name" type="xs:string"> </xs:element>
```

```
        <xs:element name="Objective" type="xs:string"> </xs:element>
        <xs:element name="Address">
            <xs:complexType>
                <xs:sequence minOccurs="1" maxOccurs="1">
                    <xs:element name="Street"      type="xs:string"/>
                    <xs:element name="City"        type="xs:string"/>
                    <xs:element name="StateProv"   type="xs:string"/>
                    <xs:element name="Country"     type="xs:string"/>
                    <xs:element name="PostCode"    type="xs:string"/>
                </xs:sequence>
            </xs:complexType>
        </xs:element>

        <xs:element name="WorkExperience">
            <xs:complexType>
                <xs:sequence minOccurs="1" maxOccurs="unbounded">
                    <xs:element name="ExpText"     type="xs:string"/>
                </xs:sequence>
            </xs:complexType>
        </xs:element>

        <xs:element name="Reference">
            <xs:complexType>
                <xs:sequence minOccurs="1" maxOccurs="unbounded">
                    <xs:element name="RefText"     type="xs:string"/>
                </xs:sequence>
            </xs:complexType>
        </xs:element>

</xs:schema>
```

4. The final step is to add a bit of T-SQL code wrapped around the entire XSD definition. Right-click the XMLExample node in the Solution Explorer and choose Add New Item. Choose to add a new Text item, name it Resume.SQL, and add it to your project. Note that when you have completed this step, you will have two files. One named Resume.XML and one named Resume.SQL.

5. Next, take all of the code in Listing 7-1 and paste it into the new Resume.SQL. Then add the following code at the very top of the document:

```
CREATE XML SCHEMA COLLECTION ResumeXSD AS
```

Next, add an N and then a single quote (') right before the first angle bracket and one after the final angle bracket as well.

```
N'<?xml version="1.0" encoding="utf-16"?>
```

and

```
</xs:schema>'
```

Finally, at the very end of the document, add a GO statement, like so:

```
GO
```

The final XML Schema Definition should appear as shown in Listing 7-2. Note that a number of elements will now show up as errors. This is because you have mixed T-SQL commands into an XML document and the XML editor does not like it.

Listing 7-2: SQL Schema Collection Definition

```
CREATE XML SCHEMA COLLECTION dbo.ResumeXSD AS
N'<?xml version="1.0" encoding="utf-16"?>
<xs:schema xmlns:xs="http://www.w3.org/2001/XMLSchema"
elementFormDefault="qualified" >

    <xs:element name="Name" type="xs:string"> </xs:element>
    <xs:element name="Objective" type="xs:string"> </xs:element>
    <xs:element name="Address">
        <xs:complexType>
            <xs:sequence minOccurs="1" maxOccurs="1">
                <xs:element name="Street"      type="xs:string"/>
                <xs:element name="City"        type="xs:string"/>
                <xs:element name="StateProv"   type="xs:string"/>
                <xs:element name="Country"     type="xs:string"/>
                <xs:element name="PostCode"    type="xs:string"/>
            </xs:sequence>
        </xs:complexType>
    </xs:element>

    <xs:element name="WorkExperience">
        <xs:complexType>
            <xs:sequence minOccurs="1" maxOccurs="unbounded">
                <xs:element name="ExpText"     type="xs:string"/>
            </xs:sequence>
        </xs:complexType>
    </xs:element>

    <xs:element name="Reference">
        <xs:complexType>
            <xs:sequence minOccurs="1" maxOccurs="unbounded">
                <xs:element name="RefText"     type="xs:string"/>
            </xs:sequence>
        </xs:complexType>
    </xs:element>

</xs:schema>'
GO
```

How It Works

An XSD allows you to specify elements and their data types (for instance, name and string). It also allows you to specify more complex items. So, for instance, you specified that Work Experience is a complex type that has a sequence of lines (with at least one line and an unlimited number of maximum lines). In an XSD you can specify a number of additional constraints and choices. In this example you have used a small but useful subset of XSD functionality.

When you wrap the XSD with the CREATE XML SCHEMA COLLECTION statement and then execute it, SSE takes the XSD and stores it for potential reference when you later create a column that uses that particular XML data type.

Note that you named your "text" file Resume.XML. The .XML extension activates the built-in XML editor in VB Express. This gives you all of the IntelliSense capabilities, which will help you prevent errors while typing in XML. If you name your file Resume.XSD, VB Express does not assume you have an XML file and you will not get any IntelliSense functionality. This is because in the higher versions of Visual Studio, the built-in graphical XSD designer is associated with .XSD extension and VB Express is set up to honor that same extension.

Because you are only creating this XSD for the purpose of entering it into SSE, you do not need to give it an .XSD extension.

Note that if you want to drop a XML Schema Definition from SSE, you do the following:

```
DROP XML SCHEMA COLLECTION ResumeXSD
GO
```

In general, you should consider using an XML data type if:

- ❑ You do not know the structure of the data (for example, someone else who owns the structure sends the XML data to you, and you store it in the database). The structure may change without warning. In this case, you would use an untyped XML data type. An example here is a purchase order document you receive from other companies. You'll want to preserve it exactly as you got it.

- ❑ The data you wish to store is purely hierarchical and does not represent data that is referenced among other tables and columns in your database. An example here is a resume. A resume is, among other things, a collection of a variable number of textual descriptions of work experience and education and so on. There is no real value in breaking each of the resume work items out into separate fields or records in a database, since it would be unlikely you'd ever reference them (via a foreign key) from another table. On the other hand, preserving the native structure of the resume is beneficial in bringing the data up in a form.

The decision about what is stored in a relational format and what is stored in an XML format is an important one. It is helpful to know that relational technology originally became widely pervasive as an answer to unthinking uses of deep hierarchical storage technologies. People did not always foresee well what information they would want to query later. So, they often created deeply nested hierarchical data stores. It turns out that querying and relating deeply nested hierarchical data is both difficult and computationally expensive. Relational technology overcame the abuses of hierarchical technologies with a conceptually simpler model that could represent all data relationships. While the relational model makes it possible, it is not always simple. Using a relational database to store natively hierarchical data, although possible and certainly frequently done, can be unwieldy. Relational technology was not the perfect technology answer to all data needs. However, judging simply from its wide acceptance alone, XML does have a clear place in today's world. In choosing how you will store your data, you are probably best choosing and working with the relational approach unless the XML approach is a clear winner.

There is a great deal about XML Schema Definitions not described here. You can define keys, relationships, and impose specific choices about which elements you will allow at certain nodes in the XML hierarchy as well.

Creating a Schema Collection in SSE

Now that you have created an XSD, you need to let SQL Server know of its existence. You have defined the XSD in an SQL script, but you haven't run it yet. If you want to create a table column of type XML, you'll also want to specify what XSD its data should be conformant to. You do this by creating a *schema collection* in SSE. You actually push the XSD into SSE. Schema collections are global in nature. They are available generally in a database, and they are not specifically restricted for use by a single table or column. Once schema collections are available, you can use them anywhere you have defined a column with an XML data type. While VB Express helps a lot in a number of areas, you can't use VB Express to create the schema collection in SSE.

Try It Out   **Creating a Schema Collection in SSE**

To create a schema collection in SSE, follow these steps:

1. Open Visual Basic Express and open the Database Explorer (View ➪ Database Explorer). Right-click the top Data Connections node and choose Add Connection. This brings up the Add Connection dialog.

2. With the Add Connection dialog open, type in the following full path and new database name: **c:\Rich.mdf**. Do NOT choose Create New SQL Server Database. Your screen should appear as shown in Figure 7-1.

Figure 7-1

3. If you have not already done so, download SSEUtil from the Microsoft download center at //www.microsoft.com/downloads/ tools/default.aspx, as described in Chapter 6. Download this utility into the same directory as your MDF.

> SSEUtil is a command line utility like sqlcmd. However, SSEUtil works directly with the user instance (rather than the main instance.) If you simply type in SSEUtil, it will list all of the options available to it. SSEUtil was developed internally at Microsoft by a developer that was working with SSE User Instances. Its command set is heavily oriented around the typical commands you, as a developer, will frequently encounter. Note that if you plan to use SSEUtil on a regular basis, you should put SSEUtil in a separate directory and then modify your Windows search path to include that directory. (Note also that if you rename SSEUtil to SQLUtil, it will work by default, with the main instance.)

4. Execute a USE statement on your database on the master database. Type **SSEUtil –c**. This will put SSEUtil into console mode. Then type **USE "c:\Rich.mdf"** and press Return. Next, type **GO** and press Return. This will execute the USE statement. Note the use of double quotes to reference the name. If the command executes successfully, you will see a statement that says Command Completed Successfully.

5. Copy Resume.SQL to your c:\ directory and then type **!Run Resume.SQL**. This will execute the SQL file that you have created.

6. Type the following code in SSEUtil. This will check that your XML schema has been accepted into SSE.

```
SELECT * FROM SYS.XML_SCHEMA_COLLECTIONS
GO
```

Running this query should show that ResumeXSD has been added as a schema collection to Rich.mdf. The Resume schema is now available in your database for you to use as an XSD.

How It Works

When you use the Create schema collection command, SSE takes the input you have given it, validates it, and then stores it for use. Now any column in your database that has an XML data type can use the Resume XSD. Your next step is to create a column that actually references this XSD.

Another important point here is how you used the Add Connection dialog to create a new SSE database. This database now lives outside any Visual Basic project. Simply typing in a new name of a database at some location (in this case you placed it directly in the root) will create a new database if it doesn't already exist.

In particular, note that you did not use the Create New SQL Server Database command. This menu command is used for service-style, or traditional, connections. You can use SQL Server Express in service-style mode. In fact, this is the traditional way people use SQL Server. If you want to create a SQL Server database this way, you need to identify the database server's name. The SSE server name is the name of the machine and then the instance name. The default instance name is SQLExpress. A shortcut for the local machine name is a dot. So, you would identify the server name on your local machine as .\SQLExpress. However, VB Express does not explicitly support the service-style type of connection. The higher versions of Visual Studio do.

Creating a Column with an XML Data Type

With an XSD stored in a schema collection, you can create a column in a table that has an XML data type and that uses the XSD that you have created. After you have created a column with an XML data type, you can store XML data that will be validated against the XSD you put into the database.

Try It Out   Creating a Column with an XML Data Type

To create a column with an XML data type, follow these steps:

1. Using VB Express, open the existing connection to Rich.mdf that you created in the previous section.

2. Create a new table. Create the first column, name it PKID, and make it an int data type. Make it the primary key.

3. Create a second column, name it Resume, and make the data type XML. Tab out of the data type column so the property section below is updated for your XML data type choice.

4. In the property section for the column, find the XML Type Specification and set the schema collection to dbo.ResumeXSD. It is available since you have added ResumeXSD as a schema collection to the database. Figure 7-2 shows what your screen should look like.

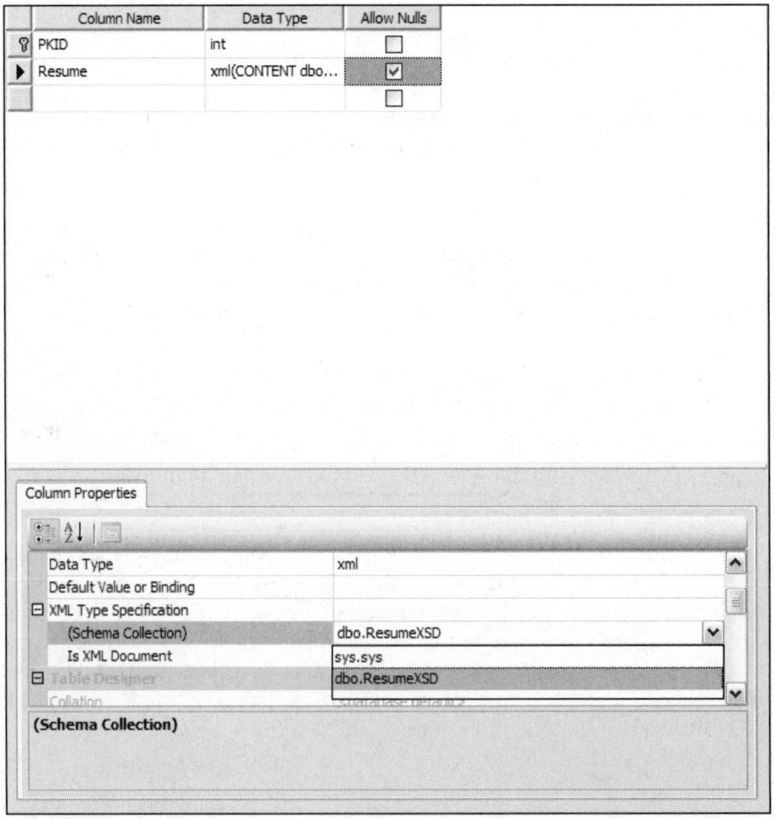

Figure 7-2

5. Select the row that defines the Resume column and then right-click on the table designer background and choose XML Indexes. Click the Add button. This will add an XML primary XML index on your column. Click Close to close the XML Index dialog.

6. Exit the table designer and save the table with the name RichTable.

Alternatively, you can perform the same task using SSEUtil. In SQL Express, enter the code in Listing 7-3.

Listing 7-3: Simple Table with XML Column CREATE Script

```
1> Use "c:\Rich.mdf"
2> CREATE TABLE RichTable
3> (
4> PKID INT PRIMARY KEY,
5> Resume XML(ResumeXSD)
6> )
7> GO
```

How It Works

Your table column Resume is now bound to the Resume.XSD you put in the database in the last section. This means that the data in the XML column must conform to the XSD.

Note that you did not make the XML column the primary key. SSE cannot compare two XML documents for equality. You can't ask SSE whether the XML data in this record is the same as the XML data in a different record. Therefore, you cannot make a column with an XML data type a primary key. In order for a data type to be a primary key, the data type instances must be comparable for equality. This also means that you also cannot have a foreign key point to or from a column with an XML data type. An additional limitation is that you cannot use an XML column in a GROUP BY statement as a grouping value.

You can do some things to work around these limitations. For instance, you can extract the data from an XML data column and then put those values in a column with a data type that can be compared or used as a primary key.

While you cannot make an XML column a primary key, you can index it. In step 5 of the preceding exercise, you added a primary XML index. Indexing provides significant speed advantages when querying. The important thing to understand about the indexing is that at the time you insert the XML data into the table, it shreds the XML data and pulls out the indexable elements into a hidden internal table, so it doesn't try and shred the data at query time. Speed is significantly increased.

Additionally, you can provide other, secondary, indexes on the same XML column. If the amount of XML data that you need to store is quite large, you may want to provide a secondary index that is optimized for paths, properties, or values you seek. To create one of these secondary indexes, however, you must first create a primary XML index — like you did in this example — and then you can create the secondary indexes.

Populating an XML Column with Data

Inserting data into an XML column is fairly straightforward. You simply need to create an XML fragment that conforms to the XSD you created.

Inserting Data into an XML Column

To add data to a column with an XML data type, follow these steps:

1.   Create an XML fragment. Enter the code in Listing 7-4 into an XML text document in VB Express and name it Insert.XML. If you have typed it in correctly, the XML editor will show only one error under the Objective node: "XML Document cannot contain multiple root level elements."

Listing 7-4: XML Fragment to Insert

```xml
<?xml version="1.0" encoding="utf-16"?>
<Name>George Washington</Name>
<Objective>Lead a country</Objective>
<Address>
    <Street>1 Cherry Lane</Street>
    <City>Washington</City>
    <StateProv>DC</StateProv>
    <Country>USA</Country>
    <PostCode>100000</PostCode>
</Address>

<WorkExperience>
    <ExpText>Country Farmer</ExpText>
    <ExpText>Led a revolution</ExpText>
    <ExpText>Army General</ExpText>
</WorkExperience>

<Reference>
    <RefText>Benjamin Franklin</RefText>
    <RefText>Layfette</RefText>
    <RefText>King Henry</RefText>
</Reference>
```

2.   Wrap the XML fragment with the following SQL text as shown in Listing 7-5. Note, in particular, the parentheses and use of the single quote (before the XML declaration and at the very end). The XML editor will not like the addition of this code since it is not legal XML.

Listing 7-5: INSERT Statement for George Washington Resume

```sql
INSERT INTO dbo.RichTable(PKID, Resume) values ('1',N'<?xml version="1.0"
encoding="UTF-16"?>
<Name>George Washington</Name>
<Objective>Lead a country</Objective>
<Address>
    <Street>1 Cherry Lane</Street>
    <City>Washington</City>
    <StateProv>DC</StateProv>
    <Country>USA</Country>
```

```
            <PostCode>100000</PostCode>
    </Address>

    <WorkExperience>
        <ExpText>Country Farmer</ExpText>
        <ExpText>Led a revolution</ExpText>
        <ExpText>Army General</ExpText>
    </WorkExperience>

    <Reference>
        <RefText>Benjamin Franklin</RefText>
        <RefText>Layfette</RefText>
        <RefText>King Henry</RefText>
    </Reference>
')
GO
```

3. Using SSEUtil, type **!run Insert.SQL**. Because this XML validates against the XSD, it will add a new row with the XML fragment in the XML column.

> **Note that it's important to have the line of insert text formatted this way:** INSERT INTO dbo.RichTable(PKID, Resume) values ('1',N'<?xml version="1.0" encoding="UTF-16"?>
>
> **And not this way:**
>
> INSERT INTO dbo.RichTable(PKID, Resume) values ('1',N'
> <?xml version="1.0" encoding="UTF-16"?>
>
> **If you do not format it correctly, SSE will throw an error stating that the first value after the N' must be the XML text.**

How It Works

Conceptually, the data for this data fragment is quite simple. In a simpler form, the data looks quite reasonable, as shown in Listing 7-6.

Listing 7-6: George Washington's Resume Data

```
Name        George Washington
Objective   Lead a country
Address
        1 Cherry Lane
        Washington
        DC
        USA
        100000
```

```
Work Experience
   Country Farmer
   Led a revolution
   Army General
References:
   Benjamin Franklin
   Layfette
   King Henry
```

If you tried to enter a different XML fragment, one that contained a different node, it would fail. For instance, if you tried to enter an XML fragment that has a node for <PhoneNumber>, it would fail because the XSD that the fragment must conform to does not allow it.

Additionally, note that you have entered an XML fragment, not an XML document. That's the reason you have the one error in the XML editor. SSE allows you to specify whether you are entering an XML fragment or an XML document. By default, if you do not specify, then SSE assumes you are entering an XML fragment (as you have above). To specify that the XML you will store in a column is an XML document, then you set the property "Is XML Document" in the table designer to yes. Alternatively, if you are specifying this in TSQL (as per Listing 7-3), it is specified as follows:

```
CREATE TABLE RichTable (PKID INT PRIMARY KEY, Resume XML(DOCUMENT ResumeXSD))
```

You should understand some things about what you have done in this example. First, a perfect and exact copy of your XML data is not what is actually stored in the database. Insignificant information is not stored. For example, white space that you introduced in noncritical places will not be preserved. Attributes will not necessarily be retrieved in the specific order you stored them. In general, the type of information that is lost should not matter since you retrieve XML data by name, not position. Additionally, an XML hierarchy in SSE cannot be deeper than 128 levels, and the size of the XML document cannot be larger than 2GB.

Querying an XML Column

Now that you have data in an XML column, you can query it. The query language for XML, XQuery, is quite extensive. And, the syntax is quite different than SQL. SSE allows you to embed XQuery into the SQL in order to retrieve data. You will only use a simple aspect of it in this example.

Traditional SQL queries on the entire row will return various columns with all of their data. If you want the entire contents of any row/column combination, use SQL syntax. Enter the following code and run it in SSEUtil:

```
SELECT *
FROM RichTable
GO
```

The result will appear like the following (the voluminous detail of the XML fragment has been removed):

```
PKID      Resume
--------------------------------------------------------
1         <Name>George Washington</Name> <Objective>Lead ...
```

This code simply returned the row and all its data. If you are going to return this row to a control in VB Express on a WinForm, this may be all you need. However, if you want to reach down inside the XML structure and pull out only specific parts of the XML structure, you need to use XQuery to get out specific parts of the XML structure. To reach in and pull out specific XML data from an XML column, create and run the following code in SSEUtil:

```
SELECT Resume.query('WorkExperience/ExpText') AS WorkExperience
FROM RichTable
GO
```

The result will appear like the following (formatted here for easy reading):

```
WorkExperience
-----------------------------------------------------
<ExpText>Country Farmer</ExpText>
<ExpText>Led a revolution</ExpText>
<ExpText>Army General</ExpText>
```

Note that the data is returned as XML data. If you want to get the data in a relational style format, you need to use a different style command after `Resume`. To get data retrieved from an XML column in a relational style format, create and run the following code in SSEUtil:

```
SELECT Resume.value('(/Name)[1]', 'VARCHAR(50)')
FROM RichTable
GO
```

The result will appear like the following:

```
Name
-----------------------------------------------------
George Washington
```

This will simply return the name George Washington as an SQL scalar value. The value must come back singly; it is the only value you can pull out of the XML column. You cannot have it return multiple data elements this way for each row in the database. However, if you have, for instance, three rows in the database, each with an XML fragment in it (such as the resumes for George Washington, Thomas Jefferson, and Abraham Lincoln) each in separate rows, then you can get a result like the following:

```
Name
------------------------
George Washington
Thomas Jefferson
Abraham Lincoln
```

SSE has an entirely different query language, XQuery, that you use to query XML data. Microsoft has gone to great lengths to tightly integrate the relational and XML story. As you can see from the examples here, you can retrieve the XML data into an XML data or relational format.

Chapter 7

Summary

This chapter has given you an overview of using the SSE XML data type. XML is a very rich storage option that you will likely need at some point.

What this chapter has not shown you, but does exist, is the rest of the very rich query functionality associated with XQuery. Some additional features for XML data types not discussed here include:

- ❑ Nested `for` XML queries
- ❑ The ability to selectively modify portions of XML data
- ❑ The ability to index the XML data

There are entire sets of books devoted exclusively to XML that you will find very instructive if you wish to delve deeper into this topic. But this chapter has covered quite a bit. In particular, this chapter explained how to:

- ❑ Create an XML Schema Definition using VB Express
- ❑ Create an XML SCHEMA COLLECTION
- ❑ Create a column with an XML data type
- ❑ Insert XML into a XML column
- ❑ Query an XML column

Exercises

Try the exercises that follow to test your understanding of the material covered in this chapter. You can find the solutions to these exercises in Appendix A.

1. You are using an XML data type to collect inter-business documents. You anticipate having to write an XQuery to quickly retrieve information from the column that is storing the XML data. Use the Visual Basic Table Editor to create an XML index on the XML data type.

2. You have invested heavily in using XML data types to collect purchase order information from your vendors. There are certain queries you make into an XML data type column that always retrieve single values. You want to speed up your queries by better indexing the XML data type column. Use the Visual Basic Table Editor to create a secondary XML index on the Resume column based on Path.

3. You are creating a database application and you want the results from an XML column to appear, programmatically, just like the other columns you retrieve in a query. Retrieve more than one SQL Scalar value from the XML column in a single select. Push the results into several columns.

Debugging Database Applications

Debugging is the process of figuring out what's wrong with your program. Unfortunately, there is no one single tool, or even a single method, that will always help you find the problem in your code. In short, debugging is a skill that requires many tricks. You will learn a number of those tricks in this chapter. The specific technique you use in debugging depends heavily on the type of data and code you have created. This chapter explores some debugging techniques aimed specifically at database-oriented applications. If you have a very simple application, your debugging efforts may be limited to simply verifying that your data was updated correctly in the database. You might update a value in your application and then look at the database, in a separate way, to verify that the values you input are actually being updated in the database. At the other extreme, you may need to follow the code as it executes not only in your application, but directly into the database as well. As with many problem-solving methods, the key in debugging is getting things set up right and knowing what the tools can help you accomplish.

In this chapter, you will learn to set up things so you can:

❑   Work with VB 2005 Express Edition for the basic verification techniques

❑   Work with SSE to trace output to the error log

❑   Work with VB Express for general debugging and T-SQL debugging

You will use VB 2005 Express Edition for this chapter. You will also need the application you built in Chapter 5. When you have finished this chapter, you will have debugged database application problems with SSE, and you should be able to use these techniques in applications you build on your own.

Basic Verification

The most basic of debugging steps for a database application is to verify what values your application has actually updated or inserted into the database. In the case of SSE and VB Express, this means the ability to verify that when you update the form that you built in VB Express, the SSE database is also correctly updated. Working with databases in Visual Basic 2005 is a little different from what most database professionals expect. While it is different, it fits nicely with the traditional compiler model. Your first goal is to understand how to check that your database is correctly updated, as outlined in the following Try It Out. Keep in mind that your Visual Basic source files and your source database live in the same directory. When you press F5 and debug your application, your Visual Basic source files are compiled into an executable application and your source database is copied into the same directory as your executable, as illustrated in Figure 8-1.

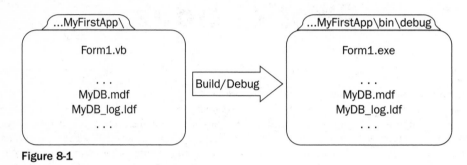

Figure 8-1

Try It Out   **Checking Your Output**

To check that your application is correctly updating the database, follow these steps:

1. Open the MyFirstApp solution you built in Chapter 5.

2. Press F5 to run your application in debug mode.

3. Type in the ID number and name of a new president: **4, Woodrow Wilson** (you can omit the other optional fields) and save the data.

4. Without stopping debugging, open Server Explorer (View ➪ Server Explorer) and right-click Data Connections to add a new connection.

5. In the Connection dialog, browse to the debug directory (see Figure 8-1). Select MyDB.mdf and click Open. Click OK to close the Connection dialog. This should create a new connection in Server Explorer with a name of MyDB.mdf1. (Note the 1 in the name as it appears in Server Explorer. Note also that this is not the file name but simply a name Server Explorer uses to keep track of the connection.)

6. Expand the nodes of the Server Explorer until you reach the Person table. Right-click on the Person table and choose Show table data. This should display the results grid with the record Woodrow Wilson added to it.

7. Return to your application and add another record: **5, Franklin Roosevelt**. Save the data to the database.

8. Navigate again to the Person table data. Right-click on the table and choose Execute SQL. Your table should now be updated with the new results.

How It Works

Remember that you must have first saved your project so that it is in a known directory (so you can navigate to it in the connection dialog). Note that in step 8, you must refresh the table view's data by choosing Execute SQL. A final key point to note is that the copy of the database that shows up in Server Explorer that is in the debug directory is added as MyDB.mdf1. If a database with a given name already appears in Server Explorer, subsequent connections have a number added to the end to distinguish them. You can determine which database the connection is for by looking at the connection property.

This method of copying the database to the output directory is a bit different from what most database professionals are used to. Most database professionals work against the database in a single location and they do not copy the database from a source location into a test or debug location for testing. VB Express does copy the database, in keeping with the normal compilation model. In the compilation model, a developer's source files in the source directory are compiled into an executable (and other files) and placed in the test or debug directory. In the VB Express example here, you have a source database (in your source directory) that is directly created by the table designer. It corresponds to the scripts used to create a database by many database developers. And, you have a test database in your output directory.

By default, the database in the source directory is only copied to the output directory if it is newer. You can change the behavior by changing the property Copy to Output Directory. (Right-click MyDB.mdf in the Solution Explorer to bring up the Property window.)

This type of debugging is pretty simple. You don't get the fine level of granularity of seeing the individual SQL statements as they go across the wire. To do that you need a different tool, as demonstrated in the next section.

Tracing Output

Sometimes you may not be sure exactly what T-SQL your application has sent to the database. It may be hard to determine in exactly what order T-SQL commands are issued, if your application issues T-SQL in several places. Alternatively, in a multi-user or multi-application scenario, you might want to catch input coming from several sources at a single point. A simple way is to use the SQL Trace flags. With these flags, you can monitor the SQL that is issued directly to the database. While there are several ways to issue a trace command, the following Try It Out uses the SSEUtil utility for this task.

Try It Out   Tracing Output

To trace the output of your SQL statements to the database, follow these steps:

1. Run MyFirstApp. You can run your app in debug mode or simply run the application straight from the bin or debug directory.

2. Select Start ⇨ Run and type **Cmd** to bring up a command window.

3. At the command prompt, type **SSEUtil −t +4054**. This will enable the 4054 trace flag.

4. Then, at the command prompt, type **SSEUtil −t +3605**. This will automatically add the trace flag 3605.

5. Enter some new data in MyFirstApp and save it to the database. Then close MyFirstApp.

6. In Windows Explorer, navigate to the following location, where <username> is your login name:

```
C:\Documents and Settings\<username>\Local Settings\Application
Data\Microsoft\Microsoft SQL Server Data\SQLEXPRESS\error.log
```

Open the most recent error.log file. (Note: to do this, you'll need to set your folder options so that you can see hidden files and folders.)

7. Towards the end of the error log, see if you can find the SQL that was issued by your application. Depending on the data you entered, it should look something like the output in the following code. In this example, the database was updated to add a record for James Monroe (just his first and last name), as indicated by the highlighted code.

```
SELECT PersonID, FirstName, LastName, FirstLine, SecondLine, City, State, Phone
FROM Person WHERE (PersonID = @PersonID)
2005-06-05 15:39:46.67 spid51        Parameter# 1:
Name=,Flags=0,Xvt=231,MaxLen=352,Len=352,Pxvar Value=@PersonID int,@FirstName
nvarchar(5),@LastName nvarchar(6),@FirstLine nvarchar(4000),@SecondLine
nvarchar(4000),@City nvarchar(4000),@State nvarchar(4000),@Phone nvarchar(4000)
2005-06-05 15:39:46.67 spid51        Parameter# 2:
Name=@PersonID,Flags=0,Xvt=56,MaxLen=4,Len=4,Pxvar Value=6
2005-06-05 15:39:46.67 spid51        Parameter# 3:
Name=@FirstName,Flags=0,Xvt=231,MaxLen=10,Len=10,Pxvar Value=James
2005-06-05 15:39:46.67 spid51        Parameter# 4:
Name=@LastName,Flags=0,Xvt=231,MaxLen=12,Len=12,Pxvar Value=Monroe
2005-06-05 15:39:46.67 spid51        Parameter# 5: Name=@FirstLine,
Flags=0,Xvt=231,MaxLen=2,Pxvar NULL
2005-06-05 15:39:46.67 spid51        Parameter# 6: Name=@SecondLine,
Flags=0,Xvt=231,MaxLen=2,Pxvar NULL
2005-06-05 15:39:46.67 spid51        Parameter# 7: Name=@City,
Flags=0,Xvt=231,MaxLen=2,Pxvar NULL
2005-06-05 15:39:46.67 spid51        Parameter# 8: Name=@State,
Flags=0,Xvt=231,MaxLen=2,Pxvar NULL
2005-06-05 15:39:46.67 spid51        Parameter# 9: Name=@Phone,
Flags=0,Xvt=231,MaxLen=2,Pxvar NULL
2005-06-05 15:39:46.67 spid51              IPC Name: sp_executesql
2005-06-05 15:39:46.67 spid51        ODS Event: execrpc : Xact 0 ORS#: 1, connId: 2
```

How It Works

There are a couple of important things to note in this example. First, you can trap the SQL commands going to SQL Server in a single location. While the SQL may be in a number of places in your code, the trace output tells you, unambiguously, exactly what SQL Server has received in SQL statements. And what's more, in what order it was received.

Another thing to note is the location of the error logs for the user instance. These files are in your Documents and Settings folder. While there are identically named files in the C:\Program Files\Microsoft SQL Server\MSSQL.1\MSSQL\LOG directory, these are not the files you are interested in for any database that is run with User Instance = True in the connection string (for attach-style connections). Note that in the error log in your Documents and Settings folder, you can find the instance name that is generated for your user instance. The instance name will be in a message of this form:

```
Server named pipe provider is ready to accept connection on [\\.\pipe\<instance
name>\tsql\query ]
```

where the instance name might be something like A169276A-A56C-40. If you are logged on as administrator, then you can see all of the child instances running on your machine by typing the following code:

```
SSEUtil -childlist
```

Behind the scenes, it is the pipe name that is being used to connect to child instances.

There are many different flags you can set via the DBCC command. (There are other ways to set it as well.) The following table shows a small subset of the interesting DBCC Trace flags you can set. SQL Server's Books Online documents all public trace flags.

Flag	Purpose
3604	Sends trace output to the client.
3605	Sends trace output to the error log.
4022	Automatically started stored procedures are skipped on start up of SQLServer.

Tracing T-SQL issued to SQL Server can help you in a number of different situations. But, if you need to see what result of a T-SQL command is actually returned to your application and how it's used internally in your application, it's best to use the VB Express Debugger.

VB Express Debugger

Launching the VB Express Debugger is pretty simple. You've already done it when you chose F5 to build and debug your application. This command is the same in all versions of Visual Studio. VB Express's integrated debugger gives you the ability to create break points, set assertions, and walk the objects currently in-memory during application execution.

Try It Out   Debugging MyFirstApp

To debug MyFirstApp, follow these steps:

1. Bring up Visual Basic 2005 Express Edition and open your project for MyFirstApp.

2. Open the Form1 designer and double-click on the grid to bring up Form1.vb.

3. In the Public Class Form1, right-click on the grey column for the Update line. Your screen should appear as shown in Figure 8-2.

4. Press F5 to start debugging your application. (This will launch your application in debug mode.)

5. Enter some data in your application and click the Save button. This will take you to the break point you set in your code.

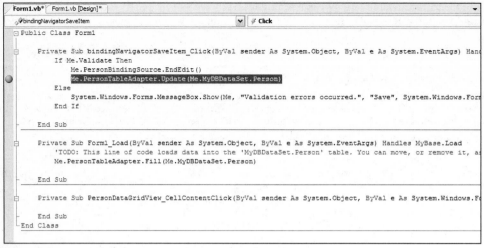

Figure 8-2

6. From the Debug menu item select Step Into or, press F11.

7. On the `Return Me.tablePerson` line, hover the mouse over the `Me.tablePerson` text. This should bring up the `Me.tablePerson` object so that you can browse it.

8. Note the little dropdown combo box on the magnifying glass on the `Me.tablePerson` object. From the dropdown, select the DataSet Visualizer. Expand the object so that you can see the properties as shown in Figure 8-3.

Figure 8-3

9. Close the DataSet Visualizer.

10. Select the `Me.tablePerson` text on the Return Me.tablePerson line. Then, from the Debug menu, select QuickWatch. This will select the `tablePerson` object and show its detailed properties as in Figure 8-4.

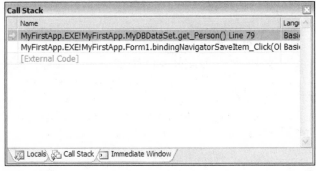

Figure 8-4

11. With the QuickWatch window up, scroll through the various items until you find Rows and expand it. You should see the number of rows that should be in the `tablePerson` data table.

12. Close the QuickWatch window. From the Debug menu, choose Windows. Open the Locals and Call Stack windows. They should appear as shown in Figure 8-5. Inspect the windows for local variable values and current call stack.

Figure 8-5

How It Works

When you debug, VB Express allows you to inspect the state of memory via the various tools you just used. As the program executes, various memory structures are created, updated, and deleted. The break point allows you to stop execution so you can inspect the memory state at that point. Then, you can incrementally step through code and watch things change.

Note that it is important to set your break point at a point where you know the data can be inspected in the right state. If you set the break point in the wrong place, you will have to use F11 a lot to get to an interesting line of code.

There are a number of tools available for debugging an application in VB Express. This example touched on the most basic ones. Using the DataSet Visualizer, you can easily check to see the values that you input into your form are committed to the dataset. Visualizers are not available for all objects. Using the Quick Watch window, however, you can inspect the object you are debugging directly.

The Locals window shows all variables that are currently in scope and their current values. So, if you are just generally debugging, the Locals window gives you the same visibility that your code has as it executes. The Call Stack window lets you see how you got where you are. If you have created an assertion, the Call Stack can tell you what set of calls got you into your current state. This set of windows (Visualizer, QuickWatch, Locals, and Call Stack) forms the most likely core set of tool windows in which you will spend most of your time in the debugger.

While break points can help a lot in debugging, you will get much more mileage out of carefully placed and created assertions.

Assertions

An assertion will stop program execution for you automatically when something you expect to be true is not. You can think of these as dynamic break points. Production code is typically filled with assertions to help prevent potential errors.

Try It Out   **Creating Assertions**

To create an assertion for your code, follow these steps:

1. Open your MyFirstApp application in VB Express.

2. Open Form1.vb and find the SaveItem code. (This is the code you added in an exercise in Chapter 5.)

3. Add a Debug.Assert statement after the EndEdit statement as shown in the following code and remove the break point:

```
Private Sub bindingNavigatorSaveItem_Click ...
   If Me.Validate Then
   Me.PersonBindingSource.EndEdit()

   Debug.Assert(Not (Me.MyDBDataSet.Person.GetChanges Is Nothing), _
           "We're trying to save Nothing ")

   Else
     System.Windows.Forms.MessageBox.Show ...
   End If

End Sub
```

4. Build and debug your application.

5. With the application up, click Save without entering any data. This should trigger the assert. If the break point is still present, simply hit F5 after it first hits the break point.

How It Works

In this example, you check for a null value from `GetChanges`. Note that null is `Nothing` in Visual Basic and you use the `Is` operator to check for equality. Forgetting to check for null is a common mistake — especially for simple values. While you can check for null and check for other range constraints you may be interested in (for example, `rowcount > 5`) all in the same assert, it is cleaner to split them out into separate, more readable lines. It's better to check for null first, before you check for other range values, because if the object does not exist, checking for detailed properties on that object in an assert may cause side effects you don't intend.

One key place you will want to use assertions is when you have a method that takes arguments. You want to ensure that those arguments exist and that they are in the ranges you expect for your code.

T-SQL Debugging

If you have written a stored procedure or function, you can debug it in VB Express. However, if you have Visual Studio Professional or a higher version, there are two key scenarios in which you may debug. If SSE is local, debugging and stepping into a stored procedure is pretty easy, as shown in the following Try It Out. On the other hand, if SSE is remote, things get more difficult. When SSE is remote, you must set up more things on both the server and on your machine, as explained later in this section.

Try It Out   Debugging a T-SQL Stored Procedure Locally

To debug a T-SQL Stored Procedure locally, follow these steps:

1. Open the solution for Chapter 15 from the CD. Its version of MyDB.mdf database has a stored procedure in it named `spGetNextPKValue`. Copy this database to your current project.

2. Open Server Explorer and add a new connection to the MyDB.mdf.

3. Expand the Stored Procedures node and double-click `spGetNextPKValue`. This will open the stored procedure in the code editor.

4. Set a break point in the stored procedure (on a `SELECT` statement) and choose Execute SQL. This will run the stored procedure. But first, it will bring up the parameters dialog.

5. In the parameters dialog, enter the value `Person` (leave the other parameter with the default value), and click OK. This will start the stored procedure and stop execution at the break point you set. Your screen should appear similar to Figure 8-6.

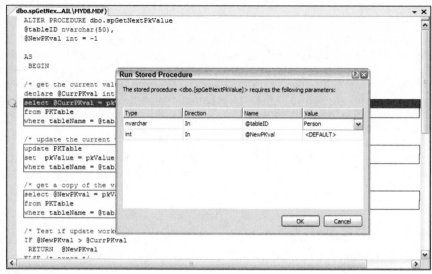

Figure 8-6

How It Works

When you are using SSE locally to debug stored procedures, VB Express and SSE can communicate with each other directly—in the same process space. This is an important point to understand. Remote debugging can be difficult to get working correctly. If you can copy the .MDF to your local machine, debugging will be much easier.

To get remote debugging to work (say, on a remote version of SSE or a fuller version of SQL Server), you must follow the additional steps. These additional steps are required to open the channels of communication across process and machine boundaries.

The first set of instructions tells you how to prepare your machine for remote debugging if you are using a Windows XP Professional SP2 machine. The second set of instructions provides instructions on basic remote debugging.

To prepare your Windows XP SP2 machine, follow these instructions. Note that the following remote debugging procedure only works if SSE is installed on a domain.

1. Ensure that SSE is running under a domain account.

2. Run `c:\Windows\system32\gpedit.msc` to open the Group Policy dialog. (Note: You may find this under c:\WinNT.)

3. In the Group Policy dialog, open the following folders in succession:

```
Local Computer Policy
    Computer Configuration
        Administrative Templates
            System
                Remote Procedure Call
```

Then disable the Restrictions for Unauthenticated RPC client property.

4. Close the Group Policy dialog.

5. Choose Start ⇨ Run and enter **regedit.exe** to bring up the registry editor.

> **Note: You should always back up your registry before making any changes.**

6. Find and delete the HKEY_LOCAL_MACHINE\Software\Policies\Microsoft\Windows NT\RPC\RestrictRemoteClients key.

7. Reboot the computer.

To use T-SQL debugging, follow these steps.

1. Open Visual Studio Professional (or higher) and establish a connection to the database.

❑ If you use a SQL login, the Windows login you logged in under on the client machine must also be an administrator on the server machine that has SSE (or higher).

❑ If you use an NT domain user (with NT authentication to log into the server), the domain account on the server must have permission to run the stored procedure sp_enable_sql_debug in SSE.

2. Open a T-SQL stored procedure to select. Right-click on the stored procedure and choose Step Into (or run to a break point).

Note that if you are using WinXPSP2, you will still see a warning dialog. Select the third firewall option to allow all machine connections to pass through the firewall.

From a security standpoint, you have to open many paths to enable remote T-SQL debugging. The main message is that if you can get the .MDF onto your local machine, it will make the job of debugging a whole lot easier. However, if you must debug remotely, it is possible.

SQL CLR Debugging

SQL CLR debugging is another situation where debugging locally is different from debugging remotely. Debugging locally is just normal debugging. Just set a break point and debug. Debugging SQL CLR remotely is similar to remote T-SQL debugging. Follow these steps:

1. Ensure that your login is a local Administrator account on the server machine with SSE.

2. Create a directory on the server machine and copy the remote debugger component that ships with Visual Studio Professional into the folder. The remote debugger component can be found on your machine with an installation of Visual Studio Professional in the following directory: C:\Program Files\Microsoft Visual Studio 8\Common7\IDE\Remote Debugger\x86.

3. Run msvsmon.exe on the server machine with SSE.

4. Follow step 1 from the preceding set of instructions to log into the server machine from the client machine.

5. In Server Explorer, right-click the connection to the server and choose Allow SQL/CLR Debugging.

6. Press F5 to debug your SQL CLR application.

Summary

In this chapter, you learned some valuable general principles of debugging and some specifics about debugging database applications.

Specifically, in this chapter, you learned how to:

❑ Verify that your database has been updated with data

❑ Use trace flags with the database

❑ Use the Visual Express debugger

❑ Use the DataSet Visualizer and the QuickWatch and Locals windows

❑ Use assertions

❑ Debug stored procedures (local and remote)

Exercises

Try the exercises that follow to test your understanding of the material covered in this chapter. You can find the solutions to these exercises in Appendix A.

1. In your build/debug cycle, you decide that the output version of the database (that ends up in the bin folder) should always be fresh and new each time you debug. (You don't want old test data in the database.) Find the properties for the MDF in the Property Window. Change the Copy Always property to Copy to Output Directory. Note performance differences.

2. You want to control the behavior of SSE on your machine through global settings. Set some of the other DBCC flags and observe the output in the error.log file.

3. VB Express handles the connection to the database for you automatically. It generates the connection string and handles all the details. However, from time to time, you may want to connect directly to the database and test certain things out. This is easy using SSEUtil. Just type in **SSEUtil** to get a list of commands you can use. Then, using SSEUtil, use the generated name of the user instance to connect to SQL Server. After you are connected, find and use the generated name of the database to query your database.

Part III:

Setup and Deployment

Chapter 9: Understanding SQL Server Express Setup

Chapter 10: Deploying Your Application

Chapter 11: Migrating from Microsoft Desktop Engine (MSDE)

Chapter 12: Migrating from Jet and Microsoft Access to MSDE and SSE

Understanding SQL Server Express Setup

In Chapter 1, you installed SQL Server Express (SSE) with the default settings using a single command line. This chapter provides an introduction to the setup and to the deployment options available in SSE. If you are planning to install the product for use on a local machine, you need to understand the configuration features supported by the setup dialogs. On the other hand, if you are an application developer or Independent Software Vendor (ISV) who plans to redistribute SSE along with the application, you need to understand the silent installation options described in this chapter. Regardless of whether you plan to use the setup user interface or the silent installation, this chapter will help you understand the setup options for networking, log files, and SQL Authentication.

In this chapter, you learn how to do the following tasks:

- ❏ Use the setup user interface to install SSE
- ❏ Silently install SSE using command line parameters and ini files
- ❏ Add or remove features to (and from) the SSE Installation
- ❏ Uninstall SSE

Installing SSE with the Setup Graphical User Interface

This section guides you through the dialogs required to successfully install SSE. It covers the various options available in each dialog and recommends actions to be taken at each step. The setup experience is streamlined with this release of the product, so that the mandatory items that the user will have to select for a successful install are minimized by default.

Verify the following conditions before starting setup:

1. Your computer satisfies the minimum hardware and software requirements described in Chapter 1.

2. The proper version of .NET Framework 2.0 is installed on the computer. This is also described in Chapter 1.

    Although the .NET Framework is not installed by SQL Express, the setup requires a certain version of the Framework to be present prior to the installation. If the Framework is not present, the setup displays an error message box, and you will have to install the appropriate version of the .NET Framework before continuing.

3. You are using the NTFS file system. NTFS is the preferred file system for installations of SSE because it is more stable and recoverable than FAT file system, although NTFS is not required. You can verify the file system in Windows XP by opening Windows Explorer and going to the drive (for example, C:\) where you want to install SSE. The Details section at the left contains details about the File System.

4. You are running setup as an Administrator on the machine.

To start the setup using the SSE 2005 CD, insert the CD into your computer's CD-ROM drive. Autorun .exe should automatically launch the Installation Wizard from the root folder. If the Installation Wizard does not launch automatically, navigate to the appropriate folder in Windows Explorer and double-click Autorun.exe. Perform the following steps to install SSE on your local machine.

1. On the End User License Agreement page, read the license agreement, and then select the check box to accept the licensing terms and conditions. By default, the EULA allows for multiple free installations of SQL Server Express on a single machine. If you are planning to redistribute SSE with your application, you should do a free registration at http://www.microsoft.com/sql/ howtobuy/default.mspx. Selecting the check box activates the Next button. Click Next

2. The SSE Component Update dialog checks for prerequisites and installs the SQL Support files (see Figure 9-1). Click Next.

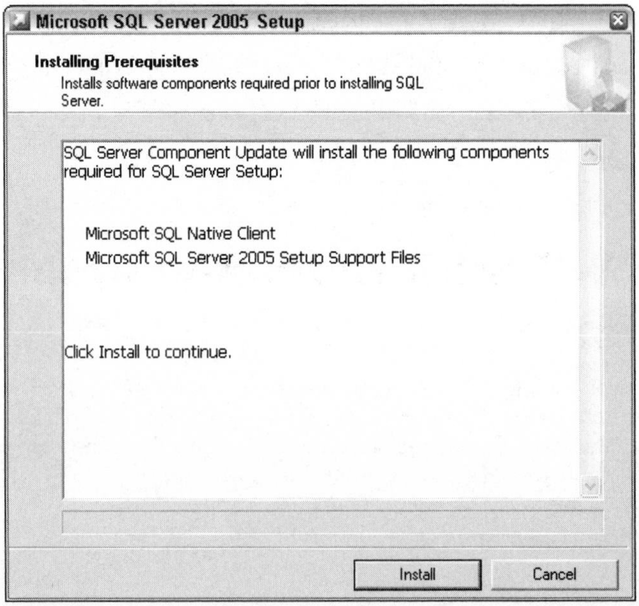

Figure 9-1

Notice there is no dependency on the Microsoft Data Access Components (MDAC), which significantly improves the serviceability story of SSE. In previous versions of SQL Server, the client incompatibilities due to the mismatch of MDAC installed with the operating system caused a lot of deployment and redistribution issues. Removing the dependency on MDAC is a big win for application developers.

3. On the Welcome page of the Installation Wizard, click Next.

4. The System Configuration Check (SCC) page (see Figure 9-2) indicates that the installation computer is being scanned for any known machine configurations that will limit the user or cause setup to fail. The intent of this dialog is to identify potential failure cases early in the install cycle, and provide a detailed report to the user. To proceed with setup after the scan completes, click Next.

The SCC dialog contains a wizard that informs the users about the checks that it is running. For instance, it will verify whether the machine meets the minimum hardware and software requirements. You will get a warning if the memory is less than 256MB, but the setup will proceed as long as the memory is 192MB or more. The items checked at this stage are described in the following table. This table also describes the remedies you should take if an error occurs.

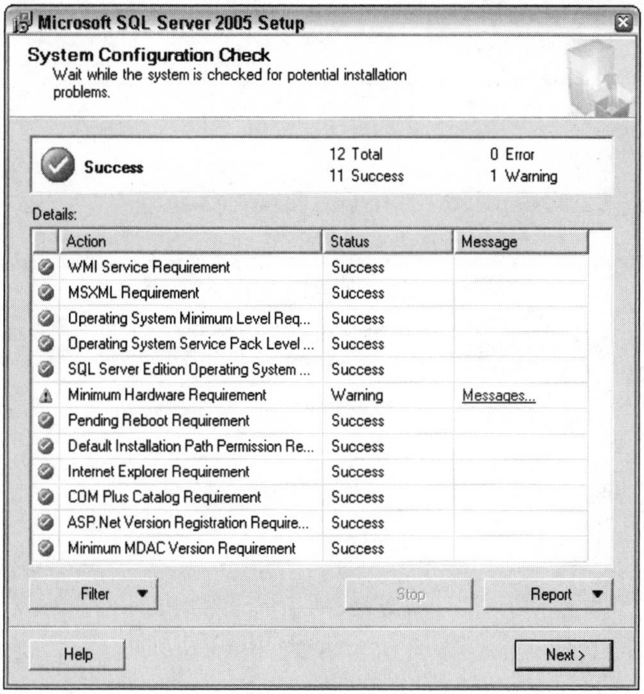

Figure 9-2

The progress symbols are intuitive to understand: an arrow symbol means that the check is in progress, a check symbol means that the check is complete, an exclamation point symbol means a warning, and an X symbol means that the check item failed.

Many users will initially encounter the Pending Reboot Requirement. This requirement arises when some system file like ODBC is being used by another application, or there is a pending reboot requirement from a previous installation. If you encounter this error, the correct action is to reboot the system and start the setup again.

The Report button is disabled while SCC is in progress. The checks can be stopped using the Stop button. You must then close the dialog, and exit setup. There is no way to restart the checks once the dialog is stopped. After SCC is complete, the Report button is enabled. If the checks identify a fatal error, the setup will exit; otherwise it will continue. By clicking the Report button, you have the option to view the report, save it to a file, copy it to the clipboard, or to send it as email. Information presented in the report (Figure 9-3) includes a list of configuration items checked and the result of each item checked. The report also contains the recommended remedy for any failed configuration checks.

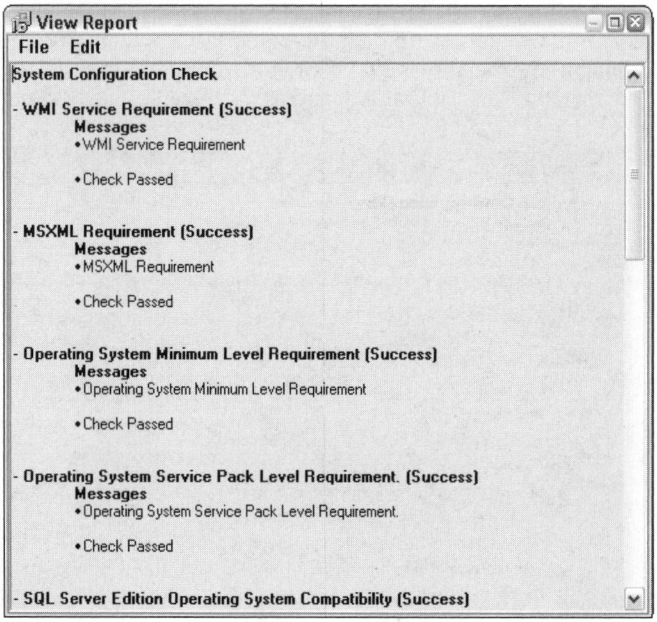

Figure 9-3

SCC Check Item	Description	Additional Information
WMI Service Requirement	Windows Management Instrumentation (WMI) service must be available; a failed check will block setup.	
MSXML Requirement	Proper version of MSXML must be present on the machine. A failed check on this item does not block setup.	You can download and install the proper version of MSXML from the Microsoft website at a later time.

SCC Check Item	Description	Additional Information
Operating system (OS) checks: Operating System Minimum Level Requirement, Operating System Service Pack Level Requirement, and SQL Compatibility with Operating System	Microsoft Windows 2000 SP4, Windows XP SP1, or Windows Server 2003 is required. Any unsupported OS causes the setup to fail. OS type must support the given SQL Server edition. For example, SQL Server Enterprise Edition can only be installed on Windows 2000 Server or higher. A failed check on this item will block setup. Typically the OS Type check is not relevant for SSE.	Refer to Chapter 1 for a list of supported operating systems. Use Windows Update Component for installing appropriate Windows Service Packs on the machine.
Minimum Hardware Requirement	Hardware must satisfy minimum CPU and memory requirements. A failed check on this item will block setup.	Refer to Chapter 1 for hardware and memory requirements.
Pending Reboot Requirement	If a previous product installation requires reboot, the Pending reboot registry key is set. SSE setup requires that this registry key be empty or nonexistent before it can start. A failed check on this item will block setup.	You should restart the machine and then run setup again.
Default Installation Path Permission Requirement	The disk drive should be formatted and uncompressed, and you should have read/ write permission. A failed check will block setup.	Make sure the disk drive is formatted, uncompressed, and not read-only.
Internet Explorer Requirement	Internet Explorer version 6.0 SP1 or later is required to install and run Business Intelligence Development Studio. Failure on this item will disable dependent components in the setup feature selection tree.	SSE is not affected by this check, and you can ignore it.
Com+ Catalog Requirement	The SCC verifies the current COM+ catalog requirement.	

5.   On the Registration Information page (Figure 9-4), enter your Name and Company information.

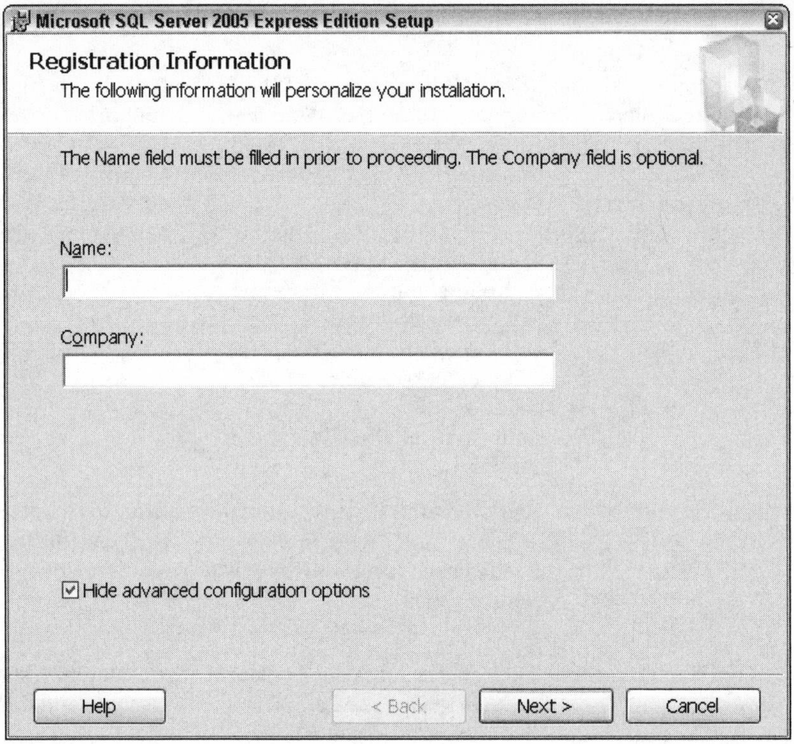

Figure 9-4

On this page is a check box unique to SSE called Hide Advanced Configuration Options. When this check box is enabled, the Service account, authentication mode, collation settings, and user instance dialogs are not shown to the user in later screens of the setup utility. Similarly, the instance name dialog is also not shown as long as there are no conflicts about the instance name. For example, if the default instance name of SQLExpress already exists on the machine, then this dialog is shown so that you can select a different instance name. Try not to change the default setting of this check box unless absolutely necessary.

Click Next to proceed.

6.   On the Feature Selection page (Figure 9-5), select the program features to install. Only the SQL Server Database Services and Data Files are selected by default (as shown in the figure). All the features that are not selected will have an X mark next to them. To change this, right-click the feature and select the Will Be Installed option.

The descriptions of the available features and subfeatures are listed in the following table. The ADDLOCAL column is explained in later sections when the setup command line parameters are covered. My recommendation is to select all components except for Replication, which should be selected only if you plan to use the SSE instance as a replication subscriber. At the lower part of the dialog, the disk cost associated with each section is mentioned.

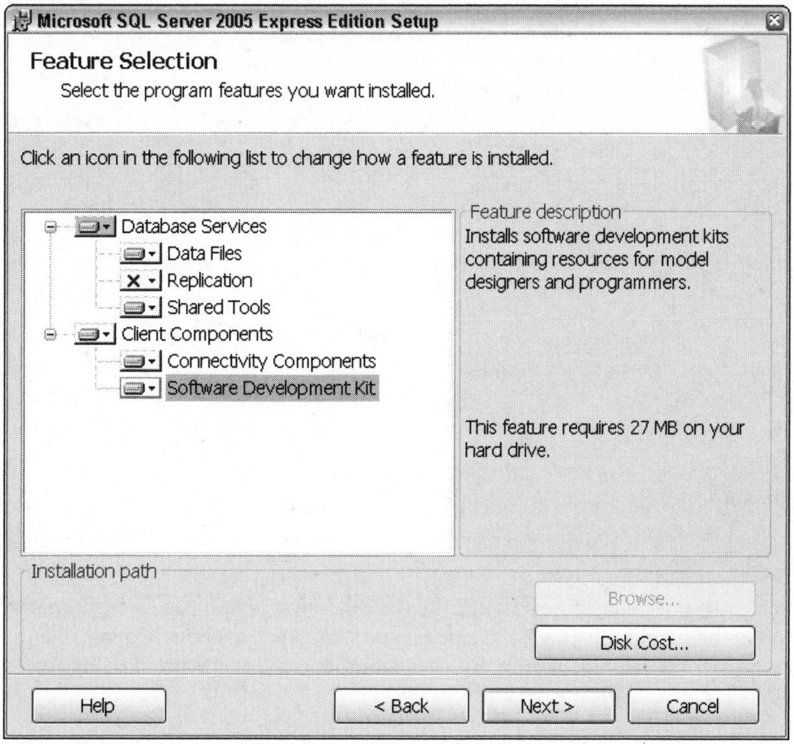

Figure 9-5

Feature Selection Component	Feature Selection Subcomponent	ADDLOCAL Feature_Selection	Description
SQL Server Database Services		SQL_Engine	Selects the SSE database engine for installation.
	Data Files	SQL_Data_Files	Selects the system data files for installation.
	Replication	SQL_Replication	Selects the replication features required for merge, transactional, and snapshot subscribers for installation.
Client Components		Client_Components	Selects connectivity components, programming models, development tools, and command line tools.

Table continued on following page

Feature Selection Component	Feature Selection Subcomponent	ADDLOCAL Feature_Selection	Description
	Connectivity Components	Connectivity	Selects components for communication between clients and servers, including SQL Native Access Components (SNAC), and network libraries for installation.
	Software Development Kit	SDK	Selects components for the software development kit and resources for model designers.

Click Next to proceed. If you selected to keep the advanced configuration options hidden in step 6, skip ahead to step 12. If you cleared the Hide advanced configuration check box, proceed with steps 7 through 11.

7. Skip this step if you did not change the default value of the Hide advanced configuration check box. On the Instance Name page (see Figure 9-6), you can choose to install a default or a named instance. It is possible to see the list of existing instances, as shown in Figure 9-7, by clicking the Installed Instances button. Click Next.

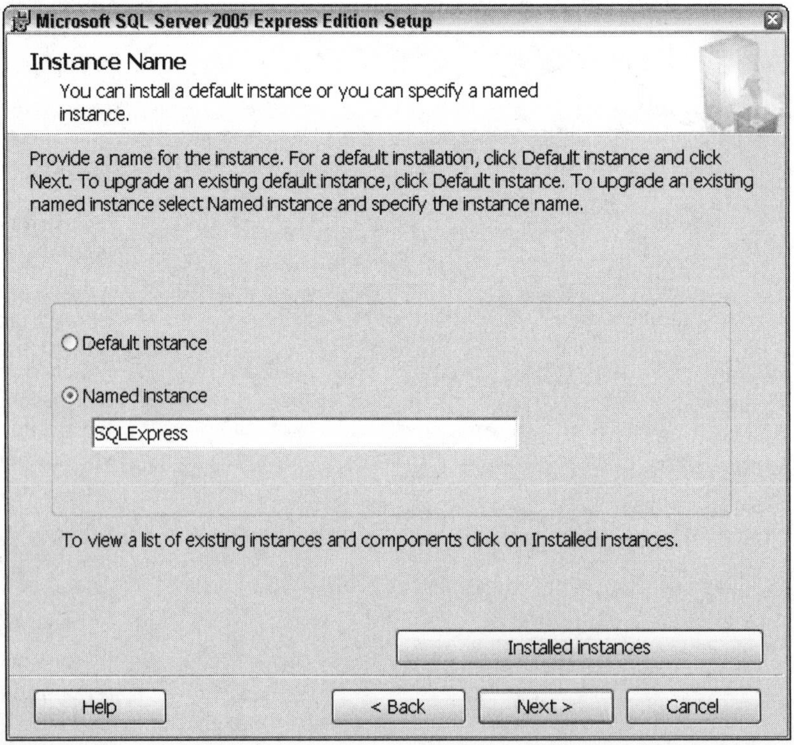

Figure 9-6

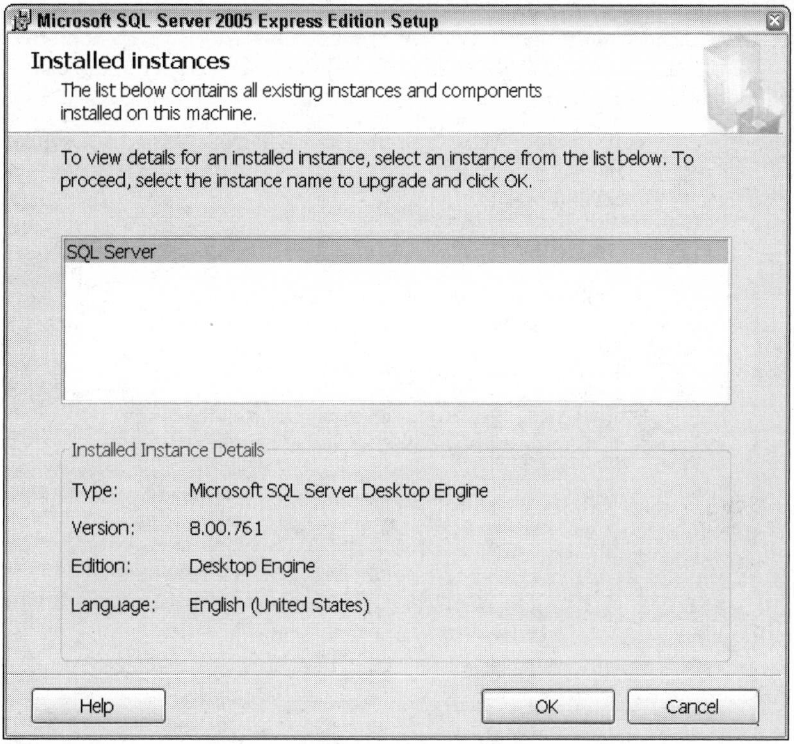

Figure 9-7

All editions of Microsoft SQL Server 2005, including SSE, support multiple installations of SQL Server on the same machine, and each such installation is called an instance. Each instance has its own set of program files and data files, while a set of common files like SQLNCLI or tools are shared among all instances on the computer. This mechanism allows different versions of SQL Server like SQL Server 7.0, SQL Server 2000, and SQL Server 2005 to co-exist on the same machine.

You can choose to uniquely name your instance, or choose a default instance name. The default instance is uniquely identified by the computer name alone, and has no separate name. Only one default instance per computer is possible. The default instance, which is also called MSSQLSERVER, is selected by default for editions of SQL Server 2005 other than SSE. This terminology can be somewhat confusing to an SSE user because they work with the named instance, called SQLExpress by default. An application developer provides a different name for the instance in the following cases:

❑   A different version of SQL Server with the same name already exists on the machine. This instance could be any edition of SQL Server 2000, MSDE, or SQL Server 2005.

❑   Your application needs some system-wide settings like SSL, which most other apps would not require.

❑   You want to control access to the particular instance of SSE for additional security.

You can supply a unique name for your SSE instance by clicking the Named Instance check box. Specify an instance name that is different from the ones already present on the machine. Instance names are limited to 16 characters, and the first character in the instance name must be a letter or an underscore (_).

If no additional features are selected for the instance name specified, the setup program will display an error message (see Figure 9-8). If you get this error message, click OK and then click Back to return to the Feature Selection page.

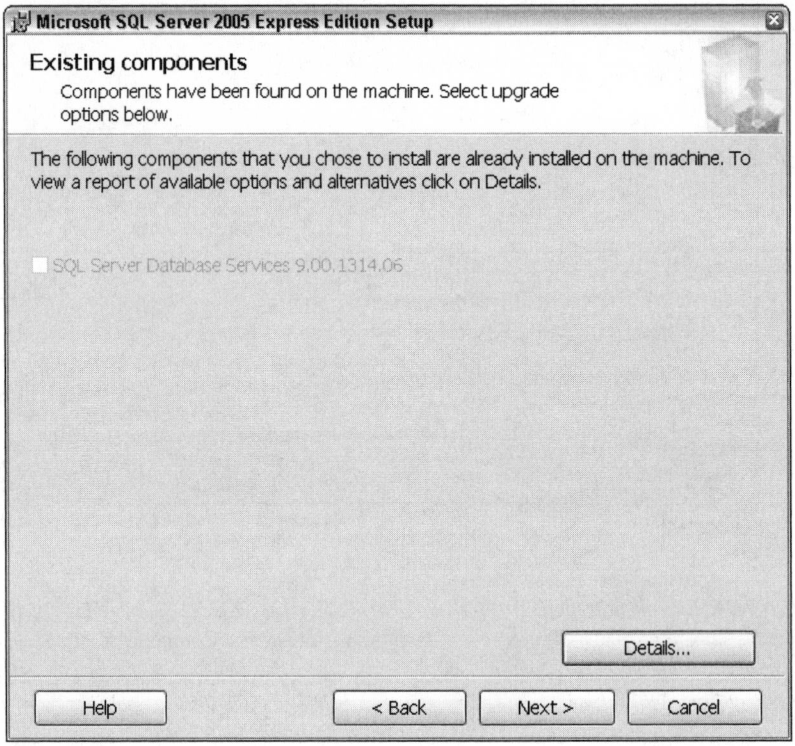

Figure 9-8

8. Skip this step if you did not change the default value of the Hide advanced configuration check box. The Service Account dialog (see Figure 9-9) allows you to specify a local or domain service account for the SQL Service.

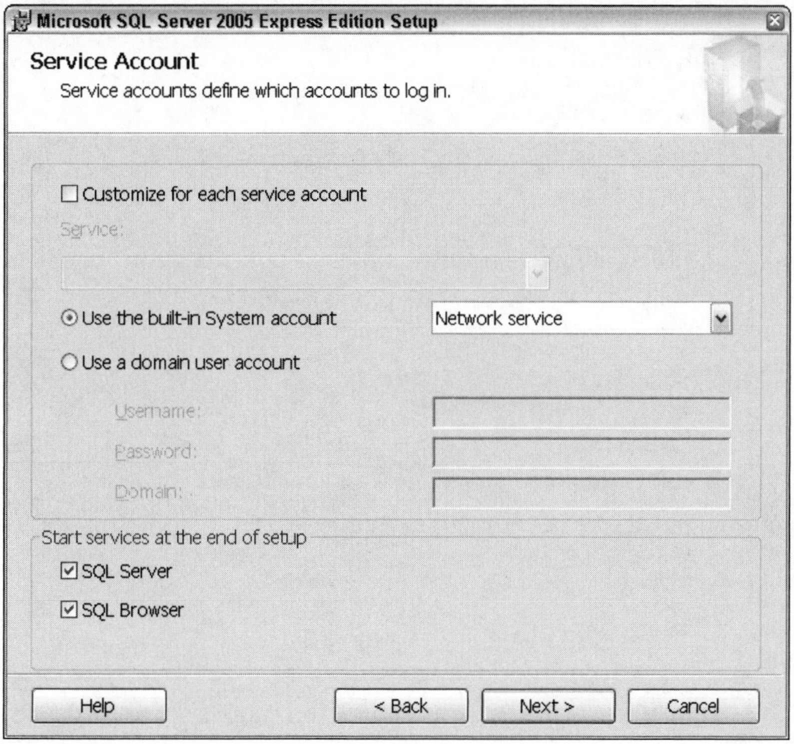

Figure 9-9

By default, SQL Service runs as Network Service in Windows XP and Windows 2003. Network Service is a special low privilege account available on these operating systems.

Windows 2000 does not have a Network Service account, and hence on that operating system, the SQL Server Service defaults to Local System account. Unfortunately, Local System is a high privilege account, and you are advised to specify a local security account that has minimal privileges.

9. Skip this step if you did not change the default value of the Hide advanced configuration check box. The Authentication Mode dialog (see Figure 9-10) allows you to select Mixed Mode Authentication so that your applications can use both Windows and SQL Authentication. Click Next.

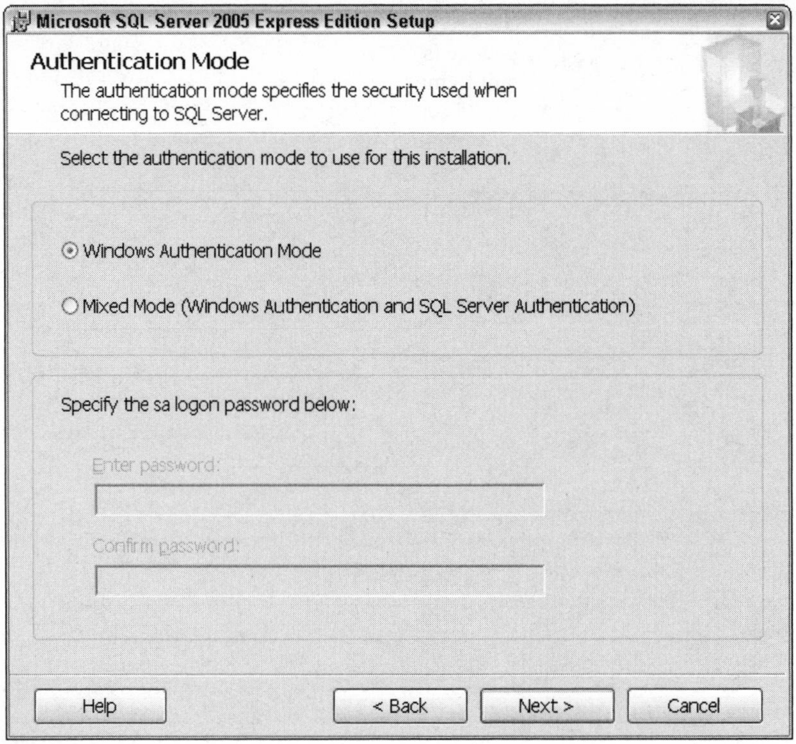

Figure 9-10

Microsoft recommends that you use Windows Authentication by default with your applications. When you select Mixed Mode Authentication, you are required to supply a password for your sa account, which is a special administrator account that is a member of the sysadmin fixed server role. We recommend a strong password that must be at least six characters long and contains a mix of uppercase, lowercase, numbers, and non-alphanumeric characters. Do not use a personal name, a login name, or a machine name as your password.

10. Skip this step if you did not change the default value of the Hide advanced configuration check box. On the Collation Settings page (see Figure 9-11), change the default Collation Designator and Sort Order only if you want to match collation settings in another instance of SQL Server. Select SQL Collations to match the sort order settings in earlier versions of SQL Server. Typically you need not change anything in this dialog. Click Next.

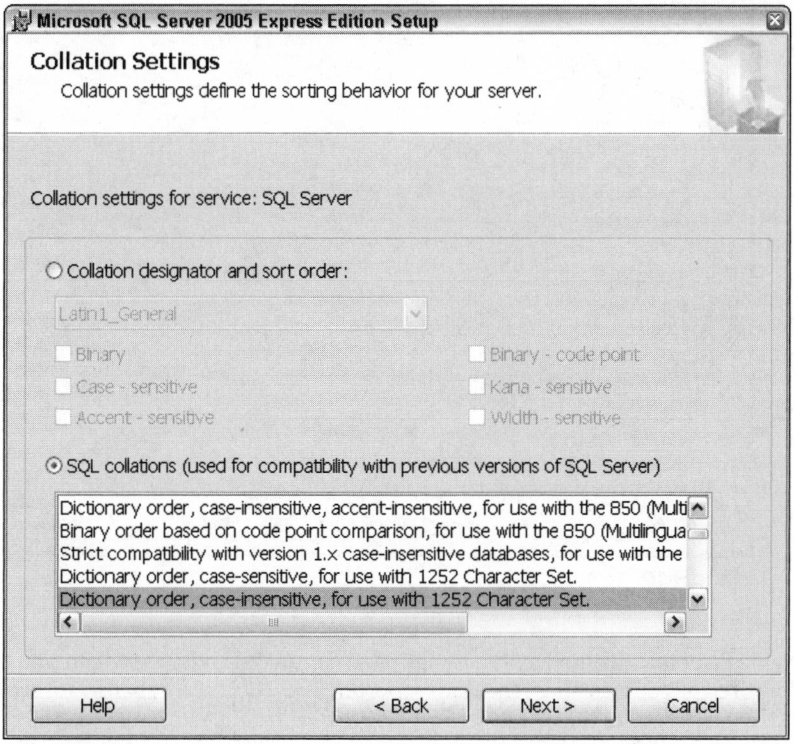

Figure 9-11

11. Skip this step if you did not change the default value of the Hide advanced configuration check box. On the User Instances dialog box (Figure 9-12), the Enable User Instance check box is checked by default. Chapter 6 covers User Instances in detail. Click Next.

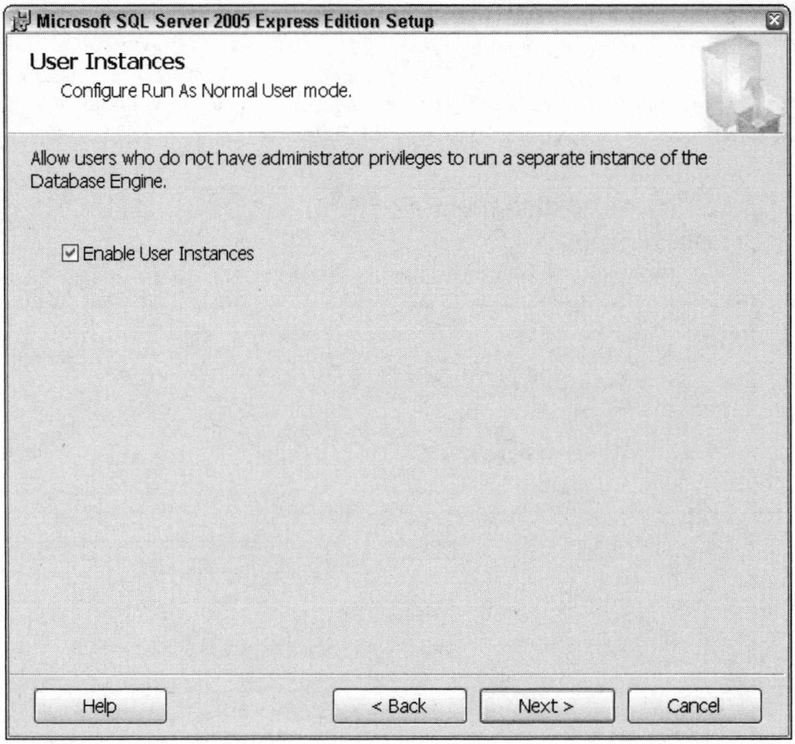

Figure 9-12

12. On the Error and Usage Report Settings page (Figure 9-13) choose whether to turn off the error reporting for your instance. The error reporting is used to report hardware error, program error and feature usage to Microsoft. To turn off error reporting, clear the check box. Typically you do not turn this off. Click Next.

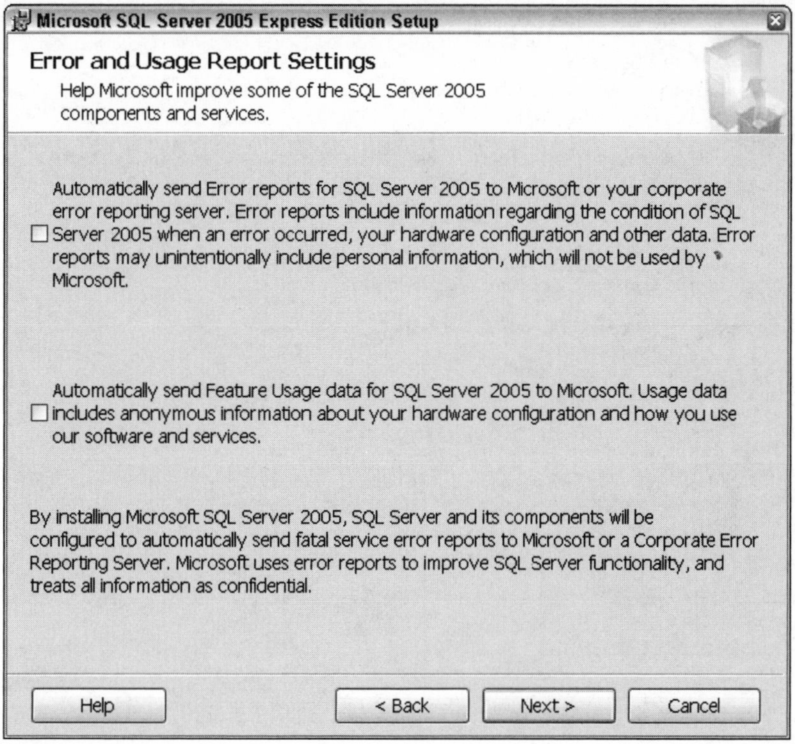

Figure 9-13

13. The Ready to Install dialog (see Figure 9-14) asks for a confirmation to start the installation. At this stage, the Installation Wizard has enough information to begin copying files. Click Install to proceed.

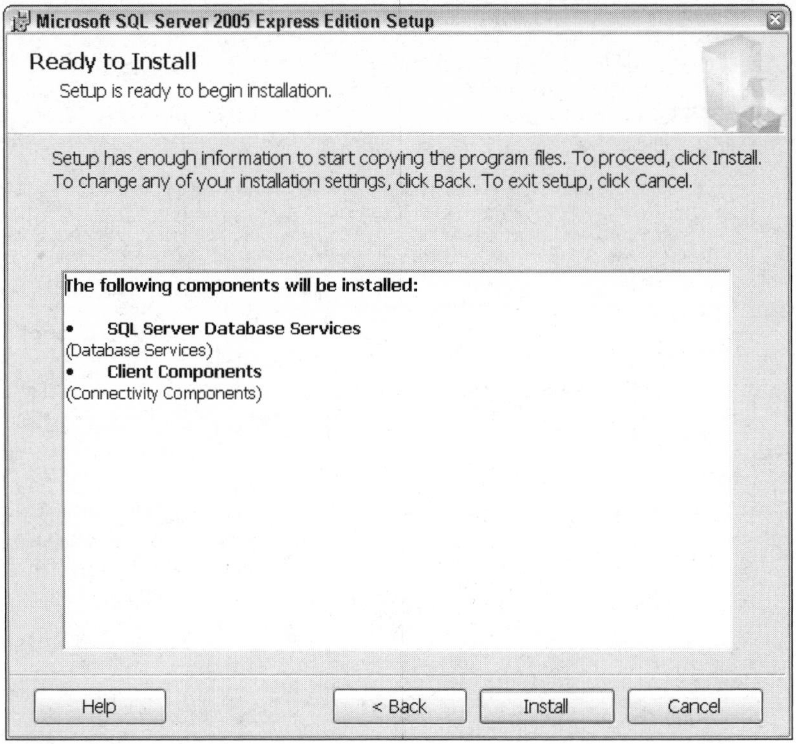

Figure 9-14

Post-Installation Verification

To verify that you have installed SSE correctly, first verify that the SQL Server Services are running. In the Control Panel, double-click Administrative Tools, and then double-click Services. Make sure the service names below are present in the service list, and verify that they are running.

❑ SQL Server (SQLEXPRESS) for a named instance with name SQLEXPRESS or SQL Server (MSSQLSERVER) for a default instance

❑ SQL Server Browser

If you installed SQL Configuration Manager, the setup creates a shortcut for it under All Programs. Go to All Programs ➪ Microsoft SQL Server 2005 ➪ Configuration Tools and click SQL Configuration Manager. Click SQL Server 2005 Services and verify that the state for SQL Server(SQLEXPRESS) service is Running.

Each instance of SSE has its own program files and data files, and it is useful to know where the setup utility installed these files. The Program Files directory structure contains most of the binaries, while the Data folder contains system database and log files, as well as directories for the system log, backup, and replication data. There are also some common files such as shared Tools that are used by all instances on a single computer. The default directories for default and named instances are as follows:

❑   For program files: systemdrive:\Program Files\Microsoft SQL
      Server\MSSQL.n\MSSQL\Binn\

❑   For data files: systemdrive:\Program Files\Microsoft SQL Server\MSSQL.n\MSSQL\Data\

❑   For common files: systemdrive:\Program Files\Microsoft SQL Server\90

MSSQL.n is called an *instance ID*; the variable *n* starts with a value of 1 so that the first instance ID generated will be MSSQL.1. Each subsequent installation of SQL Server 2005 increments the ID number such as MSSQL.2, MSSQL.3, and so on. All editions of SQL Server 2005 follow this naming scheme. The most recently installed instance will always have the highest ID number.

Silently Installing SSE

When trying to install SSE along with an application, you probably want the user to experience the application's setup, but not the SSE setup. You may prefer to totally embed the SSE setup within your application setup to improve the user experience. In this case, it makes sense to do a *silent install* of SSE so that none of the SSE setup graphical user interfaces are shown to the user during its installation. There is no visible indication of the installation progress, including any success or failure information. All status information is written to log files.

Using Command Line Parameters to Install SSE Silently

The SQL Server 2005 Express Edition is available in the web as a compressed exe package that you should extract to a folder before beginning the silent installation. To extract the setup contents to a folder, specify the /x command line option after the compressed exe package name as shown below. You will be prompted to specify a directory for the extracted files. After you enter the destination directory, click OK. The setup.exe is copied to the directory indicated.

```
Sqlexpr.exe /x
```

In the case of a silent install, the user cannot interact with the SSE setup. All the relevant parameters are passed by using command line parameters or ini files. The mandatory parameters for silent install are:

❑   The /qn switch is used to indicate a silent installation. When this is used, no user interface dialog boxes are displayed, even in cases of setup errors or failure. All SSE setup messages including errors are written to setup log files. If you prefer the basic setup graphical user interface, use the /qb switch instead.

❑   SSE requires you to specify the features that you want to install using
      ADDLOCAL=feature_selection. The values that can be used for feature_selection are
      described in the following table, and are case-sensitive. Provide a comma-delimited list of components with no spaces if you are installing multiple components. To install all components, specify ADDLOCAL=ALL. If ADDLOCAL is omitted, setup will fail. Selecting a parent feature only installs the parent feature, while selecting a child feature automatically selects the parent in addition to the child feature. If you are adding features to an existing installation, specify only those features that you are adding.

      For example, to install just the engine, and SQL data files for a default instance, type

```
start /wait setup.exe /qn ADDLOCAL= SQL_Engine, SQL_Data_Files
```

The `start /wait` command returns control to the command prompt only after setup completes.

❑ If you are planning to install a named instance, you should provide the name of the instance using the `INSTANCENAME` parameter. To install a default instance, you need not specify this parameter. Remember that you can only have one default instance per machine.

The following Try It Out shows you how to silently install SSE components.

Try It Out   Silently Install SSE

Open a command prompt window and navigate to the SSE setup directory. Execute one of the following commands:

❑ If you want to install a default unnamed instance of SSE:

```
start /wait setup.exe /qn ADDLOCAL=ALL
```

❑ If you want to install a named instance of SSE called SQLEXPRESS:

```
start /wait setup.exe /qn ADDLOCAL=ALL INSTANCENAME=SQLEXPRESS
```

How It Works

If you want to silently install a default instance of SSE, you should supply two command line parameters to setup.exe. The `/qn` parameter indicates silent mode of installation, while `ADDLOCAL=ALL` tells the setup to select all the feature components in SSE for installation. The instance name is indicated by the value of the `INSTANCENAME` parameter and is used if a default instance of SSE already exists on the machine.

Some commonly used optional parameters are as follows:

❑ **reboot=ReallySuppress** — If you do not want any reboot during the installation of SQL Server Express, you can pass the command line `reboot=ReallySuppress`. This is just a mechanism to delay the reboot so that an application setup does not reboot in the middle of an installation. It is also important that the application setup checks for the return code 3010 and reboots at the end of its installation. Note that this parameter does not prevent the reboot prompt for pending reboots since the pending reboot requirement must be taken care of prior to the start of the installation. The following line shows an example of this parameter:

```
start /wait setup.exe /qn ADDLOCAL=ALL reboot= ReallySuppress
```

❑ **DISABLENETWORKPROTOCOLS={0, 1, 2}** — SSE disables all remote networking protocols such as TCP/IP and Named Pipe by default. If you want to use SSE with MDAC clients on the same machine, the local Named Pipe functionality must be enabled. The reason is that the shared memory protocol, which is used for local connectivity, is not backwards compatible. A value of 2 must be passed to DISABLENETWORKPROTOCOL option as shown below so that your server is secure from remote connections, while at the same time enabling the local Named

Pipes protocol. Thus the legacy clients are able to connect to SSE over local Named Pipe. Use `DISABLENETWORKPROTOCOLS=0` to enable remote TCP/IP and NP protocols. You can also use SQL Server Configuration Manager to change the network settings after installation.

```
start /wait setup.exe /qn ADDLOCAL=ALL DISABLENETWORKPROTOCOLS=2
```

❑ **SECURITYMODE=SQL** — To use the mixed authentication model, you have to use the command line `SECURITYMODE=SQL`. In addition, you should pass a strong password as mentioned earlier for the sa account using the `SAPWD` parameter. The password string specified by this property is hidden and is not written to the log file. In case of Windows Authentication, there is no need to pass the `SAPWD` parameter.

```
start /wait setup.exe /qn ADDLOCAL=ALL SECURITYMODE=SQL SAPWD=<Strong password>
```

❑ **REMOVE=*feature_selection*** — Use `REMOVE=feature_selection` to remove a particular component or subcomponent from an existing installation. The `feature_selection` list is a comma-delimited list containing features listed under `ADDLOCAL`. Removing a parent feature automatically removes the child features. Use the following command to remove the SDK from the default instance.

```
start /wait setup.exe /qn REMOVE=SDK
```

When REMOVE is used as a parameter to setup.exe, there, is no need to pass the otherwise mandatory ADDLOCAL parameter.

The following table contains the setup command line parameters for SSE. The user defined parameters are italicized.

Parameters	Description	Values
ADDLOCAL=*feature_selection* ADDLOCAL=ALL	Allows you to specify the features that will be installed.	No default value.
ALLOWXDBCHAINING={1 | 0}	Turn on or off cross database ownership chaining for all databases. It is recommended that you disable this feature.	0 (Default) means disable cross database ownership chaining 1 is used to enable cross database ownership chaining. This value is not recommended for security reasons.
COMPANYNAME= *CompanyName*	Specifies the name for the company registering this product.	If this property is omitted, the company name for the operating system is used.
COLLATION=*Collation_name*	Allows you to specify the SQL Server collation.	The default collation is the collation used by the system.

Table continued on following page

Parameters	Description	Values
DISABLENETWORK PROTOCOLS={0 | 1 | 2}	Allows you to enable or disable the networking protocols.	Networking is disabled by default (value of 1).
	0 means Shared memory (SM), TCP/IP and Named Pipe (NP) is enabled.	
	1 (default) means SM is enabled while TCP/IP and NP are disabled.	
	2 means Local only named pipe is enabled in addition to shared memory. TCP/IP is disabled.	
ERRORREPORTING={1 | 0}	Allows you to enable or disable error reporting.	Error reporting is turned off by default for unattended setup. Use ERRORREPORTING=1 to enable, and ERRORREPORTING=0 to disable error reporting.
INSTANCENAME=*Instance_name*	Allows you to specify the name of the instance. If this property is omitted, the instance is installed as a default instance.	The default instance for SSE MSSQLSERVER.
INSTALLSQLDATADIR=*Dir_location*	Folder containing system database files. For all path-related parameters, a trailing backslash (\) is required.	By default the files get installed to a directory under %systemdrive%:\Program Files\Microsoft SQL Server\...\Data\.
INSTALLSQLDIR=*Dir_location*	Folder containing executable files. For all path-related parameters, a trailing backslash (\) is required.	By default, the files get installed to a directory under %systemdrive%:\Program Files\Microsoft SQL Server\...\Binn\.
LOGNAME=*File_name*	Specifies the name of the log file.	The default file name is SqlSetup<XXXX>.cab.
LOGPATH=*File_location*	Specifies the location of the log files.	If this property is omitted, setup will write log files to ...\Setup Bootstrap\Log\Files\...

Parameters	Description	Values
REINSTALL=ALL	Allows you to install all previously installed SSE features. This property must always be used with REINSTALLMODE.	The only value supported for this property is ALL.
REINSTALLMODE= { omus | amus }	Allows you to specify the level of processing performed by SSE setup.	Use REINSTALLMODE= omus when resuming a failed setup. With this option, the entire installation is verified and completed. This also rebuilds the registry for a corrupted Microsoft SSE installation.
		Use REINSTALLMODE= amus to rebuild the system databases; for example, to change the server collation or to rebuild the master database after a hard drive failure.
REMOVE=*feature_selection* REMOVE=ALL	Allows you to specify the features that will be removed from an existing installation. The feature_selection list is a comma-delimited list containing features listed under ADDLOCAL, which is described in the feature selection table earlier in this chapter.	No default value.
SAPWD=*sa_pwd*	Allows you to specify the sa password for use with the SECURITYMODE= SQL property.	No default value.
SAVESYSDB	This option is used during uninstall and a value of 1 prevents deletion of the system databases.	Default value is 0.
SECURITYMODE=SQL	Allows you to configure the installed instance to use SQL Server Authentication.	If this property is omitted, setup will use Windows Authentication.

Table continued on following page

Parameters	Description	Values
SQLACCOUNT=*domain\ login_name* SQLBROWSERACCOUNT =*domain\login_name*	Specifies the SQL Server or SQLBrowser service account domain and logon name. Some typical values include NT AUTHORITY\NETWORK SERVICE and NT AUTHORITY\ LOCAL SERVICE.	The default SQL Server service account is Network Service for XP and Windows 2003 operating systems. For Windows 2000, Local System is used as the service account.
SQLPASSWORD=*password* SQLBROWSERPASSWORD =*password*	Allows you to specify the SQL Server or SQL Browser service account password that corresponds to the logon name specified by SQLACCOUNT or SQLBROWSERACCOUNT respectively.	No default value.
SQLAUTOSTART={1 | 0} SQLBROWSERAUTOSTART ={0 | 1}	Indicates whether the SQL Server or the SQL Browser service starts automatically when the Windows operating system restarts.	You should specify a value of 1 to enable or 0 to disable the automatic start. By default, the automatic start is enabled.
SQMREPORTING={0 | 1}	Indicates whether the feature usage is reported periodically to Microsoft.	By default the value is 0 and the feature usage is not reported.
UPGRADE	Allows you to specify the product to upgrade. The common value for SQL Express installations is SQL_Engine.	No default value.
USESYSDB	This option is used during new installations to specify the location of the system databases. Typically these files were left because of a previous uninstall that used the SAVESYSDB option.	No default value.
USERNAME=*UserName*	Specifies the name for the user registering this product.	If this property is omitted, setup will use the user name for the operating system.
/qn, /qb	Switch for silent install. /qb shows basic UI-like progress bar, while /qn does not show any UI at all.	No additional values passed.
/?	Lists the command line parameters for setup.exe.	No additional values passed.

Using INI Files to Install SSE

An ini file can be used to pass configuration parameters to setup.exe When you have to run SSE setup on multiple machines with similar configuration, using an ini file is preferred over command line parameters. You can use the `/settings ini_file` argument to indicate to setup.exe that an ini file is used instead of passing all the parameters through the command line.

The following example illustrates the format of the ini file and shows the use of some of the database engine arguments. Note that the first line in the ini file consists of the header `[Options]`.

```
[Options]
USERNAME=Joe
COMPANYNAME=JoeComputerGarage
INSTALLSQLDIR="C:\Program Files\Microsoft SQL Server\"
INSTALLSQLDATADIR="C:\Program Files\Microsoft SQL Server\"
ADDLOCAL=ALL
INSTANCENAME=JoeInstance
SQLAUTOSTART=1
```

The following Try It Out shows you how to use an ini file to install SSE.

Try It Out   Using an ini File to Install a Default SSE Instance

1. Open Notepad and type the following code. Specify your name and your company name for the variables *MyName and MyCompanyName*. Save the file as `DefaultSSEIni.ini`.

```
[Options]
USERNAME=MyName
COMPANYNAME=MyCompanyName
ADDLOCAL=ALL
```

2. Open a command prompt window and navigate to the SSE setup directory. Execute the following to start SSE setup.

```
start /wait Setup.exe /qn /settings DefaultSSEIni.ini
```

How It Works

Because you are installing a default instance, the only mandatory parameter to be passed is `ADDLOCAL=ALL`. However, it is a good practice to pass the username and company name to the SSE installation. These parameters are saved to the ini file and passed to setup.exe using `/settings ini_file` argument. The `/qn` switch is used to install SSE silently.

Understanding Log Files and Dealing with Setup Errors

The log files are very useful for understanding the status of the installation, especially if there is an error during silent installation. They are created by default, and there is no need to specify any extra command line parameters. By default, the log files can be found in the %PROGRAMFILES%\Microsoft Sql Server\90\Setup Bootstrap\log\ directory. Since this is a directory shared by all editions of SQL Server 2005 instances, the log file names are uniquely numbered (denoted by [XXXX]). For summary information, look at the summary.txt in the directory. The log files are named as SQLSetup[XXXX][s]_ [Machine]_[Feature].log where [Machine] denotes the machine name, and the [Feature] could be values such as Core, MSXML6_1, SCC, SQL, SQLNCLI_1, SQLSupport, Tools, etc.

> *As a rule of thumb, to find the errors you can search the log files for "return value 3" starting at the end of the file.*

In the case of a silent installation, the application setup takes care of propagating the success and failure information about the SSE installation to the user. You can use the return value from the SSE setup.exe in this case. The two common error codes are:

❑ 0 — indicates that the installation is successful.

❑ 3010 — indicates that a reboot is required.

Detecting SSE Programmatically

It is typical for application setup programs to detect whether the proper version of SSE is already installed on the machine. This is done to determine if the application setup can skip the install of SSE. The detection can easily be done two ways:

1. The T-SQL Statement `Select SERVERPROPERTY('ENGINEEDITION')` returns a value of 4 for SSE.

2. The SQL Server 2005 WMI provider has a class called `ServerInstance` object, and from that you can get the instance name, the version, and edition information. If you are a non-administrator on the machine, you need to have extra privileges to use this object.

The following Try It Out lets you practice the first method of detecting whether SSE is already installed.

Try It Out   Using a T-SQL Statement to Detect an Installed SSE Instance

Follow these steps to determine whether SSE is already installed:

1. Open SSMS-EE and connect to the instance you just installed using the appropriate user ID and password.

2. Using the Query Editor, type the following at the command prompt:

```
Select SERVERPROPERTY('ENGINEEDITION'), SERVERPROPERTY('EDITION'),
SERVERPROPERTY('INSTANCENAME')
```

How It Works

You learned how to use the SSMS-EE query editor in Chapter 2. In this example, you are running the T-SQL statement against the instance that you installed in the previous Try It Out. If the return value that you get is 4 for the ENGINEEDITION property, then the instance is SSE. Similarly, SSE returns a value of Express Edition for the EDITION property.

Adding or Removing SSE 2005 Features

You can add or remove individual features in an instance of SSE 2005 by running the SSE setup from the CD or clicking Change under Add or Remove Programs. You can also add or remove features from the command prompt using ADDLOCAL and REMOVE parameters described earlier. You should use the ADDLOCAL property to specify features to add to an instance of SSE; use the REMOVE property to specify features to remove.

The following Try It Out shows you how to use Add or Remove Programs or the command line to add the Replication feature to an installed instance of SSE.

Try It Out   **Add Replication feature to SQLExpress SSE Instance**

To remove replication from your SSE instance, execute the following steps:

1. In Control Panel, double-click the Add or Remove Programs icon.

2. Under Currently Installed Programs, click the product listed as Microsoft SQL Server 2005 Express Edition and then click Change.

3. In the Component Selection dialog, select the instance you want to update (see Figure 9-15) and click Next.

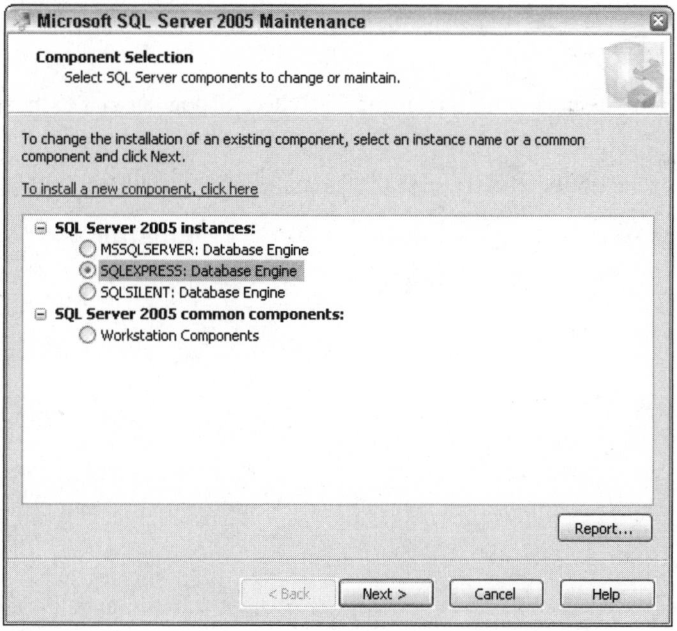

Figure 9-15

4. Select Database Engine in the Feature Maintenance dialog as shown in Figure 9-16.

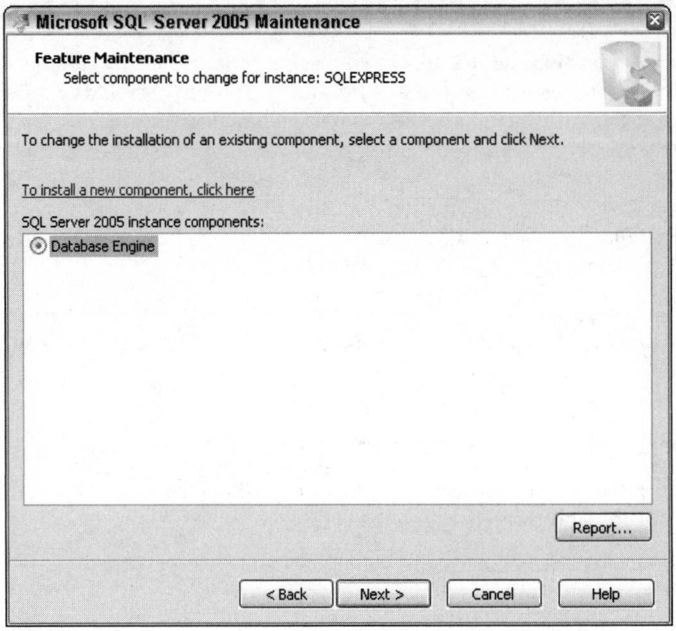

Figure 9-16

5. You will now see a welcome screen and SCC check dialogs similar to the dialogs for new installs.

6. On the Change or Remove Instance page, click Change Installed Components as shown in Figure 9-17.

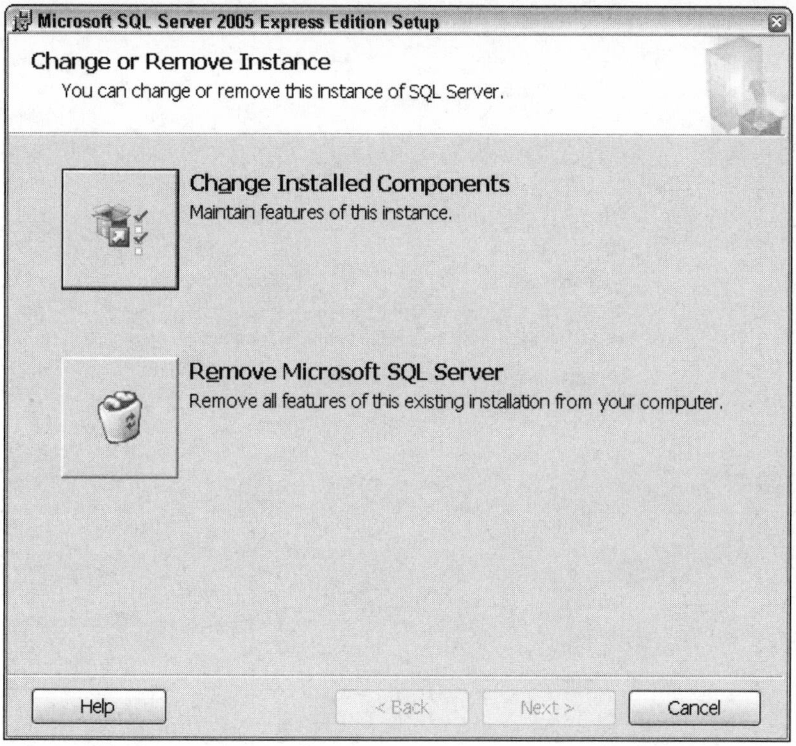

Figure 9-17

7. On the Feature Selection page, right-click the Replication entry under SQL Server Database Services. Select the Will be Installed on local hard drive option (see Figure 9-18) so that the X mark is no longer seen against that entry. Click Next.

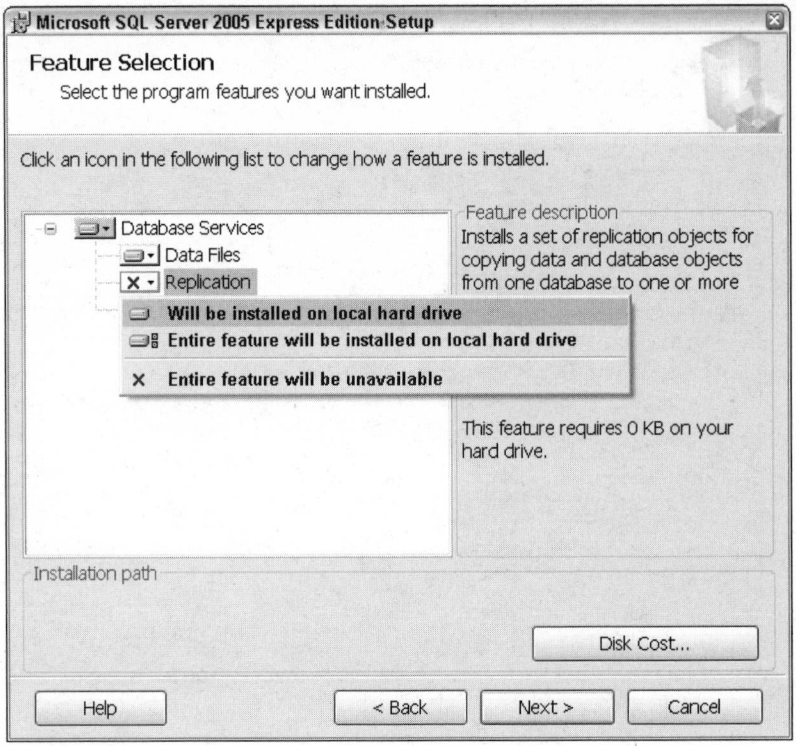

Figure 9-18

8. Click Install in the ready to install page to begin the installation.

Alternatively, you can use the following command line parameter to add replication:

```
start /wait setup.exe /qn ADDLOCAL=SQL_Replication
```

How It Works

You are using the Add or Remove Programs in the control panel to add the replication feature from the default SSE instance. In the Feature Selection page, any feature that is not currently installed will have an X mark next to it. Make sure Replication does not have this mark before clicking Next, so that the feature will be installed as part of setup.

The command line demonstrates the use of ADDLOCAL for performing the same operation silently.

If you installed SSE from a web download, you need an extra step for maintenance and repair. You should manually extract the SSE installation sources from the web download package using the command line switch /x to a local directory. Now follow the steps above using Add or Remove Programs. When the setup prompts for the location of the original sources, you should point it to the local directory. This additional step is required because maintenance and repair requires the use of original sources.

Uninstalling SSE

You can use Add or Remove Programs in Control Panel to remove an instance of Microsoft SSE, or do so from the command line. When you remove an instance of SSE, the instance-specific program files, data files, and registry keys are deleted. Even after SSE is uninstalled, some files that are shared by multiple instances, such as tools, may remain. These cannot be removed until all instances of SSE have been removed. To remove all instances of SSE, each instance must be removed individually.

The following Try It Out shows you how to uninstall SSE using the Add or Remove Programs window.

Try It Out   **Uninstalling the SSE Named Instance called SQLEXPRESS Using Add or Remove Programs**

To remove SSE using Add or Remove Programs, follow these steps:

1. Open Control Panel and Select Add or Remove Programs.

2. Under Currently Installed Programs, click the product listed as Microsoft SQL Server 2005 Express Edition and then click Remove.

3. In the Component Selection dialog, select the SQLEXPRESS instance (see Figure 9-19) and click Next. Select Workstation Components if this is the only instance of SQL Server 2005 or SSE on your computer.

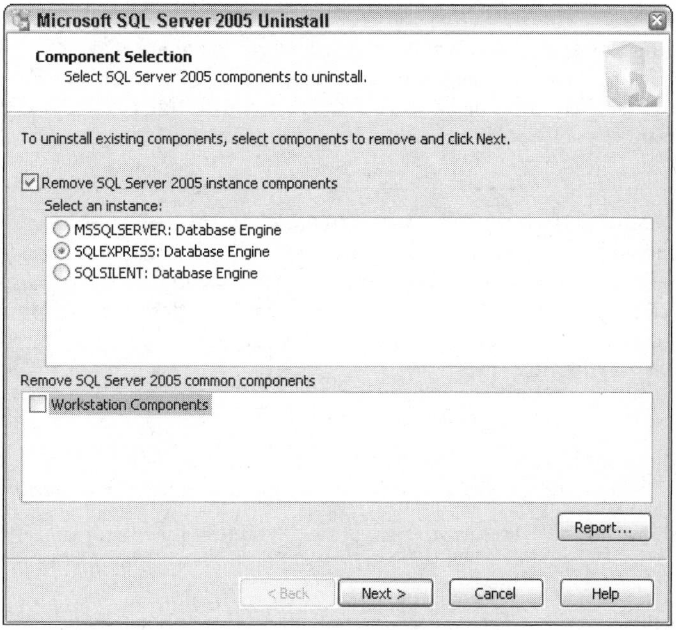

Figure 9-19

4. Click Finish in the Confirmation dialog to start the uninstall process. The components selected for uninstall are listed in the dialog as shown in Figure 9-20.

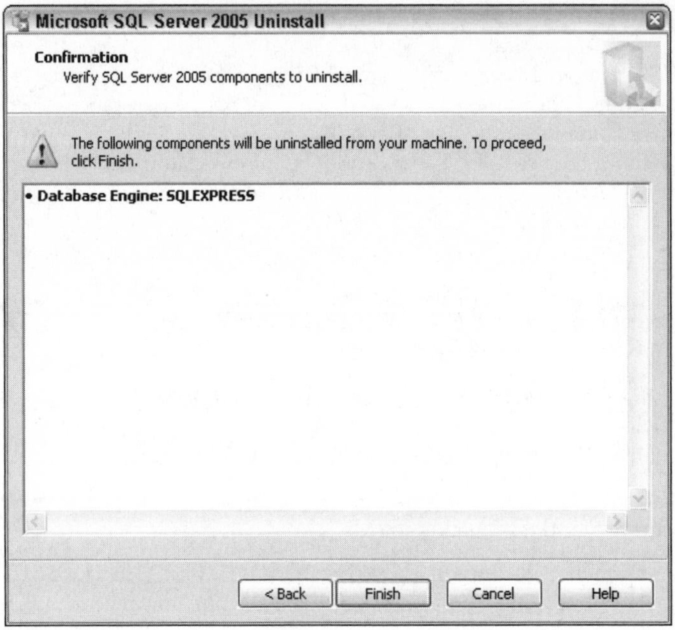

Figure 9-20

5. This is an optional step and is followed only if you have removed all the instances of SQL Server 2005 or SSE on your local machine. Select Microsoft SQL Server 2005 Setup Support Files under Currently Installed programs and click the Remove button. Click Yes in the Windows Installer dialog that asks you for confirmation.

> **All instances of SQL Server 2005 and Tools must be uninstalled before uninstalling SQL Support files. Failure to do this will break future installations, and the fix is to reinstall SQL Support files. SQL Support files warn you if you try to uninstall it before all editions of SQL Server 2005 are uninstalled. If you uninstall all SQL (engine) instances and Tools, SQL Server 2005 setup will uninstall the SQL Support files automatically.**

6. Select Microsoft SQL Native Client under Currently Installed programs and click the Remove button. Click Yes in the Windows Installer dialog that asks you for confirmation.

7. Select Microsoft .NET Framework 2.0 under Currently Installed programs and click the Remove button. Click Yes in the Windows Installer dialog that asks you for confirmation.

.NET Framework is used by other applications, including Visual Studio. If any application using .NET Framework is installed on the machine, skip this step.

How It Works

The Add or Remove Programs exposes a Remove button for all the products that are installed on the machine. In the preceding example, you are uninstalling all the files that form part of the SSE installation. You have to uninstall in exactly the sequence listed above to be successful. For instance, if you uninstall .NET Framework before uninstalling SSE, the SSE setup will not work.

Not all steps need to be done if you have multiple instances of SSE on the machine. For instance, the Setup Support files, SQL Native Client, and .NET Framework are used by all the SSE instances. Hence, steps 5 to 7 should be done only when you uninstall the last SSE instance on your machine.

The following Try It Out shows you how to uninstall SSE using command line parameters.

Try It Out   **Uninstalling the SSE Named Instance SQLEXPRESS via the Command Prompt**

Open a command prompt window and navigate to the SSE setup directory. Execute the following commands from the command prompt:

1. To remove all SSE 2005 components, type

```
start /wait setup.exe /qn REMOVE=ALL INSTANCENAME=SQLEXPRESS
```

2. To remove Microsoft SQL Native Client, type

```
msiexec /qn /X <CD Drive>\Setup\sqlncli.msi
```

3. To remove the Microsoft NET Framework 2.0, type

```
redist\2.0\dotnetfx.exe /q:a /c:"install /qu"
```

How It Works

In the first step, the REMOVE=ALL command line parameter is used to remove all components installed by SSE. The instance name of SQLEXPRESS is specified by the INSTANCENAME parameter. Since the SQL Support Files automatically get removed after the last instance of SSE is uninstalled, there is no special mention about it. The SQL Native Client and the .NET Framework should be removed only after all the applications using it are uninstalled.

Summary

SSE supports both Graphical User Interface (GUI) and silent installations. This chapter walked you through the steps required for a successful installation, and discussed the appropriateness of using the silent install during application setup. Equally important is choosing the correct settings for networking and authentication. We also covered adding and removing features as well as uninstalling the product.

In this chapter, you learned to

❑   Install a default instance or named instance of SSE using setup dialogs

❑   Install a default instance or named instance of SSE using command line parameters and ini files

❑   Specify appropriate values for networking and authentication during installation

❑   Add or remove features such as replication to an existing instance using Add or Remove Programs or command line parameters

❑   Uninstall a default or named instance of SSE using Add or Remove Programs or command line parameters

In the next chapter, you learn more about using ClickOnce installation to deploy SSE along with your applications.

Exercises

Try the exercises that follow to test your understanding of the material covered in this chapter. You can find the solutions to these exercises in Appendix A.

1.   You are the IT department head for Joe's Garage, and the Director of Marketing asks you to install SSE on his new desktop machine. You found out that he wants a named instance called SalesDBServer, and he wants to access the database server from his laptop using TCP/IP. The director wants to use the Sales Application with this instance, and you found out that the Sales Application uses SQL Authentication. The component features that the director wants installed include SQL Engine, SQL Data Files, Replication, Client Components, Connectivity, and SDK. What steps would you follow to install SSE on his machine? Assume that the director wants you to explain the setup dialogs to him while you do the installation.

2.   There are 10 marketing personnel in your company, and all of them want to install SSE using the same specifications as listed in Exercise 1. What command line parameters would you use to do a silent installation?

3.   The Director of Marketing wants to remove replication his SSE instance. Explain how you will do this with the setup dialogs. How will you proceed if you can use setup command line parameters?

4.   Explain how you will uninstall SSE from Joe's machine. You know that Joe uses the Visual Basic Express from the book CD and he does not plan to uninstall it.

10

Deploying Your Application

When you build an application, one hurdle you face is how you deploy it. As you saw in Chapter 6 on Xcopy deploying your application, you can simply copy the application. But if you have hundreds of users, this isn't a good option. If you have built a web application, this is not a problem: Users can simply connect to your website. However, if you have built a rich client application using Visual Basic, you face a deployment challenge. Fortunately, Microsoft has made this task much easier by introducing a new feature called ClickOnce. ClickOnce is the name of a deployment option that enables end-users to download your rich client application with a single click. This makes getting your application as easy for users as navigating to a website. It turns out that when you write your code against the Microsoft .NET Framework, the amount of code necessary for your application to run becomes quite small, so distributing it across the web is a viable solution. Further, keeping your application up-to-date with updates via the web is also possible. In addition to your application, you need to get the .NET Framework and SSE on the user's desktop somehow. Fortunately, ClickOnce allows for this as well.

In this chapter, you learn to:

❑   Deploy your application via ClickOnce

❑   Update your application via ClickOnce

To use ClickOnce, you need all the software you've been using for the projects in this book, such as SSE and VB Express. You also need the following:

❑   A computer running Windows Professional XP SP2 or higher that you can use as a website

❑   Internet Information Services (IIS) turned on for that computer

With a machine capable of website deployment that you can connect to from your development machine, you are ready to go.

Deploying Your Application

Safe deployment of rich client applications is a key goal of ClickOnce. You can take any of the rich client applications that you have built in previous chapters (MyFirstApp or MasterDetail) and deploy them via ClickOnce. For testing purposes, you may want to use your development machine to test out the ClickOnce functionality. To do that, however, you have to first make sure that IIS is running properly, as in the following Try It Out. (Note: the home edition of Microsoft Windows does not support IIS. You must use a higher Windows edition such as Windows XP Professional.)

Try It Out   Enabling IIS on Your Machine

To enable your machine for IIS, follow these steps:

1. Bring up your Internet browser (such as Microsoft Internet Explorer) and type **http://localhost** to initiate an attempt to connect to the local IIS service on your machine. If IIS is running, you will connect to your local machine and it will display some content. If IIS is not running, you will get a "The page cannot be displayed" error. If IIS is not running, continue with the following steps.

2. From the Start menu, select Control Panel ⇨ Add or Remove Programs to bring up the control panel.

3. On the left-hand side of the control panel, select Add/Remove Windows Components. This will show the Windows Component Wizard with a list of Windows services that have been enabled.

4. View the Internet Information Services (IIS) component. If it is not selected, proceed with steps 6 and higher. If it is already selected, you should have connectivity at this point, provided you enabled IIS *before* you installed Visual Basic Express. If you enabled IIS *after* you installed Visual Basic Express, follow steps 6 and higher. If you do not have connectivity, and IIS is selected, you have a problem with the way Windows is installed or configured.

    If you are using Windows Server 2003, the steps are slightly different. Look for Application Server. It should be enabled. The IIS component is nested inside of the Application Server component.

5. Enable the check box for the IIS component and click OK. This will enable IIS for your machine with the default options. If you select Details at the bottom of the dialog, you can see the other options available to you while running IIS.

    You enable the check box for the Application Server component if you are using Windows Server 2003.

    Because you are only now enabling IIS, and VB Express has previously been installed, you will also need to enable Visual Studio to work with IIS.

6. Go to Start ⇨ Run and type **CMD** to bring up a command window.

7. Type **dir /s aspnet_regiis.exe** and press Enter. This will locate the directory in which the regiis command is located. Find the command from the 2.0 version of the framework. It should be in a directory named something like: `C:\windows\Microsoft.Net\Framework\v2.0.<some number>`.

8. In the command window, navigate to that directory (type **cd c:\windows\microsoft.net\ framework\v2.0.<*somenumber*>** and press Enter.

9. Once in the directory, type **aspnet_regiis –i** and press Enter. This will install ASP.NET 2.0 and update the script maps, enabling Visual Basic Express to work with IIS.

How It Works

IIS is the service that enables you to host a website. There are a lot of options that must be configured just right to get things going. The default settings don't quite work for ASP.NET, so the key thing here is that ASP.NET must be configured to work with IIS. When you install Visual Basic Express, if IIS is already running, the Visual Basic Express install program configures ASP.NET appropriately. However, if IIS is not running, the Visual Basic install program will not turn on IIS for you automatically. That is a machine configuration you must make manually. So, if IIS was not running, you must take specific steps to get things running right.

Now with IIS running and Visual Basic Express configured to work with it, you are ready to publish your application to a local IIS server.

Your next step is to deploy your application, as shown in the following Try It Out.

Try It Out   **Publishing Your Application**

To publish the MasterDetail application, follow these steps:

1. Open the MasterDetail project and build the application. Choose Build ⇨ Build MasterDetail from the menu.

2. From the menu, choose Build ⇨ Publish. This will bring up the Publish Wizard, as shown in Figure 10-1. By default, the wizard will appear with the localhost IIS site and a directory for MasterDetail. Note that this may take a while. Watch the lower left-hand corner of the window to see the progress.

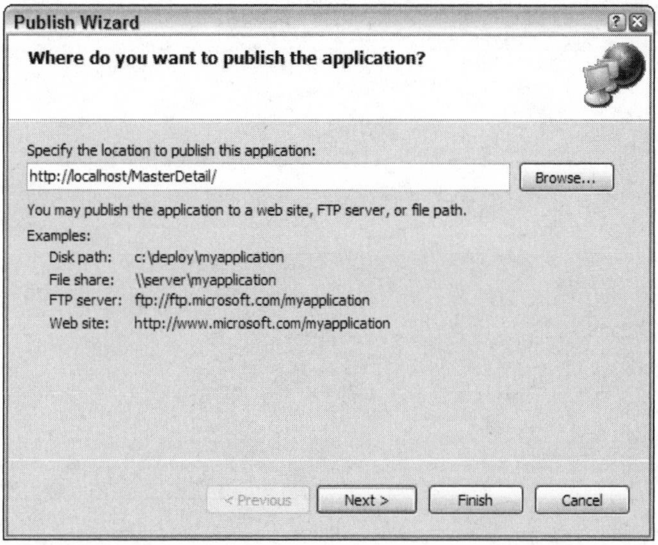

Figure 10-1

3. In the next step of the wizard, indicate that the application will be available both online and offline, as shown in Figure 10-2. This choice means that sometimes the application will have an Internet connection and sometimes it will not. Click Next to continue.

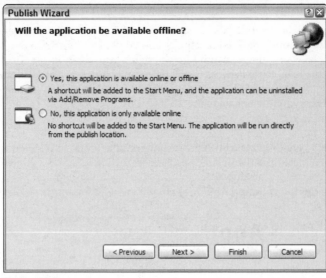

Figure 10-2

4.   Click Finish. This will bring up an Internet Explorer with an Install web page for the deployed MasterDetail, as shown in Figure 10-3.

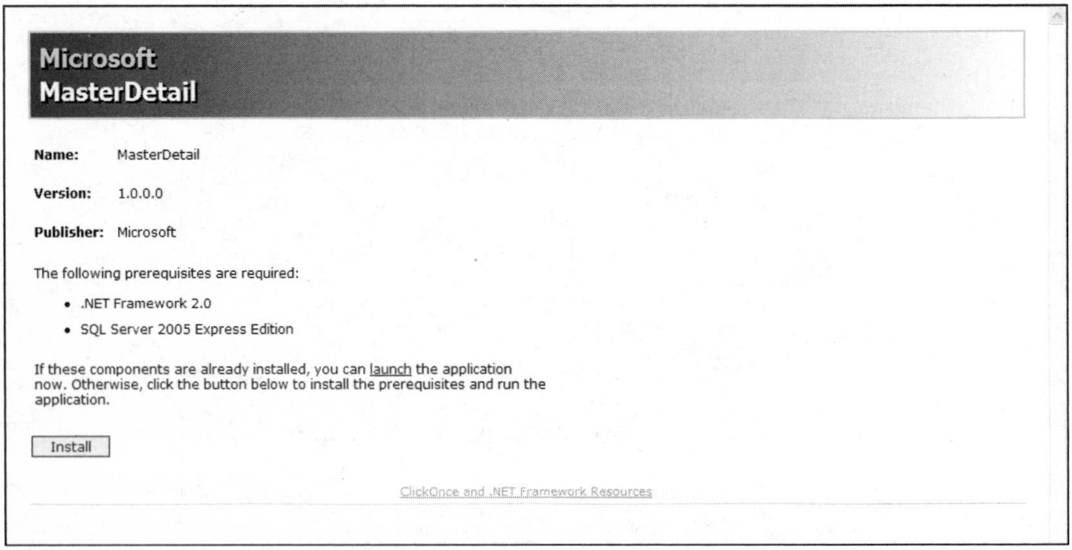

Microsoft
MasterDetail

Name: MasterDetail

Version: 1.0.0.0

Publisher: Microsoft

The following prerequisites are required:

- .NET Framework 2.0
- SQL Server 2005 Express Edition

If these components are already installed, you can launch the application now. Otherwise, click the button below to install the prerequisites and run the application.

Install

ClickOnce and .NET Framework Resources

Figure 10-3

5.   On the Install web page, click the Install button and then choose to run the application. This will install the application on your machine.

How It Works

Note that after you install your application, you can run it by choosing Start ⇨ All Programs ⇨ Microsoft ⇨ MasterDetail. It's right there on your Start menu, ready to go. Also, MasterDetail now shows up in your Add or Remove Programs list. The user can easily uninstall your application. (The application appears under Microsoft in the All Programs list by default; you can change it if you prefer.)

If you run the application a few times, note that whenever you start up the application, it looks around for updates. And, with the way it's currently configured, it will still run if not connected to the Internet.

But the experience probably seems a little less than satisfying. Do you really want your application hanging off of the All Programs menu list under Microsoft? Probably not. Fortunately, there is a way to configure and update your application.

Updating Your Application

There are a number of options you can set for ClickOnce. It's a complex area with lots of choices. Those choices are set in the project options page. Not only can you set publish options in the project options page, you can set the start up form, digitally sign the project, change the assembly name, and so on.

Try It Out   **Setting Your Publication Options**

To set your publication options, follow these steps:

1. Open the MasterDetail project and build the application. Choose Build ⇨ Build MasterDetail from the menu.

2. From the menu, choose Project and the MasterDetail properties (at the bottom). This will bring up the properties for the application.

3. On the left-hand side of the application properties, choose the Publish tab as shown in Figure 10-4.

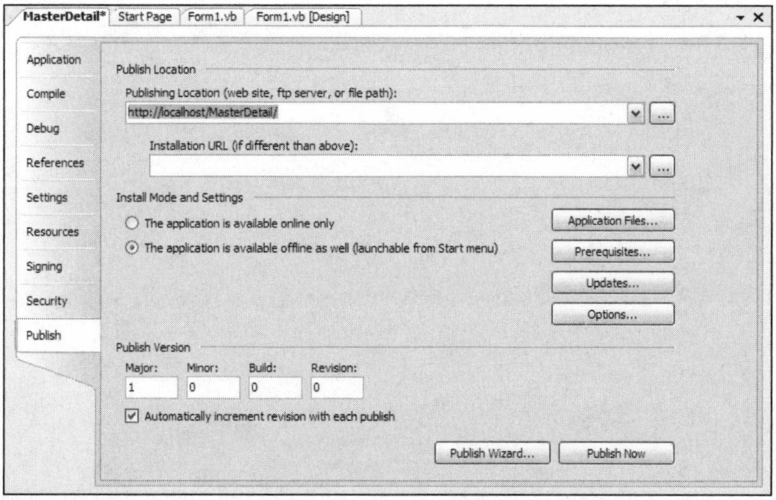

Figure 10-4

4. Click the Updates button to open the Application Updates dialog.

5. In the Application Updates dialog, select the option to allow the application to check for updates "After the application starts" (see Figure 10-5) and click OK to close the dialog. This will allow the application to launch faster. Checking for updates will happen in the background.

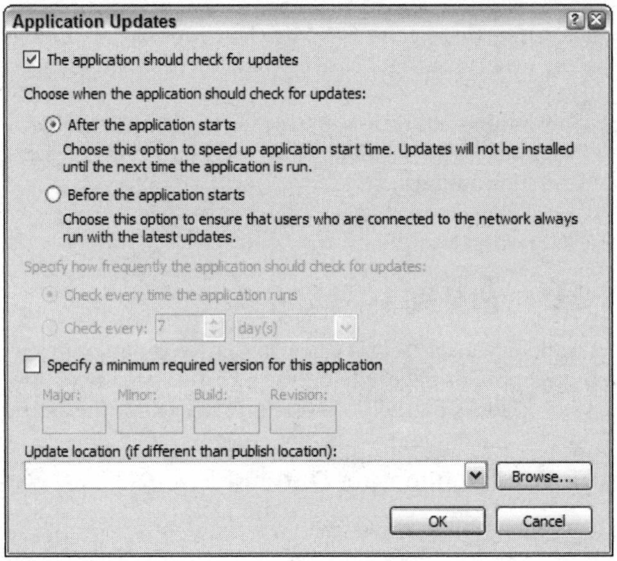

Figure 10-5

6. Click the Options button to open the Publish Options dialog.

7. In the Publish Options dialog, change the Publisher name to a fictitious name such as FamousPeopleCorp and the Product name to Famous People, as shown in Figure 10-6. Click OK to close the dialog.

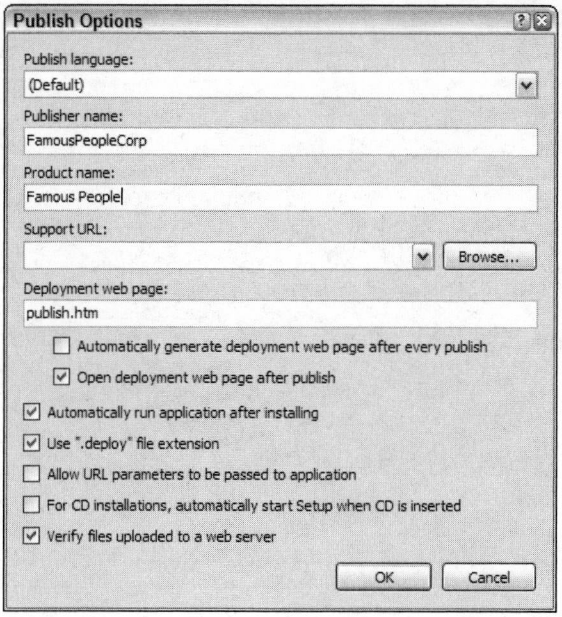

Figure 10-6

8. Click the Application Files button to bring up the Application Files dialog.

9. In the Application Files dialog, change the Publish Status of MyDB.mdf and MyDB_log.ldf to Data File, as shown in Figure 10-7. Click OK to close the dialog.

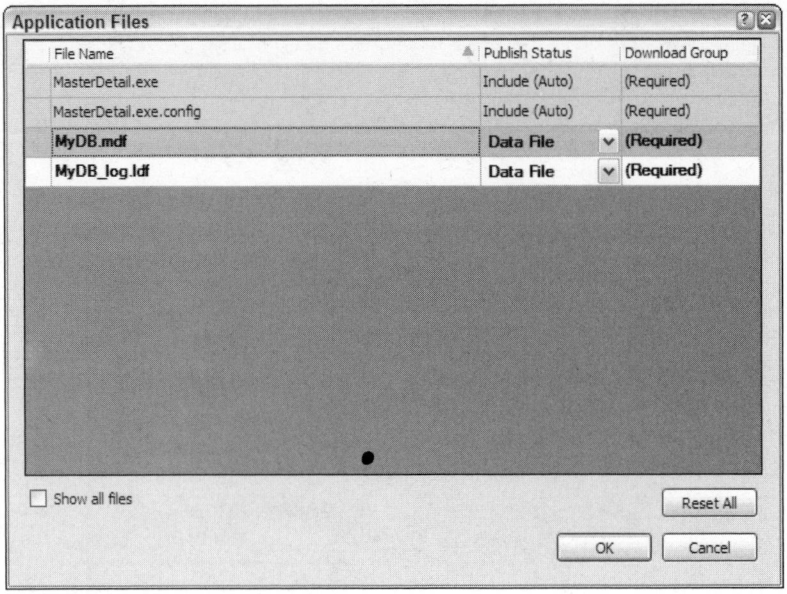

Figure 10-7

How It Works

Note that with the changes to the Publisher and Product names, the application now shows up under FamousPeopleCorp and Famous People on the All Programs menu. If you start the application a second time, you will see that the application starts up faster as well, because it does not go online first to check for updates. You can choose Publish Now (in the lower right-hand corner of the property page) and get the same results as if you had chosen Build ➪ Publish from the top-level menu. There are a lot of choices you can make in this property page area. In the Application Files dialog, you choose which specific files should be treated as Data Files. You can also choose for them to be excluded.

If you choose prerequisites, you can choose whether the prerequisites should be downloaded from the component vendor's site (the default), or whether you want to point them to a specific site or the same site as your application. This would be useful if you are working for a corporation and have an internal site for such applications.

When you installed MasterDetail, ClickOnce checked to see if SSE and the .NET framework were installed on the machine. If not, ClickOnce will prompt you to install them first. It's important to understand that both the .NET framework and SSE require that the user have full administrative rights to install. The .NET Framework is installed into the Windows directory, which is available for all applications. SSE is installed into its own application directory; however, it runs as a service, locally, that is available to all applications. So, both programs require administrative rights.

As a reminder, your application, the actual code that accesses both the .NET framework and SSE, does not require administrative rights for installation. You can both install it and run it as a normal user. Therefore, once someone has both the .NET Framework and SSE on their machine, they can install other applications that use those without needing administrative rights.

If you click the Security tab on the left side of the Properties page (see Figure 10-8), you can see what kind of trust an application may request. By default, an application is published as full trust, meaning the user trusts your application to do the right thing. The user is giving you full trust. SSE needs full trust because it needs the ability to write to disk.

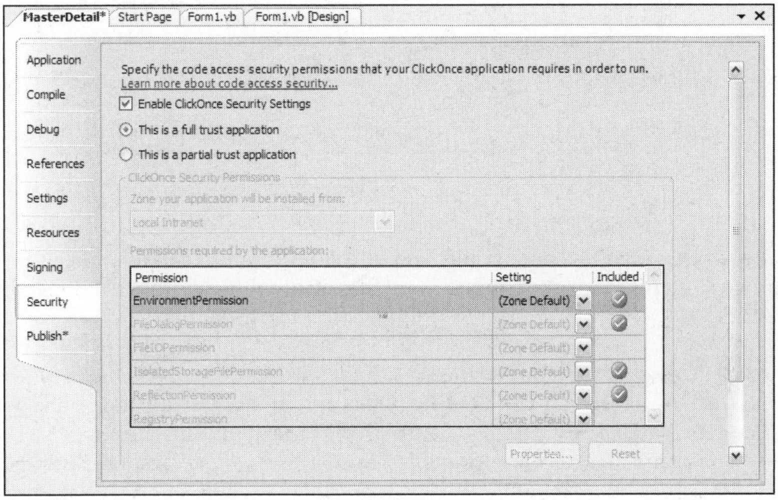

Figure 10-8

If a user only partially trusts you, he might be willing to run your application as long as you don't do certain things, like write to disk, write to the registry, and so on. Partial trust applications are safer for users because they can do less damage. They are also less powerful in providing a rich client experience.

With your publication options set, you are now ready to republish your application, as shown in the following example.

Try It Out   **Republishing Your Application**

To update and republish the MasterDetail application, follow these steps:

1. In Visual Basic 2005 Express Edition, double-click Form1.vb and open the Form Wizard. This opens the Form designer.

2. Move the existing button to a different place on the form.

3. Rebuild the application (Build ➪ Build MasterDetail).

4. Choose Build ➪ Publish from the menu to bring up the Publish Wizard. Walk through the various steps and choose Finish. This will update the executable and bring up the web page.

5. Do not install from the web page which comes up. Rather, go to Start ➪ All Programs ➪ Microsoft ➪ MasterDetail and run your application. Your application will check for updates and bring up an Update Available dialog as shown in Figure 10-9.

Figure 10-9

6. Make a copy of the MyDB.mdf and MyDB_log.ldf files and put them in a safe place. When you republish, if you have not changed these files, recopy them into the publish directory.

> The data file designation for MDF and LDF files works *as long as you do not change the data files themselves.* If you do, ClickOnce assumes that you want to republish the MDF and the LDF, so any changes the user has made to his data files will be lost. When you simply open a connection to an MDF and query for results, SSE updates the MDF with information about that so it can optimize for later queries. So, even using the Show Data command may update the MDF and LDF and put your ClickOnce Deployment at risk. If you make a copy of the MDF and LDF, and recopy it into the publish directory, you can ensure that users will keep their data files intact.

How It Works

Each time the application starts up, it checks to see if there are any updates. This functionality is built into your application when you first create it. The URL it looks for, and when it looks (at the beginning or end of when the application runs), are options you set in the property pages. Each time you choose to publish your application, the application version is automatically upgraded for you so that users can have some sense of what version they are upgrading to. If you inspect the Options page, you will see that this is a settable option. The old executable and other such files are replaced as needed and user data remains. On updates, note that data files are not automatically updated. This is so that if your user enters data, it is not destroyed on the update. If you do want to change the data file (to add a new column, for example), you will need to migrate the user's data from the old MDF to the new MDF through a series of queries. The safest way to proceed is to rename the new MDF and LDF so that the old MDF and LDF are not destroyed or lost.

Publishing Your Web Application

The preceding sections explain how to publish your rich-client application to target users over the web. Publishing for the web application is a little different. In the case of web application development, there is no Build ➪ Publish menu item. In the case of web development, simply copying the web files into the right location is all that's necessary for deployment. Then, when an http request comes in, the local IIS finds the right start page and you're on your way.

Publishing a web application poses two potential problems for web developers. First, there are several potential targets where you may copy your web application. You may copy to another location on your hard drive, a local IIS site, an FTP site (where a host might pick it up), or directly to a remote http site that has the appropriate Microsoft Front Page extensions installed on it.

The second issue is keeping track of what files on the target location are different from those you keep local. With respect to keeping your local files synchronized with those in the target location, if the site is shared, someone may have updated a file since you last took a copy, so if you blindly copy your web application up the site, you may destroy their updates.

With all this in mind, the Visual Web Developer tool helps make these two tasks easier as shown in the Try it Out below.

Try It Out   **Copying Your Web Application**

To copy your web application, follow these steps:

1. In Visual Web Developer 2005, select WebSite ⇨ Copy WebSite. This brings up the Copy Web page (see Figure 10-10). In this state, no remote website has been selected.

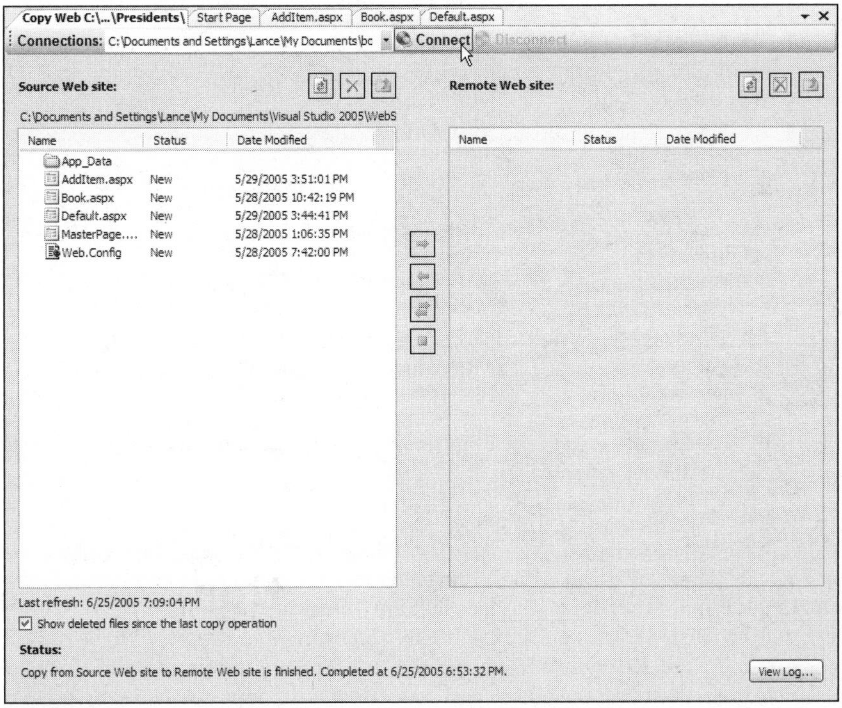

Figure 10-10

A Remote Web site is either an actual remote web location or an FTP site or even a site on the same machine. The term *remote* here is used to differentiate between the files you are copying from (the Source Web site files) and the target location for those files (the Remote Web site).

2. Click the Connect button next to the connections setting at the top of the Copy Web page. This brings up the Open Web Site dialog shown in Figure 10-11.

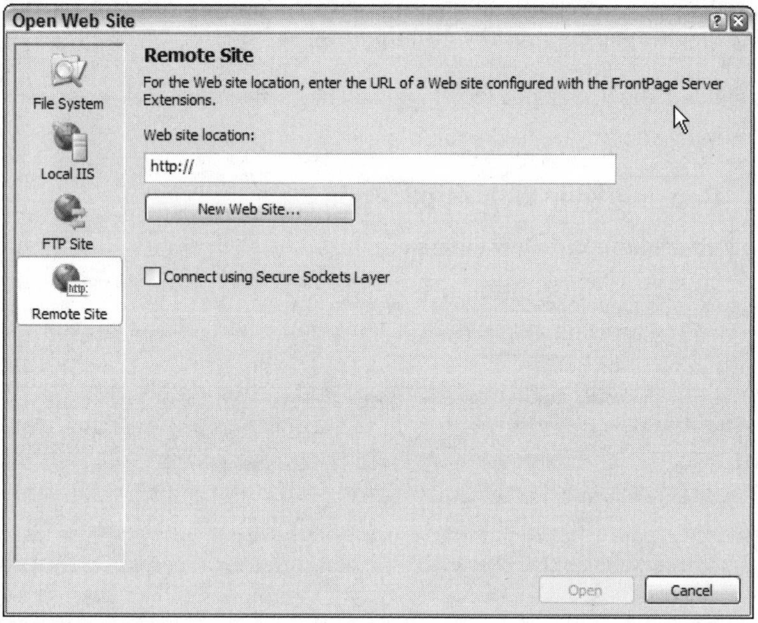

Figure 10-11

3. Enter the name of a valid Web site location and click Open. This will show all the Web Site files at the Remote Web site location. If there are already files present in the remote site, it will show them as well.

4. Copy the appropriate files to the Remote Web site location by using the arrows that sit between the Source and Remote Web Sites.

How It Works

The Copy Web Site page makes the task of connecting to your remote site and synchronizing a lot easier. It shows a graphical representation of the files that are different. The Source Web site files that do not exist on the Remote Web site have an arrow next to them suggesting that they need to be copied over to get things synchronized. And, Remote Web site files that are different from those on Source are shown with an arrow next to them (pointing the other way) suggesting that they need to be copied to the source to keep things synchronized. If the same file exists in both Source and Remote, they may show a question mark to indicate that it's not clear whether they should be copied. The Copy Web Site page also keeps track of the remote sites you have connected to so that you can easily target them again.

Summary

Using ClickOnce is a huge boon to developers writing rich-client applications. Writing a specialized setup program, getting it on a CD, creating a download site, and so on are menial tasks that often take away from the fun of writing an application. They certainly don't add any actual functionality to the program, but they must be done to get the application to customers. ClickOnce makes what once was an annoying task easy and pain-free.

In particular, this chapter showed you how to:

❑   Publish a database application using ClickOnce

❑   Set options for publication

❑   Republish a database application using ClickOnce

❑   Use the Copy Web site tool for Web applications

Exercises

Try the exercises that follow to test your understanding of the material covered in this chapter. You can find the solutions to these exercises in Appendix A.

1.   After you have published your application and installed it on your machine, run it and add some data to it. Next, in VB Express, make another simple change in the UI (for example, move the button again). Next, in the Application Files for the project properties option, mark the .MDF and the .LDF as Include (Auto). Build and republish the application.

2.   In your corporation, you maintain separate websites for support and downloads. In VB Express, republish your application but specify the separate website for support. Enter the support website URL on the Options page. Build and republish. Find out where the support URL shows up.

3.   Your application and database are very large. While publishing via the Internet is a great distribution option, it is too big a download for some customers. You want to create a CD and also push the setup to a UNC share. Using the publish options, publish the bits to a CD.

Migrating from Microsoft Desktop Engine (MSDE)

In Chapter 9, you learned how to install a new instance of SQL Server Express (SSE). This chapter briefly introduces you to Microsoft SQL Server Desktop Engine (MSDE), which is a free database based on previous versions of SQL Server. MSDE 1.0 contains the SQL Server 7.0 database engine, and MSDE 2000 contains the corresponding binaries from SQL Server 2000. The focus in this chapter is on helping you understand the differences between MSDE and SSE, so that you can decide whether to upgrade your existing applications to SSE.

If you are not currently using MSDE or do not plan to upgrade applications from MSDE to SQL Server Express, you may prefer to skip this chapter.

Unfortunately, upgrading from MSDE to SSE is not always simple. Also, SSE is not fully backwards-compatible with MSDE. There are scenarios where automatic upgrades cannot be done, so that you have to do some manual steps. In this chapter you will learn the following:

❑   Understand the differences between MSDE and SSE

❑   Introduction to SQLNCLI and the data access architecture in SSE

❑   Understand the upgrade rules to figure out if you need manual or automatic upgrades

❑   Automatically upgrade from MSDE to SSE using both the Graphical User Interface and command line

❑   Manually upgrade from MSDE to SSE using both GUI and command line

Understanding Microsoft Desktop Engine (MSDE)

MSDE is the redistributable free version of previous versions of SQL Server and is optimized for small workloads typical of a single user or workgroup. MSDE and SSE support the same programmatic APIs and T-SQL as the corresponding SQL Server editions. There is a concurrency workload governor in MSDE that limits its performance. It is important to understand how this governor works because this is a common reason for upgrading from MSDE to SSE or other SQL Server editions.

MSDE Concurrency Workload Governor

This section teaches you about the concurrency limitations of MSDE, as well as how to detect when the governor is active. The MSDE concurrency workload governor counts the number of *active operations*. The operations counted include login and logoff requests, batching of T-SQL statements, distributed transactions, and system queries such as ghost and autoshrink.

> *It is important to realize that some T-SQL statements use multiple operations. For example, the governor counts three operations from a BACKUP statement that references two backup devices: one operation for processing the batch containing the BACKUP statement and one operation against each backup device. Similarly, the governor counts four operations from a CREATE DATABASE statement that specifies a primary data file, a secondary data file, and a log file: one operation for the batch containing the CREATE DATABASE statement and one operation for each file.*

When there are more than eight active operations at the same time in the same instance of the database engine, the governor implements a slight wait before each logical read or write to a database file. Three out of the eight operations are reserved for system use, so that only five concurrent operations are available to the application. When the workload governor is active, it equally affects all connections; it is not limited to slowing down only the connections that activated the governor. The length of the wait implemented by the governor is constant; it does not vary depending on how many active operations the system has gone over the limit. The workload governor operates at the level of an instance of the database engine, not at the level of a database.

> *The MSDE workload governor depends only on the concurrent active operations, and imposes no limits on the number of users.*

The Database Consistency Checker (DBCC) statement CONCURRENCYVIOLATION(DISPLAY) displays statistics on how many times the governor was activated. An example display is given below. There are three lines to the display: The first line indicates the time frame since the counter started. The second line is a heading for the counts above 8 operations, so a value of 1 represents 9 concurrent operations; a value of 2 represents 10 operations and so on. The third line indicates the actual statistical values. In the example below, 9 concurrent operations happened four times and 10 concurrent operations happened two times. There were no concurrency violations more than 10 since the date indicated in the first line.

```
Concurrency violations since 2-10-2003 9:03:18.02
1  2  3  4  5  6  7  8  9  10-100  >100
4  2  0  0  0  0  0  0  0   0         0
```

You can enable periodic logging of concurrency violation counters in SQL Server event log by using the DBCC statement CONCURRENCYVIOLATION(STARTLOG). When logging is enabled, the event log is written every minute when the number of operations is greater than eight. After the governor is activated, the event log entries are written every minute. You can review the application event log for messages, similar to the following example:

```
2003-10-02 9:03:18.02 spid12 This SQL Server has been optimized for five concurrent
queries. This limit has been exceeded by two queries and performance may be
affected
```

> To achieve predictability with MSDE performance so that your application does not hit the workload governor limits, you can use connection pooling with a maximum limit of five. The Max Pool Size connection string option in ADO.NET can be used to indicate this. The default value of Max Pool Size is 100 and should be set to 5 when running your application with MSDE.

Usage Scenarios

The fact that MSDE has the same SQL Server engine used by other SQL Server editions, as well as the fact that it is free for redistribution, brought about high usage in both client and server database environments.

As a server data store, MSDE is used just like SQL Server when the requirements for throughput and volume are low. The scenarios include cases where MSDE is used in the evaluation or low-end versions of the application. The installation, management, and servicing of MSDE are typically exposed to the user in this scenario because of the assumption of a server administrator in these environments. As the usage or throughput requirements increase, these MSDE installations typically get upgraded to other editions of SQL Server.

MSDE is used by many client applications as a data store for application data, although it lacks usability features such as the management tools. The installation, administration, and servicing of MSDE is typically hidden to the user in this scenario because the application is totally responsible for the MSDE instance. Typically, there are no database administrators in the desktop home environment. Some key characteristics of this scenario are as follows:

❑ Named instances are used for each application to distinguish between the MSDE instances used by different applications. For example, the Joe's Garage application may name its MSDE instance "JoesGarage" to uniquely distinguish it.

❑ Many applications like to totally encapsulate the database functionality so that the end-user is not even aware that MSDE is being installed or used as a part of the application. This means silent installation and servicing of MSDE.

❑ This is typically a single-user scenario.

In many ways the usage scenarios for MSDE are similar to those of SSE. SSE is also expected to be used in both client and server environments, but the major difference is the higher usability because of the availability of SSMS-EE tools, .NET support, and the Application Xcopy feature. Another difference is User Instance, the feature in SSE which creates instances running as the user enables multiple applications to share the same default instance name instead of installing one instance per application.

Comparing MSDE and SSE

SSE is the latest version of a free database product from Microsoft, and in many ways it can be thought of as a successor to MSDE. SSE is based on the SQL Server 2005 engine, while MSDE is based on previous versions of SQL Server. Both are tuned for smaller work loads like home or workgroup use, and have performance characteristics lower than other SQL Server editions like SQL Server Standard Edition. SSE does not have any concurrency limitations, unlike MSDE which has the workload governor.

Chapter 11

There are architectural similarities between these products. You already know from the previous sections that the usage scenarios of SSE and MSDE are similar and both of them support client and server applications. They do not support enterprise class features such as Analysis Services, Business Intelligence, log shipping, clustering, and the like. Seamless upgrades to other editions of SQL Server are supported from both and no change is required from an existing application for this migration. These free editions support all the programming APIs and T-SQL exposed by the corresponding SQL Server editions.

On the other hand, there are some differences between SSE and MSDE that you should be aware of. SSE includes numerous ease-of-use features such as Application Xcopy, a setup graphical user interface, .NET support, XML data type, and SSMS-EE tools. The key differences between SSE and MSDE are described further in the following table.

SSE Features	MSDE Features
Engine Features	
Based on SQL Server 2005 engine.	Based on SQL Server 2000 or SQL Server 7.0 engine.
Supports SQL Server 2005 features such as Application Xcopy, XML data type, User Defined Types, and so on.	Does not support the new features in SQL Server 2005.
Supports usage of .NET technology inside SQL Server, such as writing stored procedures in C#.	Does not support using .NET inside SQL Server.
No replication publishing (snapshot, merge, or transactional replication) is supported.	Supports merge replication publishing.
No replication distribution.	Supports replication distribution.
Supports snapshot, merge, and transactional replication subscription.	Supports merge and transactional replication subscription.
No SQL Agent support.	SQL Agent supported.
No Data Transformation Services (DTS) run-time support.	Data Transformation Services (DTS) run-time is supported although the tools are not supported.
No concurrency workload governor.	Concurrency workload governor present which limits concurrency.
SQL Server Profiler is supported if another edition of SQL Server 2005 is installed on the same machine.	SQL Server Profiler is not supported.
Active Directory registration is supported.	Active Directory registration is not supported.
Maximum size of user database is 4GB.	Maximum size of user database is 2GB.
Memory supported is 1GB.	Memory supported is 2GB.
1 CPU supported.	2 CPUs supported.

196

SSE Features	MSDE Features
Data Access Features	
MDAC is not part of the install. However, existing native applications are not affected since they can use MDAC present on the operating system.	MDAC is part of the install.
.NET Framework is not installed, but is a requirement.	.NET Framework is not installed and is not a requirement.
SQL Native Access provider supports native access to the database and supports the new data types exposed by SQL 2005.	No SQL Native Access provider support.
Setup and Installation Features	
Windows Installer (MSI) technology supported for installations.	Windows Installer (MSI) and Merge Modules (MSM) supported for installs.
Robust and functional setup graphical user interface.	Basic graphical user interface.
64-bit machines such as x64 and ENT64 systems are supported in WOW, which allows 32-bit SQL Server binaries to run on 64-bit machines. It is not supported on IA64 systems.	There is no 64-bit support.
16 instances of SSE per machine supported.	16 instances of MSDE per machine supported.
Twelve localized languages supported.	Twelve localized languages supported.
Does not support legacy operating systems versions such as Windows 98, Windows ME, Windows 2000 RTM, Windows 2000 SP1, Windows 2000 SP2, Windows 2000 SP3, XP RTM, and Windows NT 4.0.	Supports legacy operating systems versions such as Windows 98, Windows ME, Windows 2000 RTM, Windows 2000 SP1, Windows 2000 SP2, Windows 2000 SP3, XP RTM, and Windows NT 4.0.
Supports editions of Windows such as XP Web Edition, XP Media Edition, and XP Tablet.	Does not support editions of Windows such as XP Web Edition, XP Media Edition, and XP Tablet.
Tools Support	
SSMS-EE management tool is provided as a separate web download.	No GUI management tools are provided by Microsoft for MSDE.
Support for managing Express via SQL Server Management Studio in development and production environment.	Support for managing MSDE via Enterprise Manager is limited to development environment. It cannot be used in production.
Good integration with Visual Studio for .NET development.	Loose integration with Visual Studio for .NET development.

Migrating Applications to SSE

Migration to a new database platform typically involves a migration of the user databases and the application. The user databases developed with MSDE are automatically upgraded when they are attached to SSE or any other SQL Server 2005 edition. Once the databases are upgraded, they cannot be downgraded back to MSDE. Upgrading applications to SSE is also easy because the data-access application programming interfaces (APIs) are backwards-compatible. However, it is important to understand the new providers for SSE so that new application development can use the latest APIs. Both MSDE and SSE support access via native APIs as well as managed APIs.

The native support for MSDE relies on the Microsoft Data Access Components (MDAC) that ship as part of the Windows operating systems. MDAC exposes multiple native data providers such as OLEDB and ODBC (see Figure 11-1). The ADO.NET data providers like SQL Native Client, OLE DB .NET, and ODBC .NET form the managed APIs and they also rely on the MDAC. The reliance on a Windows component increases serviceability hassles because these files are system-file protected, and an update in the form of a Windows service pack could break your application even though your SQL Server service pack remains the same.

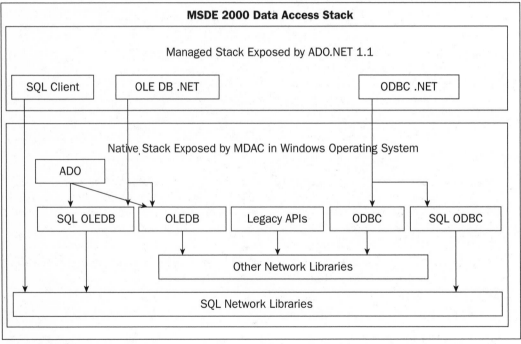

Figure 11-1

In SSE, a new provider, SQL Native Client (SQLNCLI), is introduced that has no reliance on MDAC. It is important to realize that all the previous OLEDB, ODBC, and legacy data providers continue to work with SSE, and your native application should require no modification to move to SSE. However, native support for all the new SQL Server 2005 features such as User Defined Types (UDT), the XML data type, and so on are present only in the new SQLNCLI provider. In other words, the native support for all the MDAC providers will not be updated for new SQL Server releases, and will remain fixed at SQL Server 2000 levels.

SQLNCLI is a redistributable DLL shipping with SSE and contains the SQL Server 2005 equivalent for the SQL OLEDB and SQL ODBC providers. Bulk Copy (BCP) and SQL Networking Interface (SNI) are also a part of this DLL, while legacy providers such as DBLIB and ESQL are not supported. Because SQLNCLI is designed to co-exist with the data providers included in the MDAC stack, there are new class IDs and provider names for its components. For example, the OLE DB Program ID used is SQLNCLI, and the ODBC Driver Name is SQL Native Client. There could be some backward incompatibilities between MDAC and SQLNCLI providers, but as long as you do not change your existing connection string, you are insulated from these changes.

There is significant change to the SQLClient ADO.NET provider working with SSE. Support for all the new SQL Server 2005 features, including Application Xcopy deployment, is added to this provider. In addition, the dependency on MDAC is removed by adding the SQL Networking Interfaces (SNI) to the ADO.NET infrastructure. However, the other managed providers such as OLE DB .NET and ODBC .NET continue to rely on the MDAC provided by the Windows operating system, as shown in Figure 11-2.

The SQL Networking Interface (SNI) is the new high-performance networking layer for SQL Server 2005. This layer supports the protocols such as shared memory for local data communication, as well as Named Pipes (NP) and TCP/IP used for local and remote communication. The shared memory protocol for SQL Server 2005 is incompatible with the protocol used in SQL Server 2000 and MDAC. This means that any provider that uses MDAC over shared memory cannot work with SNI and SSE. The providers affected include the MDAC SQLOLEDB, SQL ODBC, OLEDB, ODBC, ADO, DBLIB, ESQL, OLE DB .NET, and ODBC .NET. However, the Named Pipes and TCP/IP protocols are not affected.

SQL Server has protocols ordering enabled by default. If the protocol is not specified in the connection string for MSDE 2000, then local connections will first try Shared Memory, followed by Named Pipes and TCP/IP. Hence, unless you explicitly specify the networking protocols to be used in your connection string, MDAC-based applications will continue to work using Named Pipes or TCP/IP.

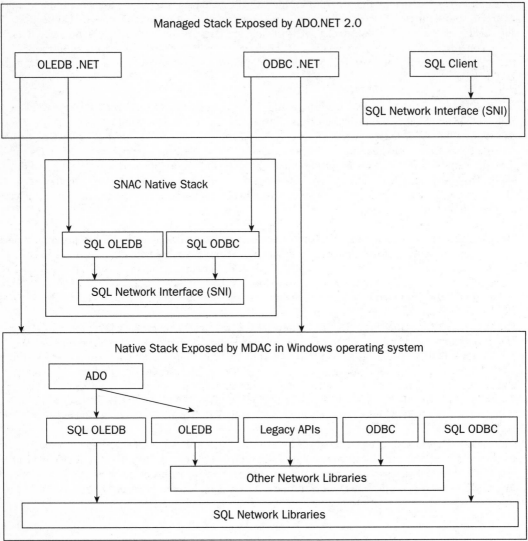

SSE Data Access Stack

Figure 11-2

By default, SSE has all the remote networking protocols turned off. This means that only the Shared Memory and Local Named Pipes are enabled. Local Named Pipes means that the Named Pipes protocol is enabled for access on the local machine only. Remote machine access is disabled by default. If you are using a data provider that uses MDAC, then the connection to SSE on the local machine happens over a Named Pipe. For SQLNCLI and SQLClient that do not rely on MDAC, the connection happens over Shared Memory.

MSDE Setup and Servicing

The distinct client and the server usage scenarios described earlier ask for different behavior from MSDE setup, which in turn led Microsoft to expose the setup in two different ways: the Windows Installer MSI package and the Merge Module (MSM). This section not only explains the two setup options, but also gives you some background on the servicing implications.

The MSDE setup executable contains a set of Windows Installer (WI) -based packages that contains all the information to install or uninstall the product. Since MSDE supports 16 instances on a machine, 16 separate installation packages are created. There are .msi files (MSI) included in each package that contains the installation database, information about the files, configuration entries, and so on. Each MSI has a separate product code and package code that uniquely identify it. The product code is a GUID that uniquely identifies the MSDE installation, while the package code is another GUID that identifies the WI package. The MSIs are named Sqlrun01.msi, Sqlrun02.msi, and so on until Sqlrun16.msi.

Although you can install MSDE by invoking MSIs directly, Microsoft recommends installing using setup.exe. The main reason is that the setup executable performs additional tasks to ensure the success of the install. For example, setup.exe does the task of enumerating all instances on the machine and picking the right MSI to install. So if there are already three instances on the box (Sqlrun01 to Sqlrun03), setup.exe picks up Sqlrun04 as the MSI package when the next instance is installed.

MSDE was also released in the form of merge modules (MSM), a mechanism to deliver the components and setup logic that can later be merged together into an installation package. The merge modules cannot be installed alone and typically the MSDE merge modules become a part of the application's MSI so that it is fully embedded in the application. In other words, MSDE is now almost invisible to the end-user and has no separate identity for installation purposes. This product does not show up in the Add/Remove Programs list.

Microsoft does regular free updates for its operating system and application software so that the computer is protected from critical bugs, viruses, and other newly discovered threats. These updates use the product and package codes to uniquely identify the product. The service packs provide convenient all-in-one access to the most recent drivers, tools, security updates, and customer requested changes. They are freely available at the Microsoft website, and contain both critical and non-critical updates. They are supposed to improve stability and enhance security, and Microsoft recommends that you install the latest service pack. Service packs are cumulative; each new service pack contains all the fixes that are in previous service packs, as well as any new fixes. You do not need to install a previous service pack before you install the latest one. For example, you do not need to install SQL Server 2000 Service Pack 3 (SP3) before you install SQL Server 2000 Service Pack 4 (SP4).

These service packs and updates can easily be applied when MSDE is installed using its setup.exe. However, when MSDE is installed as merge modules, the updates are unable to identify the installation automatically. The MSDE merge modules use the parent application's product code, which is different from the product code used by MSDE. This means that the application developer has to be involved in future servicing of applications that used MSDE merge modules.

Some users of MSDE manually change the product code of the MSIs so that they can avoid product code conflicts with any of the existing MSDE instances. They have to distribute only one MSI instead of the 16 MSIs that come with setup.exe. Unfortunately, this solution has the same servicing problems faced by merge modules since SQL service packs and patches cannot understand the new product code used by the application.

> Because of the servicing problems, Microsoft discourages the use of merge modules
> or MSIs with changed product code. There is no support for merge modules in SQL
> Server Express 2005, so that the installation and servicing is simpler.

*Advanced information about MSDE servicing and patching is described in the next paragraph. When
MSDE service packs (SP) are released, 16 patches are sent out with the names SqlRunXX.msp (Sqlrun01
.msp to Sqlrun16.msp) corresponding to the MSIs described previously. There is a one-to-one mapping
between a patch and the original install. For example, Sqlrun01.msp does not work on any install other
than from Sqlrun01.msi since the product code and package code is verified prior to patching. Setup.exe
does the task of matching the MSP to an MSI. Please refer to Microsoft KB article 314131 (available at
http://support.microsoft.com/?kbid=314131) for creating patch files if you changed the product code of
the MSI.*

*To patch a merge module install, the application developer first gets the refresh merge modules
corresponding to a service pack. These new merge modules are consumed by the application setup
so that an application patch package is generated. This is sent to the end-user as a patch from the
application vendor. SQL Server service packs and patches cannot touch these merge modules because
they belong to a different product.*

In summary, MSDE can be installed on the computer in multiple ways, depending on how its installation
is invoked. The install options are shown in the following list:

❑ Invoke setup.exe. This exe enumerates the existing installed instances and chooses the right MSI
to install. *This is the only valid scenario for SSE.*

❑ The application setup.exe invokes one of the MSDE MSIs directly. This option is used when the
application does not want to ship all 16 MSIs. The application setup is responsible for all work
done by the MSDE setup.exe, including instance enumeration. Remember that SSE does not
support installs by calling MSIs directly.

A variation of the installation involves the application setup changing the product code of the
MSDE MSI. However, this option has serious servicing issues, and should not be used.

❑ The application setup.exe invokes the MSDE merge modules directly. However, this option has
serious servicing issues, and should not be used.

The following Try It Out shows you how to detect MSDE installations on your machine.

Try It Out   Detecting Existing SQL Server Installations and Figuring Out Which Instances Are MSDE

1. Click Start and then click Run. In the Open box, type **regedit.exe** and then click OK. View all the
values under the registry key `HKEY_LOCAL_MACHINE (HKLM) \SOFTWARE\Microsoft Sql
Server\InstalledInstances`. This gives you a list of all the SQL Server installations on the
machine.

> Be careful not to modify any of the registry values when using the regedit tool.

2. Next, for each of the instance names listed, go to either of the following registry key locations: HKLM\SOFTWARE\Microsoft\Microsoft SQL Server*instance name*\Setup for a named instance or HKLM\SOFTWARE\Microsoft\MSSQLServer\Setup for a default MSDE instance. Look for a key called Product Code. If this key exists, then the instance is MSDE; otherwise, it is some other edition of SQL Server.

Any instances that are upgraded from MSDE to other SQL Server Editions have this registry key too.

How It Works

The registry key HKLM\SOFTWARE\Microsoft Sql Server\InstalledInstances lists the names of all SQL Server instances that are installed on a server machine, including SQL Server 2000, SQL Server 2005, MSDE, and SSE. In the next step, you distinguish MSDE from other SQL Server instances by using the product key registry key, which is unique to MSDE instances. After you have the product code, use the following table to identify the SQLRun MSI file used for installing MSDE.

Product Code	Original Package Name
E09B48B5-E141-427A-AB0C-D3605127224A	SqlRun01.msi
689404D2-1C94-44B3-9203-BEC5594FDA7A	SqlRun02.msi
EFB70B01-B1F3-4960-AB69-4A280084A60C	SqlRun03.msi
C2736CA7-76E1-4D0C-B590-483A7FFD18DA	SqlRun04.msi
FE7E950B-220A-4182-B5CA-19397244DCFD	SqlRun05.msi
7E5C338B-E77E-4CB4-9C1D-FB67B56B3B19	SqlRun06.msi
F07E35BF-8B03-4777-9B5E-AE90E4FF0932	SqlRun07.msi
C5B59406-E985-4187-84E8-68E2D9F89A47	SqlRun08.msi
D7CE240C-0F3B-4C40-9278-C0B90E533652	SqlRun09.msi
A519AE9C-7C79-4C5B-9127-8F46D648D5A4	SqlRun10.msi
4541DA32-2108-43E9-9915-C71B9DE77048	SqlRun11.msi
A5C1C914-4EF7-40ED-9BCE-FCEB4BB0C19D	SqlRun12.msi
9FCE5BBD-D85F-4905-8A0C-12A3A86C2434	SqlRun13.msi
F4E46404-2578-4955-B748-547957F08AB1	SqlRun14.msi
B7300824-E68F-45F1-BAC1-5F15636C346F	SqlRun15.msi
CD59EA85-6CBF-4C08-BE59-6C628B3D8F54	SqlRun16.msi

Upgrading MSDE to SSE

You might choose to upgrade from MSDE to SSE for any of the following reasons:

❑ SSE is the successor to MSDE and is the logical and easiest upgrade path.

❑ You are planning to use some of the engine features present in SSE like Application Xcopy, User Defined Types, or the XML data type.

❑ You want the enhanced productivity features in SSE such as support of .NET on the server.

❑ Your application does not rely on features like replication publishing, DTS, or SQL Agent, which are not supported by SSE.

❑ Your application is constantly encountering the concurrency workload governor limit in MSDE.

❑ You are rewriting your application, and you want to use the Visual Studio integration supported only by SSE.

❑ The support time frame for MSDE is running out and you want to move to a more recent and secure platform. You can get latest information about the support time lines at http://support .microsoft.com/gp/lifesrvr.

❑ You are planning to use features present in other editions of SQL Server 2005, and SSE is used in the evaluation or low-end edition of your product.

❑ You want to discontinue using merge modules and transition to the Windows Installer MSI technologies supported by SSE.

❑ SSE is easy to manage and administer because of the availability of SSMS-EE tools.

❑ Your application supports 64-bit operating systems, as well as editions of XP such as XP Web Edition.

> **Some editions of SQL Server 2005, including SSE, do not support Windows NT 4.0 and Windows 9x platforms such as Windows 98 or Windows ME. If your application relies on these operating system platforms, you should not upgrade to SSE.**
>
> **Features such as replication publishing, SQL Agent, and DTS are not present in SSE, although they are supported in MSDE. If your MSDE application uses any of these features, SSE may not work for you. Instead you might want to turn to some higher editions of SQL Server 2005.**

MSDE to SSE Upgrade Rules

The SSE setup follows certain upgrade rules to determine whether an existing MSDE installation qualifies for the upgrade option. The rules are described as follows.

❑ **Version rule:** If the existing instance on the box is MSDE 2000 SP4-based or higher, then it can be upgraded.

❑ **Edition rule:** The edition of the SQL Server instance to be upgraded must be lower than or equal to SSE. This means that out of all the SQL Server 2000 editions, only MSDE can be upgraded to SSE. There is no upgrade path from SQL Server Standard 2000 to SSE.

❑ **Language rule:** If version and edition rules pass, the language rule is checked. The given instance on the machine can be upgraded only if the language chosen to upgrade is the same as the language of the instance.

Both SQL Server Express and MSDE are available in 12 different languages, and Microsoft supports upgrades from these MSDE languages to the corresponding SSE ones. The languages supported are English, Brazilian Portuguese, Dutch, Swedish, Simplified Chinese, Traditional Chinese, French, German, Italian, Japanese, Korean, and Spanish. However, other editions of SQL Server 2005 and SQL Server 2000 support only 9 languages. The three additional languages supported by SSE and MSDE are Swedish, Dutch, and Portuguese-Br. Hence, based on the language rule, upgrade from a language like MSDE Swedish to SQL Server Standard 2000 or 2005 is not supported as SQL Server Standard does not support Swedish.

❑ **Product Code Rule:** SSE can upgrade an MSDE instance *automatically* only if the product code matches the default product codes that shipped with MSDE. These default product codes are given in the preceding table. If you are using merge modules or you used a product code different from those in the following table, you need to perform some manual steps during upgrade.

> **The version, edition, language, and product code rules must match before an MSDE instance can be automatically upgraded to SSE. Upgrading the version is easy because there are automatic upgrades from all previous versions of MSDE to MSDE 2000 SP4. All the languages supported by MSDE 2000 are also supported by SSE. Unfortunately, if the product code rule breaks, your only choice is manual upgrade.**

Upgrade To:					
Starting with Versions Below:	SSE 2005 32-bit	SQL Server 2005 Workgroup, Standard and Enterprise Editions	SQL Server 2005 Developer and Evaluation Editions	SQL Server 2000 SP4/MSDE 2000 SP4	Recommendation
MSDE 1.0	No	No	No	Yes	Upgrade to MSDE 2000 SP4 before upgrading to SSE.
Product Code matches the default MSDE product codes and version is MSDE 2000 RTM, SP1, SP2, or SP3.	No	No	No	Yes	Upgrade to MSDE 2000 SP4 before upgrading to SSE.
Product Code matches the MSDE product codes and version is MSDE 2000 SP4 or higher.	Yes	Yes	No	Not applicable	Automatic upgrade to SSE is possible; follow the steps described in the proceeding sections.
Uses pre- SP4 MSM does not match the MSDE product codes and version is MSDE 2000 RTM, SP1, SP2, or SP3.	No	No	No	Manual upgrade only	Upgrade to or Product Code MSDE 2000 SP4 before upgrading to SSE. Because the product codes are changed, manual steps are required while upgrading to MSDE 2000 SP4.
Uses MSM version SP4 or Product Code does not match the MSDE product codes and version is MSDE 2000 SP4 or higher	Manual upgrade only	Manual upgrade only	No	Not applicable	Only manual upgrade is , possible and the upgrade process can take care of upgrading only the binaries and system databases. Any information stored in registry keys is lost.
SSE 2005	Yes if target is higher version than SSE RTM	Yes	No	No	SSE can be upgraded to a higher edition of SQL Server 2005 automatically. No upgrades to SQL Server 2005 Developer or Evaluation edition are supported.

Automatically Upgrading MSDE to SSE

The SSE 2005 upgrade process involves upgrading the binaries, registry keys, and the system databases. User databases are untouched as part of setup upgrade, and automatic migration is done when the database is attached to the server.

Automatic MSDE to SSE upgrades of the binaries, registry keys, and the system databases are possible only if the MSDE installation is compatible with the SSE upgrade software. The compatibility is established by the upgrade rules described in the previous section. Typically, if your installation invokes MSDE setup.exe or it uses the MSIs directly without changing the default product codes, your MSDE installation is compatible. In this case, your upgrade is simple and you have only to supply the appropriate command line for silent install or point the GUI to the appropriate instance.

> **For features removed from SSE such as replication publishing, Agent, DTS, and the like, there will be no warning during the upgrade process. These features will just not work in the upgraded instance. Replication is a special case because the replication upgrade scripts will detect the SSE edition and remove all the publishing or distribution related entries from the system tables.**

It is important to understand why you should be installing using the setup.exe provided by SSE instead of directly calling MSIs as you used to do for MSDE. The main reason is that the setup architecture has changed significantly for SSE. Instead of having a single MSI that contains all the features, SSE has multiple MSIs corresponding to the features like SQL Engine, MSXML, Client Components, and so on. These MSIs are interdependent, and are invoked in a particular sequence by the setup.exe provided by SSE. In addition, the setup.exe takes care of some key installation features such as dealing with multiple instances, instance enumeration, System Configuration Checker (SCC), setup logging, and so on. It is very hard for an application developer to correctly simulate the working of SSE's setup.exe.

Some application developers want to call the SSE setup.exe from within an MSI (and not an exe). The SSE setup.exe calls multiple MSIs in sequence. One MSI calling another MSI is termed a nested MSI install and is not currently supported by Microsoft since they suffer from the same servicing issues as merge modules. The registration entries for nested installs are different from those in a normal install. The nested install has no Add/Remove Program entries, and the uninstall is tied to the parent. Hence Microsoft recommends not doing nested installs of SQL Server Express.

The following Try It Out shows you how to determine if your MSDE installation can be automatically upgraded to SSE.

Try It Out   Can Your MSDE Installation Be Automatically Upgraded to SSE?

1. **Check the Edition Rule:** Click Start, and then click Run. In the open box, type regedit.exe and then click OK. Look for existence of the Product Code registry key at either of these locations: HKLM\SOFTWARE\Microsoft\Microsoft SQL Server*instance name*\Setup for a named instance, or at HKLM\SOFTWARE\Microsoft\MSSQLServer\Setup for a default instance. If the Product Code key exists, the instance is MSDE and this check passes.

   The T-SQL Statement SELECT SERVERPROPERTY('Edition') *also gives the edition information.*

2. **Check the Version Rule:** The version of the MSDE instance must be SP4 or above to pass this check. You can check the version of the product the following ways:

❏ The T-SQL statement SELECT SERVERPROPERTY ('ProductLevel') returns a value of SP4 or higher.

❏ The T-SQL statement SELECT @@version returns 8.00.2039 or higher.

❏ Use regedit.exe to verify the version information at the following registry key locations: HKLM\SOFTWARE\Microsoft\Microsoft SQL Server*instance name*\ MSSQLServer\CurrentVersion for a named instance or HKLM\SOFTWARE\ Microsoft\MSSQLServer\MSSQLServer\CurrentVersion for a default instance.

3. Check the **Language Rule:** Click Start, and then click Run. In the Open box, type **regedit.exe** and then click OK. Look for the Language entry at either of these locations: HKLM\SOFTWARE\ Microsoft\Microsoft SQL Server*instance name*\CurrentVersion for named instance, or HKLM\ SOFTWARE\Microsoft\MSSQLServer\MSSQLSERVER\CurrentVersion for a default instance. Compare the value to the following table to determine the language of the MSDE instance. Verify that the language of SSE on the CD is the same as the language of the MSDE install.

Language Registry Value (in hexadecimal)	Language Registry Value (in decimal)	Language of That Instance
0x00000404	1028	Traditional Chinese
0x00000407	1031	German
0x00000409	1033	English
0x0000040a	1034	Spanish
0x0000040c	1036	French
0x00000410	1040	Italian
0x00000411	1041	Japanese
0x00000412	1042	Korean
0x00000413	1043	Dutch
0x00000416	1046	Portuguese (Brazil)
0x0000041d	1053	Swedish
0x00000805	2053	Simplified Chinese

4. **Check the Product Code Rule:** Get the product code value from step 1, and verify that it belongs to one of the default product codes listed in the table. If the product code matches, you pass this check.

How It Works

All the rules mentioned above have to be satisfied to ensure that the MSDE installation is automatically upgradeable to SSE. The first step makes sure that the installation you are interested in is an MSDE instance. MSDE is the only SQL Server 2000 edition that can be upgraded to SSE. Then the version information is verified to make sure the instance is at the service pack level SP4 or above. If the service pack level check failed, it is relatively straightforward to upgrade your instance to SP4 or above. Finally, the product code used must be one of the default product codes used and the language of SSE on the CD should match the language of the MSDE instance.

Similar to the SSE installs described in Chapter 9, the automatic upgrade supports both graphical user interface (GUI) and silent installs. The GUI-based install relies on the administrator providing the necessary configuration at install time. In the silent mode, the upgrade program uses the parameters supplied via the command line or .ini file so that there is no further interaction with the user during setup.

Upgrading MSDE Using the Graphical User Interface

This section guides you through the dialogs required to successfully upgrade an instance of MSDE to SSE. It discusses the various options available in each dialog and recommends actions to be taken at each step. Many of these dialogs are similar to the ones in install as presented in Chapter 9, and you may find it useful to refer to the figures in that chapter, in the section "Installing SSE with the Setup Graphical User Interface."

Before Starting Setup

Verify the following conditions before starting setup:

❑ Your computer satisfies the minimum hardware and software requirements for SSE as listed in Chapter 1.

❑ The proper version of .NET Framework 2.0 is installed on the computer.

❑ Your existing MSDE installation satisfies the upgrade rules listed previously.

❑ You have administrator rights on the machine.

The following Try It Out shows you how to silently upgrade a default instance of MSDE to SSE.

Try It Out	Upgrade a Default Instance of MSDE

Launch the SSE setup.exe and perform the following steps:

1. On the End User License Agreement page, read the licensing agreement, and select the check box to accept the licensing terms and conditions. Selecting the check box activates the Next button. Click Next.

2. SQL Server Component Update dialog checks for prerequisites and installs the SQL Support files. Click Next.

3. On the Welcome page of the SQL Server Installation Wizard, click Next.

4. On the System Configuration Check (SCC) page, the installation computer is scanned for any known machine configurations that will limit the user or cause setup to fail. To proceed with setup after the scan completes, click Continue.

5. On the Registration Information page, enter the user name and company information. Uncheck the Hide advanced configuration check box. Click Next.

6. On the Feature Selection page, select SQL Engine, SQL Data Files, Shared Tools, Client Components, Connectivity, and SDK. Click Next.

7. On the Instance Name page, specify the name of the MSDE instance to upgrade. You can also click Installed Instances button and select the instance name. The list displayed contains information about all the installed SQL Server 2005, SQL Server 2000, MSDE 2000, or SQL Server 7.0 instances. SQL Server 2005 instances can be selected to do feature maintenance or to do uninstall. SQL Server 2000 or MSDE 2000 instances can be selected to perform an upgrade. Click Next.

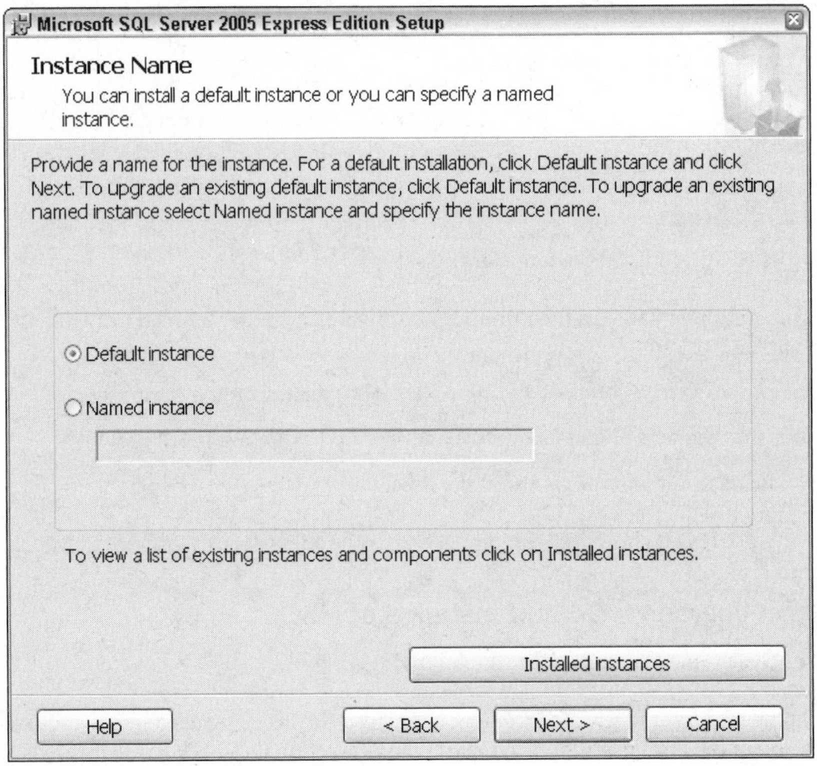

Figure 11-3

8. Select SQL Database Services, Workstation Components, Books Online and development tools in the Existing components page and click Next (see Figure 11-4). You can get details about these components if you click the Details button at the bottom of this page (see Figure 11-5).

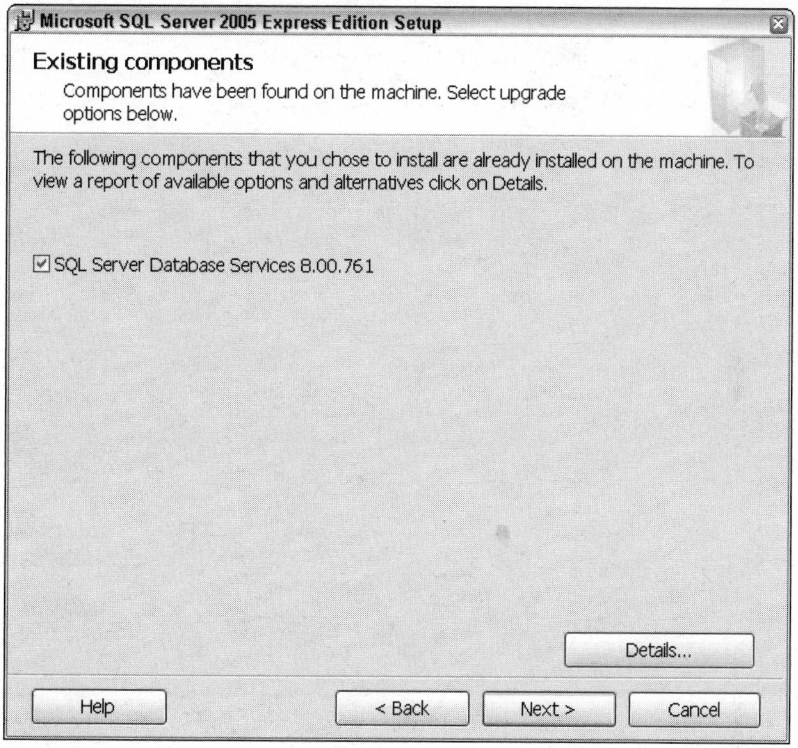

Figure 11-4

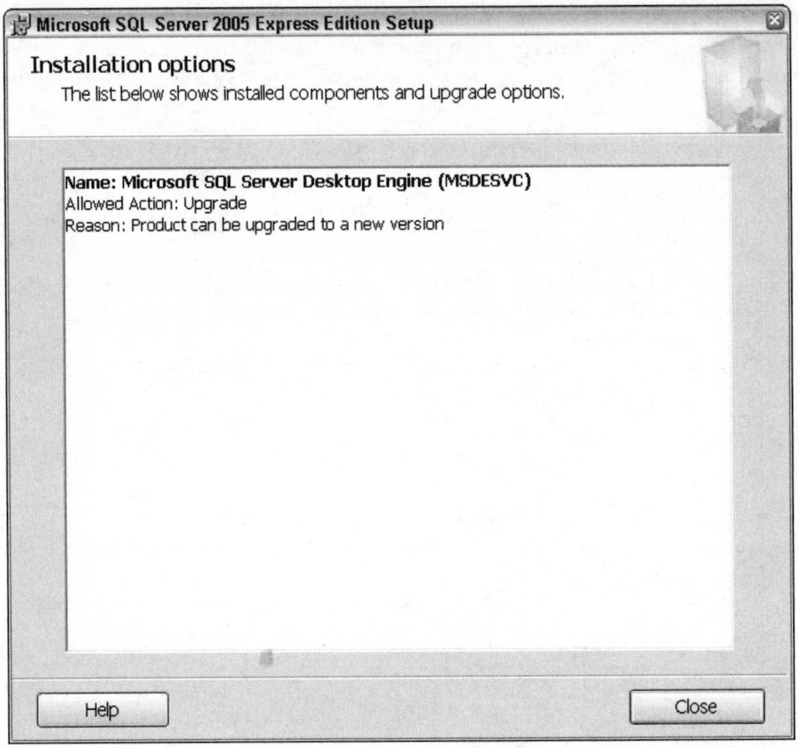

Figure 11-5

9. Select Windows Authentication Mode in the Upgrade Logon Information page. This account is used for connecting to SQL Server during the upgrade process (see Figure 11-6).

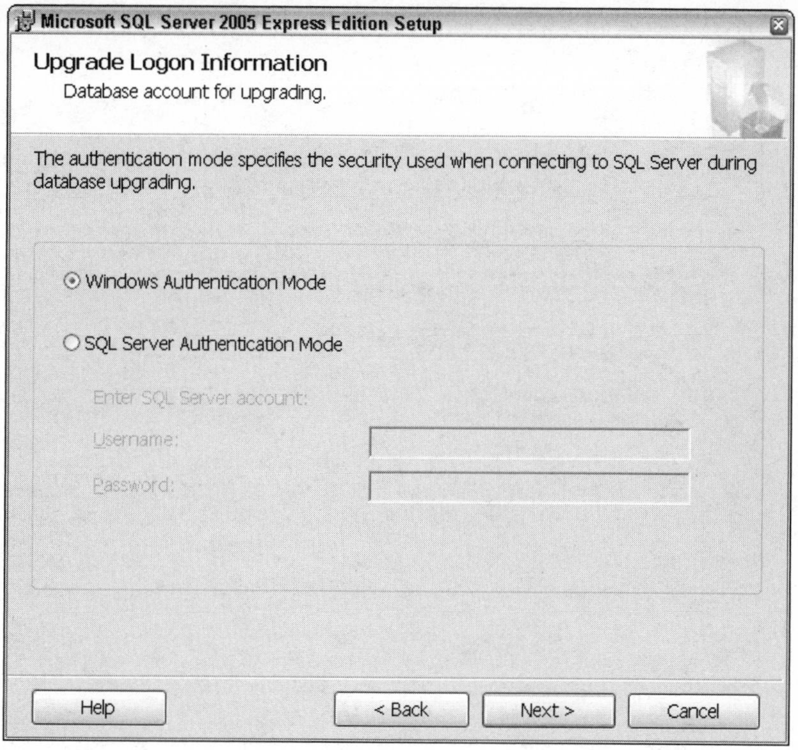

Figure 11-6

10. In the User Instance page, click Next. This dialog is similar to the User Instance dialog for clean SSE installations.

11. Click Next in the Error and Usage Report Settings. This dialog is similar to the Error dialog visible during SSE installation.

12. Click Install in the Ready To Install page to start the installation process (see Figure11-7).

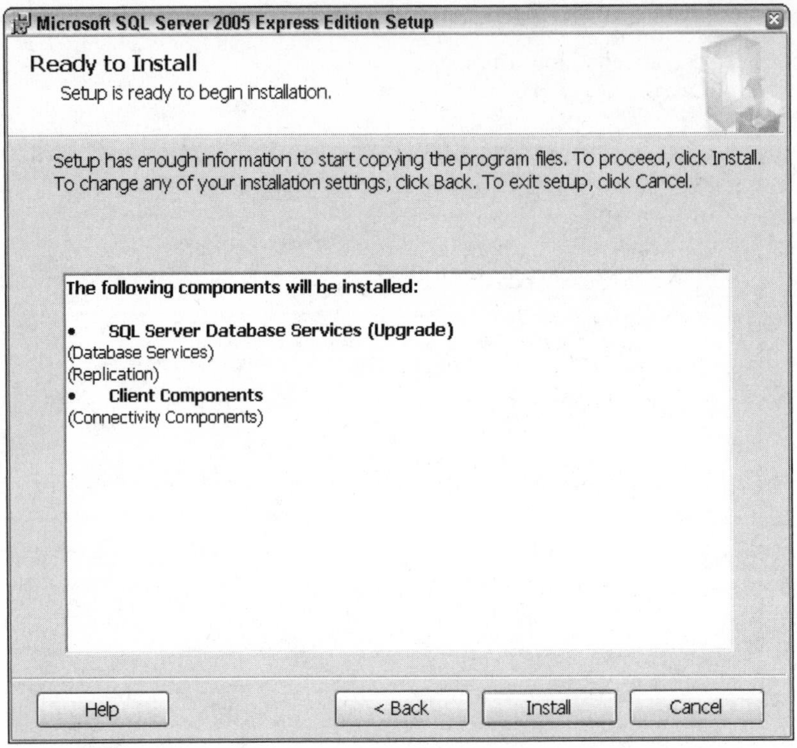

Microsoft SQL Server 2005 Express Edition Setup

Ready to Install
Setup is ready to begin installation.

Setup has enough information to start copying the program files. To proceed, click Install.
To change any of your installation settings, click Back. To exit setup, click Cancel.

The following components will be installed:

- **SQL Server Database Services (Upgrade)**
(Database Services)
(Replication)
- **Client Components**
(Connectivity Components)

[Help]   [< Back]   [Install]   [Cancel]

Figure 11-7

13.   Click Finish to complete the upgrade.

How It Works

You can see from the above Try It Out that the upgrade user interface is similar to clean installation. The difference starts with the Instance Page dialog in step 7 when you specify an existing instance on the machine instead of specifying a new name. The assumption is that you have a previous default (MSSQLSERVER) instance of MSDE already installed on the machine.

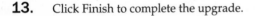

Post Installation Verification

To verify the correct installation of SSE, make sure that the SQL Server and SQL Browser services are running, as described in Chapter 9 in the section "Post-Installation Verification."

Upgrading MSDE Using Silent Installation

Silent install mode is supported when using command line parameters or ini files. The registry settings, the server settings, as well as the system database settings are preserved during the upgrade process. For example, if networking was enabled in SSE, after upgrade the SSE instance will also have networking enabled.

For silent upgrades, the command line parameters passed must include the UPGRADE command line parameter. UPGRADE indicates that the SSE setup is upgrading the instance specified by INSTANCENAME. The typical value passed to UPGRADE is SQL_Engine.

The other optional command line parameters used commonly with upgrade are as follows.

❑ **UPGRADEUSER=login_account:** This command line parameter is used to specify the SQL Authentication login account used by SSE setup when connecting to the instance. The connection is required for scenarios like upgrading the master database. If this parameter is not specified, Windows Authentication is used. The login account must be a member of the sysadmin fixed server role.

 It is recommended that you not use this parameter. Omitting this parameter forces setup to run under a Windows domain or computer account that has been included in the SQL Server sysadmin fixed server role.

❑ **UPGRADEPWD=password:** This parameter specifies a password for the login account specified by the UPGRADEUSER property setting. This can be omitted if the login account has a blank password. It is strongly recommended *not* to use a blank password.

❑ **/settings ini_file:** You can use the /settings ini_file argument to indicate to setup.exe that an ini file is used instead of passing all the parameters through the command line. You can specify the full path to the ini file if necessary and enclose it within quotes if the path contains spaces.

❑ **ARPsystemcomponent=1:** You can use this flag if you do not want to add an MSDE or SSE instance to the Add/Remove Programs list.

The following Try It Out shows you how to silently upgrade an instance of MSDE SP4 to SSE.

Try It Out   Silently Upgrading MSDE SP4 to SSE

Open a command prompt window and navigate to the SSE setup directory. Execute one of the following commands:

❑ If you are using windows authentication mode for the default instance of MSDE:

```
Setup.exe /qn UPGRADE=SQL_Engine INSTANCENAME=MSSQLSERVER
```

❑ If you are using windows authentication mode for a named instance of MSDE:

```
Setup.exe /qn UPGRADE= SQL_Engine INSTANCENAME=MyNamedInstance
```

❑ If you are using windows authentication mode for MSDE and want to explicitly turn off networking:

```
Setup.exe /qn UPGRADE= SQL_Engine INSTANCENAME=MSSQLSERVER
DISABLENETWORKPROTOCOLS=1
```

❑ If you are using Mixed Mode authentication for MSDE:

```
setup /qn UPGRADE= SQL_Engine INSTANCENAME=MSSQLSERVER SECURITYMODE=SQL
UPGRADEUSER=AnAdminLogin UPGRADEPWD=AdminPassword
```

How It Works

To silently upgrade MSDE SP4 to SSE, you are passing the UPGRADE command line parameter to SSE's setup executable. You can specify the name of the MSDE instance using the INSTANCENAME parameter. You can pass MSSQLSERVER as the value for the INSTANCENAME parameter to upgrade the default instance. If MSDE is using Mixed Authentication, you have to supply a login that is a member of the *sysadmin* fixed server role via the UPGRADEUSER parameter. The password for the login is specified by the UPGRADEPWD parameter. Use the DISABLENETWORKPROTOCOLS parameter if you want to explicitly enable or disable the remote networking. By default, the networking settings for MSDE are preserved during an upgrade, which means that if MSDE had networking turned on, then the upgraded SSE will also have the networking turned on.

Manually Upgrading MSDE to SSE

If your MSDE installation is not compatible with the SSE upgrade rules, some extra manual steps are required for the MSDE upgrade to be successful. Review the upgrade rules specified earlier in this chapter to verify whether you need to do a manual upgrade. In general, if you use Merge Modules (MSM), or you have changed the default product codes for the MSDE MSI, you will need to manually upgrade.

> **Two special MSM/MSI properties called SAVESYSDB and USESYSDB are introduced to preserve the system database settings during a manual upgrade process. These properties are described in detail in this section. Unfortunately, there is nothing offered by Microsoft to preserve the registry settings during the manual upgrade.**

SAVESYSDB=1 is a new property introduced in MSDE SP4 MSI and MSM that informs the setup to preserve the system databases like master, model, and msdb during an uninstall or upgrade. USESYSDB is another new property introduced in SSE and other editions of SQL Server 2005 that informs the setup to use the system databases left behind by the MSDE uninstall. The optional parameter allows the user to specify a custom directory containing the files. There is no graphical user interface for this parameter, so the user will have to specify this option through a command line parameter or an ini file.

The general steps for manual upgrade of MSDE SP4 are as follows:

1. Uninstall the existing MSDE installation, but specify the SAVESYSDB parameter so that the system databases are saved to a folder. Please note that you cannot use Add/Remove Programs to perform this step because it does not allow you to specify this extra parameter.

2. Do a clean install of SSE from the CD, but specify the USESYSDB parameter so that the setup can use the folder containing the system databases. Note that UPGRADE=1 is not passed here because this is a clean install.

These two steps can be automated in the application's setup program, so that the end-user need not understand the processes occurring silently. In this case, the only visible indicator is the extra time taken to upgrade. As mentioned earlier, the task of automating the upgrade falls to the application developer because the existing MSDE installation uses a product code that is different from the ones SSE setup can understand. Also the application setup may have used some custom install sequence, which is understood only by the application developer.

The following Try It Out shows you how to manually upgrade an instance of MSDE SP4 to SSE.

Try It Out Manually Upgrading Your MSDE 2000 SP4 MSI Instance to SSE

1. To start the uninstall of MSDE, you need to know the location of the MSI used to install the instance. Open a command prompt window and navigate to the MSDE setup directory. Alternatively you can provide the ProductCode obtained in the previous Try It Outs as a parameter to setup. Execute one of the following commands to uninstall:

❏ If you are using windows authentication mode for the default instance of MSDE:

```
Setup.exe /qn /x Package_Or_ProductCode SAVESYSDB=1
```

❏ If you are using windows authentication mode for a named instance of MSDE:

```
Setup.exe /qn /x Package_Or_ProductCode INSTANCENAME=MyNamedInstance SAVESYSDB=1
```

❏ If you are using Mixed Mode authentication for MSDE:

```
setup /qn /x Package_Or_ProductCode SAVESYSDB=1 SECURITYMODE=SQL
UPGRADEUSER=AnAdminLogin
UPGRADEPWD=AdminPassword
```

If any of the databases are involved in replication, you must disable publishing. To disable publishing use the SQL Server Enterprise Manager. In SQL Server Enterprise Manager, go to the instance and right-click the Replication folder. Click Configure Publishing, Subscribers, and Distribution. Click the Publication Databases tab. Clear the check box for each database that is involved in replication. This allows the databases to be detached.

2. Now you can do a clean install of SSE from the CD, using the USESYSDB parameter. Open a command prompt window and navigate to the SSE setup directory. Execute one of the following commands to install silently:

❏ If you are using windows authentication mode for the default instance of MSDE:

```
Setup.exe /qn ADDLOCAL=ALL USESYSDB=Location_Of_Datafiles
```

❏ If you are using windows authentication mode for a named instance of MSDE:

```
Setup.exe /qn ADDLOCAL=ALL USESYSDB=Location_Of_Datafiles
INSTANCENAME=MyNamedInstance
```

❏ If you are using Mixed Mode authentication for MSDE:

```
setup.exe /qn ADDLOCAL=ALL USESYSDB=Location_Of_Datafiles SECURITYMODE=SQL
UPGRADEUSER=AnAdminLogin
UPGRADEPWD=AdminPassword
```

The clean-install steps using GUI are similar to the ones described in Chapter 9 and the process is not explained further here. The only difference is that you specify the USESYSDB as a command line parameter for setup.exe.

How It Works

Manual upgrade of MSDE SP4 involves uninstalling MSDE with the SAVESYSDB parameter followed by clean installation of SSE with USESYSDB. Uninstallation from the Add/Remove Programs does not allow you to pass any additional parameters. Since the SAVESYSDB parameter needs to be passed for MSDE uninstall, you have to run setup from the command prompt. The /x Package or product code is a windows installer parameter, and uninstalls the product identified by the product or package code. (See http://msdn.microsoft.com/library/default.asp?url=/library/en-us/msi/setup/command_line_options .asp for additional information.) In this example you are passing the MSI directly instead of searching for the product code.

Once the upgrade is completed, all the user databases should be automatically upgraded and attached to the new server provided the system database settings are preserved. However, if this did not happen, the following techniques can be used to upgrade the user databases:

- ❏ **sp_attach_db and sp_detach_db:** You can use the sp_detach_db stored procedure to detach the database from MSDE, followed by sp_attach_db to attach the user database to SSE. The initial attach automatically runs the upgrade scripts on the database.

- ❏ **Backup and restore:** You can run backup on the MSDE user databases followed by running restore against SSE. The restore operation automatically runs the upgrade scripts on the database.

Summary

This chapter introduced you to the feature differences between MSDE and SSE so that you can determine the appropriateness of migrating from MSDE. You also learned about the different setup technologies used by MSDE so that you can determine whether your MSDE instance is appropriate for automatic or manual upgrades to SSE. Finally, this chapter walked through upgrade steps for both silent and graphical user interface (GUI) based installations.

In this chapter, you learned to

- ❏ Identify MSDE instances on your machine

- ❏ Understand the feature differences between MSDE and SSE

- ❏ Apply the upgrade rules to figure out if your MSDE instance qualifies for automatic upgrade

- ❏ Automatically upgrade MSDE using both GUI and silent modes of installation

- ❏ Manually upgrade MSDE using both GUI and silent modes of installation

In the next chapter, you learn more about moving from Microsoft Access and Jet to SSE.

Exercises

Try the exercises that follow to test your understanding of the material covered in this chapter. You can find the solutions to these exercises in Appendix A.

1. You are the IT manager for Joe's Garage, and your manager wants to know if there are any MSDE instances on his machine. How will you determine this?

2. How will you upgrade an instance of MSDE SP3 to MSDE SP4? Assume that you do not have a strong password for your sa account.

3. Install a new named instance of MSDE SP4 on your machine using the instance name of TestMSDE. You need only windows authentication and you do not need any remote networking. Use the Graphical User Interface to upgrade this instance to SSE.

4. Assume that your company uses accounting software that relies on an MSDE instance called AccountingDataInstance. There are five accountants in your company, and all of them have an instance of MSDE installed on their machines. What is the command line you will use to upgrade these instances silently to SSE, assuming that they qualify for automatic upgrades?

5. You are the IT manager for Joe's Garage, and your company uses a default instance of MSDE to store customer information. These MSDE installations do not qualify for automatic upgrades because the product codes of the MSIs have been changed. You are using the Windows Authentication mode and all the instances are at SP4 service pack level. How will you upgrade these instances silently to SSE?

Migrating from Jet and Microsoft Access to MSDE and SSE

In Chapter 11, you learned about migrating from MSDE. In this chapter, you learn about database development with Microsoft Access, as well as migrating from Microsoft Access and Jet to MSDE and eventually to SQL Server Express (SSE). Access and Jet provide a great beginning database development platform for client applications, but you will face difficulties when trying to scale up your application to support multiple concurrent users. Most of this chapter focuses on understanding the differences among Jet, MSDE, and SSE so that you can choose whether the migration makes sense for you. SSE is the successor to MSDE and uses the same SQL Server technologies, while Jet is very different. Hence, moving your applications from Jet to MSDE requires an Upsizing Wizard. Some manual intervention for DAO to ADO conversion is also required. If you are not currently using Jet or Access, you may choose to skip this chapter.

In this chapter, you learn:

- ❑ The feature differences among MSDE, SSE, and Jet
- ❑ How to develop simple database objects using Access and MSDE
- ❑ The mapping between DAO and ADO programming models and how it impacts the upgrade
- ❑ How to use the Upsizing Wizard to migrate a Jet application

Introduction to Microsoft Access and Jet

Microsoft Access is a powerful application that provides you with a good database development environment and user interface. It targets the desktop category of users and works best with individuals or small workgroups managing megabytes, rather than gigabytes, of data. It supports the Visual Basic for Applications (VBA) development environment, which is the standard development environment for the entire Microsoft Office suite. Powerful database engines such as Jet and MSDE are also included with the product. A database engine is the component that actually handles the data.

Jet is the default database engine supported by Access. Jet is a part of the Windows operating system, and is included in Visual Basic, Visual C++, Microsoft Access, and Microsoft Excel. It stores all data in Microsoft database (.mdb) files. These files contain not only the data, but also forms, reports, macros, and modules. Having everything in a single file makes it easy to manage data and applications. Jet is a multithreaded database engine and is very useful for small client applications. It supports formats such as ASCII text files, Microsoft Excel, dBase, FoxPro, and Paradox using the Indexed Sequential Access Method (ISAM) technology. ISAM is a technique for organizing and retrieving data in sequential or random modes. Access can also use open database connectivity (ODBC) to connect to other database servers supporting ODBC like Microsoft SQL Server, Oracle, Sybase, and so on. ODBC is a standard data access method that makes it possible to access data from any database server by using a *driver*. The driver can translate the application's queries and commands into the format required by the database engine.

There are a number of options for accessing data when using Microsoft Access:

❑ **Data Access Objects (DAO):** DAO is a programming interface for the Jet database engine. Being the first object-oriented interface exposed by Jet, it allows Visual Basic developers to directly connect to the Jet tables and other databases through ODBC. Many of the data access options in DAO are improved in ADO.

❑ **Remote Data Objects (RDO):** RDO is an easy-to-use, object-oriented interface to ODBC that is used to access relational data sources like SQL Server, Oracle, and Sybase. However, it cannot work well with Jet databases. If you are developing new applications, use ADO instead of RDO.

❑ **OLEDB:** Microsoft Access 2002 or later provides a native OLEDB programming interface to access the database. OLEDB is a component database architecture that provides efficient access to many types of data sources, including relational data, flat files, and spreadsheets. Unfortunately, OLEDB is hard to use.

❑ **ActiveX Data Objects (ADO):** ADO is an object-oriented interface that wraps the OLEDB interface to allow connectivity to all editions of SQL Server, including MSDE and SSE. It is the successor to DAO and RDO and provides a simpler object model than its predecessors. ADO does not support all of DAO's functionalities, although all of RDO's functionalities are supported.

Access client-server applications using OLEDB technologies are often created using Access (.adp) Projects. This is the preferred project mechanism to connect to SQL Server or MSDE because there is no ODBC translation layer, and the applications are directly using the SQL Server technologies. Microsoft Access allows you to easily manage all your information in an MSDE database using the following capabilities:

❑ **Store your data in a table format**: The columns in the table indicate the different fields or attributes, while a row indicates a record, or an entry in the database. A primary key or a unique id distinguishes the different records of the table. Access allows you to create and define relationships between tables by adding one table's unique id field to a related table.

❑ **Run queries against multiple tables to find and retrieve your data**: The queries are also used for adding, deleting, or updating multiple records at the same time.

❑ **Easily view, enter, and change data directly in a table using a form**: A form typically focuses on one record at a time, and you can design the layout of the form using a Form Wizard. A form can also contain buttons or custom code that prints, opens other objects, or otherwise automates tasks.

❑ **Analyze data using reports and present it in a fitting layout:** Typically you aggregate data in tables or calculate totals of relevant fields during the preparation of this report.

❑ **View, update, or analyze the data from the web using data access pages**: These pages allow interactive reporting, data entry, or data analysis from an intranet or the Internet. You can choose the layout using the Page Wizard.

Developing simple database applications with Jet is easy and straightforward. However, you should use MSDE or SSE if you are looking to scale your multi-user application or require the latest features like .NET. Database development with Access projects is covered to show how easy it is to develop projects with MSDE and Access. The examples in this chapter use Access 2002 and MSDE 2000, although they work with Access 2003 also.

However, if you have an existing Access application using Jet, migration to MSDE may not be easy. You can use the Upsizing Wizard to easily migrate the database objects such as tables to MSDE. Unfortunately, migrating application objects such as forms is not straightforward if you use DAO, and some manual intervention is required. This chapter covers some of the common areas you need to be aware of during this upgrade. Currently, the Upsizing Wizard does not support migrating directly to SSE from Jet, hence all the examples in this chapter use MSDE. Unfortunately, Access 2002 or 2003 versions do not support SSE, and there is no easy migration path for access applications to SSE.

Comparing SSE, MSDE, and Jet

Jet is a file-server database manager, which means that the database is treated just like a file. Since you are already familiar with the file-based paradigm present in Windows, it is very easy to get started with Jet. With the new Application Xcopy feature, development with SSE is as easy as with Jet for beginning users. When multiple users are using a file-based database, opening and reading information from the same file causes scalability problems. Server-based database systems like MSDE have dedicated file managers that deal with concurrency, resulting in improved application performance. Also, the Jet performance is limited by the processing power of the client machine since all the processing occurs on the client. With a server-based database system like MSDE, most requests are processed at the server, which means that there is less network traffic, high performance, and increased scalability.

The MSDE and SSE data engines are fully compatible with other editions of SQL Server so that the tables, stored procedures, and triggers will operate without modification in a SQL Server database of the same version. On the other hand, Jet applications must go through the Upsizing Wizard, which is described later in this chapter.

Microsoft Jet databases are secured with either share-level security or user-level security. In a share-level security scenario, the database is secured with a single password. All users accessing the database must specify the correct password. With user-level security, each user is assigned a user name and password to open the database. A separate workgroup information file, typically named system.mdw, is used to store user information and passwords. However, storing passwords like this is not very secure. MSDE and SSE support integrated security so that there is no need to store passwords. SSE security is covered in Chapter 13.

Jet has been in the maintenance stage for a long time, while MSDE and SSE are strategic to Microsoft. SSE contains the latest features such as .NET support and XML data type support. The following table compares the data type support between the engines.

The table on pages 226-227 compares the SSE, MSDE, and Jet features.

SQL Server Express Data Types	MSDE Data Types	Microsoft Access Data Types (Synonyms in parenthesis)	Description
bit	bit	BIT (BOOLEAN, LOGICAL, YESNO)	Stores either a 1(Yes) or 0(No)
tinyint, smallint, int, bigint	tinyint, smallint, int, bigint	TINYINT (INTEGER1, BYTE) SMALLINT (SHORT, INTEGER2) INTEGER (LONG, INT, INTEGER4)	Stores integer values
real, float	real, float	REAL (SINGLE, FLOAT4, IEEESINGLE) FLOAT (DOUBLE, FLOAT8, IEEEDOUBLE, NUMBER)	Stores positive and negative real numbers and zero
money, smallmoney	money, smallmoney	MONEY (CURRENCY)	Stores monetary values
decimal, numeric	decimal, numeric	DECIMAL (NUMERIC, DEC)	Stores decimal numbers
datetime and smalldatetime	datetime and smalldatetime	DATETIME (DATE, TIME)	Stores date and time values
int with Identity property defined	int with Identity property defined	AUTONUMBER(INCREMENT)	AutoNumber is a Microsoft Access data type that automatically stores a unique number for each record
Char, nchar, varchar(n), nvarchar(n), text and varchar(MAX)	Char, nchar, varchar(n), nvarchar(n), and text	TEXT (LONGTEXT, LONGCHAR, MEMO, NOTE, NTEXT) CHARACTER (TEXT(n), ALPHANUMERIC, CHARACTER, NCHAR, NATIONAL CHARACTER)	Stores Unicode and ANSI character data

SQL Server Express Data Types	MSDE Data Types	Microsoft Access Data Types (Synonyms in parenthesis)	Description
image	image	IMAGE (OLEOBJECT, LONGBINARY, GENERAL)	Holds binary data
uniqueidentifier	uniqueidentifier	UNIQUE IDENTIFIER (GUID)	A data type storing a unique identifier or GUID
char, nchar, varchar, or nvarchar with the Hyperlink property set to Yes	char, nchar, varchar, or nvarchar with the Hyperlink property set to Yes	HYPERLINK	A data type for storing hyperlink addresses in the format: *displaytext#address# subaddress#*
varbinary and varbinary(MAX)	Varbinary	BINARY (VARBINARY, BINARY VARYING,BIT VARYING)	Stores binary data
Timestamp	Timestamp	(no equivalent)	A data type that automatically updates every time a row is inserted or updated
sql_variant	sql_variant	(no equivalent)	Stores the values of several data types, except for text, ntext, image, timestamp, and sql_variant
XML data type	(no equivalent)	(no equivalent)	A native data type for storing XML data
.NET based user-defined data type (UDT)	(no equivalent)	(no equivalent)	Allows you to define your own data type

SSE Features	MSDE Features	Jet Features
Based on SQL Server 2005 engine	Based on SQL Server 2000 or SQL Server 7.0 engine	Jet is independent of SQL Server
Easily upgrades to other editions of SQL Server 2005	Easily upgrades to other editions of SQL Server	Requires an upgrade wizard to move to SQL Server
Supports new data types such as XML Data type, and User Defined Types	Does not support the new data types in SQL Server 2005	Does not support these data types
Xcopy and User Instance features	Does not support these features	Jet database files can be Xcopied
Supports Integrated Security	Supports Integrated Security	Does not support Integrated Security
Supports usage of .NET technology inside SQL Server, such as writing stored procedures in C#	Does not support using .NET inside SQL Server	Does not support using .NET inside SQL Server
Supports ADO.NET APIs	Support ADO.NET APIs	Does not have any .NET data access support
Merge, transactional, and snapshot replication subscription only	Merge, replication publishing, and subscription as well as transactional replication subscription supported	Supports replication
No SQL Agent support	SQL Agent supported for job scheduling	No SQL Agent support

SSE Features	MSDE Features	Jet Features
Maximum size of user database is 4G	Maximum size of user database is 2G	Maximum size of user database is 2G
1 CPU supported	2 CPUs supported	1 CPU supported
64-bit machines are supported via WOW, which allows 32-bit SQL Server binaries to run on 64-bit machines	There is no 64 bit support	No 64-bit support
Requires latest operating systems such as Windows 2000 SP4, XP SP2, and so on	Supports legacy operating systems such as Windows 98, Windows Me, Windows 2000 RTM, Windows 2000 SP1, Windows 2000 SP2, Windows 2000 SP3, XP RTM, XP SP1 and Windows NT 4.0 in addition to the later versions	Supports the legacy operating systems in addition to the latest versions
Medium redistribution size	High redistribution size	Small redistribution size
Easy to deploy	Hard to deploy	Easiest to deploy
Free to redistribute	Free to redistribute	Free to redistribute
GUI management tools available as a separate web download	No GUI management tools from Microsoft	Microsoft Access is the GUI tool

Introduction to Access Project Development with MSDE

Because Access does not support any .NET technologies or the new SQL Native Access provider, only MDAC-based providers like SQLOLEDB or SQLODBC work with MSDE. Also, Access 2003 does not understand user instances or Xcopy deployment features supported by SSE. In this section, you learn to create Access Projects using MSDE. You will develop and populate SQL Server tables, and create views and stored procedures.

To access MSDE with Access, you should create a Microsoft Access project (ADP), which is an Access data file that provides efficient access to the MSDE database through OLEDB. This file works natively with MSDE, just like an Access database file (.mdb) works with the Jet database engine. After you've connected to the MSDE database, you can easily view, create, modify, and delete objects within the MSDE database from within Access without involving any Jet or ODBC layers.

Some of the advantages of Microsoft Access projects for accessing client-server data include the following:

❑   There is no extra ODBC or Jet translation involved when accessing MSDE databases.

An alternative to using ADP involves the use of linked tables. When you use linked tables, the Access SQL statements used by the application are first translated to ODBC SQL, which may be further translated to the SQL dialect specific to the database server. The translations can be slow and error prone. In addition, the query produced may not be optimized to the database server.

❑   You can use the Access development environment that you are already familiar with for creating MSDE tables, views, database diagrams, and stored procedures. You can build forms, reports, data access pages, and modules that access MSDE data using the same development environment.

❑   The server performs most of the query processing and so the client requires fewer resources.

❑   You can use the SQL Server features supported via OLEDB such as asynchronous queries, batch updates, and integrated security, which is not available otherwise.

The disadvantages of using a Microsoft Access project are:

❑   In an Access database, you could create local tables in your .mdb file. But with ADP projects, the tables have to be created within SQL Server. This could result in unnecessary network traffic if you use inefficient queries that obtain one record at a time for operations such as populating combo boxes or list boxes. T-SQL is a set-based language that is efficient at retrieving sets of data, unlike Access SQL, which is better at retrieving records one at a time.

❑   You cannot create local queries, but have to rely on views, stored procedures, or functions defined in MSDE. It is challenging and time-consuming to rebuild complex Access queries as views and stored procedures.

> In an Access project, database objects like tables, views, user-defined functions, database diagrams, and stored procedures are stored and managed by MSDE. Your .adp file contains the application objects such as forms, reports, data access pages, macros, and modules. There is clean separation between database objects and application objects.

The Access Project files (.adp) cannot be shared between users because the first user always opens it in exclusive mode. For multi-user applications, each user should have a copy of the project. However, the underlying data and database objects inside MSDE are not copied, but are shared among these users. This is important to ensure proper security for these shared database objects, so that a malicious user cannot tamper with them. Refer to Chapter 13 for additional discussion on assigning permissions to users and groups.

Since Application Xcopy is not supported for OLEDB, the MSDE database file cannot be simply be copied to another location. Access 2003 provides database utilities on the Tools menu; these are described in the following table.

Menu Option	Description
Back Up SQL Database	Creates a backup of the MSDE database
Restore SQL Database	Restores a MSDE database from a backup database file
Drop SQL Database	Deletes a MSDE database
Copy Database File	Copies a MSDE database to another MSDE or SQL Server 2000 instance
Transfer Database	Transfers a MSDE database to another MSDE or SQL Server 2000 instance

You can create an Access project using MSDE as the data store using the following Try It Out.

Try It Out   Creating an Access Data Project

1.   Select the Project (New Data) option from the File ⇨ New menu. A screen similar to Figure 12-1 appears. Specify the name of the project (such as MyADPProject) and click Create.

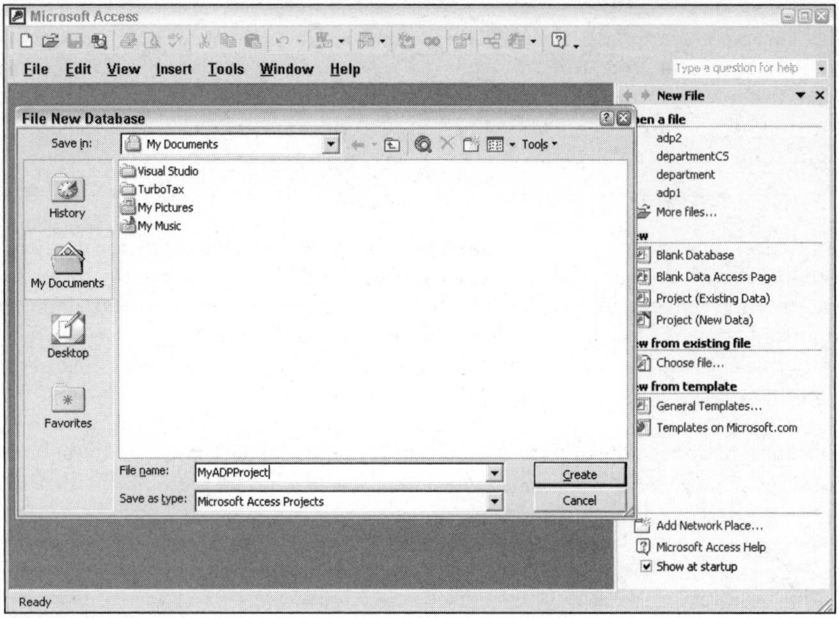

Figure 12-1

2. The Microsoft SQL Server Database Wizard dialog appears (Figure 12-2). Specify the name of your MSDE instance or select one from the list. Check the Use Trusted Connection check box to specify Windows NT Integrated Security instead of using SQL Authentication. Now specify the name of the MSDE database you want to create, and click the Next button.

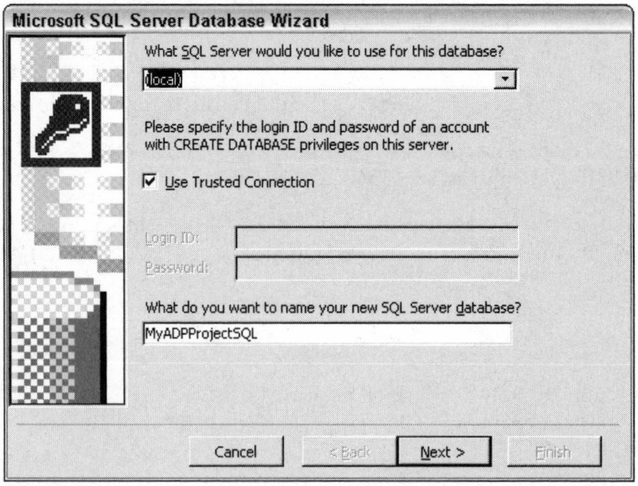

Figure 12-2

3. Click Finish in the next dialog box to create the project and the database.

How It Works

Creating an Access project is very similar to working with an Access (.mdb) database. Under File ⇨ New, you have two options to build an Access Data Project: creating an ADP file using an existing SQL Server database, or building an ADP file based on a new SQL Server database.

The Data Link Properties dialog is accessible from the File ⇨ Connection menu and lets you specify connection information about the SQL Server database that the ADP file is associated with. You should use Windows Authentication so that you do not have to pass the user id and password required for SQL Authentication. SQL Server uses your network login identity when Windows Authentication is chosen. If you want additional information about the network settings or access permissions, click the Advanced tab of the data links dialog. The All tab defines the initialization properties for the OLEDB provider. After you finish specifying all options, click Test Connection to ensure that all settings have been specified correctly.

Now that you have an Access data project, you can create tables, views, and stored procedures as in the following Try It Out.

Try It Out   Creating MSDE Database Objects Using Access 2000

Creating MSDE database objects in Access 2000 requires three tasks: building a table and adding rows; creating a stored procedure; and creating a view.

Follow steps 1-5 to create a table using MSDE and add rows to it:

1. Select the Tables Node in the database window and double-click the option Create Table in Design View.

2. Fill in the values in the Table Designer as shown in Figure 12-3.

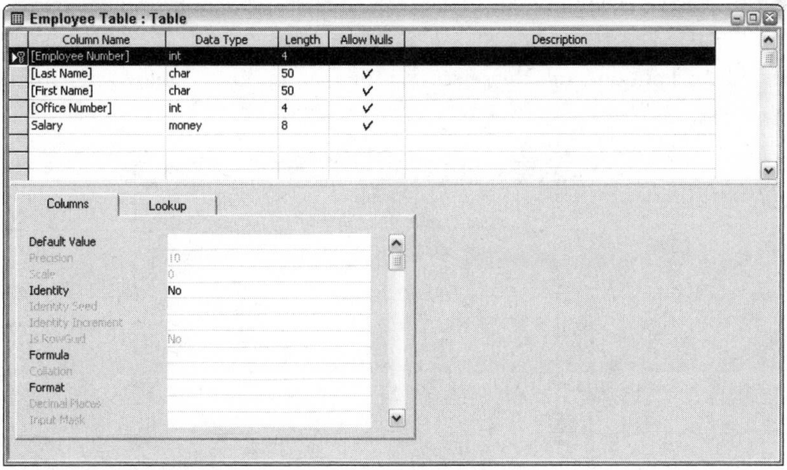

Figure 12-3

3. Click the Allow Nulls column next to the Employee Number in the Table Designer so that the tick mark is cleared indicating that NULL values are not allowed for this field. Right-click Employee Number and select the primary key option from the popup list.

4. Select File ⇨ Save and enter the table name as **Employee Table**. Click OK.

5. Select Datasheet view and populate the table by entering data in the respective fields as shown in Figure 12-4.

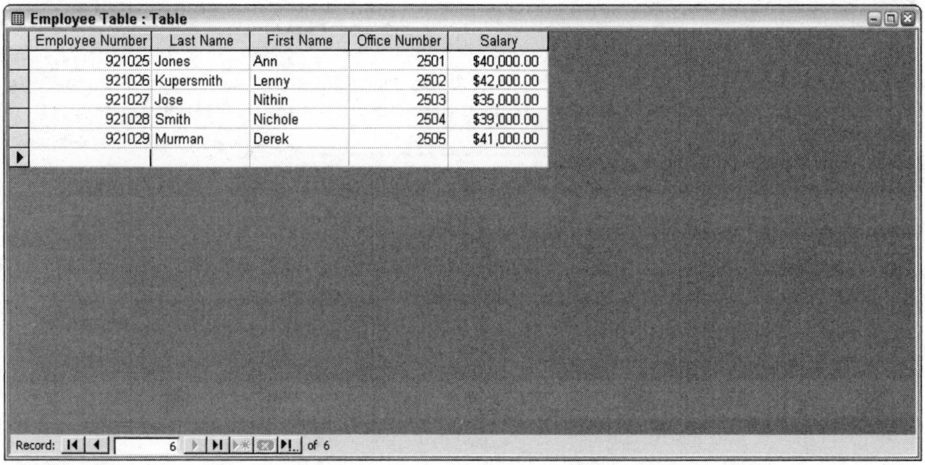

Employee Number	Last Name	First Name	Office Number	Salary
921025	Jones	Ann	2501	$40,000.00
921026	Kupersmith	Lenny	2502	$42,000.00
921027	Jose	Nithin	2503	$35,000.00
921028	Smith	Nichole	2504	$39,000.00
921029	Murman	Derek	2505	$41,000.00

Figure 12-4

Follow steps 6-9 to create a stored procedure in MSDE:

6. Select the Queries node from the database window and double-click the option Create Stored Procedure in Designer.

7. Click the Add button while the selection is on the Employee Table as shown in Figure 12-5. Click Close.

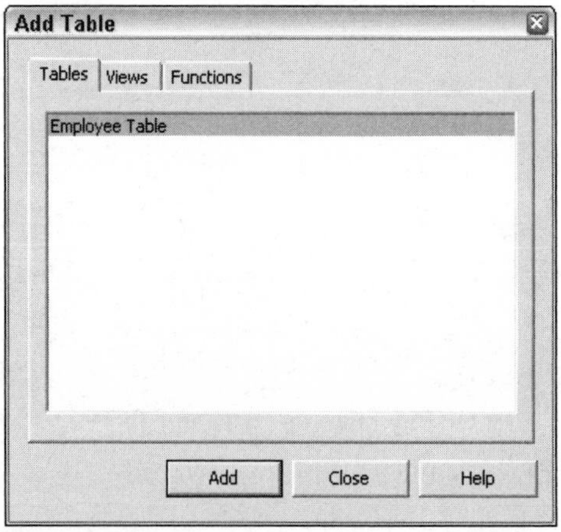

Figure 12-5

8. Click the check boxes next to Employee Number, Last Name, Office Number, and Salary so that they are selected as shown in Figure 12-6. Select File ➪ Save and save the stored procedure as sp_GetEmployeeData.

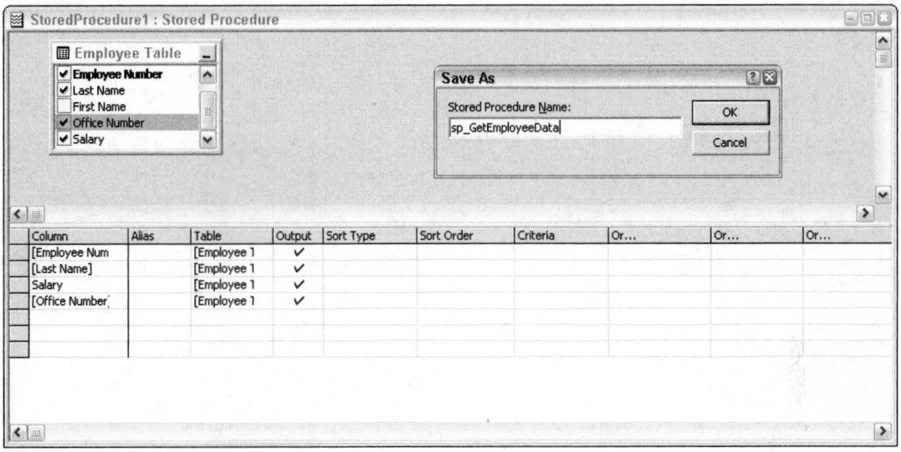

Figure 12-6

9. Select View ➪ SQL View to see the SQL statements behind the stored procedure (see Figure 12-7). Select the Datasheet view option from the View menu to run the stored procedure.

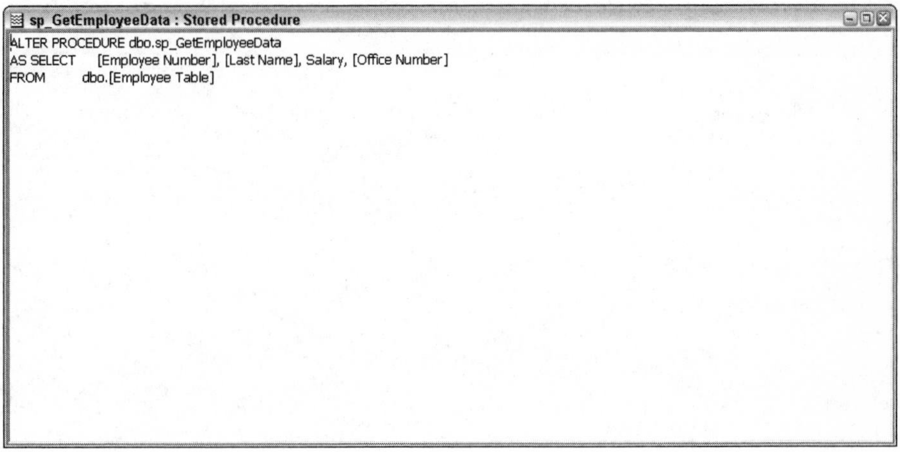

Figure 12-7

Follow steps 10-13 to create a view in MSDE.

10. Select Queries from the database window and click CreateView in Designer.

11. Click the Add button while the selection is on the Employees Table. (This is similar to step 7.) Click Close.

12. Click the check boxes next to the Employee Number, Last Name, Office Number, and Salary so that they are selected as shown in Figure 12-8. Select File ⇨ Save and save the view as **vw_EmployeeData**.

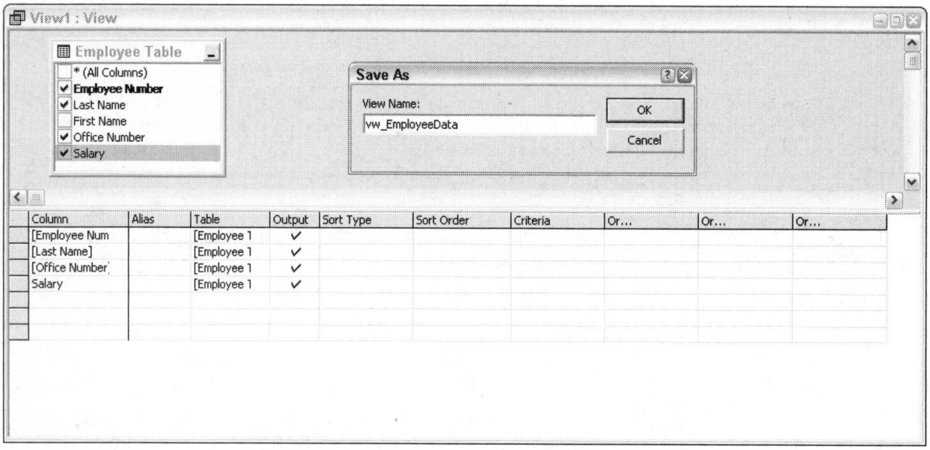

Figure 12-8

13. Select the Datasheet view option from the View menu to see the data from the view (see Figure 12-9).

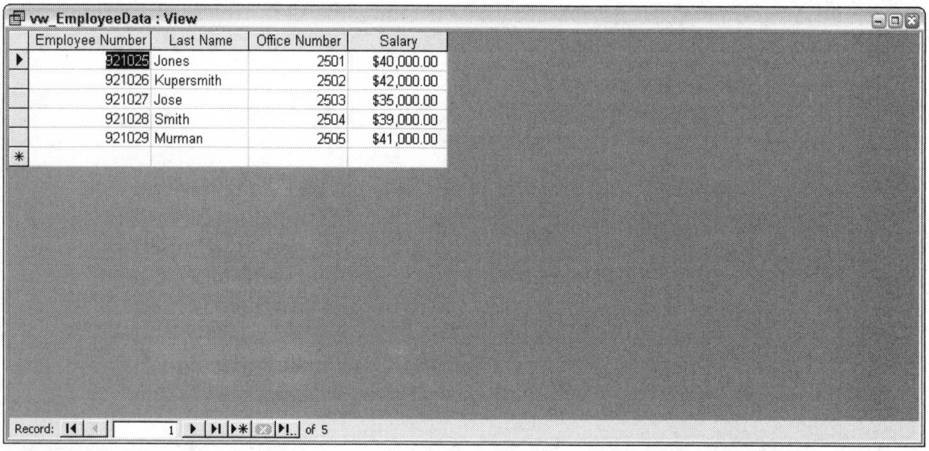

Figure 12-9

How It Works

It is easy to create MSDE database objects with Access. After you connect to an SQL Server database, you can view, create, modify, and delete tables, views, stored procedures, user-defined functions, and database diagrams by using the designers provided with Microsoft Access. This Try It Out demonstrated the usage of these wizards.

Migrating from Jet to MSDE or SSE

In the previous section, you learned about some of the features supported by Jet, MSDE, and SSE. This section teaches you how to decide whether it makes sense to move your application to use MSDE or SSE instead of Jet. You learn about upgrading from Access database (.mdb) to Access project (.adp). As mentioned earlier, all the examples in this section use MSDE because of the Upsizing Wizard limitations. You can easily move an MSDE database to use SSE. When the database developed with MSDE first attaches to SSE, it is upgraded and the transformation cannot be reversed. Unfortunately, there is no direct upgrade path to SSE and the upgrade tools are expected to come at a later time. Hence, if you want to use SSE, first the application should be converted to use MSDE. The second step is to follow the automatic upgrade process described in Chapter 11 to migrate from MSDE to SSE. Currently it is not possible to move the Access application to use SSE because of the limitations in Access 2003 support.

MSDE or SSE is preferred to Jet in the following cases:

❑ You are considering upgrading to SQL Server in the future.

❑ You are concerned about performance and throughput in a multi-user environment.

❑ You want to use .NET technologies like ADO.NET.

❑ You prefer server-based processing compared to client-based processing to reduce network traffic and improve scalability.

❑ You want higher security in the form of finer-grained control over the databases, encryption, or integrated security.

❑ You want to use the data types or features present in MSDE or SSE.

❑ You want to use a true relational database engine for storing your data.

❑ Your application is business-critical and requires features such as transaction logging, point in time recovery, or fault tolerance.

Jet is preferred over MSDE or SSE in the following cases:

❑ You are highly concerned about storage space, system memory, or web download requirements.

❑ You have multiple versions of an existing Jet application, and you do not see the requirements for larger number of concurrent users or the need for upgrading to SQL Server in the future.

An Access database (.mdb) uses Jet to store the data and application objects, while an Access project (.adp) uses MSDE for storing data. Developing Access projects is recommended in all the cases where MSDE is preferred over Jet.

Unfortunately it is not easy to migrate an Access database (.mdb) to an Access project (.adp). You have to worry about upgrading your database objects such as tables and views, as well as application objects such as modules and macros. Most of the database object translations are handled by the Upsizing Wizard. There are some variations in T-SQL syntax, such as ORDER BY usage in views that require manual upgrade. Application objects migration depends upon the choice of programming language. For instance, ADO is easy for migration to Access project, while the usage of DAO implies manual migration.

The following section covers upgrading your Jet Access application to use MSDE.

Upgrading from Access Database to Access Projects

An Access database (.mdb) contains both database objects such as tables and application objects such as forms and modules. During a migration, some or all of these objects are transferred. This section shows you how to use the Access 2003 Upsizing Wizard for upgrading from Jet. The database objects get upgraded to the MSDE database, while the application objects become part of a new Microsoft Access project (.adp). In this section, you learn about the factors to consider before using the wizard as well as the options available during the upgrade process. If you are currently using DAO, you might have to go through an additional manual step described in the "Upgrading Application Objects" section.

Upgrading Database Objects

The Upsizing Wizard that comes as part of Access migrates all the data and data definitions inside an Access (.mdb) file to MSDE. This wizard creates new SQL Server database structures for the tables, indexes, and the default settings. It also maintains the table relationships, referential integrity, and the Access validation rules. Additionally, the Upsizing Wizard tries to re-create your queries as SQL Server views or stored procedures. It is important to understand what gets upgraded when using the Upsizing Wizard. The key items that are affected by an upgrade include the following:

❑ The connection and the data binding information changes in order to work with the new SQL Server database.

❑ All Access database data types are converted to their equivalent in SQL Server. The data types table presented earlier compares the MSDE and Access data types.

❑ The Upsizing Wizard takes care of duplicate table names, delimiter differences for data types, and wildcard characters while converting databases.

❑ The VBA functions that can occur in table validation rules, field validation, or defaults convert to equivalent T-SQL functions. For example, the Asc() function in VBA gets transformed to the ASCII() function in T-SQL.

❑ Access syntax not supported in MSDE like DISTINCTROW, OWNERACCESS, TRANSFORM, or PARAMETERS is removed from the T-SQL statements during upgrade.

❑ There is no simple upgrade path for Access features like the switchboard manager form or Dynamic Data Exchange (DDE).

❑ Custom command bars and startup properties are upgraded.

❑ The Upsizing Wizard upgrades all unique and nonunique indexes in the Access file so that they become unique and nonunique SQL Server indexes. All the primary keys in the Access file are converted to Microsoft SQL Server nonclustered, unique indexes and they are marked as SQL Server primary keys. If you link the upsized SQL Server table to your Access database, the Upsizing Wizard automatically adds the prefix aaaaa to ensure that this index is prioritized over existing ones. Any illegal characters are replaced with the underscore (_) character. All other indexes retain their names. MSDE does not support ascending or descending indexes.

❑ The Upsizing Wizard upgrades all Default Value properties to ANSI equivalents.

❑ The table relationships are migrated using Declarative Referential Integrity (DRI) or Triggers.

  ❑ Declarative Referential Integrity (DRI) enforces referential integrity through primary and foreign key constraints. The Upsizing Wizard only establishes DRI relationships between related tables that upsize at the same time, but it cannot establish relationships between those tables and pre-existing tables on the MSDE. Hence DRI prevents you from overwriting related tables that are already upsized due to a previous upgrade.

  ❑ Triggers are used to execute custom validation code when there is an operation on a table like INSERT, UPDATE, or DELETE. Triggers can also replace the functionality of cascading updates and deletes, something that DRI does not support. Each table relation may become part of several triggers or each trigger may contain code to emulate the functionality of several referential integrity rules. Insert triggers are typically used on child tables while delete triggers are present on parent tables.

Use triggers for table relationships (instead of DRI) if your Microsoft Access table relationships have cascading updates or deletes defined.

❑ All the Access validation rules transform to update and insert triggers. Each Access validation rule may become part of several triggers, or each trigger may contain code to emulate the functionality of several validation rules.

❑ All SELECT queries convert to a user-defined function or view depending on the presence of the ORDER BY clause. Other types of queries, like UPDATE, APPEND, or DELETE, convert to stored procedures or inline user-defined functions.

Views are used as virtual tables to allow you to create queries without directly implementing the complex joins that underlie the query. However, MSDE does not allow parameters or ORDER BY clauses in views. Hence, if the SELECT query contains an ORDER BY clause, an equivalent user defined function is used instead of a view. See the following Try It Out for additional details.

❑ The SQL pass-through queries, data definition queries, crosstab queries, or deeply nested queries are not updated by the wizard, and you have to manually update them. All of these can be implemented with a combination of a T-SQL SELECT statement, a stored procedure, or a view.

Some Access queries are created on top of other queries in a nested fashion. Nested queries in Access become nested views in SQL Server. Since the ORDER BY clauses cannot be part of a view definition, you must create a stored procedure that contains a SELECT statement that queries the view appended by an ORDER BY clause. The process is similar to the following Try It Out.

Try It Out   Converting an Access Query to Its MSDE Equivalent

Suppose you have an Access query that contains an ORDER BY clause as shown:

```
SELECT *
FROM CUSTOMERS
WHERE TERRITORY = ,"WestCoast,"
ORDER BY LAST_NAME
```

Before running the Upsizing Wizard, the query must be converted to its SQL Server equivalent using view and a stored procedure as follows:

```
CREATE VIEW WEST_CUSTOMERS AS
SELECT * FROM CUSTOMERS
WHERE TERRITORY = ,"WestCoast,"

CREATE PROCEDURE WEST_CUSTOMERS_ORDER AS
SELECT * FROM WEST_CUSTOMERS ORDER BY LAST NAME
```

How It Works

Since views in SQL Server do not support the ORDER BY clause directly, a stored procedure is created in addition to the view. The first T-SQL statement creates a view of all customers whose territory matches WestCoast. The stored procedure WEST_CUSTOMERS_ORDER uses the ORDER BY clause to obtain results similar to the Access statement.

Upgrading Application Objects

The Upsizing Wizard offers three options for upgrading application objects:

❏ **Create a new Client Server Application:** A new Access project file (.adp) is created by the Upsizing Wizard. The default name of this file is the current Access database name with a CS suffix. The forms, reports, and data access pages that refer to the local database are converted to use the newly upsized SQL Server tables, views, and stored procedures. Any references to databases other than the current database are unchanged after upsizing.

This approach requires some manual application changes to the code after the upgrade is complete if you are currently using a DAO programming model for your Access (.mdb) database. Please refer to the next section for additional details.

❏ **Use the local Access file with linked tables to MSDE:** The existing MDB database is modified so that the queries, forms, reports, and data access pages use linked tables to connect to the upsized tables in the new MSDE database. The original MDB table is renamed with the suffix _local. For example, if you upsize a table named Sales, the table is renamed Sales_local while the new linked MSDE table is named Sales. Queries, forms, reports, and data access pages based on the original MDB Sales table will now use the linked MSDE Sales table. This approach requires very little application modification since the code is still using the Jet DB engine.

❏ **Do not change your application:** You can use this option if you want to migrate only your data and not make any other changes to your existing Access database application.

Running the Upsizing Wizard is not a perfect process. There are incompatibilities between Access databases and SQL Server databases that cannot be fully handled by the Wizard. Therefore, you need to understand the design considerations as well as the items that cannot be converted automatically. Some key factors to keep in mind while upgrading the application objects include:

❏ The SQL statements in RecordSource, ControlsSource, and RowSource properties for forms, reports, and controls are kept in place and are not converted to a stored procedure or user-defined function.

❏ The Upsizing Wizard does not make any changes to modules and macros, which means you have to deal with them manually.

❑ If your existing Access database (.mdb) uses DAO, then you need to manually convert code that uses record sets from DAO to ADO in your modules.

❑ The Upsizing Wizard does not upsize SQL Data Definition Language (DDL). You should manually revise any table and query design code using the ADOX provider.

❑ You should also decide whether to use client-side cursors or server-side cursors. A client-side cursor uses the client computer to hold the result sets. While this allows for disconnected scenarios, new records that are added since the last query are not visible to the client in certain cases. MSDE supports server-side cursors where the result set is located on the server itself. Using server-side cursors will improve performance in certain scenarios, such as scrolling through the records in a record set, and you will be able to see records added to tables without having to re-query the record set.

If the Upsizing Wizard experiences a problem during the upsizing process, the wizard does not stop, but instead records the error and then continues. After the upsizing process is complete, the wizard displays a report that describes the error. When using the Upsizing Wizard, it is important to review all changes made to tables, views, forms, and reports. It is equally important to verify the logic used in any stored procedures that are created, and to review any declared table relationships.

Mapping DAO to ADO

Many Access applications were written using Microsoft Visual Basic for Applications (VBA) or the Visual Basic for Applications Access user interface. Applications that use VBA as the development environment run against SQL Server using the Jet ODBC driver. Applications that use the forms and reports in the Access user interface can access SQL Server using linked tables. However, these applications are not optimal for the client/server environment. For example, if you run an unmodified Access application on SQL Server, you send suboptimal T-SQL to the database by using Data Access Objects (DAO) with the Jet ODBC driver. For example, a DELETE statement that uses the Jet ODBC driver to delete 10,000 rows makes 10,000 calls to the database, which negatively impacts performance. Also, creating queries against a mix of Jet and SQL Server using linked tables is very resource-intensive. It is better to go directly against SQL Server by using ADO. This section gives you a brief introduction to ADO and points out the similarities between the ADO and DAO models. The assumption is that you already know DAO, and no attempt is made to explain it.

Three distinct object models in ADO together provide the functionality found in DAO. These three models are ADO (ADODB), Microsoft ADO Extensions for DDL and Security (ADOX), and Microsoft Jet and Replication Objects (JRO). Many applications will need just one of these subsets of functionality. By splitting the functionality, applications do not need to incur the overhead of loading unnecessary information into memory.

The ADODB object model is less hierarchical than the DAO model, which means that different ADODB objects provide the functionality you expect from a DAO object. For example, the data access functionality provided by the DAO Database object is distributed in Connection and Recordset objects exposed by ADO. The object relationships are shown in the following table. You could also expect slight differences in the corresponding properties and methods. Since ADO is used against multiple data providers, its connection string will contain an additional provider tag indicating the OLEDB provider to use. Also, unlike DAO, most ADO objects can be created independently. The exceptions include ADO Error and Field objects, since they depend on the corresponding Connection and Recordset objects, and hence cannot be created independently.

There are also slight changes in behavior when moving from DAO to ADO. For example, DAO and ADO behave differently when a new record is added. With DAO, the record that was current before you inserted the new one continues to remain current even after insertion. With ADO, the newly inserted record becomes the current record and there is no need to explicitly reposition on the new record to get information. Another difference is the behavior of the Update method. In DAO, if Update is not called before moving to the next record, all changes are lost. In ADO, the changes are automatically committed unless CancelUpdate is explicitly invoked.

DAO Object	ADODB Objects with Corresponding Methods/ Properties
DBEngine	Connection
Workspace	Connection
Database	Connection, Recordset
Recordset	Recordset
QueryDef	Command, Recordset

In ADOX, the Catalog object is the container for the data-definition collections, including Tables, Procedures, Views, Columns, Indexes, Keys, and so on. It also contains the security collections for Users and Groups so that an administrator can control database schema and grant relevant permissions to users and groups. In DAO, the Database object contains the data-definition collections while the Workspace object contains the security collections. Another difference is that the DAO Workspace may contain multiple databases, while a Catalog object cannot.

The JRO provider works only with a Jet database, and provides features for creating, modifying, and synchronizing replicas. The primary object in the JRO model is the Replica object, which has the corresponding feature supported by the Database object in DAO.

Now you are ready to use the Upsizing Wizard on the department sample Access database as described in the Try It Out. The department Access application is provided on Wrox website as a part of the code accompanying this book.

Try It Out   Using the Upsizing Wizard to Migrate Access Database (.mdb) to Access Project (.adp)

In this example, you run the Access Upsizing Wizard against the sample department Access file. Before you start the migration wizard, verify the following.

❑   You have a backup for your Access (.mdb) database.

❑   You have adequate unused disk space of at least two times the size of the Access database.

❑   Each Access table has a unique index or primary key.

This step is necessary because the unique indexes are created by the Upsizing Wizard only if a primary key or a unique index already exists in the .mdb database to be upgraded. Without a unique index, a linked table is not updateable in Microsoft Access.

❑   You should have READ and DESIGN permissions on the Access database objects.

❑   You should have relevant permissions on SQL Server like CREATE TABLE, CREATE DEFAULT, and CREATE DATABASE. In addition, you should have SELECT permissions on system tables in the Master database.

❑   The name used for each database object follows the MSDE rules and is not a reserved key word. Refer to Chapter 2 for additional information about naming database objects.

❑   MSDE is already installed on the desktop and you are aware of the instance name.

The steps to upgrade sample database using the Upsizing Wizard are as follows:

1.   Download the department Access application from the Wrox website and save it to a local folder. Double-click department.mdb to open the department Access sample database.

2.   Select Tools ⇨ Database Utilities ⇨ Upsizing Wizard. The Upsizing Wizard opens. Select Create new database and click Next to continue.

3.   Choose the instance name of MSDE you want to use from the drop-down list. Click the check box next to Use Trusted Connection (see Figure 12-10). The wizard suggests a database name based on the original Access database name. You can either accept this name or provide a new one. Click Next to continue.

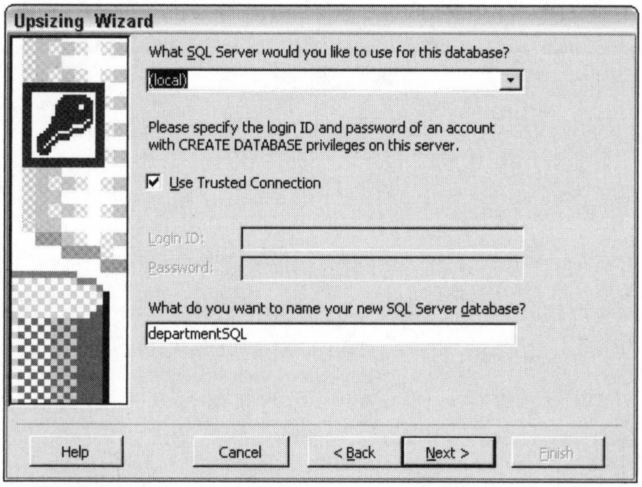

Figure 12-10

4. From the dialog box that appears, select the tables you want to migrate from the list on the left pane and click the arrow pointing to the right so that the selected table is now a part of the Export to SQL Server list. Repeat for all the Available Tables until all the tables have been moved to the Export list, as in Figure 12-11. Click Next.

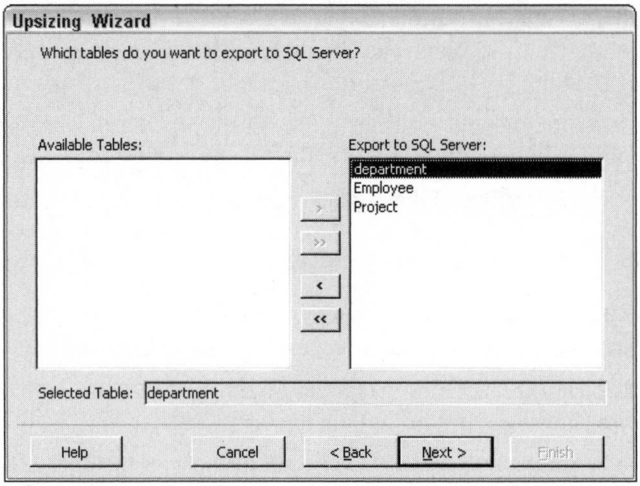

Figure 12-11

5. Check the boxes next to the table attributes to be converted, as shown in Figure 12-12. By default, all attributes are already selected. Verify that the Use DRI button under the Table Relationship check box is enabled. Do not change the default setting for timestamp fields. Click Next to continue.

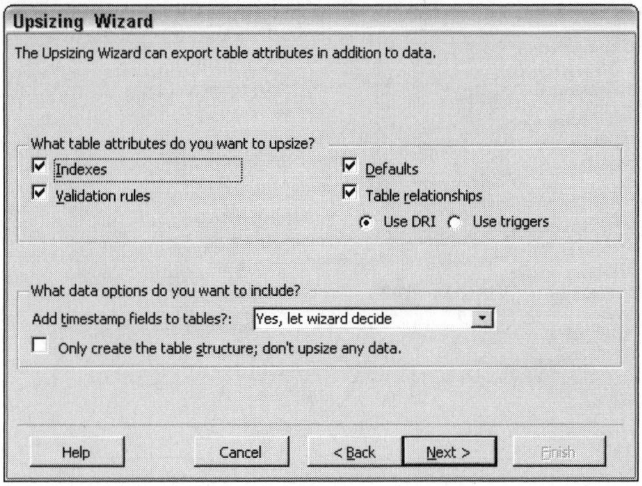

Figure 12-12

6. In the next dialog, by default, Access chooses the option Create a New Access Client/Server Application and specifies the location of the new Access Project to use (see Figure 12-13). Click Next.

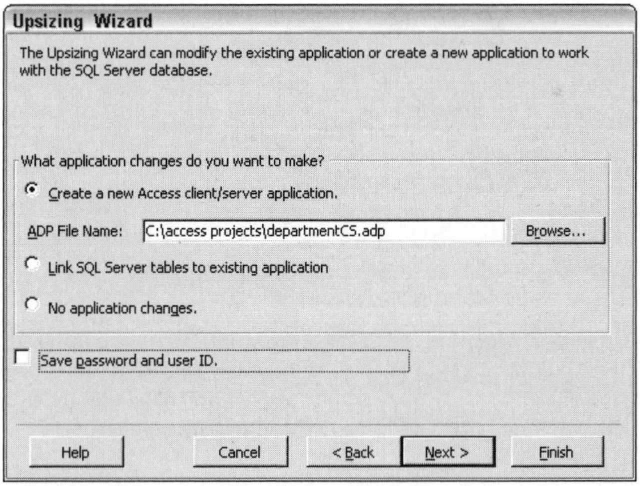

Figure 12-13

As a security measure, do not enable the Save password and User Id check box in step 6. You do not want user id and password stored as part of the application.

7. In the next dialog, leave the default choice, Open the New ADP File, checked, and click Finish to start the upgrade.

A report is displayed at the end of the upgrade operation as shown in Figure 12-14.

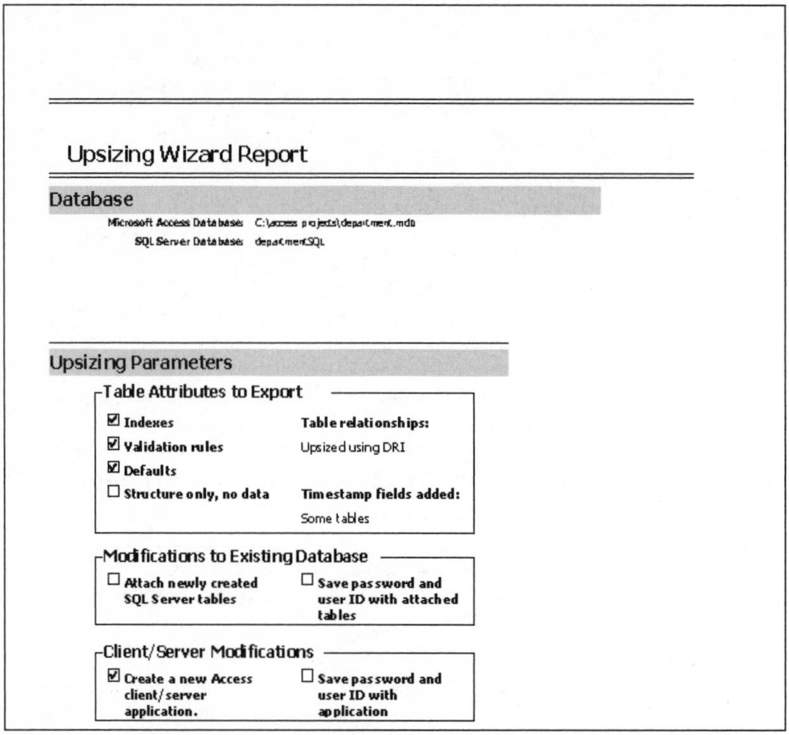

Upsizing Wizard Report

Database

Microsoft Access Database: C:\access projects\department.mdb
SQL Server Database: departmentSQL

Upsizing Parameters

Table Attributes to Export

- ☑ Indexes
- ☑ Validation rules
- ☑ Defaults
- ☐ Structure only, no data

Table relationships:
Upsized using DRI

Timestamp fields added:
Some tables

Modifications to Existing Database

- ☐ Attach newly created SQL Server tables
- ☐ Save password and user ID with attached tables

Client/Server Modifications

- ☑ Create a new Access client/server application.
- ☐ Save password and user ID with application

Figure 12-14

How It Works

The Upsizing Wizard gets information about the Access database to be upsized as well as the connection information about the MSDE instance in steps 1 to 3. You select the database objects to be upgraded in steps 4 and 5. In step 6 you choose the appropriate application object upgrade strategy. The underlying events of the steps are described in detail in the following paragraphs.

The Available Tables list box in step 4 includes all linked tables except for MSDE tables already in a MSDE database. Any table that has a name ending in "local" is excluded from the list of available tables to prevent upsizing tables that have already been upsized. The hidden tables and system tables are also excluded from upsizing.

In step 5, the timestamp field is a data type whose value gets updated automatically every time anything changes in the record containing the field. This is very useful to determine if a record was changed. The timestamp list box in the Upsizing Wizard provides three choices:

❑ **Yes, let wizard decide:** This is the default value. If the Microsoft Access table contains a Single or Double floating-point, Memo, or OLE Object field, then a timestamp field is automatically added to the table during upgrading.

❑ **Yes, always:** A timestamp field is always added to the table regardless of existing data types in the table.

❑ **No, Never:** If this option is chosen, a timestamp field is never added to the table automatically during upgrade.

By default all the table attributes (in step 5) are selected for upgrade. If you do not choose any table attribute, the Upsizing Wizard converts Microsoft Access field names and data types to the MSDE equivalents; the other attributes are not changed. If you select the Only Create Table Structure; Don't Upsize Any Data check box in step 5, only the data structure is upsized.

The Upsizing Wizard creates a report snapshot that provides a detailed description of all objects created, upsizing parameters used, and table information, and also reports any errors encountered during the process. Some of the errors could be due to inadequate permissions, skipping of a validation rule, a relationship not enforced, or the inability to convert a query to MSDE. This report has the same name as the Access database with a .snp extension (for example, Northwind.snp), and is stored in the default database folder. This report contains confidential or sensitive information and should be protected from a malicious user.

Summary

This chapter introduced you to the differences between MSDE, SSE, and Jet so that you can determine the appropriateness of migrating from Jet. Developing new MSDE applications with Access is easy, and you created simple database objects like tables, stored procedures, and views inside an Access project. Finally, you used the Upsizing Wizard to upgrade the Access (.mdb) database to an Access (.adp) project.

In this chapter, you learned:

❑ The advantages and disadvantages of migrating to MSDE and SSE from Jet

❑ How to create an Access (.adp) project that uses MSDE as its data store, and how to create tables, stored procedures, and views in MSDE using Microsoft Access

❑ The difference between database objects and application objects when using the Upsizing Wizard

❑ The object model mapping of ADO and DAO

❑ How to use the Upsizing Wizard against a sample database

In the next chapter, you learn about the SSE security concepts and securing your multi-user database application.

Exercises

Try the exercises that follow to test your understanding of the material covered in this chapter. You can find the solutions to these exercises in Appendix A.

1. Create an Access Project called MyOrderDBProject to store information about your orders and shipping details. Create the following tables and use appropriate data types for the fields.

Table Name	Field Names	Primary Key
Customer	CustomerNumber, Balance, CustomerDescription	CustomerNumber
ShipTo	Address, CustomerNumber	Address
Order	OrderNumber, Address, Date	OrderNumber
Order Details	OrderNumber, LineNumber, ItemNumber, Quantityordered	OrderNumber, LineNumber
Item Details	ItemNumber, Description	ItemNumber

2. Create views for each of the tables in Exercise 1 so that you can see the data in each table. Select all the fields for the view.

3. What is the ADO equivalent of the following DAO Recordset values?

- ❑ Cursor type of dbOpenSnapshot
- ❑ Cursor type of dbOpenForwardOnly
- ❑ Option value for dbAppendOnly
- ❑ Option value for dbInconsistent
- ❑ Lock type of dbReadOnly
- ❑ Lock type of dbOptimistic

Part IV:

Developing Multi-User Applications

Chapter 13: Securing Your Multi-User Database Application

Chapter 14: Upgrading from SSE to Other SQL Server 2005 Editions

Chapter 15: Building Robust Multi-User Database Applications

Securing Your Multi-User Database Application

Understanding and dealing with SQL Server 2005 security is a challenging task for most developers. In Chapter 6, you learned about the file permissions model used by the user instance model. The user instance model simplifies the security experience when you develop single-user database applications. However, when you use SSE in the service mode for a multi-user application, you should understand the authentication and authorization security models that are described in this chapter. If you only plan to develop single-user applications with user instances, you may choose to skip this chapter.

SSE manages a hierarchical collection of objects including the server itself, the databases, and the database objects such as tables and views. Each of these objects is owned by individuals or groups, who are authenticated by the server. To develop secure applications, you must understand the rules SSE uses to allow access to these objects. This chapter addresses the following topics:

- ❑ Logins and Roles
- ❑ SQL authentication and Windows authentication
- ❑ The permissions model in SSE
- ❑ The SSE Objects hierarchy and how it is applicable to security
- ❑ The SSE security model

Introduction to SSE Security

SSE has a rich security infrastructure to protect its resources. This section introduces you to the hierarchical model in which these resources are defined. The hierarchy is applicable not only to objects like database and tables, but also to the permissions applicable to Logins and Users.

SSE Objects Hierarchy

An SSE instance contains a hierarchical collection of objects defined within it. The SSE objects hierarchy is described in the following list and is illustrated in Figure 13-1.

❏ *Server Level*: Applies to an instance of the SSE Server. Objects with a server-wide scope such as Logins and Server Roles are defined at this level. This is the highest level in the hierarchy.

❏ *Database Level*: Each Server has multiple databases. Objects with database-wide scope such as Users, Database Roles, Application Roles, Assembly, Certificates, and the like are defined at this level.

❏ *Schema Level*: Each database has multiple schemas. A *schema* is a container of database objects. The database objects are created in the User's default schema if no schema is explicitly specified. Objects with a schema-wide scope such as tables, views, stored procedures, functions, and user-defined types are defined at this level.

❏ *Object Level*: Subobjects such as a column are defined at this level.

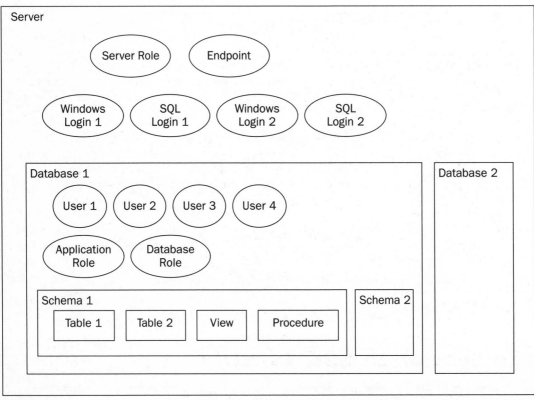

Figure 13-1

> You must have sysadmin level permission to execute any T-SQL code at the server level; db_owner permission is required to execute the T-SQL examples at the database level. The granular permissions required for each of the T-SQL statements are outside the scope of this introductory chapter on security.

The following Try It Out is a review of creating and deleting objects with SSE. Notice the objects created at different levels of the object hierarchy.

Try It Out   Creating and Deleting Database Objects

1. Open SSMS-EE, and in the Connect to Server dialog, specify the name of the SSE instance you desire. Choose Windows Authentication. Open the Query Editor by clicking New Query from the File menu.

2. To create a database, enter and execute the following code in the Query Editor:

```
CREATE DATABASE myDB
```

3. To create a schema inside myDB along with table and a view, enter and execute the following code in the Query Editor:

```
USE myDB
GO
CREATE SCHEMA mySchema CREATE TABLE mySchemaTable(Value INT PRIMARY KEY) CREATE
VIEW mySchemaView AS SELECT * FROM mySchemaTable
```

To view the table you just created, open the Tables node under Databases ⇨ myDB in the Explorer window of SSMS-EE. Similarly, the Databases ⇨ myDB ⇨ Views option in SSMS-EE shows you the view you just created. Notice that both the table and view have a prefix of mySchema indicating the schema they are associated with.

4. Create a table and view without explicitly specifying a schema:

```
CREATE TABLE myTableUseDefaultSchema(Value INT PRIMARY KEY)
GO
CREATE VIEW myViewUseDefaultSchema AS SELECT * FROM myTableUseDefaultSchema
```

View the tables and views you just created, similar to step 3. These objects are created in the default schema, which is dbo for a sysadmin.

5. To drop the schema created in step 3, execute the following in the Query Editor:

```
DROP VIEW mySchema . mySchemaView
DROP TABLE mySchema . mySchemaTable
DROP SCHEMA mySchema
```

How It Works

In Chapter 2, you learned how to create databases, tables, and views. In this example, a schema called mySchema is created in the myDB database using CREATE SCHEMA. The interesting fact is that CREATE SCHEMA provides a way to create tables and views and to grant permissions for objects with a single statement. If errors occur when creating any of the objects or when granting any permission specified in a CREATE SCHEMA statement, none of the objects are created.

The DROP SCHEMA statement is used to delete the schema you just created. This will only succeed if the schema is empty and does not contain any objects. Hence you must first drop the table and the view contained in the schema.

There is a *default schema* for Users in a database, used when you do not explicitly specify a schema. The default schema is used during name resolution, which is the algorithm that SSE uses to resolve an object when no schema is explicitly specified with the object name. SSE first tries to find the object in the default schema, and if it does not find an object there, it looks in the dbo schema.

Principals Who Can Access the SSE Objects

The consumers who can access SSE are defined in a hierarchy depending on whether they operate at a server or database level, and are often referred to as *principals*. Some principals can operate at the server-level and some at the database-level. A server-level principal is used for logging into SSE and for operating on objects at the server level. Accessing any object at the database level requires a principal defined at the database level. The following table shows four common principals and their scope of operation.

Principal	Scope of Operation	Comments
Windows Login	Server	Windows Logins are defined in the local machine or the domain that SSE is a part of. The management of these subjects is not within the scope of SSE.
SQL Server Login	Server	SQL Server Logins are defined within a particular SSE instance and are undefined outside the scope of that SSE instance. These are visible across all databases in the instance and can be used for authorization of resources in any database in the instance.
User	Database	A database User is defined for a database and typically has a Login corresponding to it. A User is not recognized outside the database for which it is defined.
Application Role	Database	Application Roles are database scoped, but have no mapped Login. They are restricted to a database and are identified by an Application Role name and password.

This Try It Out illustrates the creation of the principals described in the table.

Try It Out   Creating Logins, Users, and Application Roles

1. Open a new query window by clicking New Query from the File menu.

2. To create a Windows login, type and execute the following code in the Query Editor

```
CREATE LOGIN "MachineOrDomainName\WindowsTestLogin" FROM WINDOWS
```

Substitute your machine name or domain name for MachineOrDomainName. This will only work if the WindowsTestLogin is already present on your machine or domain. If the Login is not present, you will get an error message:

```
'Windows NT User or Group 'MachineOrDomainName\ WindowsTestLogin' not found. Check
the name again.'
```

To see the Login you just created, select Security ⇨ Logins in the Explorer window of SSMS-EE. Right-click Logins and select the Refresh option if the new Login does not appear. The following T-SQL also shows the object you created.

```
SELECT * from syslogins WHERE name = 'MachineOrDomainName\WindowsTestLogin'
```

3. To create a SQL Server Login, type and execute the following in the Query Editor:

```
CREATE LOGIN "SQLTestLogin" WITH PASSWORD = 'TEST', CHECK_EXPIRATION=ON,
CHECK_POLICY=ON
```

To see the Login you just created, select Security ⇨ Logins in the Explorer window of SSMS-EE. The following T-SQL also shows the object you created.

```
SELECT * FROM syslogins WHERE name = 'SQLTestLogin'
```

4. To create a User, type and execute the following in the Query Editor. Substitute your machine name or domain name for MachineOrDomainName.

```
USE myDB
GO
CREATE USER "WindowsTestUser" FOR LOGIN "MachineOrDomainName\WindowsTestLogin"
```

To see the User you just created, select Databases ⇨ myDB ⇨ Security ⇨ Users in the Explorer window of SSMS-EE. Right-click Users and select the Refresh option if the new User does not appear. The following T-SQL also shows the object you created.

```
SELECT * FROM sysusers WHERE name = 'WindowsTestUser'
```

5. To create an Application Role, type and execute the following in the Query Editor:

```
CREATE APPLICATION ROLE "AppRoleTest" WITH PASSWORD= 'AppRoleTestPwd'
```

You can use the following T-SQL to see the newly created Application Role.

```
SELECT * FROM sysusers WHERE name = 'AppRoleTest'
```

6. To delete the Windows and SQL Server Logins, execute the following in the Query Editor. Substitute your machine name or domain name for MachineOrDomainName.

```
DROP LOGIN "MachineOrDomainName\WindowsTestLogin"
DROP LOGIN "SQLTestLogin"
```

Verify that the Logins are deleted by refreshing the Logins option under Security ➪ Logins in the SSMS-EE Explorer window. You can also use the following T-SQL.

```
SELECT * FROM syslogins WHERE name= 'SQLTestLogin' OR name= 'MachineOrDomainName
\WindowsTestLogin'
```

7. To delete the User and Application Roles, type and execute the following in the Query Editor:

```
DROP USER "WindowsTestUser"
DROP APPLICATION ROLE "AppRoleTest"
```

Verify that the User is deleted by refreshing the Users option under Databases ➪ myDB ➪ Security ➪ Users in the Explorer window. You can also use the following T-SQL:

```
SELECT * FROM sysusers WHERE name= 'WindowsTestUser' OR name = 'AppRoleTest'
```

How It Works

The CREATE LOGIN statement is used to create Windows and SQL Server Logins. The keyword FROM WINDOWS tells SSE that the account is a pre-existing Windows local or domain account. The syntax for SQL Server Logins allows you to specify multiple options. For more information about the following syntax refer to the SQL Server books online.

```
CREATE LOGIN Login_name
WITH PASSWORD = 'password' [HASHED] [MUST_CHANGE] [, options [,...]]
        [CREDENTIAL = CredentialName]
options::= | SID = sid | DEFAULT_DATABASE = dbname | DEFAULT_LANGUAGE = language |
CHECK_EXPIRATION ={ON | OFF}   | CHECK_POLICY ={ON| OFF}
```

The options used for SQL Server Logins are described in the following list. These do not apply to Windows Logins.

❑ MUST_CHANGE is used to enforce password change when the User first logs in. Both CHECK_EXPIRATION and CHECK_POLICY must be on if this is used. If you are not running Windows 2003 or higher, you get an error when using this option.

❑ CHECK_EXPIRATION and CHECK_POLICY specify whether password expiration and policy will be enforced for this Login and are on by default. These are only enforced in the presence of the password policy API available with Windows 2003. If CHECK_POLICY is off, then CHECK_EXPI-RATION cannot be on.

❑ HASHED specifies that the password is already hashed. *Hashing* is the process by which a string of variable length is transformed to a different fixed size string by using a function called a hash function. SSE will automatically hash the password supplied if this option is omitted.

❑ SID refers to the security identifier to be assigned to this Login. A SID is a unique value that can identify a principal such as the Login. SSE will assign a SID internally if this option is omitted.

The following options are available to both SQL and Windows Logins:

❑ DEFAULT_DATABASE is the default database assigned to the Login. If this option is not specified, the default database is set to MASTER.

❑ DEFAULT_LANGUAGE is the default language assigned to the Login. If not specified, this is set to the default language of the server. Changing the server's default language does not change the default language for existing Logins.

The database access is granted with a CREATE USER statement in SSE. The User is associated with a corresponding Login; the login name specified must be a valid Login in the SSE instance. When the Login enters this database in order to access a resource, it uses the credentials of the User as its database context. All access to tables, views, and stored procedures within the database is done under this User's context.

The DROP statement is used to delete Logins, Users, and Application Roles. Only Users or Application Roles that do not own database objects can be dropped from the database. Assign a new owner for these objects, or drop them before deleting a Login or a User. The syslogins and sysusers views contain information about the current Logins and Users, respectively.

Application Roles allow the database administrator to restrict user access to data based on the application that the User is using. The application proves its identity to SSE by executing the sp_setapprole stored procedure, which takes two parameters: Application Role name and password. The Application Role password is known only to the application. If the Application Role name and password are valid, the Application Role is activated. At this point, all permissions currently assigned to the User are dropped and the security context of the Application Role is assumed. Since only the application knows the password for the Application Role, only the application can activate this role and access objects to which the role has permissions. However, it is dangerous to store the password within the application unless it is encrypted.

Application Roles work with both authentication modes. Users cannot be associated with Application Roles, as the application requests the Application Role's security context using the sp_setapprole stored procedure. Application Roles provide the security context within which the database object permissions are checked, but the identity of the actual database user is not lost. If an Application Role attempts to access another database, that Application Role will only be granted the privileges of the guest account in that database. After an Application Role is activated with sp_setapprole, the role cannot be deactivated in the current database until the user disconnects from SSE.

Try It Out   Application Roles

1. Open a new query window by clicking New Query from the File menu in SSMS-EE.

2. Enter and execute the following in the Query Editor:

```
CREATE APPLICATION ROLE "TestAppRole" WITH PASSWORD= 'TestAppPwd'
EXEC sp_setapprole 'TestAppRole', 'TestAppPwd'
```

Now you are in the Application Role context. Any T-SQL Statement you execute, like the following , fails.

```
SELECT * from sysusers
```

3. Disconnect the query window to be de-activated from the Application Role.

How It Works

In this Try It Out, you created an Application Role using the CREATE statement. Executing the stored procedure sp_setapprole puts you in the context of the Application Role. However, since you did not previously grant any additional permission to this role, its permissions are those of the guest account. To get out of this Application Role context, close the connection to SSE.

Built-In SQL Server Logins

All SSE instances have built-in SQL Server Logins with special purposes. These Logins are:

❑ The `sa` Login is the system administrator's account for SSE and has ownership over all objects defined within SSE. This account is used for administration of the server in SQL Authentication mode, and is disabled by default in a new SSE installation.

❑ The database owner (`DBO`) is the User who creates a database and is implicitly granted all permissions on the database. They can grant these permissions to other Users. The DBO User cannot be deleted and is always present in every database. The `sa`, or the system administrator's account, is automatically given database owner privileges for all the databases within the SSE instance.

❑ The `guest` User account is a special account that is not created by default in a new database. If this account is present, it allows a valid SQL Server Login to access a database using the identity of `guest`. Permissions apply to the guest User as if it were any other user account. The guest User can be deleted and added to all databases except the master and tempdb, where it must always exist.

Roles and Groups

SSE also supports the notion of Groups or Roles where the consumers defined earlier can be aggregated for the purpose of giving permissions. *Role* is an administrative unit within SSE that can contain SQL Server Logins, Windows Logins, Windows Groups, or other Roles. The Roles are typically defined in a hierarchical system, so that the security settings defined for a Role are applied to all members of that Role. When a Role is a member of a higher-level Role, all members of the Role inherits the security settings of the higher-level Role in addition to the security defined for the Role itself.

The concept of a Role within SSE is similar to a Windows Security Group. Groups are easier to manage compared to individual Logins, since the Groups can easily map to functional roles such as Manager, Secretary, Web User, and so on. For instance, a Secretary role may have the permission to see the Employee roster, while the Manager role may have permissions to modify the list of employees. These objects can be thought of as containers of permissions since they cannot directly access any SSE objects. This is demonstrated in the following Try It Out.

Try It Out   Creating and Dropping Secretary and Manager Roles

1. Open a new query window by clicking New Query from the File menu in SSMS-EE.

2. To create a Login and User for Emily and Ann, execute the following in the Query Editor.

```
USE myDB
CREATE LOGIN "Emily" WITH PASSWORD = 'TEST'
CREATE USER Emily
CREATE LOGIN "Ann" WITH PASSWORD = 'TEST'
CREATE USER Ann
```

3. Create the Roles `Secretary` and `Manager`:

```
CREATE ROLE Secretary
CREATE ROLE Manager
```

4. Add Emily to the `Secretary` Role, and add Ann to the `Manager` Role:

```
EXEC sp_addrolemember 'Secretary', 'Emily'
EXEC sp_addrolemember 'Manager', 'Ann'
```

5. Delete the `Secretary` and `Manager` Roles:

```
EXEC sp_droprolemember 'Secretary', 'Emily'
EXEC sp_droprolemember 'Manager', 'Ann'
DROP ROLE Secretary
DROP ROLE Manager
```

How It Works

Use the CREATE ROLE statement to create the `Secretary` and `Manager` Roles. Emily is added to the `Secretary` Role, while Ann is added to the `Manager` Role using the stored procedure sp _addrolemember. Emily and Ann are valid Users inside the database. The permissions applied to the Role are inherited by its members. Applying permissions to the Roles is explained in the next section. To delete a Role, use the statement DROP ROLE. However, before using this, you must first remove Emily and Ann from their respective Roles using sp_droprolemember.

Fixed Server and Database Roles

There are some predefined Roles within SSE both at the server and database levels. The local administrator group, or sysadmin, for example, has ownership of all the objects defined within the SSE instance. Its members include the sa account or any other Users who are set to administer the system locally. Windows Users who are members of the BUILTIN\Administrators Group are also members of the sysadmin Role so that an administrator on the machine can administer SSE.

Fixed server Roles are pre-defined Roles at the server level and, their scope includes all objects defined in the instance. Any member of a fixed server Role can add other SQL Server or Windows Logins to this Role. The following table describes the fixed server Roles.

Fixed Server Role	Description
sysadmin	This is the administrator of SSE and may perform any activity in SSE. The permissions of this Role span all other fixed server Roles.
serveradmin	Server administrators configure server-wide settings and can shut down the server.
setupadmin	Setup administrators may add or remove linked servers, and execute some system stored procedures, such as sp_serveroption.
securityadmin	Security administrators may manage Logins, create database permissions, and read error logs.
processadmin	Process administrators may manage processes running in an instance of SSE and can kill any processes.
dbcreator	Database creators may create, delete, rename, and alter databases and log files.
diskadmin	Disk administrators manage disk files.
bulkadmin	Bulk Insert administrators may execute the BULK INSERT command.

Fixed database roles are defined at the database level and exist in each database. You can add any valid Windows or SSE User account as a member of a fixed database role. Each member gains the permissions applied to the fixed database role. Any member of a fixed database role can add other Users to the Role. The following table describes the fixed database roles.

Pre-defined Role	Description
db_accessadmin	Add or remove Logins from the database.
db_backupoperator	Back up the database and run selected DBCC commands such as DBCC CHECKDB and DBCC CHECKCATALOG.
db_datareader	SELECT data from any table in the database.
db_datawriter	DELETE, INSERT, or UPDATE any database objects.
db_ddladmin	Run any data definition language (DDL) queries for adding, modifying, or dropping objects in the database.
db_securityadmin	Manage Users and Roles, statement and object permissions in the database.
db_denydatareader	Deny permission to select data in the database.
db_denydatawriter	Deny permission to change data in the database.
db_owner	Permission spans all of the other fixed database roles. Members own all the objects in the database.

Try It Out   Adding and Dropping Users from Fixed Server Roles

1. Open a new query window by clicking New Query from the File menu in SSMS-EE.

2. To add Ann to the securityadmin fixed Server Role, execute the following statement in the Query Editor.

```
EXEC sp_addsrvrolemember 'Ann', 'securityadmin'
```

3. To drop Ann from the securityadmin fixed Server Role, execute the following statement in the Query Editor.

```
EXEC sp_dropsrvrolemember 'Ann', 'securityadmin'
```

How It Works

In this example, the stored procedures sp_addsrvrolemember and sp_dropsrvrolemember are used to add and remove a valid User Ann from the fixed Security Role securityadmin.

Permissions

Permissions are a mechanism by which the owner of an object allows another beneficiary User the ability to perform one or more operations on the object or its subordinate objects. The permissions provided determine the actions that a User can perform within SSE. The following table gives a brief description of the common permissions you will encounter.

Object Permission	Description	Applies to SSE Objects
ALTER	Allows you to create, drop, or modify the object. In the case of a container like the Schema, this permission allows you to create, drop, or modify any of the objects it contains.	Application Role Assembly Certificate Login Procedures (T-SQL and .NET) Role Schema Symmetric Key Tables Views Scalar and Aggregate Functions (T-SQL and .NET) Table-Valued Functions (T-SQL and .NET) User XML Schema Collection
CONTROL	Allows all operations on the object although you are not the owner. You can now grant any permission on the object and such a grant is recorded as being done on behalf of the owner.	Application Role Assembly Certificate Login Procedures (T-SQL and .NET) Role Schema Symmetric Key Tables Views Scalar and Aggregate Functions (T-SQL and .NET) Synonyms Table-Valued Functions (T-SQL and .NET) Type User XML Schema Collection
DELETE	Allows you to delete data.	Schema Synonyms Tables and columns Views and columns

Table continued on following page

Object Permission	Description	Applies to SSE Objects
EXECUTE	Allows you to execute code, typically in a function or stored procedure.	Assembly Procedures (T-SQL and .NET) Scalar and Aggregate Functions (T-SQL and .NET) Schema Synonyms Type XML Schema Collection
IMPERSONATE	Allows you to impersonate another User. You need not be a sysadmin or DBO for impersonating a User or Login.	Login User
INSERT	Allows you to insert new data.	Schema Synonyms Tables and columns Views and columns
REFERENCES	Allows you to make foreign key references to primary key and unique columns of a table. It also allows SCHEMABINDING references from views and functions.	Assembly Certificate Schema Symmetric Key Tables and columns Table-Valued Functions (T-SQL and .NET) and columns Type Scalar and Aggregate Functions (T-SQL and .NET) Views and columns XML Schema Collection
SELECT	Allows you to view the data.	Schema Synonyms Tables and columns Table-Valued Functions (T-SQL and .NET) and columns

Views and columns

Object Permission	Description	Applies to SSE Objects
TAKE OWNERSHIP	Allows you to take ownership of the object. This operation can be initiated even if the grantor is not a DBO or sysadmin	Assembly Certificate Procedures (T-SQL and .NET) Role Tables. Views Scalar and Aggregate Functions (T-SQL and .NET) Schema Symmetric Key Synonyms Table-Valued Functions (T-SQL and .NET) Type XML Schema Collection
UPDATE	Allows you to modify the data.	Schema Synonyms Tables and columns Views and columns
VIEW DEFINITION	Allows you to see the catalog views or the metadata even if you do not have any other permission on the object.	Application Role Assembly Certificate Login Procedures (T-SQL and .NET) Role Schema Symmetric Key Synonyms Tables Type Views Scalar and Aggregate Functions (T-SQL and .NET) Table-Valued Functions (T-SQL and .NET) User XML Schema Collection

For example, SELECT permissions on a table allow you to view the data inside the table. However, you cannot insert, delete, or update rows from the table unless you have INSERT, DELETE, or UPDATE permissions, respectively. VIEW DEFINITION is a new permission in SQL Server 2005 that allows you to see the table structure (metadata) even if you have no other permissions on the table. To add a column to the table, you need the ALTER permission; to execute a stored procedure, you need the EXECUTE permission; and so on. As you can easily imagine, the list could get big very fast. Instead, if you have CONTROL permissions on the table, you can do all possible operations on the table. However, if it makes sense for you to own the table, the DBO could use the TAKE OWNERSHIP statement to make you the owner.

Access Control

An owner of a resource uses GRANT, DENY, and REVOKE statements to control access to the resource. The permissions are granted to a SQL Server Login, Windows Group, Database User, Database Role, or an Application Role on instances of objects such as Schema, Assembly, Type, or Login. The keywords are described in the following table and the Try It out explains the usage of these statements.

Owner Action	Description
GRANT	The beneficiary can perform an operation that requires this permission.
DENY	The beneficiary is denied permission to perform this operation.
REVOKE	Any previous GRANT or DENY permissions are taken away.

Try It Out   Using GRANT, DENY, and REVOKE

We will use the User Emily created in the database myDB to illustrate the GRANT, DENY, and REVOKE statements on a table. Emily does not have any permission at the beginning of this example.

1.   Open a new query window by clicking New Query from the File menu in SSMS-EE. Type and execute the following code in the Query Editor to create a table:

```
use myDB
CREATE TABLE SecurityCheckTable(Value INT PRIMARY KEY);

--Add values to the table using number field from an existing table in master
INSERT SecurityCheckTable SELECT DISTINCT number FROM master.dbo.spt_values WHERE
number < 1000 GROUP BY number
```

Verify that Emily does not have permissions. The following SELECT statement should fail:

```
EXECUTE AS USER='Emily'
SELECT * FROM SecurityCheckTable
REVERT
```

2.   Grant Emily SELECT privileges:

```
GRANT SELECT ON SecurityCheckTable TO Emily

-- Check if Emily has SELECT permission.
EXECUTE AS USER='Emily'
SELECT * FROM SecurityCheckTable
REVERT
```

3. Grant Emily INSERT permissions:

```
GRANT INSERT ON SecurityCheckTable TO Emily

-- Check if Emily has INSERT permission.
EXECUTE AS USER='Emily'
INSERT SecurityCheckTable VALUES (1000)
REVERT
```

4. Grant Emily CONTROL permissions:

```
GRANT CONTROL ON SecurityCheckTable TO Emily

-- Check if Emily has ALTER permission.
EXECUTE AS USER='Emily'
ALTER TABLE SecurityCheckTable ADD Description varchar(20) NULL
REVERT
```

5. Deny the ALTER permissions, and verify that Emily cannot alter the table:

```
DENY ALTER ON SecurityCheckTable TO Emily
-- Verify that Emily does not have ALTER permission. The statement below fails.
EXECUTE AS USER='Emily'
ALTER TABLE SecurityCheckTable DROP COLUMN Description
REVERT
```

6. Add Emily to a newly created SecurityCheckManager Role, and give ALTER permissions to this Role. Emily still cannot alter the table since the DENY has precedence.

```
CREATE ROLE SecurityCheckManager
EXEC sp_addrolemember 'SecurityCheckManager', 'Emily'
GRANT ALTER ON SecurityCheckTable TO SecurityCheckManager

-- Verify that Emily does not have ALTER permission. The statement below fails.
EXECUTE AS USER='Emily'
ALTER TABLE SecurityCheckTable ADD RelatedTo varchar(20) NULL
REVERT
```

7. Revoke the DENY of ALTER permissions and verify that Emily can alter the table:

```
REVOKE ALTER ON SecurityCheckTable FROM Emily

-- Check if Emily has ALTER permissions.
EXECUTE AS USER='Emily'
ALTER TABLE SecurityCheckTable DROP COLUMN Description
REVERT
```

How It Works

In one of the previous examples, the User Emily was created, but was not granted any permission on the database myDB. When Emily tries to SELECT from the newly created SecurityCheckTable in step 2, the operation fails because Emily has no permissions on the table.

The EXECUTE AS statement in SSE allows you to specify a security context in which your statements can execute. If you are the sysadmin on SSE, you automatically run in the context of db_owner (DBO) for the database. When you use EXECUTE AS USER='Emily', you tell SSE to change the user context to Emily. Any subsequent statements are executed in the context of Emily until REVERT is invoked. The REVERT keyword changes the security context back to the original User so that you are no longer running under the context of Emily.

After you grant SELECT or INSERT permissions to Emily, the corresponding statements in steps 2 and 3 are successfully run. The principals to whom the permissions are granted are indicated after the TO keyword. A SQL Server Login, Windows Group, Database User, Database Role, or an Application Role can be specified after the TO clause. The permissions apply to objects such as Schema, Assembly, Type, or Login, which are specified after the ON clause. In step 4, Emily is granted the CONTROL permission, which is a broad permission that allows all operations to succeed against the table. Hence Emily can execute the ALTER statement to add a column to the table.

> DENY *always takes precedence regardless of the order or hierarchy in which it is defined.*

In step 5, since the ALTER permission is denied to Emily; she cannot execute the ALTER statement for deleting the newly added column even though she has the broad CONTROL permissions. Step 6 demonstrates how DENY takes precedence even if the ALTER permission is available to Emily through the SecurityCheckManager Role. When the DENY permission for ALTER on Emily is revoked in step 7, she is able to execute the ALTER statement. Principals such as the User or Login are specified using the FROM clause instead of the TO clause in a REVOKE statement.

> *It is easy to remember that REVOKE removes a previous permission GRANT. However, many forget that REVOKE removes a previous DENY permission also.*

SSE Security Model

You can combine the concepts presented in the first parts of this chapter to understand the security model of SSE. Other than the user instance security model, the SQL Server 2005 security model is similar to SSE security model. To access any resource in a database, the consumer has first to login to the SSE instance. During the login process, SSE validates and establishes the identity of the consumer expressing the desire to access a resource. (The authentication modes supported by SSE are explained in a later section.) After the consumer is authenticated and authorized at the server level, SSE verifies her credentials at the database level. Finally, a permissions check is done at the database, schema, and the object level when you try to access a resource from the database. This is illustrated in Figure 13-2.

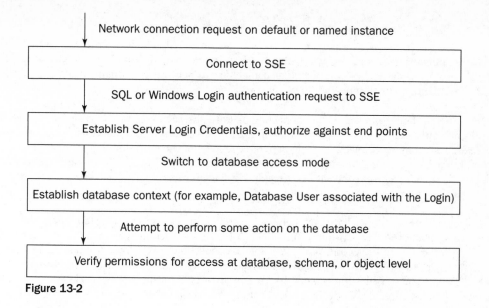

Figure 13-2

Connecting to SSE

The client makes a network connection request to SSE in a step known as *pre-login*, which happens prior to login. Connection to a SQL instance requires only the information about the server machine name and the instance name. The instance name can be omitted for the default instance of MSSQLSERVER.

Connection on the local machine using Shared Memory is easy and requires no lookup. When networking is enabled, the instance identification process becomes more complicated and requires a service called SQL Browser. By default, the first instance of SSE listens on the TCP port 1433. The SSE instances installed after this each obtain the next available dynamic ports, so the client may not know which port to connect to. SQL Browser is a lookup service that maps the SSE instance names to the ports they are listening on. SQL Browser listens over port 1434, and the clients connect to this port during the pre-login to determine the actual port to connect to. Once the correct port is determined, the connection request proceeds.

If you have pre-SP3 versions of MSDE or SQL Server 2000 on the same machine as SSE, SQL Browser may not work. The workaround is to upgrade all SQL Server 2000/MSDE instances on the machine to SP3 or higher. SQL Server 7.0 has no conflicts with SQL Browser.

Authentication Modes Supported by SSE

SSE supports authentication using the user id and password defined and maintained within it. This mode of authentication is called SQL Authentication, and you should supply the password every time a new connection is made. Many applications using SQL Authentication store the password internally, which could be a security concern if the password is not encrypted.

SQL Authentication is often used for connecting over the Internet or from nontrusted domains. You can configure applications that connect from the Internet to use specific SQL Server accounts, which are typically passed in the connection string. Upon receiving a new connection request, SSE first determines whether the User is connecting using a valid SQL Server Login. If the User has a valid login and has the proper password, the user connection is accepted. If the User has a valid login but has an improper password, the user connection is refused.

SSE also supports Windows-based Authentication so that the Windows login credentials of the User are used for authentication. Every time you log on to a Windows machine, you are uniquely identified by your login user id and password. When you open a connection in Windows Authentication mode, these credentials are automatically verified by SSE; no additional information is required. The application need not store any sensitive information like the password. Similarly, SQL Server does not store any password information for Windows Authentication. You cannot use Windows Authentication to connect from the Internet.

Password management is easy if you use Windows Authentication, since passwords are stored only with Windows. Your Windows password is subject to any password expiration and strong password rules of your domain. Also, it is easy for the administrators to enforce security since they have to understand and manage only the Windows security policy. If changes are made to the accessibility rights of a connected user, the changes become effective the next time the User connects to SSE.

> **Microsoft recommends the use of Windows Authentication unless you have legacy applications using SQL Authentication. Users connecting to SSE from untrusted domains or the Internet also use SQL Authentication.**

Your SSE instance can be configured in two authentication modes depending on whether SQL Authentication is supported or not. These modes are:

❏　**Windows Authentication mode**: In this mode, SQL Authentication is disabled, so that you use your Windows credentials for connections to SSE. Any application using SQL Authentication fails to connect to SSE. This is the default authentication mode supported by SSE.

❏　**Mixed Authentication mode:** In this mode you can use both Windows Authentication and SQL Server Logins. Use this mode if you have legacy or Internet applications that use SQL Authentication.

Regardless of the authentication mode, you should connect using the least privileged account. Use an account that has just enough privileges to do the operations required. Never use the system administrator or sa account in practice unless you are actually administering the server.

Permissions Hierarchy

It is important to recognize that the permissions are defined and verified at various levels of the SSE objects hierarchy. For example, server-level permissions are defined on the server; database-level permissions are defined on a particular database, and so on. A permission defined at a higher level controls all the objects defined within that level. For example, the DBO Role defined at database level has control over all instances of schema level objects defined under it. However, the DBO Role is not sufficient to deal with a Login object since the Login is scoped at a higher level. The access request to a resource succeeds only if the permissions checks are successful in all the levels. The hierarchy is described in the following table.

> **The GRANT, DENY, and REVOKE statements can be used at any level of the SSE Object hierarchy to manipulate the permissions available to a principal.**

SSE Objects Hierarchy	Controlled by (Owner)	SSE Objects Scoped by the Level	Typical Permissions Applied to Objects at This Level
Server Level	sysadmin	Login Server Role	ALTER CONTROL TAKE OWNERSHIP VIEW DEFINITION IMPERSONATE (only for Login)
Database Level	DBO	Assembly XML Schema Collection User Application Role Asymmetric Key Symmetric Key Certificate	ALTER CONTROL EXECUTE REFERENCES TAKE OWNERSHIP VIEW DEFINITION IMPERSONATE (Only for User)

Table continued on following page

SSE Objects Hierarchy	Controlled by (Owner)	SSE Objects Scoped by the Level	Typical Permissions Applied to Objects at This Level

Schema Level	Any User who is granted control privileges on one or more objects	Table
		View
		Table Functions
		Table Functions
		Table Functions
		Procedure
		Function
		Extended Stored
		    Procedures
		Assembly Stored
		    Procedure
		Assembly Table
		    Valued Functions
		Assembly Scalar
		    Functions
		Query Statistics
		Aggregate Functions
		Rule
		Synonyms
		Default
		Triggers
		User Defined Types
			ALTER
			CONTROL
			DELETE
			EXECUTE
			INSERT
			REFERENCES
			SELECT
			TAKE OWNERSHIP
			UPDATE
			VIEW DEFINITION

Object Level	Any User who is granted control privileges on part of an object	Column	Permissions are applied in conjunction with Table, View, or Table Valued Functions.

Not all the permissions at a given level can be applied to the objects at that level. For instance, you can only apply ALTER, CONTROL, or VIEW DEFINITION permissions to the Application Role object. You will get an error if you try to apply TAKE OWNERSHIP, EXECUTE, or REFERENCES permissions to it although these permissions are generally available at the Database Level where Application Role is defined.

While somewhat outside the scope of this book, some of the permissions set that can be applied to an instance of the Server, Database, or Schema objects is shown in the following table.

Permissions on SERVER	Permissions on DATABASE	Permissions on SCHEMA
ADMINISTER BULK OPERATIONS	ALTER	ALTER
ALTER ANY CREDENTIAL	ALTER ANY APPLICATION ROLE	CONTROL
ALTER ANY DATABASE	ALTER ANY ASSEMBLY	DELETE
ALTER ANY LINKED SERVER	ALTER ANY ASYMMETRIC KEY	EXECUTE
ALTER ANY LOGIN	ALTER ANY CERTIFICATE	INSERT
ALTER RESOURCES	ALTER ANY ROLE	REFERENCES
ALTER SERVER STATE	ALTER ANY SCHEMA	SELECT
ALTER SETTINGS	ALTER ANY SYMMETRIC KEY	TAKE OWNERSHIP
ALTER TRACE	ALTER ANY TRIGGER	UPDATE
AUTHENTICATE SERVER	ALTER ANY USER	VIEW DEFINITION
CONTROL SERVER	ALTER ANY XML SCHEMA COLLECTION	
CREATE ANY DATABASE	ALTER OPTIONS	
EXTERNAL ACCESS	AUTHENTICATE	
SHUTDOWN	BACKUP DATABASE	
VIEW ANY DEFINITION	BACKUP LOG	
VIEW SERVER STATE	CHECKPOINT	
	CONTROL	
	CREATE AGGREGATE	
	CREATE ASSEMBLY	
	CREATE CERTIFICATE	
	CREATE DATABASE	
	CREATE DEFAULT	
	CREATE FUNCTION	
	CREATE PROCEDURE	
	CREATE ROLE	
	CREATE RULE	
	CREATE SCHEMA	
	CREATE SYMMETRIC KEY	
	CREATE SYNONYM	
	CREATE TABLE	
	CREATE TYPE	
	CREATE VIEW	
	CREATE XML SCHEMA COLLECTION	
	DELETE	
	EXECUTE	
	INSERT	
	REFERENCES	
	SELECT	
	SHOWPLAN	
	TAKE OWNERSHIP	
	UPDATE	
	VIEW DATABASE STATE	
	VIEW DEFINITION	

Permissions like CONTROL are present at all the levels; however, the scope of the permission changes depending on the level in which it is defined. This is illustrated in the following Try It Out:

Try It Out   Granting Permissions at Different Hierarchy Levels

Open a new query window by clicking New Query from the File menu in SSMS-EE. Execute the following statements in the Query Editor.

1. Create a new Login called TestLogin and a User called TestUser for this example:

```
USE myDB
CREATE LOGIN "TestLogin" WITH PASSWORD = 'TEST'
CREATE USER "TestUser" FOR LOGIN "TestLogin"
```

2. Server Level: Grant the TestLogin the CONTROL SERVER permissions, which is same as sysadmin:

```
USE master
GRANT CONTROL SERVER TO TestLogin

-- Restore the initial value for Test Login before the next step.
REVOKE CONTROL SERVER TO TestLogin
```

3. Database Level: Grant CONTROL to all objects in the current database to TestUser:

```
USE myDB
GRANT CONTROL TO TestUser

-- Restore the initial value for Test User before the next step.
REVOKE CONTROL TO TestUser
```

4. Schema Level: Grant CONTROL on all objects in a schema to TestUser:

```
CREATE SCHEMA TestSchema
GRANT CONTROL ON SCHEMA::TestSchema TO TestUser

-- Restore the initial value for Test User before the next step.
REVOKE CONTROL ON SCHEMA::TestSchema TO TestUser
```

5. Object Level: Grant CONTROL on the TestTable to TestUser:

```
CREATE TABLE TestTable(Value int PRIMARY KEY, Description varchar(20));
GRANT CONTROL ON TestTable TO TestUser

-- Restore the initial value for Test User before the next step.
REVOKE CONTROL ON TestTable TO TestUser
```

6. Column Level: Grant SELECT permissions on the Value column:

```
GRANT SELECT (Value) ON TestTable TO TestUser
```

How It Works

This example demonstrates applying the CONTROL permission to the different levels of the SSE object hierarchy. The operations that the beneficiary User can perform using the CONTROL permissions depend on the hierarchy. In step 2, the CONTROL SERVER permission is granted to the Login at the Server level.

This permission is the same as the system administrator of SQL Server. When CONTROL is granted at the database level in step 3, the TestUser can do operations on all objects defined in the database. Similarly, the CONTROL defined at the Schema Level has permission on the schema, while the CONTROL defined on the table has permissions only on the table. The User and Login are initialized at the end of each step in the example so that you can remove the permission changes done in that step.

Verifying Permissions

There is a very useful function, has_perms_by_name, exposed by SSE that enables you to verify whether a User has the relevant permissions against a particular object. A successful permission would mean any of the following:

❑   User has a previous GRANT but not a DENY.

❑   The User's Role has a previous GRANT but not a DENY.

❑   A higher-level permission is held by the User and there is no DENY.

The syntax is as follows:

```
has_perms_by_name(target object name, class description, permission name, [sub
object name], [sub object class description] )
```

The target object name specified in the first parameter is an object instance at the Server, Database, or Schema Level. A NULL server or database level object name implies the current server or current database, respectively. However, NULL is not allowed for a schema-scoped object. The class description represents the kind of object that we are targeting like SERVER, DATABASE, SCHEMA, OBJECT, APPLICATION ROLE, LOGIN, USER, ROLE, and so forth. The permission name represents the permission that you are checking, like SELECT or ALTER. *Subobjects* are used for columns. The subobject name and subobject class descriptions are optional parameters used when the subobject class description is COLUMN. The default value for these parameters is NULL.

Try It Out   Using has_perms_by_name to Check for Permissions

Open a new query window by clicking New Query from the File menu in SSMS-EE. Execute the following statements in the Query Editor.

1.   Check whether you are able to IMPERSONATE the Login TestLogin:

```
SELECT has_perms_by_name('TestLogin','LOGIN','IMPERSONATE')
```

2.   Check whether you have any permission on the current database:

```
SELECT has_perms_by_name(db_name(),'DATABASE', 'ANY')
```

3.   Check whether the User TestUser has any permissions on the database myDB:

```
USE myDb
EXECUTE AS USER='TestUser'
SELECT has_perms_by_name(db_name(),'DATABASE', 'ANY')
REVERT
```

4.   Check whether you have ALTER permissions on a table called TestTable.

```
SELECT has_perms_by_name('TestTable','OBJECT', 'ALTER')
```

5.   Check whether you can SELECT from the column Value in the table TestTable.

```
SELECT has_perms_by_name('TestTable','OBJECT', 'SELECT','Value', 'COLUMN')
```

How It Works

A return value of 1 means that the caller has the permission; a value of 0 means that the caller does not have the permission. A NULL return value means that an error has occurred because an invalid value has been passed to any of the parameters.

Summary

This chapter introduced you to the multi-user security model in SSE. It started with an explanation about the hierarchical object structure in SSE, followed by the usage of Users and Logins. Next, permissions at the different levels of the security hierarchy were explained. Finally, the chapter discussed how all of this fits together in the SQL Security model.

In this chapter, you learned to

- ❑   Create objects at various hierarchies like the Server Level, Database Level, Schema Level, and Object Level

- ❑   Create and use principals such as Windows and SQL Server Login, User, and Application Role

- ❑   Use Roles to map individual users to functional Roles so that permissions can be applied to the Roles

- ❑   Understand the various SQL Server permissions

- ❑   Use the access control mechanisms to control the permissions at various levels of the hierarchy

- ❑   Understand the authentication modes and how to change them

- ❑   Understand the SQL Server Security model

In the next chapter, you learn more about upgrading to higher versions of SQL Server 2005.

Exercises

Try the exercises that follow to test your understanding of the material covered in this chapter. You can find the solutions to these exercises in Appendix A.

1.   Suppose your organization uses a table called Sales and you want to enable two salespersons, Burt and Ernie, to view the sales data. Create a Role called ViewSalesData and assign permissions to view data from the Sales table. Create new Logins and Users called Burt and Ernie. Add Burt and Ernie to the ViewSalesData Role.

2.   Add Ernie to the fixed Server Role for creating and altering databases.

3.   Create a new schema called SalesReportSchema and give Burt control on the schema.

Upgrading from SSE to Other SQL Server 2005 Editions

In Chapter 13, you learned about the various security concepts necessary for developing multi-user applications. This chapter introduces you to the different editions supported by SQL Server 2005 and explains some of the manageability, availability, scalability, and performance features offered by these editions. You will learn the main reasons to upgrade from SSE, and the process of upgrading your SSE application to use these SQL Server editions.

Upgrading from SSE to the other SQL Server 2005 editions is automatic as far as the setup is concerned. However, you will need to make some changes for your application to perform well in the upgraded environment, especially if you are using Xcopy deployment and User Instances. You will learn about the main differences between SSE and other editions, as well as the important settings that enable your application to utilize the upgraded environment. This chapter will help you:

❑   Determine when you should consider upgrading from SSE to other SQL Server 2005 editions

❑   Understand the features offered by the different SQL Server 2005 Editions

❑   Use tools such as Surface Area Configuration and Configuration Manager to enable remote networking and features such as CLR Integration

❑   Understand the key changes required to enable your application to work well in the upgraded environment

❑   Learn how to upgrade SSE to other SQL Server 2005 editions using the setup GUI

Introducing SQL Server 2005 Editions

SSE is the free edition of SQL Server 2005 that introduces you to the capabilities and rich features offered by the SQL Server 2005 family. The SQL Server 2005 family includes the Workgroup, Standard, Enterprise, and Developer editions. Each product is offered in both 32-bit and 64-bit Windows operating systems. Only SSE is free for use in development, production, and redistribution. The Developer edition is sold for a nominal fee, but can be used only for development. All the other editions are used in production, and you must purchase a license to use them.

The key features supported by the different SQL Server 2005 editions are shown in Figure 14-1. You can see that the higher-level editions offer enterprise-level availability, manageability, and scalability features. Each higher-level edition contains all the features offered by the edition immediately below it in the hierarchy. For example, the Workgroup edition offers features such as SQL Server Agent and Backup Log Shipping, in addition to the features offered by SSE. The only exceptions to this rule are the User Instance and Xcopy deployment features that are present only in SSE.

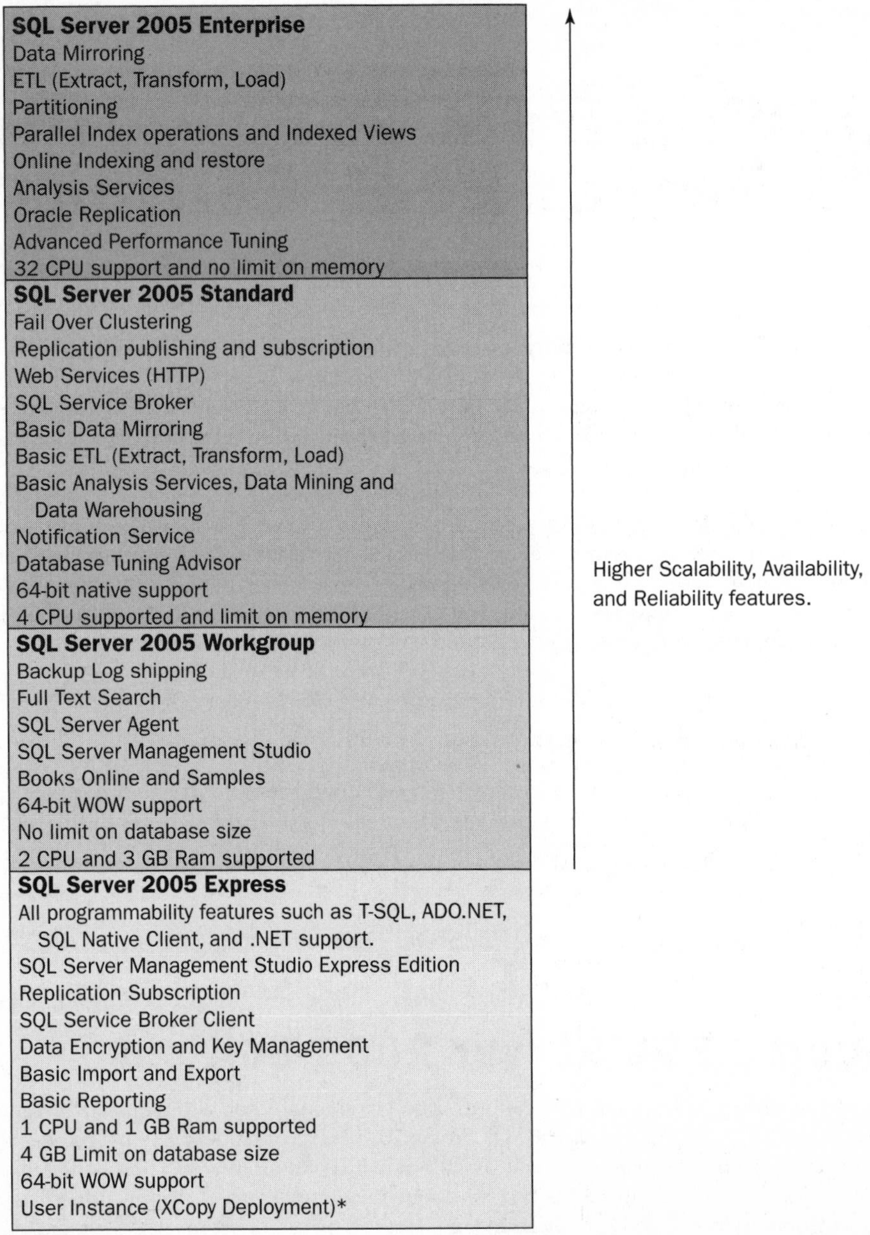

SQL Server 2005 Enterprise
Data Mirroring
ETL (Extract, Transform, Load)
Partitioning
Parallel Index operations and Indexed Views
Online Indexing and restore
Analysis Services
Oracle Replication
Advanced Performance Tuning
32 CPU support and no limit on memory

SQL Server 2005 Standard
Fail Over Clustering
Replication publishing and subscription
Web Services (HTTP)
SQL Service Broker
Basic Data Mirroring
Basic ETL (Extract, Transform, Load)
Basic Analysis Services, Data Mining and
    Data Warehousing
Notification Service
Database Tuning Advisor
64-bit native support
4 CPU supported and limit on memory

SQL Server 2005 Workgroup
Backup Log shipping
Full Text Search
SQL Server Agent
SQL Server Management Studio
Books Online and Samples
64-bit WOW support
No limit on database size
2 CPU and 3 GB Ram supported

SQL Server 2005 Express
All programmability features such as T-SQL, ADO.NET,
    SQL Native Client, and .NET support.
SQL Server Management Studio Express Edition
Replication Subscription
SQL Service Broker Client
Data Encryption and Key Management
Basic Import and Export
Basic Reporting
1 CPU and 1 GB Ram supported
4 GB Limit on database size
64-bit WOW support
User Instance (XCopy Deployment)*

Higher Scalability, Availability, and Reliability features.

*All the features except for User Instance (XCopy Deployment) are present in higher level editions.

Figure 14-1

Windows CE and similar devices are supported by SQL Server Mobile Edition version 3.0. Development of this edition is independent of the rest of SQL Server 2005 editions. An application using the Mobile Edition can also run on tablets, desktops, and laptops under certain conditions. The mobile edition is beyond the scope of this chapter.

Reasons to Upgrade from SSE

SSE is an excellent database server for client applications and servers requiring support of a small user base. It supports almost all of the programmability features in SQL Server 2005, making it very useful for beginning developers. Independent Software Vendors use the redistribution capabilities and rich features offered by SSE and bundle SSE along with their applications. However, when your application grows to support larger numbers of users, you may need to consider moving to a higher version of SQL Server 2005. Some of the common reasons for upgrading from SSE are:

❑ You are hitting the performance limitations because SSE supports only one CPU and 1GB RAM. Although there is no limit to the number of users that can connect to SSE, the hardware restrictions limit the performance of the database server under load. Higher-level editions support parallel operations, performance optimizations, and faster networking protocols such as VIA.

❑ Your application database is growing towards 4GB, which is the limit per database supported by SSE. Many of the new features supported by SQL Server 2005 such as .NET Assemblies can quickly fill up the available space. Standard, Enterprise, and Developer Editions of SQL Server 2005 do not have any limitations on the database size.

❑ Your application requires scalability or availability features found only in other editions of SQL Server 2005. When your application grows and becomes critical to the business, it becomes important that the server is available continuously, and can scale to peak user load. Higher-level editions support availability features such as Data Mirroring and Online operations as well as scalability features such as partitioning and snapshot isolation level.

❑ Your application requires replication. Since SSE supports only replication subscription, you require a SQL Server 2005 server to act as the replication publisher.

❑ You want to develop Web Services in the database tier using the HTTP capabilities in SQL Server 2005. This feature allows a SOAP client to connect to SQL Server and execute commands.

❑ You want to use SQL Service Broker or Notification Services for building your messaging or notification applications.

❑ You want to use the rich reporting facilities offered by the SQL Server Reporting Services.

❑ You want to use the Analysis Services features, especially OLAP, data warehouse, and data mining, to analyze business data.

❑ The Extract, Transform, and Local (ETL) capabilities of SQL Server 2005 Integration Services become important if you work with heterogeneous data.

❑ You want to administer and manage your SQL Server instances using the rich GUI features provided by the SQL Server Management Studio.

❑ You need capabilities to profile and tune your applications using SQL Server Profiler and Showplan, which are present only in higher SQL Server editions.

❑ You have different versions of SQL Server for different editions of your application. For example, you may ship SSE with the evaluation edition of your application, but use SQL Sever Standard or SQL Server Enterprise for the production application.

Before you learn about upgrading to SQL Server 2005 editions, it is useful to understand the different features offered by the editions so that you can determine which edition is most appropriate for you.

Features Offered by SQL Server 2005 Editions

This section describes many of the features offered by the different SQL Server 2005 editions. A table at the end of this section explains the feature availability per edition. It is important to realize that almost all of the programmability features such as T-SQL, NET support, and SQL Management Objects (SMO) are supported by all editions of SQL Server, including SSE.

Manageability

Manageability refers to the capability of being administered or governed, and typically relates to the availability of Graphical User Interface (GUI) tools used for administration. SSE supports the SQL Server Management Studio Express Edition (SSMS-EE), which is an easy-to-use lightweight GUI targeted at developers. Other editions of SQL Server 2005 contain SQL Server Management Studio, which is an integrated suite of management tools focused for database administrators (DBAs) and database developers. The following list describes some of the management tools supported:

❑ **SQL Server Management Studio Query Editor:** Similar to the query editor supported by SSMS-EE, but has advanced capabilities such as Multidimensional Expressions (MDX) that are used in Analysis Services.

❑ **Database Tuning Advisor (DTA):** A new index tuning tool that has the ability to suggest index and table partition changes to a database structure.

❑ **SQL Profiler:** Can be used to profile your application code for greater performance and provide visibility into the server, like capturing events raised by Analysis Services. SQL Profiler can also correlate performance monitor counters with SQL Server or Analysis Services events.

❑ **SQL Server Showplan:** A great tool for analyzing queries and determining whether or not more performance tuning needs to be done. The Showplan results, including Deadlock events and trace results, are saved in an XML format so that they can be saved, transferred to another location, and viewed without the need to have an underlying database.

❑ **Dedicated Administrator Connection (DAC):** A very useful administrator feature that connects to a running SQL Server even if the server is not responding or unavailable through normal connections.

❑ **Database Mail:** Provides a mechanism to send, receive, delete, and process email messages. The messages can contain query results and files.

❑ **Full-Text Search:** Allows fast and flexible indexing for keyword-based queries of data. Although SQL Server supports multiple languages and multiple document formats, this technology is typically used against unstructured text data.

❑   **SQL Server Agent Service:** Allows for running specific SQL Server tasks called *jobs* that are scheduled to occur at specific time intervals. It can also detect and respond to specific conditions of interest to an administrator.

Scalability

Scalability refers to the load SQL Server can process before it breaks down or requires additional hardware or software. For a server system, it typically refers to the number of users supported without reducing the performance characteristics. *Scale up* means improving the scalability of the system using bigger and more expensive hardware, while *scale out* means improving scalability using larger number of connected hardware. The features offered by SQL Server 2005 for scalability include:

❑   **Scale Up Partitioning:** In SQL Server 2005, tables and indexes can be divided into partitions across file groups based on value ranges. *Horizontal partitioning* allows division of a table into smaller groupings that are more manageable because you can focus on individual partitions. Maintenance operations can now perform against single partitions instead of an entire table or index. Query performance for very large databases (VLDB) improves when using partitions because blocks of data are transferred more efficiently. Partitioning in SQL Server 2005 does not support scale-out; all partitions of one table or index must reside in the same database.

❑   **Distributed Partition View (DPV):** Joins horizontally partitioned data across one or more servers so that you see a single view of all the data. Currently SSE users cannot insert, delete, or update against the view.

❑   **Snapshot Isolation Level:** Allows users to access the last row that was committed, by using a transactionally consistent view of the database. This increases the data availability for read-only applications, and nonblocking read operations are allowed in an Online Transaction Processing (OLTP) environment.

❑   **Replication:** Allows copying, distribution, and synchronization of databases or database objects between a publisher and a subscriber. A publisher is a server that makes data available for replication, and has responsibility for synchronizing the data. The subscriber is a server that receives the database objects published by a publisher. This is a scale-out technology; the machines could be at remote locations and the users can be mobile. There are three types of replication supported by SQL Server 2005. *Snapshot replication* is typically used for static data and offline scenarios, and involves complete refresh of the dataset for the subscribers. *Transactional replication* is used for connected scenarios and involves regular transactional updates to the subscriber. *Merge replication* allows both online and offline scenarios by tracking the updates to both subscriber and publisher along with synchronization at regular intervals. SSE supports only replication subscription, and SSMS-EE does not support configuration of replication.

High Availability

High Availability refers to the ability to service a component in SQL Server 2005, without having the stop the service or reboot the machine, so that the service is available continuously. The high availability features supported by SQL Server 2005 are:

❑   **Clustering:** A *failover cluster* is a group of independent servers that runs Microsoft Cluster Service and works collectively as a single system. If one of the servers in the cluster becomes unavailable, resources and applications move to another available cluster node, so that the application downtime is small during server failures and planned outages. The individual computers in a cluster system are often referred to as *nodes*. SQL Server 2005 supports a maximum of 8-node failover clusters on 32-bit systems, and 4-node clusters on 64-bit systems.

❑ **Backup Log Shipping:** Allows the transaction logs from the primary online database to be constantly fed to a destination database that could be located at a remote physical location. This allows you to have a standby server in case the primary goes down. The failover mechanism is manual, and could take a few minutes.

❑ **Database Mirroring:** An enhanced version of backup log shipping that provides creation of hot standby database servers. It requires three servers that are running SQL Server. The servers may be in one of the following roles: the primary server that the applications connect to, the mirroring server that is the target of transaction log records, or the witness server that acts as an arbiter that enables automatic failover. Transaction log records can be applied to the mirroring server either synchronously or asynchronously. If the primary system fails the failure is detected very fast and the applications reconnect to the database on the secondary server. The automatic failover reduces the downtime and increases availability for applications. This technology is easier to manage than failover clusters, works on standard server hardware, and requires no special storage or controllers.

❑ **Online Operations:** The online restore feature allows you to access databases when a partial database restore is being performed on a database. Only the part of the database being restored is unavailable; the rest of the database remains online and available. The online index option allows concurrent updates, deletes, or inserts to the underlying table or index. For example, while a clustered index is being rebuilt, you can continue to make updates to the underlying data and perform queries against the data.

❑ **Database Snapshots**: Offer an efficient way to record the current state of the data in a database as if all active transactions were rolled back. The snapshot then records all data changes from that point forward. If an accidental change, like mistakenly dropping a large table, happens, the snapshot can be used to recover the change.

Performance

One common reason for upgrading to other SQL Server 2005 editions is the high performance features offered, including:

❑ **Memory and Processor Support:** SSE is limited to one CPU, 1GB memory, and 4GB size for the user database. The Standard, Enterprise, and Developer editions support a maximum of 64GB RAM and have no limitations on the size of the user databases. Two CPUs are supported by the Workgroup, 4 by the Standard, and 32 by the Enterprise version.

❑ **Dynamic Address Windowing Extensions (AWE):** A Windows feature that allows support of large physical memory available on the machine. Dynamic AWE allows instances of SQL Server 2005 to dynamically adjust the amount of memory they use based on the current workloads.

❑ **Hot-Add Memory:** Allows the SQL Server 2005 instance to use new memory added to a computer while it is running. No rebooting of the machine or restarting the SQL Server service is required when you add new memory, so you can keep up with the production demands for systems that require continuous availability. Specific hardware is required to use this feature.

❑ **Networking Protocols:** Allow communication to remote machines. SSE supports TCP/IP and Named Pipes. HTTP and VIA are two additional protocols supported by other SQL Server 2005 editions. With HTTP, you can develop Web services in the database tier by making SQL Server an HTTP listener. In this mode, the middle tier layers such as Microsoft Internet Information Services (IIS) are not needed. Highly reliable, fast, and efficient network layers are supported by SQL Server 2005 using the hardware based on the Virtual Interface Architecture (VIA), such as the hardware from Giganet. Third-party VIA providers can easily add their support to SQL Server using a registration mechanism.

❑ **Parallel Operations:** Since SSE is limited to one CPU, it does not take advantage of the parallel operations possible in other editions like parallel DBCC and parallel Index creation. The MAX-DOP clause is specified on index data definition language (DDL) statements for controlling the number of parallel operations used by that statement. The value of MAXDOP is 1 in SSE by default because of the single CPU support.

❑ **Indexed Views (materialized views):** These are views with a clustered index and are specified using the SCHEMABINDING clause in T-SQL. When you create the view's index, the data selected by the view is materialized and kept persistent and up-to-date by SQL Server 2005. SELECT statements from this view are faster because the data is persistent. The optimizer in SSE does not make use of the index when determining a query plan.

Business Intelligence

Business Intelligence (BI) software enables users to easily obtain information relevant to the history, current status, or future projections of the enterprise by tightly integrating querying, reporting, OLAP, data mining, and data warehousing functions. To support BI functionalities, data from the production databases may be copied at regular intervals to data warehouses (special databases supporting huge amounts of data). The key features offered by the SQL Server Business Intelligence (BI) system are as follows:

❑ **Reporting Services:** Enables creating, modifying, and delivering interactive reports using web services. It allows application programming interfaces (APIs) for embedding reports or integrating the solution in diverse IT environments.

❑ **SQL Server Integration Services (SSIS):** Extract, transform, and load (ETL) software that allows you to read data from multiple sources and apply formatting rules in order to load the data to single or multiple target databases. A simple example of the use of this feature is an import from a Jet database to SQL Server tables.

❑ **Online Analytical Processing (OLAP):** Allows you to analyze multidimensional information using multidimensional expressions (MDX) that can define, query, and manipulate multidimensional data. For example, OLAP tools are used to perform trend analysis on sales and financial information.

❑ **Unified Dimensional Model:** Combines the best characteristics of relational and OLAP models to provide an integrated view of data to the end-users.

❑ **Key Performance Indicator (KPI) Framework:** Allows you to define corporate measures very easily. A KPI consists of expressions for value, goal, current status, and trends.

❑ **Data Mining Algorithms:** Discover knowledge by searching for previously unknown patterns and relationships in a multidimensional database. SQL Server 2005 supports algorithms like Association Rules, Time Series, Regression Trees, Sequence Clustering, Neural Nets, and Naïve Bayes. These algorithms can be used to solve problems such as classification, segmentation, association, time series forecasting, prediction, and deviation analysis.

❑ **XML for Analysis (XML/A):** A standards-based protocol used for communication between the client and the Analysis server.

❑ **Business Intelligence Development Studio:** An integrated development environment designed for the BI developer. It provides debugging, source control, script and code development for a BI application.

Messaging and Notification

Other key features that are useful for special types of applications include SQL Service Broker and Notification services.

❑ **SQL Service Broker:** Enables reliable, asynchronous messaging between database instances; used by applications to improve response time and throughput when dealing with resource intensive tasks. SSE can only send or receive messages from a non-SSE instance. In other words, two SSE instances cannot reliably send messages to each other; these messages are dropped automatically. The resulting error messages are shown using a trace.

❑ **Notification Services:** Enables you to build applications that generate and send notifications to users in a timely manner. The user subscribes to a service such as a stock market alert, and specifies preferences like the schedule of delivery and the condition for generating the notification. When the pre-specified condition is satisfied, a notification is generated and sent to the device specified by the user such a mobile phone, personal digital assistant (PDA), Microsoft Windows Messenger, or an email account.

You can get more information about the features supported in the different SQL Server 2005 editions at http://www.microsoft.com/sql/2005/productinfo/sql2005features.mspx.

Upgrading from SSE to Editions of SQL Server 2005

There are two key steps to upgrading from SSE to other SQL Server 2005 editions. First, you should understand some of the key differences between the editions so that your application is ready to use the upgraded database. The second step is the actual upgrade of the database using the setup GUI or the silent installation features. These steps are described in detail in the following sections.

Upgrading Your Database Application

The following sections detail some of the key difference of SSE from other editions of SQL Server 2005, and show you the changes you must make to upgrade your database application. Although the programming features are similar in all SQL Server 2005 editions, there are some differences in the default values that you should be aware of before upgrading.

Instance Name

SSE typically is installed with the instance name of SQLExpress, while the other SQL Editions use the default instance (MSSQLServer) or a named instance whose name is chosen by the administrator. All applications developed with Visual Basic Express and SSE automatically use the SQLExpress instance name. If you upgrade your SQLExpress instance to higher editions, you risk breaking other applications that rely on the User Instance feature.

All editions of SQL Server 2005 support named instances, allowing you to specify a unique name for your SQL Server instance. Any such uniquely named SSE instance can be upgraded to other editions of SQL Server 2005. So you are affected only if you are using a named instance of SQLExpress, in which case you have to modify your application to use a different instance name before upgrading to other SQL Server 2005 editions. You must change the connection string entry SERVER so that the new instance name is specified.

Networking Support

All networking protocols such as TCP/IP and Named Pipes (NP) are turned off by default in SSE, while they are on by default in other editions. You should enable these protocols explicitly during upgrade using the DISABLENETWORKPROTOCOL command line switch, or you can use the SQL Server Configuration Tools. The Try It Out below uses SQL Server Configuration Manager to enable networking.

Try It Out   **Using SQL Server Configuration Manager to Enable Networking**

The following steps enable TCP/IP and NP for the SQLExpress instance.

1.   Select All Programs ⇨ SQL Server 2005 ⇨ Configuration Tools ⇨ SQL Server Configuration Manager.

2.   Click SQL Server 2005 Network Configuration, and then double-click Protocols for SQLEX-PRESS (See Figure 14-2.)

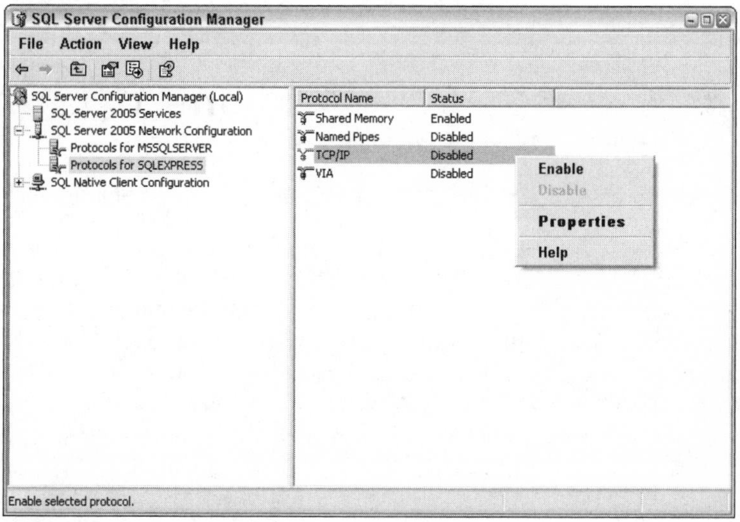

Figure 14-2

3.   Right-click Tcp and select Enable.

4.   Right-click IP1 and select Enable. Similarly, right-click IP2 and select Enable.

5. Right-click NP and select Enable.

6. Find the node SQL Server under SQL Server 2005 Services, right-click SQL Server (SQLExpress), and select Restart.

How It Works

SQL Server Configuration Manager is a GUI tool that allows you to start and stop services, change the passwords for the accounts used by the SQL Server services, and modify the networking parameters for the SSE instance. The high-level options available to the users when you open the GUI are as follows:

❑ **SQL Server 2005 Services:** Allows you to view all the services running on your machine. The only service of interest to SSE users is SQL Server. You can start and stop this service, as well as modify some of the startup parameters using this tool.

❑ **SQL Server 2005 Network Configuration:** Allows you to enable, disable, or set the properties of the different protocols supported by the SSE instance. SSE supports three protocols: Shared Memory (SM), Named Pipe (NP), and TCP/IP (TCP). VIA is a high-performance protocol that is not supported by SSE.

❑ **SQL Native Client Configuration:** Allows you to enable, disable, or set the properties of the SQL Native Client provider (SQLNCLI). These protocols refer to the client provider as opposed to the server network properties specified by the previous option.

In the preceding Try It Out, you are enabling the networking options of the SSE instance using the SQL Server 2005 Network Configuration option. Alternatively, you can also use the SQL Server Area Configuration for Services and Connections tool to enable networking. The Try It Out below guides you through the steps involved.

Try It Out   Using Surface Area Configuration Tool to Enable Networking

The following steps enable TCP/IP for the SQLExpress instance.

1. Select All Programs ➪ SQL Server 2005 ➪ Configuration Tools ➪ SQL Server Surface Area Configuration.

2. Click the Link for the Surface Area Configuration for Services and Connections.

3. Select SQLEXPRESS ➪ Database Engine ➪ Remote Connections ➪ Local and remote connections (see Figure 14-3). By default Using TCP/IP only option is selected. This is the recommended option when remote networking is enabled. However, if you have clients that use named pipes, then select the option Using both TCP/IP and named pipes. Click OK.

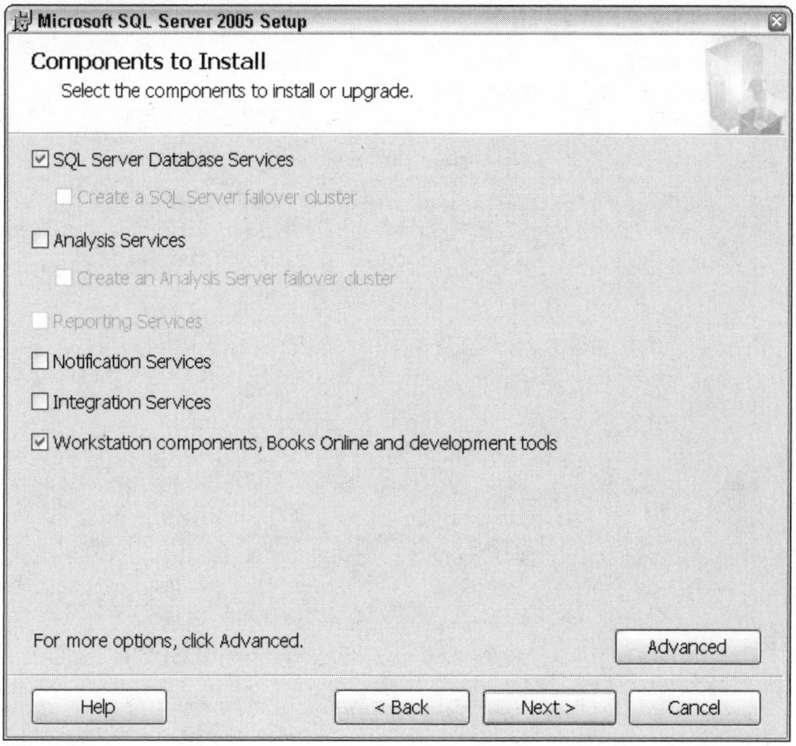

Figure 14-3

How It Works

SQL Server Area Configuration for Services and Connections is a simpler GUI than SQL Server Configuration Manager for enabling remote networking. This tool also offers the capability to start, pause, or stop the SQL and SQL Browser services. Selecting the Service option under SQLEXPRESS ⇨ Database Engine shows you a GUI similar to Figure 14-4. You can click the Start, Stop or Pause button to change the running status of the service.

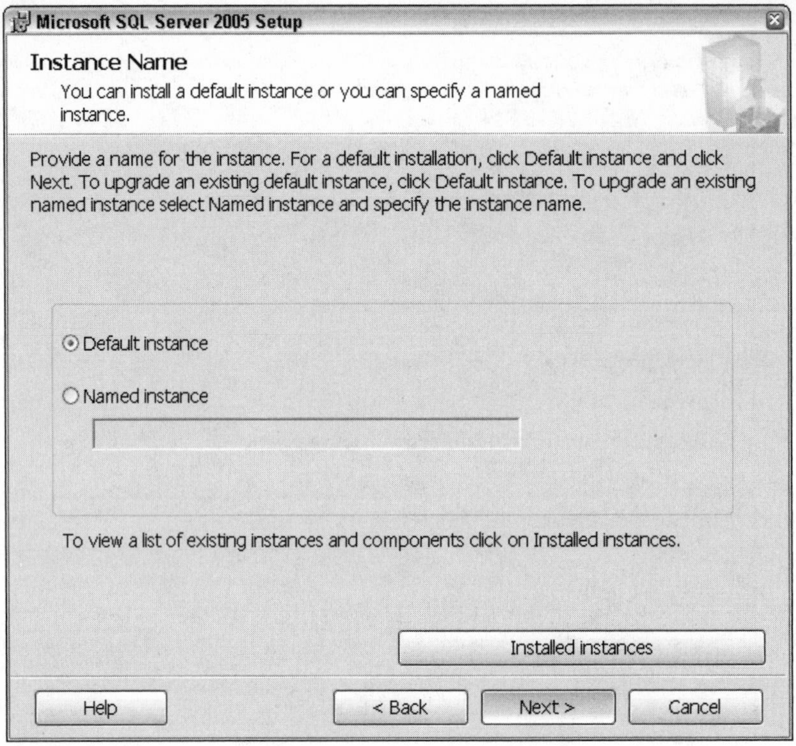

Figure 14-4

In the Try It Out above, you are enabling remote networking for the SQLEXPRESS instance. If you want to enable the remote networking protocols for a different instance, you should select the appropriate instance name. After the networking properties are changed, the server must be restarted for the changes to be effective. You can verify that the instance is listening on TCP/IP by connecting to it from another machine using SSMS-EE. If you are unable to connect, you may have a firewall configured on the computer where SSE is running. The steps to enable the firewall for SSE traffic are as follows:

1. Launch the Windows Firewall configuration tool from the control panel.

2. Click the Exceptions tab and then click the Add Programs button to add sqlservr.exe from the location where you initially installed SSE.

Service Account

SSE is installed to run as Network Service by default on Windows XP and Windows 2003, which is a low privileged account. The lower privilege account provides increased security. You can use the SQLAC-COUNT command line switch during installation to specify the service account if you want to use a different service account.

Configuration Options

SSE differs from the other SQL Server 2005 editions in the defaults for some of the configuration options, including tracing and recovery models. Tracing allows you to record various operations or events in SQL Server. Tracing is off by default in SSE since it consumes space on disk and there is no SQL Profiler to represent the trace output graphically.

Recovery models determine your data backup strategy and exposure to data loss. Simple Recovery recovers data to the most recent backup, but the changes since then are lost. Bulk-logged Recovery does minimal logging of bulk or image operations done using the T-SQL SELECT INTO, BULK INSERT, WRITE-TEXT, and UPDATETEXT statements. The data changes after the last backup are lost for both the options in case of a failure. Full Recovery provides complete protection against data loss and allows the database to be recovered to the point of failure. However, the logs require a lot of disk space. SSE uses the Simple Recovery mode, compared to the Full Recovery mode used by other editions.

The following Try It Out demonstrates the use of sp_configure to change the configuration options.

Try It Out   Using sp_configure to Change Configuration options

1.   Open the Query Editor in SSMS-EE and type the following:

```
USE master
exec sp_configure 'show advanced options', 1
reconfigure
exec sp_configure
```

2.   To change the default trace, type the following.

```
exec sp_configure ''default trace enabled', 1
reconfigure
```

How It Works

A stored procedure called sp_configure is used to change the common configuration options. First, you must run sp_configure with show advanced options set to 1 so that you can list the advanced options by using the stored procedure. The RECONFIGURE command updates the currently configured value of a configuration option. sp_configure without any parameters displays all the global configuration settings for the current server.

Use the default trace enabled option to enable or disable the Default Trace that provides a rich, persistent log of activity and changes. Use maximum server memory to reconfigure the amount of memory (in megabytes) in the buffer pool used by an instance of SQL Server.

Not all features are enabled by default for SSE. For example, CLR integration is not enabled in a new installation of SSE. You can use the SQL Server Surface Area Configuration for Features Tool to enable these features. The Try It Out below demonstrates the use of this tool to enable CLR Integration.

Try It Out   Using Surface Area Configuration for Features Tool to Enable CLR Integration

1.   Select All Programs ⇨ SQL Server 2005 ⇨ Configuration Tools ⇨ SQL Server Surface Area Configuration.

2. Click the Link for the Surface Area Configuration for Features.

3. Select SQLEXPRESS ⇨ Database Engine ⇨ CLR Integration (see Figure 14-5). Click Enable CLR Integration check box and press the OK button.

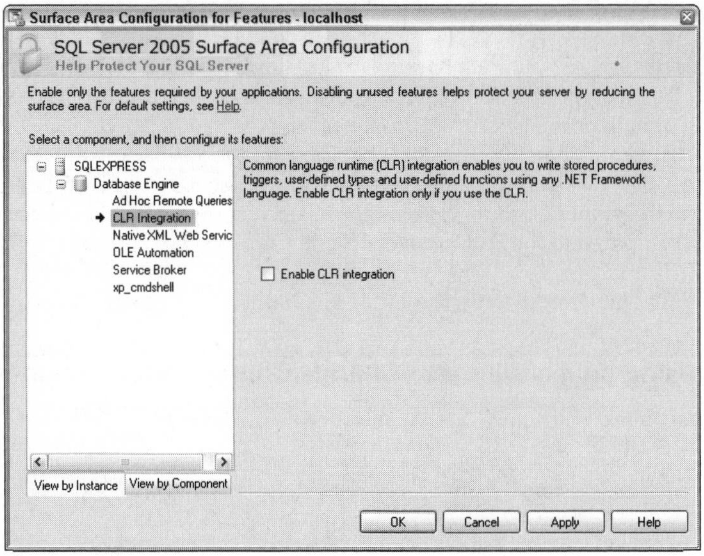

Figure 14-5

How It Works

SQL Server Surface Area Configuration for Features is a simple to use GUI for enabling features such as CLR Integration, Adhoc Remote Queries, OLE Automation, etc. You can click the corresponding check box to enable these features.

64-Bit Support

There is no native 64-bit support for SSE, but it can run on 64-bit machines using the Windows on Windows (WOW) feature. However, native 64-bit editions of SQL Server 2005 are available. These 64-bit machines support larger amount of memory compared to their 32-bit equivalents. So if you want your applications to use the native features in 64-bit machines, choose a 64-bit version of SQL Server 2005.

Visual Studio Support

Programming using Visual Studio is different than with other SQL Server 2005 editions because the User Instance and Xcopy features are available only in SSE. Nonadministrators on the machine require proper permissions and privileges to use an instance of SQL Server 2005; these security concepts are described in detail in the previous chapter. Also, you must explicitly attach and detach the database before copying or moving to another location, and you cannot rely on the AttachDBFileName functionality.

Visual Studio local data features rely on SSE and are not available if you use SQL Standard. For example, you cannot use Add New Item to add an .mdf file to your project. If the .mdf is not in your project, you do not get all of the functionality associated with it, like modifying tables or viewing the database using the Server Explorer.

Upgrading SSE Using the Graphical User Interface

This section guides you through the dialogs required to successfully upgrade an instance of SSE to other editions of SQL Server 2005. Many of these dialogs are similar to the ones in a clean install as described in Chapter 9.

Verify the following before starting setup:

❑　Your computer satisfies the minimum hardware and software requirements for the edition of SQL Server 2005 that you are planning to upgrade to.

❑　You are running setup as an administrator on the machine.

The following Try It Out shows you how to silently upgrade a default instance of SSE to SQL Server 2005 Standard Edition.

Try It Out　　Upgrade a Default Instance of SSE

Follow the steps below to perform the upgrade.

1.　Insert the SQL Server 2005 Standard Edition CD into your computer's CD-ROM drive. If the Installation Wizard does not launch automatically, double-click Autorun.exe.

2.　On the End User License Agreement page, read the licensing agreement, and select the check box to accept the licensing terms and conditions. Selecting the check box activates the Next button. Click Next to continue.

3.　The SQL Server Component Update dialog checks for prerequisites and installs the SQL Support files. Click Next.

4.　On the Welcome page of the SQL Server Installation Wizard, click Next.

5.　On the System Configuration Check (SCC) page, click Continue. This is similar to the SCC run during the SSE installs. If you encounter any errors at this stage, you should restart the setup after fixing the problem.

6.　On the Registration Information page, enter the user name, company information, and the Product Key. The Product Key is typically found on the yellow sticker on the CD liner or the CD sleeves. Click Next.

7.　On the Components to Install page, select SQL Server Database Services, Workstation Components, Books Online and development tools (see Figure 14-6).

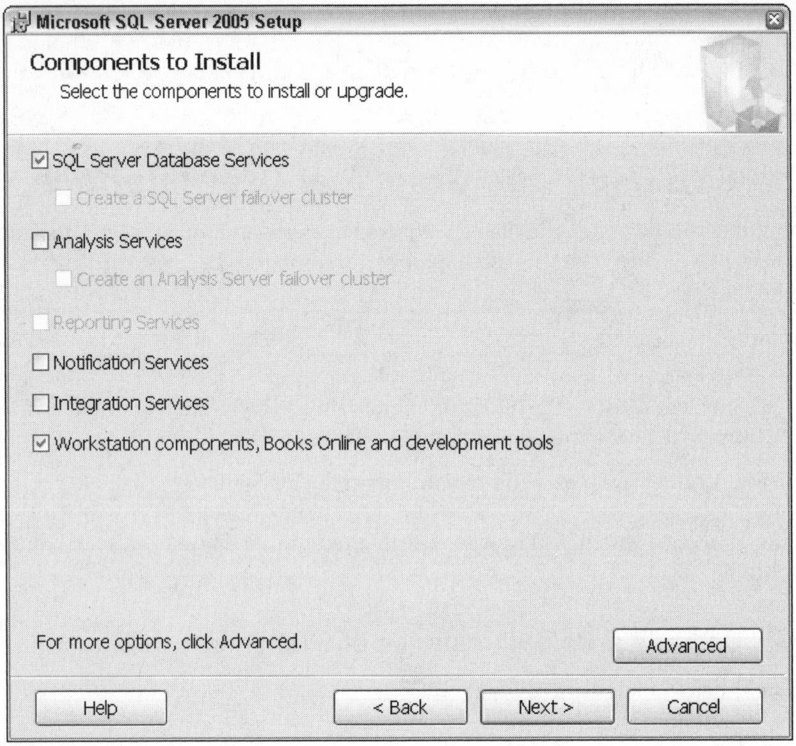

Figure 14-6

8. On the Instance Name page, choose to install the default instance and click Next (see Figure 14-7).

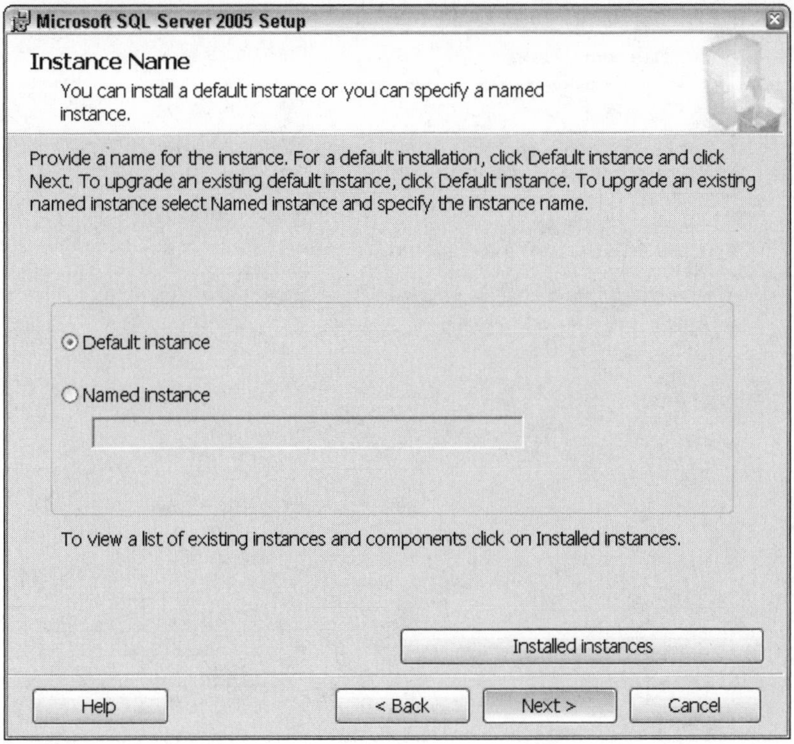

Figure 14-7

9. Select SQL Database Services, Workstation Components, Books Online and development tools in the Existing components page and click Next (see Figure 14-8). You can get details about these components if you click the Details button at the bottom of this page. Clicking the details button pops up a new dialog as shown in Figure 14-9.

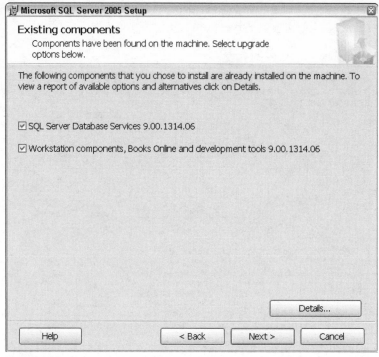

Figure 14-8

Microsoft SQL Server 2005 Setup

Installation options

The list below shows installed components and upgrade options.

> **Name: Microsoft SQL Server 2005 Express Edition**
> Allowed Action: Upgrade
> Reason: Product can be upgraded to a new version
>
> **Name: Microsoft SQL Server 2005 Tools Express Edition**
> Allowed Action: Upgrade
> Reason: Product can be upgraded to a new version

Help   Close

Figure 14-9

10. Select Windows Authentication Mode in the Upgrade Logon Information page. This account is used for connecting to SQL Server during the upgrade process (see 14-10).

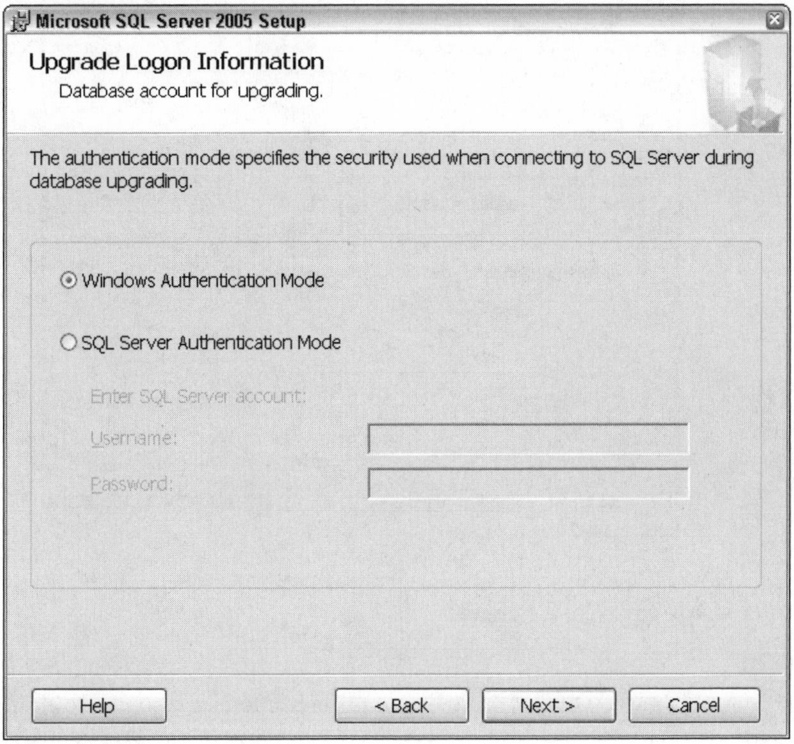

```
Microsoft SQL Server 2005 Setup

Upgrade Logon Information
   Database account for upgrading.

The authentication mode specifies the security used when connecting to SQL Server during
database upgrading.

   ⊙ Windows Authentication Mode

   ○ SQL Server Authentication Mode

      Enter SQL Server account:
      Username:  [_____]
      Password:  [_____]


   Help              < Back    Next >     Cancel
```

Figure 14-10

11. Click Next in the Error and Usage Report Settings. This dialog is similar to the Error dialog visible during SSE installation.

12. Click Install in the Ready To Install page to start the installation process. You will notice the progress bar and click Next when the upgrade is complete (see Figure 14-11).

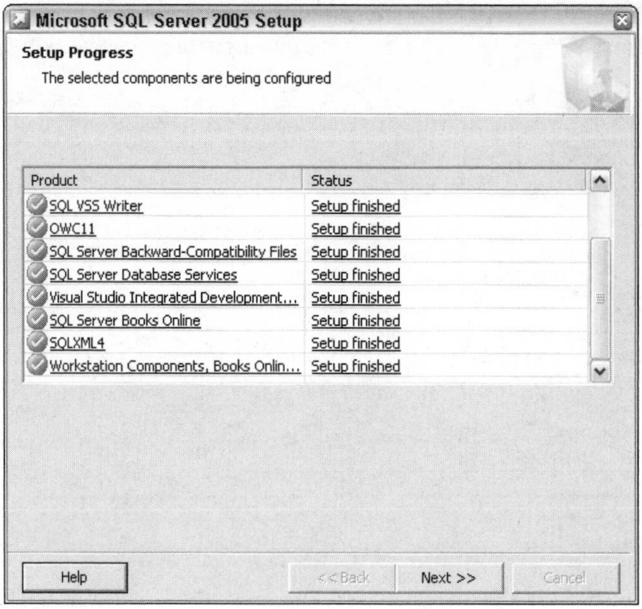

Figure 14-11

13. Click Finish to complete the upgrade.

How It Works

You can see from the above Try It Out that the upgrade user interface is similar to clean installation. The difference starts with the Instance Page dialog in step 8 when you specify an existing instance on the machine instead of specifying a new name. The assumption is that you have a previous default (MSSQLSERVER) instance of SSE already installed on the machine.

If you want to install additional feature in SQL Server 2005 Standard edition, please select additional features such as Analysis Services so that these also get installed as a part of the upgrade.

Summary

This chapter introduced you to the feature differences between SSE and other editions of SQL Server 2005 so that you can determine the appropriateness of migrating from SSE. You also learned about the key areas you should understand to migrate your application to the new database server. Finally, you walked through upgrade steps for using the setup graphical user interface (GUI).

In this chapter, you learned to

❑   Understand the different editions of SQL Server 2005

❑   Understand the features offered by other editions of SQL Server 2005

❑ Using Surface Area Configuration tool to enable networking and features such as CLR Integration

❑ Migrate your application to use SQL Server 2005

❑ Automatically upgrade SSE using GUI installation

In the next chapter, you learn more about developing robust multi-user applications.

Exercises

Try the exercises that follow to test your understanding of the material covered in this chapter. You can find the solutions to these exercises in Appendix A.

1. You are the IT manager for Joe's Garage, and your manager wants to know if your database application should be upgraded to use SQL Server Standard. Currently the application uses SSE. What are the additional features offered by the SQL Server Standard edition compared to SSE?

2. How would you upgrade a default instance (instance name of MSSQLSERVER) of SSE to another edition of SQL Server 2005 silently? You need only windows authentication and you do not need any remote networking.

3. How would you upgrade a named instance (instance name of SalesDBServer) of SSE to another edition of SQL Server 2005 using the setup GUI? You need only windows authentication and you do not need any remote networking.

Building Robust Multi-User Database Applications

The applications you have built so far in this book are single-user applications. SSE can handle both multiple users and multiple applications. To enable multiple users, you must turn on networking as described in Chapter 14. However, simply turning on networking isn't all you need to worry about if you want to enable multiple users. You certainly need to worry about security, which is addressed in Chapter 13. But you also need to worry about the design of your application and your database. And, to really make your database robust, you should also worry about the scenario where different applications are updating the same database. Once you have a database that multiple people can use, you will often find other applications you can create that should share some of the data you have created for your first application. And, once applications are sharing data, one of the best ways to ensure that data isn't accidentally corrupted by one of the applications is to push some of the validation logic into the database. Therefore, when you design your database for multiple users and multiple applications, there are a number of key design issues you should keep in mind.

In this chapter, you learn:

❑   How to choose and create the right primary keys for multi-user applications

❑   How to ensure that your insert, updates, and deletes are properly transacted

❑   Other common techniques for building multi-user applications

Choosing and Creating Primary Keys

In the earlier chapters on creating an application, the design for the primary key value is a manually input integer value. A primary key value should uniquely identify a record in the database. A manually input integer value can work. However, you cannot rely on the user to enter a value that will necessarily be unique. For instance, what happens when multiple users try to manually insert a primary key value that is the same? Or if they try and update data at the same time? What happens if you accidentally try to insert a new record with a primary key that already exists in the database?

To keep the system robust, you must guarantee it. In a multi-user scenario, where the application requires a live connection to the database, the only thing that you can count on to remain common among the various users is the database itself. It sits at the center of the various users and can coordinate which primary keys a user may use. Therefore, you must generate the primary key from the database and give it to the user. And, to do that, you must create a stored procedure from which it can be generated, as shown in the following Try It Out.

Try It Out   Creating a Stored Procedure

In this example, you will implement a stored procedure that stores the next primary key value in a separate table. The stored procedure will return the next value to you and increment the value in the table. To create a stored procedure, follow these steps:

1. Close Visual Basic 2005 if it is open. Navigate to your Documents and Settings folder, and then to the *<your name>*\My Documents\Visual Studio 2005\Projects folder. Find the folder that has your MasterDetail application. Copy the entire folder to a new directory and name it MultiUserApp.

> Note that the application name "MasterDetail" will still be the same. It will just be in a different folder.

2. Open Visual Basic 2005 and choose Open Project. Navigate to the MultiUserApp directory and find the MasterDetail.SLN (Solution) file. Double-click it to open your project.

3. Open the Server Explorer and open the connection to MyDB.MDF.

> Note: If you have trouble opening the connection in Server Explorer, simply delete the connection and recreate it by double clicking on the database in the Solution Explorer. If Server Explorer thinks a database if offline (say if you get a time out), it will put the connection in a state where it won't reopen it for you.

4. Right-click the Tables folder. Create a new table named PKTable with the columns and data types shown in the following table. Save the table.

Column Name	Data Type	Allow Nulls
pktableID	int	No
tableName	nvarchar(50)	No
pkValue	int	No

5. Right-click the PKTable table node in Server Explorer and choose Show Table Data. Populate the table as shown in Figure 15-1 and save the data.

PKTableID	TableName	pkValue
1	Person	20
2	Book	20

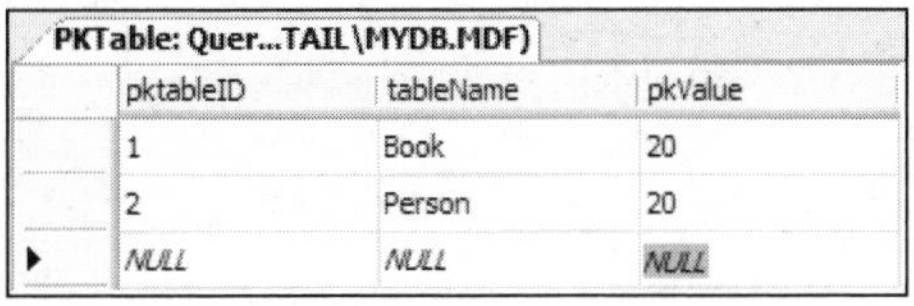

PKTable: Quer...TAIL\MYDB.MDF)		
pktableID	tableName	pkValue
1	Book	20
2	Person	20
NULL	NULL	NULL

Figure 15-1

6. Right-click the Stored Procedure node in Server Explorer and choose Add New Stored Procedure.

7. Replace the default code that comes up in the editor with the code in Listing 15-1, and save it. After you save it, it will show up in the Server Explorer in the Stored Procedure folder.

Listing 15-1: Stored Procedure spGetNextPkValue

```
CREATE PROCEDURE dbo.spGetNextPkValue
@tableID nvarchar(50),
@NewPKval int = -1

AS
 SET NOCOUNT ON
 BEGIN

/* get the current value of the id and place it in a temporary variable*/
declare @CurrPKval int
select @CurrPKval = pkValue
from PKTable
where tableName = @tableID

/* increment the current value*/
update PKTable
set  pkValue = pkValue + 1
where tableName = @tableID

/* get a copy of the value just updated */
select @NewPKval = pkValue
from PKTable
where tableName = @tableID

/* Test if update worked, and return new value or error (-1) */
IF @NewPKval > @CurrPKval
 BEGIN
   SELECT pkValue from PKTable where tableName = @tableID
   RETURN  0
 END
ELSE /* error */
 RETURN -1
END
```

8. Find spGetNextPkValue in Server Explorer and click Execute. This brings up the Run Stored Procedure dialog, shown in Figure 15-2.

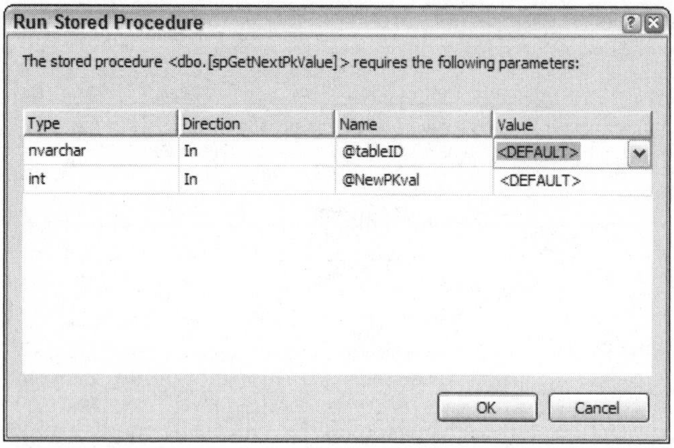

Figure 15-2

9. Enter the name of a table (for example, Person) and click OK. This runs the stored procedure and puts the output into the Output Window. Note, do not put in a value for NewPKValue. NewPKValue is the return value and is set to -1 by default. The Output Window shows the return value of the stored procedure. It also tells you how many rows were affected, as shown in Figure 15-3. (If the Output Window is not visible, you may need to move some windows around to show it.)

```
Running dbo.[spGetNextPkValue] ( @tableID = Person, @NewPKval = -1 ).

pkValue
-----------
21
No rows affected.
(1 row(s) returned)
@RETURN_VALUE = 0
Finished running dbo.[spGetNextPkValue].
```

Figure 15-3

10. Check the PKTable for updated values. Navigate to the Tables folder, find PKTable, right-click on it, and choose Show Table Data. The Person row should be updated with a new value.

How It Works

When you start using this stored procedure in your application, you can ensure that your application has a unique primary key that is generated from the database. As long as all applications that use this database call this stored procedure to generate the primary key for the records they are trying to insert, then there will no collisions with existing records when you are inserting a new record.

In this example, you created a separate table to keep track of the next primary key value and then used a stored procedure to access it and update the table with a new value. You will see how to use this stored procedure in your code in the next Try It Out. There are several methods used to get the next primary key. SSE has a built-in automatic primary key generator for columns called Identity. This works well for cases where, when you are entering the data, you don't care to know what the identifier is before you save your data. Most websites work this way. You will get a confirmation sent to you after you submit your order. The confirmation email will have the identifier. However, this scheme does not work well if you want to know the primary key value, or record number, up front. The DataSet in-memory model needs a unique identifier before you commit it to the DataSet. So, you need a primary key value before you can accept changes into the DataSet. The business examples that involve wanting to know the primary key value up front center on potentially disconnected situations. For example, if your connection to the database aborts after you have sent the information to the server, but before you get a confirmation, you can use the DataSet to preserve your work. As you will see in a later section, if you need a fully disconnected scenario, you will need yet another primary key value scheme.

This scheme also does not ensure that there will always be a sequential set of numbers for a primary key. That is, if an application requests a `spGetNextPkValue` and does not use it (for example, the user aborts the transaction or the computer crashes), that value is lost and will never exist in the database. Some people really like a guaranteed sequential set of numbers. Yet, this is not very easy to do. If someone starts a transaction and gets a value, but does not finish the transaction for a couple of hours, you could negate their number and reissue it. But, if you start thinking through the error cases here, you can see that this type of scheme can get very messy very fast.

The separate PKTable scheme works well and is pretty simple. The only real issue with it is making sure that the PKtable and the target table (such as Person) are in synch. That is, if the PKTable or the target table must ever be backed up separately, or one restored from the other, you need to make sure that the next PK value in the PKTable will work with the value actually in the target table.

Using a stored procedure allows you to customize the primary key value with additional information as well. The primary key must be unique, but you might also add information to the unique part of the primary key. For instance, if you were tracking sales Person orders, you might preface the primary key value with a code for the territory (say "W" for West). In this case, the Primary key value might be something like W0001.

You can make the primary key as involved as you want. You can make the value unique, and just add or concatenate information to it (for example, you can have W0001 and E0002). Alternatively, you can segment the values by code (W0001 and E0001). If you use this type of approach, you need to keep separate table entries in the PKTable for E and W to ensure that they stay unique.

Now that you know your stored procedure works, and that you can return a value you want reliably, you need to integrate this into your code. As mentioned earlier, by using the stored procedure in your application to automatically get the next primary key, you will avoid collisions between users.

Try It Out   Calling the Stored Procedure in Code

To call the `spGetNextPKValue` stored procedure from your code, follow these steps:

1. Navigate to the DataSources window. Right-click and choose Configure DataSet with Wizard to bring up the DataSet Configuration Wizard.

2. Step through the wizard and update it for all new objects. In particular, be sure to select the stored procedure you just added.

3. Open the Data Set Designer MyDBDataSet.xsd and select the spGetNextPKValue stored procedure in the Queries TableAdapter. Right-click on it and choose Properties. Set the Execute mode to Scalar.

4. Navigate to the Solution Explorer and choose Show All Files (the second icon on the top of the Solution Explorer bar).

5. Navigate to MyDBDataSet.xls. Right-click it and choose View Code to bring up MyDBDataSet.vb.

> This may seem a little counterintutive. It might not seem that viewing the code on a XSD would open a .vb file. The way to think about this is that MyDBDataSet.xsd represents a XML representation of your DataSet. But Microsoft wants you to edit the XML file to extend it. Microsoft wants you to work with a partial class to extend the functionality. That's why it opens a .vb file.

6. Add the code in Listing 15-2 to the Partial Class (inside the existing Partial Class for MyDBDataSet).

Listing 15-2: Calling a Stored Procedure to Set the Primary Key

```
Partial Public Class MyDBDataSet

    Partial Public Class PersonDataTable

        Private Sub PersonDataTable_NewRow(ByVal sender As Object, _
            ByVal e As System.Data.DataTableNewRowEventArgs) Handles Me.TableNewRow

            Dim NewPersonRow As PersonRow = TryCast(e.Row, PersonRow)
            Dim SpObject As MyDBDataSetTableAdapters.QueriesTableAdapter = _
                New MyDBDataSetTableAdapters.QueriesTableAdapter

            If NewPersonRow IsNot Nothing And SpObject IsNot Nothing Then
                NewPersonRow.PersonID = SpObject.spGetNextPkValue("Person", -1)
            End If

        End Sub

    End Class

End Class
```

7. Set the ReadOnly property of the PersonIDTextBox to True.

8. Save your files and debug/run your code by pressing F5. This should bring up your form with the primary key ready to be generated for new records.

9. Create a new record (use the Add New Record button) and note the new record number.

How It Works

Stored procedures are treated a little differently than other objects in a DataSet. For instance, table adapters are automatically created for tables. Therefore, when you use IntelliSense in your code, you can find things like PersonTable or BookTable. This is not true for stored procedures.

If you look in the DataSet graphical designer, you can see a table adapter named Queries. (It is often scrolled off on the far right so it may be hard to find.) The DataSet knows about the stored procedure, but it has not created an object for you to use at run-time the same way it does for tables.

So, in the previous code, note that you have to actually create a New MyDBDataSetTableAdapters .QueriesTableAdapter to use in executing the stored procedure for NewPersonRow.PersonID. This is instructive, as this will be the case for any stored procedure that you want to call and use in this way. You will have to create a new QueriesTableAdapter object dynamically.

Another thing to note here is where you put your code. You put your code in the MyDBDataSet.vb file. This file is a safe place for you to put your code. If you expand the MyDBDataSet.xsd node, you will see several files. The file next to it, MyDBDataSet.Designer.vb, is an auto-code generated file. If you put your code in that file, it will get overwritten the next time you change the DataSet. Say, for instance, you want to update the DataSet with another stored procedure. When the data set is regenerated, your code in the MyDBDataSet.vb is not overwritten.

The code you put in here used the key prefix word "Partial" in front of the class definition. You have created a partial class, which extends the existing PersonDataTable class. As long as the PersonDataTable class exists in your DataSet, your code will not be orphaned (even though the PersonDataTable may be updated with new columns).

There are other options for what you use as a primary key as well. The examples so far have all assumed that you are connected somehow to the server. This is not always true. There are disconnected scenarios that are very important. Consider a salesman who wants to make a sale but doesn't have Internet access. You'd like to ensure that the salesman can make the sale and give the customer a printed copy of the invoice, even if he doesn't have access to the Internet.

For these kinds of scenarios, you need a primary key that allows for disconnected applications. You need to ensure that your primary key is unique globally. Creating a GUID (globally unique identifier) is one way to do this. GUIDs are not a perfect guarantee of uniqueness, but they are so close that they are used through computer science for that very purpose. The following example starts with the use of a GUID.

Try It Out   Creating a GUID as the Primary Key

To use a GUID as a primary key in your solution, follow these steps:

1. Close Visual Basic 2005 if it is open. Navigate to your Documents and Settings folder and find the *<your name>*\ My Documents\Visual Studio 2005\Projects folder. Find the directory that has your MultiUserApp application. Copy the entire project to a new directory and name it GUIDApp.

2. Open Visual Basic 2005 and choose Open Project. Navigate to the GUIDApp directory and find the .sln (Solution) file. Double-click it to open your project.

3. Open the Server Explorer and open the connection to MyDB.MDF.

4. Right-click the Tables folder and delete the Person, Book, and PKTable tables.

5. Create the tables as you did in Chapters 3 and 4, but instead of using an int for the data type, use UniqueIdentifier in both the Person and the Book (for the column that refers to the Person table: AuthorID) tables. In the property section for the UniqueIdentifier, set the IsRowGuid property to true. Keep the same column names. Do not populate the tables with data. For your reference, the correct structures and data types are shown in the following table. Be sure to re-add the foreign key relationship between Person and Book.

Person Table

Column Name	Data Type	Allow Nulls
PersonID	uniqueidentifier	No
FirstName	nvarchar(50)	Yes
LastName	nvarchar(50)	Yes
Firstline	nvarchar(50)	Yes
Secondline	nvarchar(50)	Yes
City	nvarchar(50)	Yes
State	nchar(50)	Yes
Phone	nvarchar(50)	Yes

Book Table

Column Name	Data Type	Allow Nulls
BookID	Int	No
BookTitle	nvarchar (50)	No
AuthorID	uniqueidentifier	No

> You need to delete the tables (in step 4) and start over (in step 5) because you can't change a primary key from an Int to a unique identifier (the data type you will use to store a GUID) after you have already created the table. You have to start with a new table.

6. Navigate to the Data Sources Window and rerun the Configure Data Set wizard. The first time you run it, it will think there are no changes. You must first unselect the Book and Person table check boxes in the wizard. Let the wizard finish, and then rerun it and pick up the Book and Person tables again. Select the Person and Book table check boxes again and click Finish to complete the wizard. This should leave the data set with the correct expectations about what the database types are.

7. In the existing partial class you created in the previous example, remove the code necessary for calling the stored procedure spGetNextPkValue, and replace it with a single call to Guid.NewGuid, as shown in Listing 15-3.

Listing 15-3: Using Guid.NewGuid for a Primary Key Value

```
Partial Public Class MyDBDataSet

    Partial Public Class PersonDataTable
        Private Sub PersonDataTable_NewRow(ByVal sender As Object, _
            ByVal e As System.Data.DataTableNewRowEventArgs) Handles Me.TableNewRow

            Dim NewPersonRow As PersonRow = TryCast(e.Row, PersonRow)

            If NewPersonRow IsNot Nothing Then
                NewPersonRow.PersonID = Guid.NewGuid
            End If

        End Sub
    End Class

    Partial Public Class BookDataTable
        Private Sub BookDataTable_NewRow(ByVal sender As Object, _
            ByVal e As System.Data.DataTableNewRowEventArgs) Handles Me.TableNewRow

            Dim NewBookRow As BookRow = TryCast(e.Row, BookRow)

            If NewBookRow IsNot Nothing Then
                NewBookRow.BookID = Guid.NewGuid
            End If

        End Sub
    End Class

End Class
```

> **Note:** If you have problems with the code editor recognizing the Handles Me.TableNewRow, it may be that VB Express does not think you need access to the detailed set of events associated with the Book TableAdapter. Try going to the DataSet Wizard and double-clicking on the BookTable. This will generate code for a RowChanging Event for the BookTable. You should then have access to the right events in your code. You can delete the RowChanging Event code and just work with the Handles Me. TableNewRow.

How It Works

Note that you changed the database types to explicitly store the GUID. You could have used Guid .NewGuid.ToString and stored the GUID in a database type like NChar(128). However, using the native SQL type support is generally a better idea. The more that SQL knows about a data type, the better support it can give you.

Note also that you had to rerun the Data Configuration Wizard. The Data Configuration Wizard is simplistic in its evaluation of changes to the database. Note that you completely dropped the tables, gave them the same names, but changed the data types. If you had not dropped the Book and Person tables, it still would have expected the primary keys of each to be integers. This is an important point to understand in working with the Data Configuration Wizard and data sets in general. You can let the wizard work for you, but you need to know its limitations.

Now you are using a GUID as the primary key. The interesting thing about GUIDs is that while they are globally unique, they aren't really very human friendly. You can read them all right, but it's difficult to compare one GUID to another. Can you imagine reading one of these things over the phone to a friend? "I have order number 69aff3d3-d580-4847-9a5f-ec798685c06e. Is that the same one you've got?" They just aren't fit for human consumption. So, using them in your application as a display item isn't a very attractive option.

But in terms of ensuring you have a globally unique identifier, you have only a few other choices for actually uniquely identifying a record. One other choice, mentioned briefly earlier, is to use a prefix and then a unique identifier. So, for instance, you could assign each Person who has access to the system a unique id. It could be a system login name (that you never let be used by anyone else — ever). Or, you could use the current date (2005Mar19). Then, you need to find some way of ensuring a unique number per that prefix. It can be very hard to ensure uniqueness.

A good way to go, however, is to use a GUID as a hidden id and then a more human-friendly identifier in addition as an alternate identifier. The GUID need not be visible on your example form. However, you should be able to see how to get your form built this way. Programmatically, you can use the alternate identifier for searches and the like, since humans are not going to remember how to search for 69aff3d3-d580-4847-9a5f-ec798685c06e. If you are using a GUID as a hidden identifier, it is useful to toss in a couple of additional human-friendly identifiers to help humans distinguish between records. For instance, adding a date/time stamp, the name of a person or machine from which it came, and so on, all help in deciphering the difference between records when you're trying to figure out where that record came from. This is a bit longer discussion that you've encountered on other identification schemes. However, GUIDs are a very important identification scheme in building a multi-user and multi-application database.

Creating Alternate Keys

When you use a multi-user and multi-application database, performance can become paramount. It is common for people to be oblivious to minor performance design mistakes in a single user database. However, in a multi-user and multi-application database, even minor performance design errors can be costly as the heavy demand of many users often taxes system resources uniformly. If you have alternate identifiers in your database, remember to add indexes for them in the database. An example of an alternate identifier for people who have an employee IDis a Social Security number. Your employee ID uniquely identifies you (and, in this example is the primary key). But, your Social Security number also uniquely identifies you. If people are going to use it as a primary way to search for you, you should identify it as an alternate key with an index.

Indexes take up more room on disk and use more memory. However, in general, if there is any field you are going to search on frequently, you should have an index on it. The following Try It Out shows you how to add an index for the alternate identifiers.

Adding Additional Indexes

To create an alternate key, follow these steps:

1. Open the Table Definition for the Book table; double-click the Books node to open it. Right-click on the table designer background and choose Indexes/Keys to bring up the Index/Keys dialog.

2. Choose to add a new index. In the Columns property on the right, select the Browse button to bring up the Index Columns dialog. Choose BookName and close the dialog. Then choose the IsUnique property and set it to true.

How It Works

As mentioned earlier, you want an alternate index on frequently used fields. But you can also specify that an alternate index should be unique as well. Note that you specified in the earlier example that BookName should be unique. This could work well for this example. Consider the example database you created with the list of presidents: it's unlikely that a President of the United States would read two books with exactly the same title. And you might say that for your database, this rule holds true. This rule wouldn't work well, though, for the Library of Congress.

Creating Constraints

In a multi-user application, you have a choice on where you enforce certain rules about your database. As mentioned in the beginning of this chapter, enforcing constraints in the database becomes much more important in a multi-application environment because it reduces the chance that an application does not properly enforce a rule. In the example you've been using, you might say that that you only want to allow users to enter a Person that is from D.C., Illinois, or Virginia. You could put this code in your application directly by checking for state code values that are valid for those states.

But once you have a database, someone can create a second application that accesses and updates your data and it may not have all of the same constraints that your code does.

Enter check constraints. Check constraints are a way of ensuring that your data stays pure at the source.

Creating a Check Constraint

To create a check constraint, follow these steps:

1. Open the Table Definition for the Person table; double-click the Person node to open it. Right-click on the table designer background and choose Check Constraints to bring up the Check Constraints dialog.

2. Choose Add a New Check Constraint and then select the Expression property on the right-hand side. Click the Browse button to bring up the Check Constraint Expression dialog.

3. Enter the following expression into the Check Constraint editor and click OK.

```
State IN ('DC','IL','VA')
```

4. Run your application again and try and enter a state value that is invalid. Try CA, for instance. This should bring up an exception.

How It Works

When your application code tries to insert or update a record with a value that violates the constraint clause, it will fail. At the time of the insert or update, SSE checks to see if there are any constraints associated with the column and runs the data against them if they exist. Thus, by using Check Constraints you can ensure that the values in the database conform to your rules. The type of constraints you can express in a check clause are almost all the kinds of things you can put in a WHERE clause. The following table shows some simple examples:

Expression Type	Examples
Comparison	Age >= 40, BirthDate < DeathDate
Limits	Between 1 AND 3

There is often debate about where such constraints should live. In general, you will give the user a better experience if the check is done in the application code. But you are more protected if the check is done in the database. Most databases that will have multiple people using them from various applications will make heavy use of check constraints, views, and stored procedures to ensure good data integrity. These types of applications will put constraints in both places. Data rules, rules that check for the integrity of the data, generally belong in the database. Rules that must be computed dynamically at run-time generally belong in the application code.

Views

In a multi-user environment, there may be some information you don't want some users to see. For instance, you may want payroll people to be able to see a salary column in an Employee table, but you probably don't want everyone to see the salary information. SSE supports the ability to create views of your data. Views are like prewritten queries that you can reliably call upon. By default, they are no faster than simply issuing a query directly either in code or directly to SSE. But views can be useful in hiding complex aspects of your table structure and in hiding information that you don't want certain users to see. After you create a view, you can use the GRANT functionality to only grant exclusive access to the table to specific users, but grant wide access to the view as described in Chapter 13. Creating views is not hard, and you can do it in either XM or VB Express. In the following Try it Out, you use VB Express.

Try It Out   Creating and Using a View

To create and use a view, follow these steps:

1. Using the MasterDetail project in the MultiUserApp folder you've been working in, open the Database Explorer, navigate to the Views folder, right-click it, and choose Add New View. This opens the View Designer and the Add Table dialog.

2. In the View Designer, add the Person table and close the Add Table dialog. This will place the Person table on the diagram pane of the View Designer.

3. Check PersonID, FirstName, and LastName in the Person table.

4. In the Column pane, add SecondLine, and in the filter column add IS NOT NULL, or simply add the following text in the SQLPane:

```
Where Secondline IS NOT NULL
```

5. Execute the SQL for the view. The results should appear as shown in Figure 15-4.

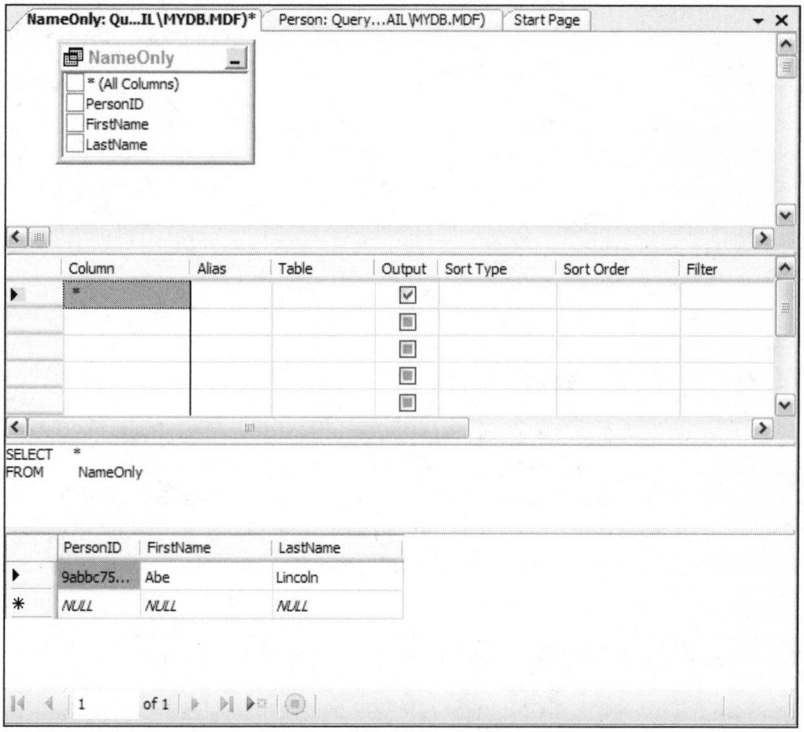

Figure 15-4

6. Save the view and name it NameOnly. It should appear as a node in the Views folder.

7. Navigate to the Data Sources Window and right-click. Select the Configure DataSet with Wizard.

8. Add the NameOnly view to the DataSet and finish the wizard.

9. Right-click on the Data Sources window and see that the NameOnly View has been added to the list of Data Sources and is available for use.

How It Works

In this example, you created a new view that you use in your application. If you can get a data item to show up in the Data Sources window, you can use it in your application as you have in previous exercises. You do need to be careful as to how your data item can be updated.

To actually use this view in your code, you treat it like you do a table. You can drag and drop the view from the Data Sources window onto a form. If the other columns in the table are optional or have default values, you can update and insert values directly on the view as if it were the table itself. However, if the view represents the join of several tables, you cannot use INSERT statements on it.

In this case, you have simply created a subset of the number of columns that are in the table. This can be useful when you want to provide programmatic access to data, but not all of it. So, for instance, this Person table might include sensitive data such as birth date, Social Security number, or pay rate that you do not want generally known. In fact you might have one program that accesses the more common information, such as you created in your view, and a different program that allows someone with the right authorization level to view, update, or delete the sensitive information.

In theory, you could store this sensitive information in a separate table. But a view gives you the ability to write one program that accesses only the data available via the view and the ability to update the full range of columns to a different program. So, using views, you can better protect sensitive data.

Similarly, if you need to provide a constant, correct view of some complex set of tables, a view might be a good choice as well.

Table-Valued Functions

In addition to views, there are other objects you can use in a multi-user environment to limit access to data. In a similar vein to views, user-defined functions — especially those functions which return a table (known as table-valued functions) — are useful in providing prewritten functionality that you can access at run-time. Like views, you can use them to limit information access to certain people. But table-valued functions have additional functionality as well. The process of creating them is similar to the process for creating a view.

Try It Out **Creating a Table-Valued User-Defined Function**

To create and use a table-valued user-defined function, follow these steps:

1. Using the same project you've been working in, open the Database Explorer, navigate to the Functions folder, right-click it, and choose Add New, Table-valued Function. This will open the editor for you to enter your code.

2. In the editor, add the code in Listing 15-4 to the point where the SELECT has been entered.

Listing 15-4: Table-Valued Function

```
CREATE FUNCTION dbo.funNameOnly ()
RETURNS TABLE
AS
   RETURN (SELECT PersonID, FirstName, LastName
           FROM   Person)
```

3. When you start to enter the SELECT statement, note that it is surrounded by a blue outline. Right-click in the blue outline area and choose Design SQL Block. This will open the Query Designer. You can design the T-SQL statement in the Query Designer. Closing the designer will update the T-SQL SELECT statement you are working on.

4. When you are finished, run it from SSEUtil. Open a command window, launch SSEUtil, attach the MDF and run the table valued function. It should appear like Listing 15-5.

Listing 15-5: Executing a Table-Valued Function

```
SSEUtil -c
1> use "C:\Documents and Settings\<UserName>\My Documents\Visual
Studio\Projects\GUID App\MasterDetail\MyDB.MDF"
2> go

Command completed successfully.

1> select * from dbo.funNameOnly()
2> go
```

The result should appear as shown in Figure 15-5.

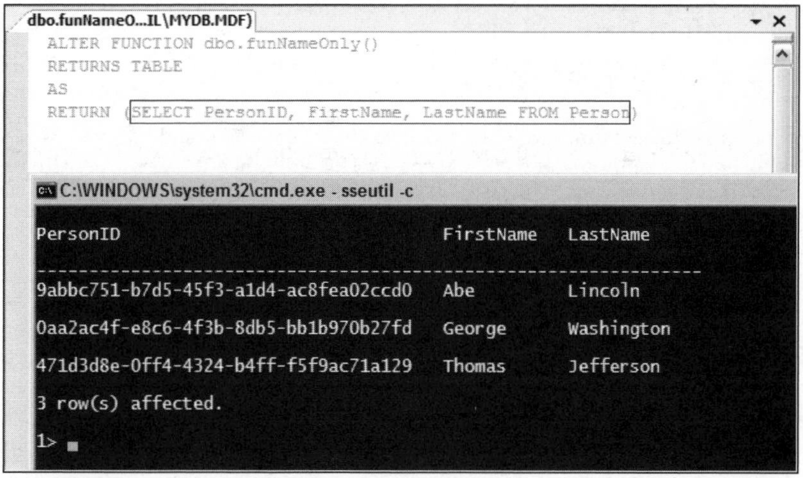

Figure 15-5

How It Works

Table-valued functions (TVFs) are essentially stored procedures that return a single well-known table structure. As such, they can provide much of the same functionality we reviewed for views. However, TVFs can be parameterized, and they can be recursive in nature as well—calling themselves.

Much of the preceding discussion about the advantages of views applies here. Once you have created a TVF, it shows up in your Data Source window and you can drag and drop it onto a form. TVFs are available as objects to code against in the data set. TVFs, however, provide much of the flexibility of stored procedures and views into a regularly defined computer science concept of functions.

Transactions

At the heart of application integrity is the ability to ensure that whatever is committed to a database is atomic; that is, you don't have half-committed records in the database. A partially committed transaction can easily occur. For instance, if you entered three records with the constraint we entered in the preceding exercise, and one of them did not conform (say, the Person from California), the first two records would be committed but the third would not. Depending on what you intended as a transaction, that might be okay and then again, it might not. It depends on what you, as the application designer, consider to be an atomic transactional unit. If you are only updating a single table, DataSets provide you basic transaction integrity at the Update statement level. If you want to encompass a larger unit of work, you need to use the System.Transactions namespace and DLL.

In a single-user environment, transactions are also important. DataSets give you basic transactional capabilities around each individual `Update` statement. In a multi-user environment, however, it's important that you be very explicit about what you consider to be a transaction because a competing update, from a different user, can interfere with your updates.

In the following Try It Out, you wrap the updates to the database in a transaction. If for any reason the database cannot accept the update, all updates will be rolled back in the database and it will be left in the state it was before you attempted the update.

Try It Out   **Custom Transactions**

To create a custom transaction, follow these steps:

1. Log on as an administrator to your machine if you are not already logged in as such. Click Start, right-click My Computer, and click Manage. This will open the Computer Manager.

2. Find the Services and Applications node and open it. Click the Services node. This will display all of the services running on the machine.

3. Find the Distributed Transaction Coordinator. Start the service. If you normally use a different account, return to the login that you normally use.

4. Using the MasterDetail project in the MultiUserApp folder you've been working in, open the Solution Explorer and open the References section. Right-click the References node and add System.Transactions from under the .NET tab.

> References tell the VB Express project where to find code that you are referencing in your project. By default, VB Express has a number of components that it already knows about. If you use a component it doesn't know about, you must add it to the list.

5. Add the highlighted lines from the code in Listing 15-6 to your existing code. You will find this in the code for Form1.vb.

Listing 15-6: Update on Save Code with System.Transactions

```
Imports System.Data
Public Class Form1
```

```vb
Private Sub bindingNavigatorSaveItem_Click(ByVal sender As System.Object, _
        ByVal e As System.EventArgs) Handles bindingNavigatorSaveItem.Click

    If Validate() Then

        Me.BookBindingSource.EndEdit()
        Me.PersonBindingSource.EndEdit()

        Dim transScope As New System.Transactions.TransactionScope
        Dim TxFailure As Boolean = False

        Using transScope

            Try
                Dim Changes As New DataTable()

                ' First delete any records in child table: Books
                Changes = Me.MyDBDataSet.Book.GetChanges(DataRowState.Deleted)
                If Not (Changes Is Nothing) Then
                    Me.BookTableAdapter.Update(Changes)
                End If

                ' Then take care of any and all insert, update, and deletes
                ' in the parent table: Person
                Changes = Me.MyDBDataSet.Person.GetChanges
                If Not (Changes Is Nothing) Then
                    Me.PersonTableAdapter.Update(Changes)
                End If

                '  Finally, take care of any modifications or additions in the
                '  child table: Books.
                Changes = Me.MyDBDataSet.Book.GetChanges(DataRowState.Added _
                        Or DataRowState.Modified)
                If Not (Changes Is Nothing) Then
                    Me.BookTableAdapter.Update(Changes)
                End If

                transScope.Complete()

            Catch ex As Exception
                MessageBox.Show(ex.Message)
                TxFailure = True
            End Try
        End Using

        If TxFailure = False Then
            MessageBox.Show("Accept changes got called")
            Me.MyDBDataSet.AcceptChanges()
        End If

    End If
End Sub
...
```

6. Add the code shown in Listing 15-7 at the bottom of the file, right before the End Class statement, and then choose to Save All. You may have done this in Chapter 4.

Listing 15-7: Data Error Code Book Row Updates

```
    . . .
Private Sub BookDataGridView_DataError(ByVal sender As Object, ByVal e _
            As System.Windows.Forms.DataGridViewDataErrorEventArgs) _
            Handles BookDataGridView.DataError

        MessageBox.Show("Error: Check that a valid record number has been input.
Save Person information first ")

End Sub
End Class
```

How It Works

Note that you have replaced almost all of the update code. The original code updated the DataSet in place by selecting those rows that had been updated and then selectively pushing them to the database for update. This code behaves differently. It copies the changes into a separate DataTable called Changes (replacing the contents for each separate update). This leaves the state of the DataSet unchanged for each update because the update is occurring from the Changes DataTable, not MyDBDataSet. The only problem is that since the DataSet itself is not coordinating all of the changes, you must separately ensure that a new Person record must be saved before any of its new book rows are created. This is why you add the code in Listing 15-6.

Using System.Transactions allows you to wrap the entire transaction, for both the parent and child rows, into a single transaction that gets updated. The way it works is that ADO.NET submits the change to the database on your behalf and then watches for an exception. If there is an exception, ADO.NET rolls back the transaction in the database for you. The DataSet, however, is still left in a state where it thinks the values have been committed. At this point, with an exception from the database, you can either refresh the data from the database into the DataSet, or you can potentially show the user an error.

Moving Your SSE Application to a Server

When your application has robust data protection in place, and you have secured it with the right permissions (see Chapter 13), then you may move your database to a central server location where multiple people can use it.

Actually moving the database is a pretty simple task since you have Xcopy deployment capabilities with SSE. It is simply a matter of copying the database to the server. If you are using SQL Server Express as the central database, you must turn on networking on the server as well as SQL Browser as described in Chapter 14.

When SSE is available from the network, you need to copy your database to the server and update your application to point to the correct location. If you have SSE running on a server with network access, you can use the following Try It Out.

Try It Out   Moving the Database and Updating Your Application

To move your database and update your application, follow these steps:

1. Copy MyDB.MDF to your server computer. Attach it to the instance of SSE running as a network server using either XM or SSEUtil. Below, in Listing 15-8, is an example of attaching using SSEUtil where the location of the MDF on the server machine is C:\myfolder and the database name is MyDB.mdf. (You must be an administrator to attach this way.)

Listing 15-8: Attaching an MDF to the Main Instance

```
SSEUtil -m -c
USE MASTER
GO

sp_detach_db MyDB
GO

CREATE DATABASE MyDB ON PRIMARY (NAME = MyDB, FILENAME = 'C:\myfolder\MyDB.mdf')
LOG ON (Name = 'MyDB_log.ldf', FILENAME = 'C:\myfolder\MyDB_log.ldf')
FOR ATTACH
GO

Use MyDB
GO
```

2. Find the connection string in your app.config file. (Open your app.config file and search on SQLExpress.)

3. Change the connection string in your configuration file. You must change the connection string in three ways:

   a. You must change the dot to the server machine name. In this example, we've been using George for the machine name.

   b. You must change the AttachDbFilename path from a relative path to your application to the logical name of the database on the server. In this case, the logical name is simply MyDB. (See the preceding attach script.)

   c. Finally, you must remove the User Instance = True. The connection string will change from something that looks like this

```
connectionString="Data  Source= .\SQLExpress;AttachDbFilename=
|DataDirectory|\MyDB.mdf; Integrated Security=True; User Instance=True"
```

   to this:

```
connectionString="Data Source=George\SQLExpress;AttachDbFilename=MyDB; Integrated
Security=True;"
```

4. Run your application on the client machine. It should connect to the database that is on the server.

How It Works

When you run your application locally, the `AttachDBFilename` parameter in the connection string tells SQL Server Express to attach the database. The dot specifies the machine name and the path specifies the location on the machine. Additionally, the `UserInstance = true` means that a local instance of SQL Server will run inside your user account. When you run your application with SSE running inside your user account, SSE will auto-close your database after a period of inactivity. This means that you still have Xcopy functionality of the database. When no one is logged into the machine, you can copy the database.

In contrast, if you want your database to always be attached on the server, you must either use Express Manager or SSEUtil to attach it. Higher versions of SQL Server 2005 run in this fashion with the database always attached. Higher-level versions of SQL Server will not auto-close the database for you. When you run your database with the SSE service running for multiple users (as shown previously), you will not be able to Xcopy the database after a period of inactivity. When a database is attached to SSE, SQL Server locks the file and it is inaccessible for other file operations, regardless of what read/write permissions you may have set on the file. In higher versions of SQL Server 2005, the auto-close functionality is off by default. In order to detach the database, once it is in this state, you can either use XM or use SSEUtil again as shown:

```
SSEUtil -m -d MyDB
```

Summary

It is not that hard to write your application so that it can be used in multi-user and multi-application scenarios. But, you need to be very aware at design-time of the choices you must make. First, you need to be careful about how you identify your data. You must decide if your application will be in a mostly connected or in a disconnected state. You also need to decide whether data will be available via views, through TVFs, or by direct access to the tables. Much of the decision here depends on how sensitive the data is. Finally, you need to decide where to check for the validity of your data. Most of the data integrity checks can be done directly in the database itself. Designing your database for multi-user and multi-application scenarios is not that difficult; it just requires forethought and good design.

In particular, this chapter showed you how to:

❑   Correctly use primary keys for multi-user and multi-application scenarios

❑   Create a stored procedure that auto-generates a primary key

❑   Use GUIDs as primary keys

❑   Create and use stored procedures in VB Express for your application

❑   Create Check Constraints in the database from VB Express

❑   Create and use views in VB Express for your application

❑   Create and use Table Valued Functions in VB Express for your application

❑   Create and use custom transactions using System.Transactions

❑   Move your database to the server and access it from your application

Exercises

Try the exercises that follow to test your understanding of the material covered in this chapter. You can find the solutions to these exercises in Appendix A.

1. This chapter showed you how to use a stored procedure to automatically generate the primary key for the Person table. The table you created to do this also has a field for the Book table. Copy the code you created for the Person table and paste it below the code for Person. Then, replace the references to Person with Book and finish adding the code necessary for the Book table to have its primary key generated automatically as well.

2. Chapter 2 showed you how to create a view using T-SQL. In this chapter, you learned how to use a view that has been created in a DataSet. Create a new view of the Books table using code rather than the View Designer in the database. Then, use the DataSet Configuration Wizard to find it and add it to your DataSet.

3. A common performance trick with SQL Server is to put the LDF file on a different drive than the MDF. This allows each drive to work independently to update the log file and the actual database. Using the SSEUtil script from this chapter, create the script necessary to put the LDF on a different drive. Assume you have, in addition to the C drive, a D drive.

A

Exercise Answers

Chapter 1

Exercise 1

You are the chairperson for a university alumni association and want to figure out the appropriate SQL Server 2005 edition to use for a photo album application. This application is an interface for digital photographs and is expected to be installed on each member's desktop. There is no sharing of the application between members, as each person gets a personal copy of the database and the application. Annually the databases are updated and emailed to each member. What edition of SQL Server 2005 would you use?

Solution

You can use SQL Server 2005 Express Edition because the Xcopy functionality is perfect for the intended scenario.

Exercise 2

You are the IT department head of Joe's Auto Parts. Your 75 retail shops are distributed in multiple states across the United States, and each retail shop requires two checkout counters that have the latest information about the catalog. The central office requires daily updates of sales information from the retail shops. What editions of SQL Server would you use in the retail and central offices?

Solution

The retail checkout counters would use SSE, while the central office would use SQL Server 2005 Enterprise or Standard Edition. Replication would be set up between the central and retail offices.

Exercise 3

You are an ISV deploying server applications to small businesses with one to five users. You want to move to the medium business segment supporting larger number of users. Currently you are using SSE in the multi-user mode. How easy is it to move to higher editions of SQL Server?

Solution

It is easy to move an application using SSE in multi-user mode to other editions of SQL Server 2005. The programming stack is similar for all editions of SQL Server 2005. Your existing application will continue to work with all editions of SQL Server 2005 (without changing a line of code) as long as you use the same instance name for your database server. Upgrades are supported from SSE to all other editions of SQL Server 2005 other than the Developer and Evaluation editions.

Chapter 2

Exercise 1

Create an Employees table. Each Employee is defined by an Employee ID and has a Last Name, First Name, office number, and salary as attributes. Insert five distinct rows into the table. Create a stored procedure that updates the salary of all the employees. A numeric number passed as a parameter to this stored procedure indicates the percentage salary increase. Increase the salary of all the employees by 5% using this stored procedure.

Solution

```
USE testDb
CREATE TABLE Employees (EmployeeID int PRIMARY KEY, LastName varchar(20) NULL,
FirstName varchar(20) NULL, OfficeNumber int, Salary numeric)
GO
--Insert Rows
INSERT INTO Employees VALUES (1,'Joe', 'Smith', 202, 40000)
INSERT INTO Employees VALUES (2,'Sally','Jones', 203, 55000)
INSERT INTO Employees VALUES (3, 'Sara', 'Parker', 204, 37000)
INSERT INTO Employees VALUES (4,'Abraham', 'Varky', 205, 50000)
INSERT INTO Employees VALUES (5,'Lisa', 'Kim', 206, 42000)
GO
SELECT * FROM Employees
GO
--Create and use the stored procedure
CREATE PROC sp_updateSalary @percentSalary numeric AS UPDATE Employees SET
salary=salary+@percentSalary*Salary/100
GO
sp_updateSalary 5
SELECT * FROM Employees
```

Exercise 2

Find all the employees with a last name starting with *S* (hint: use LIKE).

Solution

```
use testDB
SELECT EmployeeID, LastName, FirstName
FROM Employees
WHERE LastName LIKE 'S%';
```

The percent sign, %, is used to represent any possible character or set of characters that might appear after the S.

Exercise 3

Create an Office table that has the attributes of office number, area in square feet, phone number, and whether it has a window or not. Insert five rows into the table. Write a query to find out which employees have a window in their office.

Solution

```
USE testDb
CREATE TABLE Office (OfficeNumber int PRIMARY KEY, Area numeric, phoneNumber
varchar(15) NULL, isWindow bit)
GO
--Insert Rows
INSERT INTO Office VALUES (202, 110, '425-1111111', 0)
INSERT INTO Office VALUES (203, 122, '425-1111112', 1)
INSERT INTO Office VALUES (204, 98, '425-1111113', 0)
INSERT INTO Office VALUES (205, 140, '425-1111114', 1)
INSERT INTO Office VALUES (206, 100, '425-1111115', 0)
GO
SELECT * FROM Office
GO
--Find employees having office with a window
SELECT LastName, FirstName FROM Employees AS E JOIN Office AS O ON
E.OfficeNumber=O.OfficeNumber WHERE O.isWindow=1
```

Exercise 4

Create a view on the Employees and Office tables such that such that the Office number is matched from both the tables.

Solution

```
use testdb
GO
CREATE VIEW EmployeeOfficeView AS
(SELECT EmployeeID, LastName, FirstName, E.OfficeNumber, Salary,
O.Area, O.phoneNumber, O.isWindow
FROM Employees AS E JOIN Office AS O ON E.OfficeNumber=O.OfficeNumber)
GO
SELECT * from EmployeeOfficeView
```

Chapter 3

Exercise 1

Assume you want to use an existing database for your application instead of creating a new one. Try adding an existing one with Add ➪ Existing Item. (Hint: Search your machine for *.mdf files.)

Solution

As with adding a new database, you start in the Solution Explorer.

1. Follow the steps outlined in the chapter to create a new application. With VB Express running, select the File menu, Choose New Project, and then select Windows Application.

2. After you have created your application, right-click the top node in the Solution Explorer and choose Add ⇨ Existing Item from the context menu. This will bring up a browse dialog that you can use to find the MDF you want to add. Find your database and choose Add.

   There are a few things you should note. First, make sure that the Files of Type filter at the bottom of the dialog is set to Data Files. Second, if you are adding an existing database, make sure that it is not currently attached to an SQL Server database. If it is, it will be locked and you will be unable to copy it. Finally, if you are attaching an existing MDF that is SQL 2000-based, it SSE will automatically upgrade it. That may take a few seconds. So, your initial connection may fail with a timeout. The upgrade will continue in the background, and you will be able to attach when the upgrade is complete.

Exercise 2

Assume you want to take a starter kit approach and build off of other people's applications. Using File ⇨ New Project, in the New Project section, create a new database application using the My Movie Collection Starter Kit.

Solution

When you use the Movie Collection Starter Kit, you can build on an already existing starter kit that others have started. As with the example in Exercise 1:

1. Follow the steps to create a new application. With VB Express running, select the File menu, Choose New Project, and then select My Movie Collection Starter Kit.

2. Build and run your application. It should be readily usable.

Exercise 3

Using File ⇨ New Project, create and build your own database structure and sample data from scratch and create a new sample read-only database.

Solution

This exercise is an invitation to get your own application going. If you would like a specific example, try the following: Create a database with a single table called Tasks. Add a column called TaskID with a data type of int and make it the primary key. Then, add a column named TaskDescription with a data type of nvarchar(500).

Remember, in this chapter, we made the application read-only. You can leave the application directly updateable. Follow the steps to create your own Windows application, and then use the Database Explorer to create your own table and structure. A couple of notes:

❑ Be sure to choose a field as a primary key.

❑ Don't just take the default field length as the size for your data. Think about how much room you'll really need.

Chapter 4

Exercise 1

Add more dialogs, menus, and such to finish up your application. Each dialog may either allow you to work with a specific table in your database or display certain information. Start by creating an About dialog that you can launch from the menu and that will display appropriate credit information.

Solution

1. To add a new dialog to your application, right-click the top node in the Solution Explorer and choose Add New Item. Choose to add a new dialog.

2. Add a new Help menu item, and then an About menu item below that in the main form.

3. Double-click the About menu item to create a menu handler, and then add the following code to the event handler:

```
Dialog1.Show()
```

4. Open the dialog and double-click OK. Add the following code:

```
Me.Close()
```

5. In the dialog, delete the Close button.

6. Drag a RichTextBox onto the dialog. Find the Lines property and select the builder button. This will open a text box where you can enter credit information. Change the ReadOnly property to True.

7. Save, build, and debug your application.

Exercise 2

Make sure that your application is accessible to those that cannot use a mouse well. This means that you must add accelerators to the menu and ensure that tabbing works throughout the application in a smooth manner. Start by adding accelerators to the existing Print and File menus. Use the ShowShortCutKeys property. When you add an ampersand to a menu name, the ampersand marks the accelerator key for the menu entry (for example, &Print).

Solution

1. Select the File menu and change the word File to &File in the Text property. Under Misc., set the ShowShortCutKeys property to True.

2. Select the Print menu and change the Text property to &Print. Under Misc., set the Shortcut property to Ctrl F. Set the ShowShortCutKeys property to True.

When your application comes up and has focus, hold down the Alt key for several seconds. The accelerators should appear.

Exercise 3

There are several printers available to your users. You need to make your application capable of using all those printers. There is code readily available on the Internet that can help you add the code you need.

As a hint, go to http://msdn.microsoft.com/library and search for PrintDialog.ShowDialog. Add the Print Dialog component to your application and allow the user to choose a Printer.

Solution

This solution is a little harder. Open the event handler for printing and add the following code:

```
Dim PrintDialog1 As New PrintDialog()
PrintDialog1.Document = PrintDocument1
Dim diagResult As DialogResult = PrintDialog1.ShowDialog()

If (diagResult = DialogResult.OK) Then
    PrintDocument1.Print()
End If
```

Chapter 5

Exercise 1

Specify the order in which the query results are returned, using the Order By button. Order the results by Last Name.

Solution

To specify the order in which results are returned from the database, you need to start by configuring your Data Source. You can choose to configure the grid for either the Person or the Book table. For this example, use the Person grid.

1. Open the GridView tasks menu for the Person grid and click Configure Data Source to bring up the Configure Data Source Wizard.

2. In the Choose your data connection page, accept the existing connection and click Next.

3. In the Configure Select Statement page, click the ORDER BY button. This brings up the Add Order by Clause dialog.

4. In the first Sort by field, select LastName and click OK.

5. Click Next in the wizard. This will take you to the Test Query page.

6. Test your query by clicking the Test Query button.

If the results come back sorted by last name you have succeeded. The way the results show up here is the way they'll show up in the grid when run. To complete this exercise, simply click Finish on the wizard.

Exercise 2

Add some records (for example, you can invent new presidents) and then add additional controls to filter. Use an OR conditional between WHERE statements instead of an AND conditional.

Solution

You can add records pretty easily, either directly in Web Express by running your application and directly inserting values, or through the Database Explorer in the Show Table Data grid. The following table shows a couple of records you can add.

Person ID	First Name	Last Name	Firstline	Second line	City	State	Phone
4	John	Adams	1 Federalist Way	NULL	Massachusetts Bay Colony	MA	1 000 4567890
5	James	Madison	13 Framer Ave	NULL	Orange County	VA	1 000 5678901

Exercise 3

Change the properties for the LinkButton to make it look more like a traditional button.

Solution

The simplest solution to this problem is to use a Button control from the Standard group in the ToolBox. You set the postback URL in the same way to you do for a LinkButton. The difference is that a LinkButton has the text underlined so that you know it's a hyperlink. However, you can set the properties of a LinkButton to make it look close to a system button. Here are some properties you can set; simply select the LinkButton and then set the following properties to get something a little closer to a traditional button:

- ❑ BackColor: ButtonFace
- ❑ BorderColor: InactiveBorder
- ❑ FontName: Tahoma
- ❑ Font Size: Smaller
- ❑ ForeColor: Black

Exercise 4

With the FormView up, choose Edit Templates. You will see a list of templates that are used for Insert, Edit, and so on. Edit the Insert template with different label names and arrange the fields more attractively than the default layout.

Solution

First, navigate to the AddItem page you created. This page has the FormView on it. Then:

1. Open the FormView Tasks context menu and select Edit Templates to bring up the form in Template Editing mode.

2. Open the FormView Tasks context again, while in Template Edit mode, and change the display from ItemTemplate to InsertTemplate.

3. Select the outer bound around the FormView and stretch it to increase the width.

4. Move the fields around using the spacebar and using cut, copy, and paste.

5. When you are finished editing, bring up the FormView Tasks context menu and click End Template Editing.

This procedure will change the way the records are displayed on your web page both when you work with the page in design mode and when the page is run.

Chapter 6

Exercise 1

List the attached databases to a user instance as well as its parent instance.

Solution

1. Open a command line prompt and type the following to list all databases attached to the user instance:

```
SSEUtil -l
```

2. Type the following to list all databases attached to the parent SSE instance:

```
SSEUtil -m -l
```

The –m flag in SSEUtil is used to connect to the parent instance. Note that you must be logged on as an administrator to access the parent instance (use the –m option).

Exercise 2

Verify that the version of the parent instance and the user instance are the same.

Solution

1. Open a command line prompt and type the following to get the version of the user instance:

```
SSEUtil -version
```

2. Type the following to get the version of the parent SSE instance:

```
SSEUtil -m -version
```

Note that you must be logged on as an administrator to access the parent instance (use the –m option).

Exercise 3

List all SQL Server and SSE instances running on the local machine.

Solution

Open a command line prompt and type the following to get the list of SQL Server and SSE instances:

```
SSEUtil -listsrv
```

Exercise 4

Detach all databases with names starting with d:.

Solution

Open a command line prompt and type the following to detach all databases with names starting with d:. Note that most of the databases in this list were attached using the AttachDBFIleName syntax and autonamed by SSE since the autonaming feature takes into consideration the full path of the file.

```
SSEUtil -d d:
```

Chapter 7

Exercise 1

You are using an XML data type to collect inter-business documents. You anticipate having to write an XQuery to quickly retrieve information from the column that is storing the XML data. Use the Visual Basic Table Editor to create an XML index on the XML data type.

Solution

1. Open the Table Designer for the table with an XML column and select the row that has an XML data type defined for it.
2. Right-click on the background of the table designer and choose XML indexes.
3. Select Add a new XML index. Note that the property is Primary is set to Yes.

Exercise 2

You have invested heavily in using XML data types to collect purchase order information from your vendors. There are certain queries you make into an XML data type column that always retrieve single values. You want to speed up your queries by better indexing the XML data type column. Use the Visual Basic Table Editor to create a secondary XML index on the Resume column based on Path.

Solution

Add these steps to the solution to Exercise 1:

4. Add a second XML index. Note that the property is Primary is set to No.
5. Choose the Secondary Type property and set the property to Value.

Exercise 3

You are creating a database application and you want the results from an XML column to appear, programmatically, just like the other columns you retrieve in a query. Retrieve more than one SQL Scalar value from the XML column in a single select. Push the results into several columns.

Solution

There are several possible solutions for the exercise in this chapter. One is shown here:

```
SELECT Resume.value('(/Name)[1]', 'VARCHAR(50)'),
       Resume.value('(/Objective)[1]', 'VARCHAR(50)'),
       Resume.value('(/Address/PostCode)[1]', 'VARCHAR(50)')
FROM RichTable
GO
```

Chapter 8

Exercise 1

In your build/debug cycle, you decide that the output version of the database (that ends up the bin folder) should always be fresh and new each time you debug. (You don't want old test data in the database.) Find the properties for the MDF in the Property Window. Change the Copy Always property to Copy to Output Directory. Note performance differences.

Solution

To always copy the MDF to the output directory, find the Copy to Output Directory and set it to Copy Always. The Copy If Newer option will only copy the MDF from the source directory if it is newer than the one in the output directory. Be careful about establishing connections to the database in the output directory and then leaving them open. If you leave them open, SSE will touch the file timestamp and you may not get the behavior you want.

Exercise 2

You want to control the behavior of SSE on your machine through global settings. Set some of the other DBCC flags and observe the output in the `error.log` file

Solution

There are a number of trace flags you can choose from. In previous versions of SQL Server, many of these were undocumented. If you have downloaded the SSE documentation, try searching it for trace flags. For this exercise, open a command window. At the command prompt, type **SSEUtil –t +3605**.

Exercise 3

VB Express handles the connection to the database for you automatically. It generates the connection string and handles all the details. However, from time to time, you may want to connect directly to the database and test certain things out. This is easy using SSEUtil. Just type in **SSEUtil** to get a list of commands you can you use. Then, using SSEUtil, use the generated name of the user instance to connect to SQL Server. After you are connected, find and use the generated name of the database to query your database.

Solution

Use the Rich.mdf you created in the previous chapter. Then, using SSEUtil, follow these steps.

1. Open a command window.

> Note that if you have not had much practice using command windows, start in the root directory (c:\>) and type CD Doc and then press the tab key. It will complete the directory name for you so you can just press enter and navigate to the directory you want. To go back a directory level, type CD .. and press Return. This will take you back a directory level.

2. Type **SSEUtil –l** to list all of the databases that you have attached to from your user account.

3. Type **SSEUtil -a "c:\rich.mdf to"** attach the database.

4. Type **SSEUtil –c** to put SSEUtil in console mode.

5. Type the following code to orient SSE to use c:\rich.mdf as the database:

```
Use "c:\rich.mdf"
GO
```

6. Type the following code to list all the contents of RichTable:

```
SELECT * from RichTable
GO
```

Chapter 9

Exercise 1

You are the IT department head for Joe's Garage and the Director of Marketing asks you to install SSE on his new desktop machine. You found out that he wants a named instance called SalesDBServer, and he wants to access the database server from his laptop using TCP/IP. The director wants to use the Sales Application with this instance, and you found out that the Sales Application uses SQL Authentication. The component features that the director wants installed include SQL Engine, SQL Data Files, Replication, Client Components, Connectivity, and SDK. What steps would you follow to install SSE on his machine? Assume that the director wants you to explain the setup dialogs to him while you do the installation.

Solution

1. To begin the installation process, click Install SSE.

2. On the End User License Agreement page, click the check box to accept the license and then click Next.

3. On the SQL Server Component Update, click Next.

4. On the Welcome page of the SQL Server Installation Wizard, click Next.

5. On the System Configuration Check (SCC) page, click Continue.

6. On the Registration Information page, enter the user name and company information. Uncheck the Hide advanced configuration check box. Click Next.

7. On the Feature Selection page, select SQL Engine, SQL Data Files, Replication, Client Components, Connectivity, and SDK. Click Next.

8. On the Instance Name page, choose to install a named instance and specify the name **SalesDBServer**. Click Next.

9. On the Service Account dialog, enable networking and click Next.

10. On the Authentication Mode dialog, select Mixed Mode authentication and supply a strong password. Click Next.

11. On the Collations page, click Next.

12. On the Error Reporting page, click Next.

13. The ready to install dialog asks for a confirmation to start the installation. At this stage, the Installation Wizard has enough information to begin copying files. Click Install.

Exercise 2

There are 10 marketing personnel in your company, and all of them want to install SSE using the same specifications as listed in Exercise 1. What command line parameters would you use to do a silent installation?

Solution

The command line parameters are:

```
start /wait setup.exe /qn INSTANCENAME=SalesDBServer SECURITYMODE=SQL SAPWD=Strong
password DISABLENETWORKPROTOCOLS=0 ADDLOCAL=SQL_Engine,SQL_Data_Files,
SQL_Replication,Client_Components,Connectivity,SDK
```

Exercise 3

The Director of Marketing wants to remove replication from his SSE instance. Explain how you will do this with the setup dialogs. How will you proceed if you can use setup command line parameters?

Solution

1. In the Control Panel, double-click the Add or Remove Programs icon.

2. Under Currently Installed Programs, click the instance of SSE to configure, and then click Change.

3. In the Component Selection dialog, select the SalesDBServer instance and click Next.

4. Select Database Engine in the Feature Maintenance dialog. You will see a welcome screen and SCC check dialogs similar to the dialogs for new installs. Click Next.

5. On the Change or Remove Instance page, click Change Installed Components.

6. On the Feature Selection page, right-click the Replication entry under SQL Server Database Services. Select the Will not be Installed option so that an X mark shows up against that entry. Click Next.

7. Click Install in the ready to install page to begin the installation

To install silently, use the following setup command line parameters:

```
start /wait setup.exe /qn REMOVE=SQL_Replication
```

Exercise 4

Explain how you will uninstall SSE from Joe's machine. You know that Joe uses the Visual Basic Express from the book CD, and he does not plan to uninstall it.

Solution

1. Open Control Panel and Select Add or Remove Programs.

2. Under Currently Installed Programs, click the product listed as Microsoft SQL Server 2005 Express Edition and then click Remove.

3. In the Component Selection dialog, select the instance to remove and click Next. Please select Workstation Components also if this is the only instance of SQL Server 2005 or SSE on Joe's computer.

4. Click Finish in the Confirmation dialog to start the uninstall process.

5. If there is no other instance of SSE or SQL Server 2005 on your machine, select Microsoft SQL Native Client under Currently Installed programs and click the Remove button. Click Yes in the Windows Installer dialog that asks you for confirmation.

Chapter 10

Exercise 1

After you have published your application and installed it on your machine, run it and add some data to it. Next, in VB Express, make another simple change in the UI (for example, move the button again). Next, in the Application Files for the project properties option, mark the .MDF and the .LDF as Include (Auto). Build and republish the application.

Solution

This exercise illustrates what ClickOnce will do with data files. If no data files exist, it will install them; if a data file already exists, it will not overwrite it. This is particularly important for your database files. You do not want to overwrite user's data on an upgrade.

Exercise 2

In your corporation, you maintain separate websites for support and downloads. In VB Express, republish your application but specify the separate website for support. Enter the support website URL on the Options page. Build and republish. Find out where the support URL shows up.

Solution

The support URL shows up at the bottom of the Install web page and it shows up on the All Programs menu under MasterDetail.

Exercise 3

Your application and database are very large. While publishing via the Internet is a great distribution option, it is too big a download for some customers. You want to create a CD and also push the setup to a UNC share. Using the publish options, publish the bits to a CD.

Solution

1. In the Prerequisite dialog, specify Download Prerequisites from the Same Location as My Application.

2. Run the Publish Wizard and enter a local file location. Click Next.

3. Select the From a CD-ROM or DVD-ROM option and click Next.

4. Add the website where the application should look for updates (if not already present).

Chapter 11

Exercise 1

You are the IT manager for Joe's Garage, and your manager wants to know if there are any MSDE instances on his machine. How will you determine this?

Solution

1. Click Start, and then click Run. In the Open box, type `regedit.exe` and then click OK. View all values under the registry key `HKEY_LOCAL_MACHINE (HKLM)\SOFTWARE\Microsoft Sql Server\InstalledInstances`. This gives you all the SQL Server installations on the machine.

2. Now for each of the instance names listed, go to either of the following registry key locations: HKLM\SOFTWARE\Microsoft\Microsoft SQL Server*instance name*\Setup for the named instance or HKLM\SOFTWARE\Microsoft\MSSQLServer\Setup for the default MSDE instance. Look for a key called Product Code. If this key exists, then the instance is MSDE; otherwise, it is some other edition of SQL Server.

Exercise 2

How will you upgrade an instance of MSDE SP3 to MSDE SP4? Assume that you do not have a strong password for your sa account.

Solution

Open a command prompt window and navigate to the MSDE 2000 SP4 setup directory. Execute one of the following commands:

For a default instance using Windows Authentication Mode:

```
setup /upgradesp sqlrun DISABLENETWORKPROTOCOLS=1 SAPWD=strong password
```

For a named instance using Windows Authentication Mode:

```
Setup /upgradesp sqlrun INSTANCENAME=InstanceName DISABLENETWORKPROTOCOLS=1
    SAPWD=strong password
```

For a default instance using Mixed Mode:

```
setup /upgradesp sqlrun SECURITYMODE=SQL UPGRADEUSER=AnAdminLogin
UPGRADEPWD=AdminPassword DISABLENETWORKPROTOCOLS=1 SAPWD=strong password
```

For a named instance using Mixed Mode:

```
setup /upgradesp sqlrun INSTANCENAME=InstanceName SECURITYMODE=SQL
UPGRADEUSER=AnAdminLogin UPGRADEPWD=AdminPassword DISABLENETWORKPROTOCOLS=1
SAPWD=strong password
```

Exercise 3

Install a new named instance of MSDE SP4 on your machine using the instance name of TestMSDE. You need only windows authentication and you do not need any remote networking. Use the Graphical User Interface to upgrade this instance to SSE.

Solution

Open a command prompt window and navigate to the MSDE 2000 SP4 setup directory. Execute the following command to install a new instance of MSDE:

```
Setup.exe INSTANCENAME=TestMSDE SAPWD=strongpassword
```

To upgrade this instance of MSDE to SSE, launch setup.exe and follow the steps below.

1. On the End User License Agreement page, accept the license by clicking the check box and then click Next.

2. On the SQL Server Component Update dialog, click Next.

3. On the Welcome page, click Next.

4. On the System Configuration Check (SCC) page, click Continue.

5. On the Registration Information page, enter the user name and company information. Uncheck the Hide advanced configuration check box. Click Next.

6. On the Feature Selection page, select everything except replication. Click Next.

7. On the Instance Name page, specify TestMSDE. Click Next.

8. Select SQL Database Services, Workstation Components, Books Online, and development tools in the Existing components page and click Next.

9. Select Windows Authentication Mode in the Upgrade Logon Information page.

10. In the User Instance page, click Next.

11. Click Next in the Error and Usage Report Settings.

12. Click Install in the Ready To Install page to start the installation process.

13. Click Finish to complete the upgrade.

Exercise 4

Assume that your company uses accounting software that relies on an MSDE instance called AccountingDataInstance. There are five accountants in your company, and all of them have an instance of MSDE installed on their machines. What is the command line you will use to upgrade these instances silently to SSE, assuming that they qualify for automatic upgrades?

Solution

```
Setup.exe /qn UPGRADE=SQL_Engine INSTANCENAME=AccountingDataInstance
```

Exercise 5

You are the IT manager for Joe's Garage, and your company uses a default instance of MSDE to store customer information. These MSDE installations do not qualify for automatic upgrades because the product codes of the MSIs have been changed. You are using the Windows Authentication mode and all the instances are at SP4 service pack level. How will you upgrade these instances silently to SSE?

Solution

1. Click Start, and then click Run. In the Open box, type **regedit.exe** and then click OK. Obtain the Product Code from the registry key at HKLM\SOFTWARE\Microsoft\MSSQLServer\Setup.

2. Open a command prompt window and navigate to the MSDE setup directory. Execute the following command to uninstall:

```
Setup.exe /x ProductCode SAVESYSDB=1
```

3. Carry out a clean install of the SSE from the CD, using the following command:

```
Setup.exe /qn ADDLOCAL=ALL USESYSDB=Location_of_Datafiles
```

Chapter 12

Exercise 1

Create an Access Project called MyOrderDBProject to store information about your orders and shipping details. Create the tables described in the following table and use appropriate data types for the fields.

Table Name	Field Names	Primary Key
Customer	CustomerNumber, Balance, CustomerDescription	CustomerNumber
ShipTo	Address, CustomerNumber	Address
Order	OrderNumber, Address, Date	OrderNumber
Order Details	OrderNumber, LineNumber, ItemNumber, Quantityordered	OrderNumber, LineNumber
Item Details	ItemNumber, Description	ItemNumber

Solution

1. Select Project using the Project (New Data) option from the File ➪ New menu. Specify the name of the project as **MyOrderDBProject** and click Create.

2. Specify the name of your MSDE instance in the Data Link Properties dialog. Now specify the name of the MSDE database you want to create and click Next.

3. Click Finish in the next dialog box to create the project and the database.

Repeat the following steps for each of the tables described.

1. Select the Tables Node in the database window and double-click the option Create Table in Design View.

2. Fill in the values in the Table Designer for the fields.

3. Click the Allow Nulls column next to the primary key field indicated by the following table, so that the tick mark is cleared. Right-click the same field and select the primary key option from the pop-up list.

4. Select Save in the File menu and enter the table name. Click OK.

Table Name	Field Name with Datatype in Parenthesis	Primary Key
Customer	CustomerNumber (int), Balance (money), CustomerDescription (nvarchar)	CustomerNumber
ShipTo	Address(nvarchar), CustomerNumber (int)	Address
Order	OrderNumber(int), Address(nvarchar), Date(datetime)	OrderNumber
Order Details	OrderNumber(int), LineNumber(int), ItemNumber(int), Quantityordered (int)	OrderNumber, LineNumber
Item Details	ItemNumber(int), Description(nvarchar)	ItemNumber

Exercise 2

Create views for each of the tables in Exercise 1 so that you can see the data in each table. Select all the fields for the view.

Solution

Repeat the following steps for each of the tables listed in the previous exercise.

1. Select Queries from the database window and click CreateView in Designer.

2. Use the Add button to add the table. Click Close.

3. Select the all the columns and save the view.

Exercise 3

What is the ADO equivalent of the following DAO Recordset values?

- ❑ Cursor type of dbOpenSnapshot
- ❑ Cursor type of dbOpenForwardOnly
- ❑ Option value for dbAppendOnly
- ❑ Option value for dbInconsistent
- ❑ Lock type of dbReadOnly
- ❑ Lock type of dbOptimistic

Solution

DAO Recordset Values	ADO Recordset Properties or Parameters
Cursor Type	
dbOpenSnapshot	CursorType=adOpenStatic
dbOpenForwardOnly	CursorType=adOpenForwardOnly
Option Values	
dbAppendOnly	Properties("Append-Only Rowset")
dbInconsistent	Properties("Jet OLEDB:Inconsistent") = True
Lock Type Values	
dbReadOnly	adLockReadOnly
dbOptimistic	adLockOptimistic

Chapter 13

Exercise 1

Suppose your organization uses a table called Sales and you want to enable two salespersons, Burt and Ernie, to view the sales data. Create a Role called ViewSalesData and assign permissions to view data from the Sales table. Create new Logins and Users called Burt and Ernie. Add Burt and Ernie to the ViewSalesData Role.

Solution

Execute the following from the SSMS-EE Query Window:

```
--To create a Login and User for Burt and Ernie
USE mydb
CREATE LOGIN "Burt" WITH PASSWORD = 'TEST'
CREATE USER Burt
CREATE LOGIN "Ernie" WITH PASSWORD = 'TEST'
CREATE USER Ernie

--Create the Role ViewSalesData
CREATE ROLE ViewSalesData

--Add Burt and Ernie to the ViewSalesData Role
EXEC sp_addrolemember 'ViewSalesData', 'Burt'
EXEC sp_addrolemember 'ViewSalesData', 'Ernie'

--Grant SELECT Permissions on Sales table
GRANT SELECT on Sales TO ViewSalesData
```

Exercise 2

Add Ernie to the fixed Server Role for creating and altering databases.

Solution

The fixed Server Role that gives permission to create and alter databases is dbcreator. Execute the following line from the SSMS-EE Query window:

```
EXEC sp_addsrvrolemember 'Ernie', 'dbcreator'
```

Exercise 3

Create a new schema called SalesReportSchema and give Burt control on the schema.

Solution

Execute the following from the SSMS-EE Query window:

```
USE mydb
GO
CREATE SCHEMA SalesReportSchema

--Give Burt control on the schema
GRANT CONTROL ON SCHEMA::SalesReportSchema TO Burt
```

Chapter 14

Exercise 1

You are the IT manager for Joe's Garage, and your manager wants to know if your database application should be upgraded to use SQL Server Standard. Currently the application uses SSE. What are the additional features offered by the SQL Server Standard edition compared to SSE?

Solution

Some of the advantages offered by SQL Server Standard edition over SSE include:

❑ Data Mirroring and backup log shipping

❑ Fail over Clustering

❑ SQL Server Agent

❑ Reporting services

❑ SQL Service Broker

❑ SQL Server Management Studio

❑ Web Services

❑ Basic ETL

❑ Notification Service

❑ Native 64-bit support

❑ Four CPUs are supported and there is no limit on RAM or database size

However, the User Instance and Xcopy features are not available in the Standard edition.

Exercise 2

How would you upgrade a default instance (instance name of MSSQLSERVER) of SSE to another edition of SQL Server 2005 silently? You need only windows authentication, and you do not need any remote networking.

Solution

Open a command prompt window and navigate to the SQL Server 2005 setup directory. Execute the following commands:

```
Setup.exe /qn UPGRADE=SQL_Engine INSTANCENAME=MSSQLSERVER ADDLOCAL=ALL
DISABLENETWORKPROTOCOLS=0
```

Exercise 3

How would you upgrade a named instance (instance name of SalesDBServer) of SSE to another edition of SQL Server 2005 using the setup GUI? You need only windows authentication and you do not need any remote networking.

Solution

1. Insert the SQL Server 2005 Standard Edition CD into your computer's CD-ROM drive.

2. On the End User License Agreement page, read the licensing agreement, and select the check box to accept the licensing terms and conditions. Click Next.

3. On the SQL Server Component Update dialog box, click Next.

4. On the Welcome page of the SQL Server Installation Wizard, click Next.

5. On the System Configuration Check (SCC) page, click Continue.

6. On the Registration Information page, enter the user name, company information, and the Product Key. Click Next.

7. On the Components to Install page, select SQL Server Database Services, Workstation Components, Books Online, and development tools.

8. On the Instance Name page, choose SalesDBServer and click Next.

9. Select SQL Database Services, Workstation Components, Books Online, and development tools in the Existing components page and click Next.

10. Select Windows Authentication Mode in the Upgrade Logon Information page.

11. Click Next in the Error and Usage Report Settings.

12. Click Install in the Ready To Install page to start the installation process.

13. Click Finish to complete the upgrade.

Chapter 15

Exercise 1

This chapter showed you how to use a stored procedure to automatically generate the primary key for the Person table. The table you created to do this also has a field for the Book table. Copy the code you created for the Person table and paste it below the code for Person. Then, replace the references to Person with Book and finish adding the code necessary for the Book table to have its primary key generated automatically as well.

Solution

As described in the exercise instructions, getting the stored procedure to work with Book is a matter of adding a second partial class below the existing partial class for Person. You can do this quickly by copying all of the Person class and then simply changing all of the occurrences of Person to Book.

```
Partial Public Class BookDataTable

  Private Sub BookDataTable_NewRow(ByVal sender As Object, _
      ByVal e As System.Data.DataTableNewRowEventArgs) Handles Me.TableNewRow
    Dim NewBookRow As BookRow = TryCast(e.Row, BookRow)
    Dim SpObject As MyDBDataSetTableAdapters.QueriesTableAdapter = _
      New MyDBDataSetTableAdapters.QueriesTableAdapter

    If NewBookRow IsNot Nothing SpObject isNot Nothing Then
      NewBookRow.Bookid = SpOjbect.spGetNextPKValue("Book", -1)
    End if
End Sub

End Public Class
```

Exercise 2

Chapter 2 showed you how to create a view using T-SQL. In this chapter, you learned how to use a view that has been created in a DataSet. Create a new view of the Books table using code rather than the View Designer in the database. Then, use the DataSet Configuration Wizard to find it and add it to your DataSet.

Solution

You can use SSMS-EE to create the view definition in your database. If your MyDB MDF file is situated in the root drive of your machine, you can use the following script with SSEUtil:

```
SSEUtil -c
USE  "c:\MyDB.MDF"
GO
CREATE VIEW BookView
AS SELECT BookID, BookTitle, AuthorID
From Book
GO
```

❑ After you have created the view in the database, launch VB Express. Verify that your view is present by finding it in the Database Explorer. If VB Express is already running, refresh the Database Explorer by right-clicking the connection node for the database and clicking Refresh.

❑ Open the Data Sources Window and right-click on the background of the window. Click the Configure DataSet with Wizard menu item. This will add your view to the DataSet.

Exercise 3

A common performance trick with SQL Server is to put the LDF file on a different drive than the MDF. This allows each drive to work independently to update the log file and the actual database. Using the SSEUtil script from this chapter, create the script necessary to put the LDF on a different drive. Assume you have, in addition to the C drive, a D drive.

Solution

To make this work, you must first physically put the LDF file on the drive you want it to be on. Then you can run this script:

```
SSEUtil -m -c
USE MASTER
GO

sp_detach_db MyDB
GO

CREATE DATABASE MyDB ON PRIMARY (NAME = MyDB, FILENAME = 'C:\myfolder\MyDB.mdf')
LOG ON (Name = 'MyDB_log.ldf', FILENAME = 'D:\myfolder\MyDB_log.ldf')
FOR ATTACH
GO

Use MyDB
GO
```

Index

SYMBOLS

+ (addition) operator, 32
/ (division) operator, 32
= (equals) operator, 32
> (greater than) operator, 32
>= (greater than or equal to) operator, 32
< (less than) operator, 32
<= (less than or equal to) operator, 32
% (modulo) operator, 32
* (multiplication) operator, 32
<> (not equal to) operator, 32
!= (not equal to) operator, 32
!> (not greater than) operator, 32
!< (not less than) operator, 32
- (subtraction) operator, 32
/? (question mark) parameter, 168

A

Access (Microsoft)
  features, 221–223
  project development with MSDE, 228–234
accessing objects
  access control, 262–264
  groups, 256–257
  permissions, 259–262
  principals, 252–256
  roles, 256–258
ActiveX Data Objects (ADO)
  defined, 222
  mapping DAO to ADO, 239–240
Add Connection dialog, 124–125
Add New Item dialog, 46

adding
  databases, 46–47, 85
  features, 171–174
  tables, 94–96
addition (+) operator, 32
ADDLOCAL=ALL parameter, 165
ADDLOCAL=feature_selection parameter, 163, 165
ADO (ActiveX Data Objects)
  defined, 222
  mapping DAO to ADO, 239–240
ADO.NET extensions, 107
after triggers, 38
aggregate functions, 35–36
ALLOWXDBCHAINING={1 | 0}, 165
ALTER command, 29–31
ALTER permission, 259, 262
alternate key, 304–305
AND operator, 32
Application Files dialog, 185–186
application replication, 10–11
Application Role principal, 252–255
application roles
  authentication modes, 255
  creating, 253–255
  deleting, 253–255
  name, 255
  passwords, 255
Application Server component, 180
Application Updates dialog, 184
applications
  building, 53
  debugging, 53, 133–141

applications (continued)
moving to server, 312–314
printing functionality, 77–78
testing, 55
ASP.NET applications
Internet Information Services (IIS), 180–181
single-user, 11–12
third-party hosting, 12–13
assertions, 140–141
attach step (database connectivity), 102
`AttachDBFilename` **connection string, 102**
Authentication Mode dialog, 157–158
authentication modes
application roles, 255
Mixed Authentication, 157–158, 266
setting, 157–158
SQL Authentication, 22–23, 266
Windows Authentication, 22–23, 157–158, 266
AutoClose feature, 102, 104
automating connectivity to SSE instance, 102–104
auto-naming database and log files, 103
`AverageQuantity` **function, 36–37**
`AVG ()` **function, 35**

B

base tables, 40–41
batch terminator, 34
batches, 34
BCP (Bulk Copy) tool, 7
BI (Business Intelligence), 279–280
bigint data type, 28
binary data type, 28
BindingNavigator component, 52–53
BindingSource component, 52, 73
bit data type, 28
break points, 137–140
building applications, 53
built-in logins, 256
Bulk Copy (BCP) tool, 7
`bulkadmin` **role, 257**
Business Intelligence (BI), 279–280

C

C# 2005, 14
Call Stack window, 140
changing file permissions, 109–110

char data type, 28
check constraints, 305–306
checking permissions, 271–272
child instance, 107
ClickOnce deployment option
Internet Information Services (IIS), 180–181
publication options, 183–187
publishing web applications, 181–183, 188–189
republishing web applications, 187–188
setup.exe file, 10
software requirements, 179
updating web applications, 187–188
collation settings, 159
`COLLATION=Collation_name` **parameter, 165**
column names in tables, 60
columns (fields)
alternate key, 304–305
data types, 61
defined, 19
foreign key, 20, 61–63
naming, 60
optional, 61
primary key, 20, 295–304
unique identifiers, 61
XML data type
creating, 126–127
populating, 128–130
querying, 130–131
Com+ Catalog Requirement SCC check item, 151
command line
parameters
`ADDLOCAL=ALL`, 165
`ADDLOCAL=feature_selection`, 163, 165
`ALLOWXDBCHAINING={1 | 0}`, 165
`COLLATION=Collation_name`, 165
`COMPANYNAME=CompanyName`, 165
`DISABLENETWORKPROTOCOLS={0 | 1 | 2}`, 164, 166
`ERRORREPORTING={1 | 0}`, 166
`INSTALLSQLDATADIR= Dir_location\`, 166
`INSTALLSQLDIR=Dir_location\`, 166
`INSTANCENAME=Instance_name`, 166
`LOGNAME=File_name`, 166
`LOGPATH=File_location\`, 166
`/qb`, 168
`/qn`, 163–164, 168
`/?`, 168

REINSTALL=ALL, 167
REINSTALLMODE={ omus | amus }, 167
REMOVE=ALL, 167
REMOVE=feature_selection, 165, 167
SAPWD=sa_pwd, 167
SAVESYSDB, 167
SECURITYMODE=SQL, 165, 167
SQLACCOUNT=domainlogin_name, 168
SQLAUTOSTART ={1 | 0}, 168
SQLBROWSERACCOUNT=domainlogin_name, 168
SQLBROWSERAUTOSTART ={0|1}, 168
SQLBROWSERPASSWORD=password, 168
SQLPASSWORD=password, 168
SQMREPORTING={0|1} parameter, 168
UPGRADE, 168
USERNAME=UserName, 168
USESYSDB, 168
SQLCMD tool, 7
SSEUtil utility, 124–125
COMPANYNAME=CompanyName parameter, 165
components
Application Server, 180
BindingNavigator, 52–53
BindingSource, 52, 73
DataSet, 50–52, 74–75
DataTable, 74–76
Internet Information Services (IIS), 180–181
PrintDocument, 77–78
TableAdapter, 52, 76
concurrency
operations, 5
optimistic concurrency, 87
users, 5
concurrency workload governor (MSDE),
193–195
configuring Data Source, 50–51
connecting to databases
attach step, 102
AttachDBFilename connection string, 102
automating connectivity to SSE instance,
102–104
database connection string, 103
detach step, 102
initial catalog connection string, 103
logical names of databases, 56, 103
physical names of databases, 56
user instance connection string, 107

connecting to SSE, 265–266
constraints, 305–306
CONTROL permission, 259, 262
controls
BindingSource control, 52
DataGridView control, 52
FormView control, 91–93
GridView control, 86–87
reporting control, 78
ToolStrip control, 52
copying web applications, 189–190
COUNT(*) function, 36
CREATE command, 29–31
creating
application roles, 253–255
columns with XML data type, 126–127
constraints, 305–306
DataSet, 50–51
functions, 37
indexes, 21
logins, 253–254
master-detail form, 63–66
objects, 251
roles, 256–257
schema collections, 124–125
schemas, 251
stored procedures, 34–35
tables, 47–48, 60–61
user instance, 107–108
users, 253–255
views, 40–41, 306–308
web applications, 82–83
WinForm forms, 44–45, 52
XML Schema Definition (XSD), 120–122
custom queries, 96–98

D

Data Access Objects (DAO)
defined, 222
mapping DAO to ADO, 239–240
Data Definition Language (DDL), 27, 29–31
Data Manipulation Language (DML), 27, 31–34
data migration
Jet to SSE or MSDE, 235–245
Microsoft Desktop Engine (MSDE) to SSE,
198–200
Data Source Configuration Wizard, 50–51

data sources
configuring, 50–51
databases, 51
DataSet, 50–52
objects, 51
web services, 51
Data Sources window (Visual Basic 2005 Express edition), 44–45
data types
bigint, 28
binary, 28
bit, 28
char, 28
columns (fields), 61
datetime, 28
decimal, 28
float, 28
image, 29
int, 28
money, 28
nchar, 28
ntext, 28
numeric, 28
nvarchar, 28
nvarchar(MAX), 28
real, 28
smalldatetime, 28
smallint, 28
smallmoney, 28
sql_variant, 29
text, 28
timestamp, 29
tinyint, 28
uniqueidentifier, 29
user-defined, 6, 29
varbinary, 28
varbinary(MAX), 28
varchar, 28
varchar(MAX), 6, 28
XML
columns (fields), 126–131
description, 29
range/size, 29
support for, 5–6
uses for, 123
database **connection string, 103**
database connectivity
attach step, 102
AttachDBFilename connection string, 102

automating connectivity to SSE instance, 102–104
database connection string, 103
detach step, 102
initial catalog connection string, 103
logical names of databases, 56, 103
physical names of databases, 56
user instance connection string, 107
database engines
defined, 221
Jet, 6, 222
SQL Server 2005, 5
Database Explorer (Visual Basic 2005 Express edition), 44–45, 47–49
database objects. See objects
database-level principal, 252
databases
adding, 46–47, 85
columns (fields)
alternate key, 304–305
data types, 61
defined, 19
foreign key, 20, 61–63
naming, 60
optional, 61
primary key, 20, 295–304
unique identifiers, 61
XML data type, 126–131
constraints, 305–306
data sources, 51
de-normalized, 21
designing, 59–60
filtering data
rows (records), 69–71
web applications, 88–91
indexes
creating, 21
defined, 21
uses, 61
inserting data, 91–92
log file, 46–47
logical names, 56, 103
normalized, 21
physical names, 56
relational databases, 19
rows (records)
defined, 19
filtering, 69–71
finding, 72

navigating, 72
sorting, 71
tables
adding, 94–96
base tables, 40–41
column names, 60
creating, 47–48, 60–61
data entry, 49–50
defined, 19
joining, 39–40
linking, 61–63
naming, 60
querying, 38–39
relationships, 37–38
three normal forms, 20–21
views
creating, 40–41, 306–308
defined, 40
web applications, 88–91
|DataDirectory| macro, 102
DataGridView control, 52
DataNavigator, 52–53
DataSet
creating, 50–51
editing, 74–75
MyDBDataSet component, 52
populating, 51
references, 52
DataSet Visualizer, 138–140
DataTable component, 74–75
datetime data type, 28
db_accessadmin role, 258
db_backupoperator role, 258
DBCC command, 137
dbcreator role, 257
db_datareader role, 258
db_datawriter role, 258
db_ddladmin role, 258
db_denydatareader role, 258
db_denydatawriter role, 258
db_owner roles, 258
db_securityadmin role, 258
DDL (Data Definition Language), 27, 29–31
debugging
assertions, 140–141
break points, 137–140
debug mode, 53
defined, 133

error logs, 136
functions, 141–142
integrated debugger, 137–141
remote debugging, 142–143
SQL CLR debugging, 143–144
stored procedures, 141–143
tracing output, 135–137
T-SQL (Transact-SQL), 141–143
verification method, 134–135
decimal data type, 28
declarative language, 21
dedicated hosting, 12
Default Installation Path Permission Requirement
SCC check item, 151
default schema, 252
DELETE command, 31–33
DELETE permission, 259, 262
deleting
application roles, 253–255
logins, 253–255
objects, 251–252
roles, 257
schemas, 251–252
users, 253–255
de-normalized database, 21
DENY statement, 262–264
deployment
ClickOnce
Internet Information Services (IIS), 180–181
publication options, 183–187
publishing web applications, 181–183,
188–189
republishing web applications, 187–188
setup.exe file, 10
software requirements, 179
updating web applications, 187–188
Xcopy
automating connectivity to SSE instance,
102–104
availability of in higher level editions of SQL, 4
features, 6, 101–102
designing databases, 59–60
desktop users, 8
detach step (database connectivity), 102
detecting
Microsoft Desktop Engine (MSDE), 202–203
SSE, 170
Developer edition (SQL Server 2005), 3

`DISABLENETWORKPROTOCOLS={0 | 1 | 2}`, **164, 166**

disk utilization, 3

`diskadmin` **role, 257**

division (/) operator, 32

DML (Data Manipulation Language), 27, 31–34

downloading

  SQL Server Management Studio Express Edition (SSMS-EE), 22

  SSEUtil utility, 124

`DROP` **command, 29–31**

E

editing DataSet, 74–75

enabling Internet Information Services (IIS), 180–181

Enterprise edition (SQL Server 2005), 3–4

equals (=) operator, 32

error codes, 170

error logs, 136

error reporting, 160–161

`ERRORREPORTING={1 | 0}`, **166**

errors

  "The page cannot be displayed" error, 180

  "Timeout expired" error, 46

Evaluation edition (SQL Server 2005), 13

`EXEC` **command, 35**

`EXECUTE` **permission, 260, 262**

F

features

  adding, 171–174

  removing, 171–174

  selecting, 152–154

fields. See columns (fields)

file permissions

  changing, 109–110

  user instances, 108–110

files

  auto-naming database and log files, 103

  error logs, 136

  log files, 46–47, 169–170

  projects, 45–46

filtering data

  rows (records), 69–71

  web applications, 88–91

finding data, 72

fixed database roles, 257–258

fixed server roles, 257–258

float data type, 28

foreign key, 20, 61–63

Foreign Key Relationships dialog, 61

forms

  master-detail form

    adding tables, 94–96

    creating, 63–66

    updates, 66–69, 96

  WinForm

    BindingSource, 52

    creating, 44–45, 52

    DataGridView control, 52

    DataNavigator, 52–53

    TableAdapter, 52

    ToolStrip control, 52

FormView control, 91–93

functions

  aggregate functions, 35–36

  `AverageQuantity`, 36–37

  `AVG ()`, 35

  `COUNT(*)`, 36

  creating, 37

  debugging, 141–142

  `MAX ()`, 35

  `MIN ()`, 36

  `STDEV`, 36

  `SUM ()`, 35

  table-valued functions (TVFs), 308–309

  T-SQL (Transact-SQL), 21, 34

  `VAR`, 36

G

globally unique identifiers (GUIDs), 301–304

`GRANT` **statement, 262–264**

graphical user interface setup

  authentication modes, 157–158

  Collation Settings, 159

  Error and Usage Report Settings, 160–161

  Feature Selection, 152–154

  Instance Name, 154–156

  Registration Information, 151–152

  Service Account, 156–157

  SQL support files, 148–149

  System Configuration Check (SCC), 149–151

  user instances, 159–160

greater than (>) operator, 32
greater than or equal to (>=) operator, 32
GridView control, 86–87
Group Policy dialog, 142–143
groups, 256–257
GUIDs (globally unique identifiers), 301–304

H

hardware requirements
  SQL Server 2005 Express edition, 15
  Visual Basic 2005 Express edition, 15–16
hierarchy of objects, 250–251
hierarchy of permissions, 267–271
high availability, 277–278
hosting
  dedicated, 12
  third-party providers, 12–13
HTTP paths, 103

I

identifier names, 29
IIS (Internet Information Services), 180–181
image data type, 29
`IMPERSONATE` **permission, 260**
Indexed Sequential Access Method (ISAM)
  technology, 222
indexes
  alternate index, 304–305
  creating, 21
  defined, 21
  uses, 61
`initial catalog` **connection string, 103**
`INSERT` **command, 31–34**
`INSERT` **permission, 260, 262**
inserting data, 91–92
Installation Wizard, 148–149
installing
  Microsoft Desktop Engine (MSDE), 202
  NET Framework 2.0, 15
  SQL Server 2005 Express edition
    authentication modes, 157–158
    collation settings, 159
    error reporting, 160–161
    Feature Selection, 152–154
    ini file, 169
    installation steps, 16–18
    Installation Wizard, 148–149

    Instance Name, 154–156
    multiple installation support, 155
    post-installation verification, 162–163
    Registration Information, 151–152
    service account, 156–157
    setup graphical user interface, 147–162
    silent install, 163–169
    SQL Support files, 148
    System Configuration Check (SCC), 149–151
    user instances, 159–160
  SSEUtil utility, 111
  Visual Basic 2005 Express edition, 16–18
`INSTALLSQLDATADIR=` *Dir_location*
  parameters, 166
`INSTALLSQLDIR=`*Dir_location* **parameter,**
  166
instance ID, 163
`INSTANCENAME=`*Instance_name* **parameter,**
  166
instead-of triggers, 38
int data type, 28
IntelliSense functionality, 123
Internet Explorer Requirement SCC check item,
  151
Internet Information Services (IIS), 180–181
ISAM (Indexed Sequential Access Method)
  technology, 222
ISVs, 8

J

Jet database engine
  comparison to SSE and MSDE, 223–227
  Microsoft Access, 221–222
  migration to SSE or MSDE, 6, 235–245
joining tables, 39–40

L

language independence, 6
less than (<) operator, 32
less than or equal to (<=) operator, 32
licensing, 5, 14
`LIKE` **operator, 32**
linking tables, 61–63
Locals window, 140
log files, 46–47, 169–170
logical names of databases, 56, 103

logins
built-in, 256
creating, 253–254
deleting, 253–255
pre-login, 265
LOGNAME=*File_name* **parameter, 166**
LOGPATH=*File_location* **parameter, 166**

M

manageability, 276–277
management tools
SQL Bulk Copy (BCP) tool, 7
SQL Server Configuration Manager, 7
SQL Server Management Studio Express Edition
(SSMS-EE), 5, 7
SQLCMD command line tool, 7
mapping DAO to ADO, 239–240
master pages, 83–85
master-detail form
adding tables, 94–96
creating, 63–66
updates, 66–69, 96
MAX ( ) **function, 35**
memory utilization, 3
messaging, 7, 280
Microsoft Access
features, 221–223
project development with MSDE, 228–233
Microsoft Desktop Engine (MSDE)
Access project development, 228–234
comparison to SSE, 195–197
concurrency workload governor, 193–195
detecting, 202–203
installing, 202
migration to SSE, 198–200
setup, 201
SSE as a replacement, 3, 5
updates, 201–202
upgrading to SSE
automatically upgrading, 207–209
graphical user interface setup, 209–214
manually upgrading, 216–218
reasons for upgrading, 204–205
recommendations, 206
silent installation, 214–216
upgrade rules, 204–206
usage scenarios, 195
Microsoft SQL Server Database Wizard, 230

migration
Jet to SSE or MSDE, 235–245
Microsoft Desktop Engine (MSDE) to SSE,
198–200
MIN ( ) **function, 36**
**Minimum Hardware Requirement SCC check
item, 151**
Mixed Authentication mode, 157–158, 266
modulo (%) operator, 32
money data type, 28
moving applications to server, 312–314
MSDE. See Microsoft Desktop Engine (MSDE)
MSXML Requirement SCC check item, 150
multiple installation support, 155
multiplication (*) operator, 32
multi-user SSE, 9–10, 13
MyDBDataSet component, 52

N

naming conventions, 60
navigating databases, 72
nchar data type, 28
.NET Framework 2.0, 15
.NET support, 5–6
network shares, 103
New Web Site dialog, 82
normalized database, 21
not equal to (!=) operator, 32
not equal to (<>) operator, 32
not greater than (!>) operator, 32
not less than (!<) operator, 32
NOT **operator, 32**
notification services, 280
ntext data type, 28
numeric data type, 28
nvarchar data type, 28
nvarchar(MAX) data type, 28

O

Object Explorer (SSMS-EE), 23–25
objects
accessing
access control, 262–264
groups, 256–257
permissions, 259–262
principals, 252–256
roles, 256–258

creating, 251
data sources, 51
deleting, 251–252
hierarchy, 250–251
OLEDB, 222
Open Web Site dialog, 190
operators, 32
optimistic concurrency, 87
optional data, 61
OR **operator, 32**
OS (operating system) SCC check items, 151

P

parameters
ADDLOCAL=ALL, 165
ADDLOCAL=*feature_selection*, 163, 165
ALLOWXDBCHAINING={1 | 0}, 165
COLLATION=*Collation_name*, 165
COMPANYNAME=*CompanyName*, 165
DISABLENETWORKPROTOCOLS={0 | 1 | 2}, 164, 166
ERRORREPORTING={1 | 0}, 166
INSTALLSQLDATADIR= *Dir_location*, 166
INSTALLSQLDIR=*Dir_location*, 166
INSTANCENAME=*Instance_name*, 166
LOGNAME=*File_name*, 166
LOGPATH=*File_location*, 166
/qb, 168
/qn, 163–164, 168
/?, 168
REINSTALL=ALL, 167
REINSTALLMODE={ omus | amus }, 167
REMOVE=ALL, 167
REMOVE=*feature_selection*, 165, 167
SAPWD=*sa_pwd*, 167
SAVESYSDB, 167
SECURITYMODE=SQL, 165, 167
SQLACCOUNT=*domainlogin_name*, 168
SQLAUTOSTART ={1 | 0}, 168
SQLBROWSERACCOUNT=*domainlogin_name*, 168
SQLBROWSERAUTOSTART ={0|1}, 168
SQLBROWSERPASSWORD=*password*, 168
SQLPASSWORD=*password*, 168
SQMREPORTING={0|1}, 168
UPGRADE, 168
USERNAME=*UserName*, 168
USESYSDB, 168

parent instance, 107
Pending Reboot Requirement SCC check item, 151
performance, 278–279
permissions
ALTER, 259, 262
checking, 271–272
CONTROL, 259, 262
defined, 259
DELETE, 259, 262
EXECUTE, 260, 262
hierarchy, 267–271
IMPERSONATE, 260
INSERT, 260, 262
REFERENCES, 260
SELECT, 260, 262
TAKE OWNERSHIP, 261–262
UPDATE, 261–262
user instances, 110–111
verifying, 271–272
VIEW DEFINITION, 261–262
physical names of databases, 56
populating
columns with XML data type, 128–130
DataSet, 51
post-installation verification, 162–163
pre-login, 265
Preview Data dialog, 75–76
primary keys
choosing, 295–296
defined, 20
GUIDs (globally unique identifiers), 301–304
stored procedures, 296–301
principals, 252–256
PrintDocument component, 77–78
printing functionality, 77–78
privileges, 110–111
procedural language, 21
processadmin **role, 257**
programming languages
C# 2005, 14
Structured Query Language (SQL), 21
Visual Basic 2005, 14
projects
creating, 44
files, 45–46
properties, 53–55
Properties window (Visual Basic 2005 Express edition), 44–45, 53–55

Publish Options dialog, 184–185
Publish Wizard, 181–182, 187
publishing web applications, 181–183, 188–189

Q

/qb parameter, 168
/qn parameter, 163–164, 168
queries, 96–98
Query Builder, 74–75, 96–98
Query Designer, 49–50
Query Editor (SSMS-EE), 25–27
querying
   columns with XML data type, 130–131
   tables, 38–39
question mark (/?) parameter, 168
QuickWatch window, 139–140

R

RDO (Remote Data Objects), 222
Ready to Install dialog, 161–162
real data type, 28
records. See rows (records)
REFERENCES permission, 260
Registration Information, 151–152
registry editor, 143
REINSTALL=ALL parameter, 167
REINSTALLMODE={ omus | amus }, 167
relational databases, 19
Remote Data Objects (RDO), 222
remote debugging, 142–143
remote Web site, 190
REMOVE=ALL parameter, 167
REMOVE=feature_selection parameter,
   165, 167
removing features, 171–174
replication, 10–11
replication subscription, 5, 7
reporting control, 78
republishing web applications, 187–188
REVOKE statement, 262–264
roles
   bulkadmin role, 257
   creating, 256–257
   db_accessadmin role, 258
   db_backupoperator role, 258
   dbcreator role, 257
   db_datareader role, 258

db_datawriter role, 258
db_ddladmin role, 258
db_denydatareader role, 258
db_denydatawriter role, 258
db_owner roles, 258
db_securityadmin role, 258
deleting, 257
diskadmin role, 257
fixed database roles, 257–258
fixed server roles, 257–258
securityadmin role, 257
serveradmin role, 257
setupadmin role, 257
sysadmin role, 257
rows (records)
   defined, 19
   filtering, 69–71
   finding, 72
   navigating, 72
   sorting, 71

S

SAPWD=sa_pwd parameter, 167
SAVESYSDB parameter, 167
scalability, 277
SCC (System Configuration Check), 149–151
schema collections, 124–125
schemas
   creating, 251
   default schema, 252
   defined, 250
   deleting, 251–252
security
   authentication modes, 266
   built-in logins, 256
   features overview, 7
   groups, 256–257
   objects hierarchy, 250–251
   permissions, 259
   principals, 252–256
   roles, 256, 258
   security model, 264–265
securityadmin role, 257
SECURITYMODE=SQL parameter, 165, 167
SELECT command, 31–33
SELECT permission, 260, 262
selecting features, 152–154

server database application, 13
serveradmin **role, 257**
server-level principal, 252
Service Account dialog, 156–157
setting
  authentication modes, 157–158
  properties, 53–55
setup
  authentication modes, 157–158
  Collation Settings, 159
  Error and Usage Report Settings, 160–161
  Feature Selection, 152–154
  Instance Name, 154–156
  Microsoft Desktop Engine (MSDE), 201
  Registration Information, 151–152
  Service Account, 156–157
  SQL support files, 148–149
  System Configuration Check (SCC), 149–151
  user instances, 159–160
setup options, 7
setupadmin **role, 257**
silent install, 163–169
single-user ASP.NET application, 11–12
single-user SSE, 8–9
smalldatetime data type, 28
smallint data type, 28
smallmoney data type, 28
software requirements
  ClickOnce deployment option, 179
  SQL Server 2005 Express edition, 15
  Visual Basic 2005 Express edition, 15–16
Solution Explorer (Visual Basic 2005 Express edition), 44–45
sorting data, 71
SQL Authentication mode, 22–23, 266
SQL Bulk Copy (BCP) tool, 7
SQL CLR debugging, 143–144
SQL Server
  Developer edition, 3
  Enterprise edition, 3–4
  Evaluation edition, 13
  Express edition
    detecting, 170
    features, 3–7
    hardware requirements, 15
    installing, 16–18, 147–169
    licensing, 5, 14
    software requirements, 15

  support, 14
  uninstalling, 175–177
  Standard edition, 3–4
  Workgroup edition, 3–4
SQL Server 2005 database engine, 5
SQL Server Books Online, 61
SQL Server Configuration Manager, 7
SQL Server Login principal, 252–253, 255–256
SQL Server Management Studio Express Edition (SSMS-EE)
  connection dialog, 22–23
  downloading, 22
  features, 5, 7, 22
  Object Explorer, 23–25
  Query Editor, 25–27
  SSE login options, 22–23
  versions, 22
SQL Service Broker, 7, 280
SQL (Structured Query Language), 21
SQL support files, 148–149
SQLACCOUNT=*domainlogin_name* **parameter, 168**
SQLAUTOSTART ={1 | 0}**, 168**
SQLBROWSERACCOUNT=*domainlogin_name* **parameter, 168**
SQLBROWSERAUTOSTART ={0|1}**, 168**
SQLBROWSERPASSWORD=*password* **parameter, 168**
SQLCMD command line tool, 7
SQLPASSWORD=*password* **parameter, 168**
sql_variant data type, 29
SQMREPORTING={0|1} **parameter, 168**
SSE Component Update dialog, 148
SSE (SQL Server Express)
  detecting, 170
  features, 3–7
  hardware requirements, 15
  installing
    authentication modes, 157–158
    collation settings, 159
    error reporting, 160–161
    Feature Selection, 152–154
    ini file, 169
    installation steps, 16–18
    Installation Wizard, 148–149
    Instance Name, 154–156
    multiple installation support, 155
    post-installation verification, 162–163

SSE (SQL Server Express) (continued)
Registration Information, 151–152
service account, 156–157
setup graphical user interface, 147–162
silent install, 163–169
SQL Support files, 147
System Configuration Check (SCC), 149–151
user instances, 159–160
licensing, 5, 14
software requirements, 15
support, 14
uninstalling, 175–177
SSEUtil utility
downloading, 124
installing, 111
options, 125
renaming, 125
tracing output, 135–137
user instances, 111–113, 125
SSMS-EE (SQL Server Management Studio Express Edition)
connection dialog, 22–23
downloading, 22
features, 5, 7, 22
Object Explorer, 23–25
Query Editor, 25–27
SSE login options, 22–23
versions, 22
Standard edition (SQL Server 2005), 3–4
STDEV **function, 36**
stored procedures
creating, 34–35
debugging, 141–143
primary keys, 296–301
support for, 5
triggers, 5, 38
T-SQL (Transact-SQL), 21, 34–35
Structured Query Language (SQL), 21
subtraction (-) operator, 32
SUM () **function, 35**
support, 14
sysadmin **role, 257**
System Configuration Check (SCC), 149–151

T

Table Editor (Visual Basic 2005 Express edition), 47–48
table relationships, 37–38

TableAdapter component, 52, 76
TableAdapter Configuration Wizard, 74
tables
adding, 94–96
base tables, 40–41
column names, 60
creating, 47–48, 60–61
data entry, 49–50
defined, 19
joining, 39–40
linking, 61–63
naming, 60
querying, 38–39
three normal forms, 20–21
Tables and Columns dialog, 61
table-valued functions (TVFs), 308–309
TAKE OWNERSHIP **permission, 261–262**
Task List (Visual Basic 2005 Express edition), 44–45
technical support, 14
testing applications, 55
text data type, 28
"The page cannot be displayed" error, 180
third-party hosting, 12–13
three normal forms, 20–21
"Timeout expired" error, 46
timestamp data type, 29
tinyint data type, 28
ToolStrip control, 52
trace flags, 135–137
tracing output, 135–137
transactions, 310–312
Transact-SQL (T-SQL)
batch terminator, 34
batches, 34
Data Definition Language (DDL), 27, 29–31
Data Manipulation Language (DML), 27, 31–34
debugging, 141–143
functions, 21, 34
how it works, 21
operators, 32
Query Builder, 96–98
Query Editor (SSMS-EE), 25–27
stored procedures, 21, 34–35
trace flags, 135–137
triggers, 5, 38
TVFs (table-valued functions), 308–309
typed XML, 119

U

UDT (user-defined data type), 6, 29
UNC (Universal Naming Conventional) remote databases, 103
uninstalling SSE, 175–177
unique identifiers, 61
uniqueidentifier data type, 29
untyped XML, 119
Update Available dialog, 187–188
UPDATE command, 31–33
UPDATE permission, 261–262
updates
 master-detail form, 66–69, 96
 Microsoft Desktop Engine (MSDE), 201–202
 web applications, 187–188
UPGRADE parameter, 168
upgrading
 Microsoft Desktop Engine (MSDE) to SSE
  automatically upgrading, 207–209
  graphical user interface setup, 209–214
  manually upgrading, 216–218
  reasons for upgrading, 204–205
  recommendations, 206
  silent installation, 214–216
  upgrade rules, 204–206
 SSE to editions of SQL Server 2005
  configuration options, 285–286
  default instance of SSE, 287–292
  feature comparisons, 273–275
  instance name, 280–281
  networking support, 281–284
  reasons to upgrade, 275–276
  service account, 284
  64-bit support, 286
  Visual Studio support, 286–287
Upsizing Wizard
 migration from Jet to MSDE, 236–245
 support for migration from Jet to SSE, 223
user instance connection string, 107
user instances
 ADO.NET extensions, 107
 child instance, 107
 comparison to SSE instances running as services, 113–115
 creating, 107–108
 defined, 4, 6–7
 error logs, 136
 file permissions, 108–110
 how they work, 104–106
 memory limits, 105
 multi-user or third-party hosting, 13
 parent instance, 107
 permissions, 110–111
 privileges, 110–111
 setup, 159–160
 SSEUtil utility, 111–113, 125
 T-SQL extensions, 115–116
 when to use, 106–107
User Instances dialog, 159–160
User principal, 252–255
user-defined data types (UDT), 6, 29
USERNAME=UserName parameter, 168
users
 concurrent, 5
 creating, 253–255
 deleting, 253–255
 desktop users, 8
 ISVs, 8
 multi-user SSE, 9–10, 13
 single-user SSE, 8–9
 Web developers, 7
USESYSDB parameter, 168

V

VAR function, 36
varbinary data type, 28
varbinary(MAX) data type, 28
varchar data type, 28
varchar(MAX) data type, 6, 28
VBE (Visual Basic Express). See Visual Basic Express (VBE)
verification, 134–135
verifying permissions, 271–272
VIEW DEFINITION permission, 261–262
views
 creating, 40–41, 306–308
 defined, 40
Visual Basic 2005 programming language, 14
Visual Basic Express (VBE)
 applications
  building, 53
  debugging, 53
  testing, 55
 Data Source
  configuring, 50–51
  DataSet, 50–52

Visual Basic Express (VBE) (continued)
  Data Sources window, 44–45
  Database Explorer, 44–45, 47–49
  databases
    adding, 46
    tables, 47–50
  features, 14–15
  hardware requirements, 15–16
  installing, 16–18
  integration with SQL Server 2005, 5
  IntelliSense functionality, 123
  projects
    creating, 44
    files, 45–46
  properties, 53–55
  Properties window, 44–45, 53–55
  Query Designer, 49–50
  software requirements, 15–16
  Solution Explorer, 44–45
  Table Editor, 47–48
  Task List, 44–45
  WinForm forms, 44–45, 52
  XSD graphical editor, 120
Visual Web Developer 2005 Express
  features, 5
  web applications
    copying, 189–190
    creating, 82
    databases, 85, 91–92
    filtering data, 88–91
    FormView control, 91–93
    GridView control, 86–87
    master detail, 93–96
    master pages, 83–85
    publishing, 181–183, 188–189
    republishing, 187–188
    updating, 187–188
  web server, 83

W

web applications
  copying, 189–190
  creating, 82–83
  databases
    adding, 85
    inserting data, 91–92
  filtering data, 88–91
    FormView control, 91–93
  GridView control, 86–87
  master detail, 93–96
  master pages, 83–85
  publishing, 181–183, 188–189
  republishing, 187–188
  updating, 187–188
Web developers, 7
Web Express 2005. *See Visual Web Developer 2005 Express*
web services, 51
WHERE **command, 31–33**
Windows Authentication mode, 22–23, 157–158, 266
Windows Component Wizard, 180
Windows Login principal, 252–254
WinForm forms
  BindingSource, 52
  creating, 44–45, 52
  DataGridView control, 52
  DataNavigator, 52–53
  TableAdapter, 52
  ToolStrip control, 52
wizards
  Data Source Configuration Wizard, 50–51
  Installation Wizard, 148–149
  Microsoft SQL Server Database Wizard, 230
  Publish Wizard, 181–182, 187
  TableAdapter Configuration Wizard, 74
  Upsizing Wizard
    migration from Jet to MSDE, 236–245
    support for migration from Jet to SSE, 223
  Windows Component Wizard, 180
WMI Service Requirement SCC check item, 150
Workgroup edition (SQL Server 2005), 3–4

X
Xcopy deployment option
  automating connectivity to SSE instance, 102–104
  availability of in higher level editions of SQL, 4
  features, 6, 101–102
XML
  advantages of using, 119
  typed, 119
  untyped, 119

XML data type
  columns
    creating, 126–127
    populating, 128–130
    querying, 130–131
  description, 29
  range/size, 29

  support for, 5–6
  uses, 123
XML Schema Definition (XSD)
  creating, 120–122
  definition, 120–122
  how it works, 122–123
  schema collections, 124–125
XSD graphical editor, 120